# Geography of the Holy Land

## Jerusalem, Regional Cities, Small Towns, and Rural Places

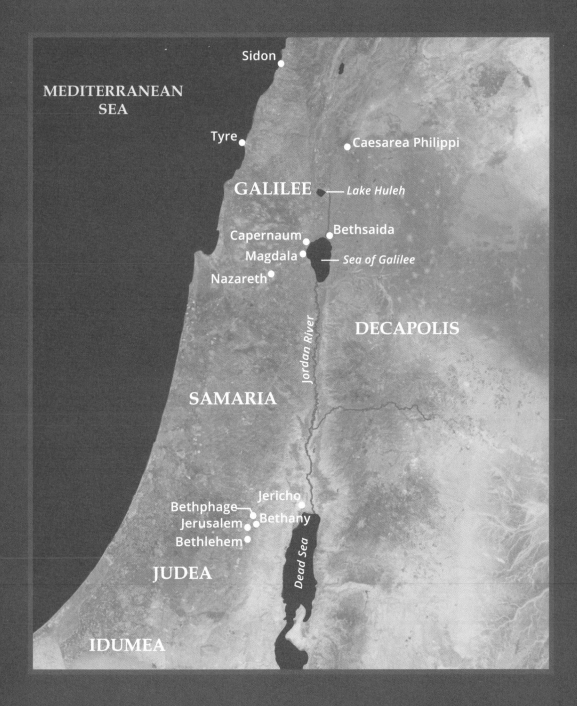

**William A. Dando   Caroline Z. Dando   Jonathan J. Lu**

Published by the Holy Light Theological Seminary Press
2 Henan Second Road, Kaohsiung 80050, Taiwan
For the:
Bible Geography Specialty Group
The Association of American Geographers

*Dedicated to Ronald R. Boyce for his scholarly contributions, his dedication, and his support of Bible Geography and the Bible Geography Specialty Group of the Association of American Geographers from its founding in New Orleans, Louisiana at the AAG Annual Meeting in 1978.*

# Book Preface

In response to many requests from the Bible Geography Specialty Group members, we published in 2005 a 488-page book on topics presented at annual meetings of the Association of American Geographers (AAG) entitled *Geography of the Holy Land: Perspectives*. It was Volume I of what we hoped to be a many volume series, and it was edited by Dr. William A. Dando, his wife Caroline Z. Dando, and Dr. Jonathan J. Lu. The book was well received and eight years later in 2013, Dr. Dando, Caroline, and Dr. Lu again dedicated themselves to bring to fruition our second volume, *Geography of the Holy Land: New Insights*, a 451-page book comprised of 22 chapters. It was a requested book and it was our hope that this new book would provide in-depth information and insights readers sought from current research ideas by specialty group members. As was Volume I, Volume II was distributed free to all new and old members of the Bible Geography Specialty Group (BGSG) of the AAG, the National Council for Geographic Education (NCGE), as well as those who teach and research on Bible geography topics worldwide and who had worked with the BGSG.

This third volume in the Geography of the Bible series, *Geography of the Holy Land: Jerusalem, Regional Cities, Small Towns, and Rural Places*, is approximately 447-page book, published in 2019, written to be an exploratory study of the urban system in Roman Palestine at the time of Jesus Christ's ministry. This volume differs from Volume I in that the first volume was composed of 45 diverse chapters. It differs from Volume II in that the second volume was made up of 22 in-depth chapters while this one is composed of 19 lengthy chapters focused on the topics of settlement geography and linkages between places.

Volume III is dedicated to Dr. Ronald R. Boyce. Professor Boyce is a very well respected urban geographer, an excellent researcher and writer, and a prolific author. Working with Dr. Jonathan J. Lu and others in the early 1970s, he was among a group of professional geographers who strongly advocated geographers teach, present professional papers, research, and publish on geography of the Bible topics and found a Bible Geography specialty group in the Association of American Geographers. Because of their efforts, the AAG Council approved their request to form an official Geography of the Bible Specialty Group. They did so, and the first session of five papers was presented in New Orleans, Louisiana at the 1978 AAG Annual Meeting.

# Geography of Holy Land: Jerusalem, Regional Cities, Small Towns, and Rural Places

## Table of Contents

## PART ONE: INTRODUCTION

Prologue: The Nature of Cities

Preface to a New Theology of the City

Seeds on the Road to Sychar: Stunning Answers to "Where" Trigger Questions

In Search of More Precise Name and Place Name Identifiers

## PART TWO: URBAN PLANNING AND CONNECTIVITY

## PART THREE: URBAN FOOD SECURITY, URBAN WARFARE, AND FAMINE

## PART FOUR: EPILOGUE

Brief snapshots of regional cities, small towns, and rural places of special interest during the early period in the spread of the Christian message are located at the conclusion of the chapter, "A Cartographic Analysis and Brief Description of 'Preacher Point' and 'Miracle Site' Cities, Towns, Villages, and Rural Places Cited in the Four Gospels" in Part One.

# List of Figures

# PART TWO: URBAN PLANNING AND CONNECTIVITY

## Damascus, Hazor, and Bashan: Northern Gateways of the Land of Israel

## Defenses and Wars of the Judean Kings

## Parables: Food, Agriculture, and Feeding the Cities

Food Security in the Roman Empire and Faith-Based Response
to Human Needs: The 46 C.E. Famine in Jerusalem

Urban Famines in Samaria and Jerusalem During Periods of
Civil Unrest, Food Plundering, and Siege Warfare

# PART FOUR: EPILOGUE

Looking Back to 2002: Katsav, Arafat, and a Biblical Solution
to the Arab/Israeli Conflict

# List of Tables

## PART THREE: URBAN FOOD SECURITY, URBAN WARFARE, AND FAMINE

# About This Book

William A. Dando, Caroline Z. Dando, and Jonathan J. Lu

## THE HOLY LAND

The Holy Land is a very special, and in many ways, unique human-defined and delimited region of the world. It is large, extending from the Nile River Valley in Egypt east to Iran (Persia). A crescent-shaped entity, it is bounded on the northwest by the Mediterranean Sea, on the east by the Carpathian Mountains and Caspian Sea, on the south by the Arabian Desert, and on the west by the sands of the Egyptian deserts. Its elevation ranges from minus 1,300 feet or so at the base of the Dead Sea to over 9,200 feet at the top of Mount Harmon. Only one river crosses this region. The 200 mile-long Jordan River sluggishly winds its way from near Mount Harmon on the extreme northeast and empties eventually into the Dead Sea. It does not drain into the Red Sea. Climates range in this narrow region from Cb forest mountain-moist subtropical, Cs Mediterranean-dry summer mixed forest-subtropical, BSh grassland steppe-very dry summer subtropical, BWh desert-extremely dry summer subtropical to Ca Jordan River Valley and Oases-dry summer subtropical. Soils and vegetation types basically conform to temperature and moisture ranges of each climatic region. Climates, soil, and topographic variability led a resourceful and intelligent people to grow a wide array of food crops, raise a range of food animals, and construct roads to exchange foods and products, and slowly develop settlements to process the products of the land (Figure 1).

The land, watered primarily in two periods of the winter months, sustained plants that provided a wide array of food crops, nutritious grasses for livestock which supplied milk and meat, hides and fleece for clothing, and runoff that supplied water for food fish and edible birds of many kinds. The Promised Land, within the Fertile Crescent and within

Figure 1. The Holy Land

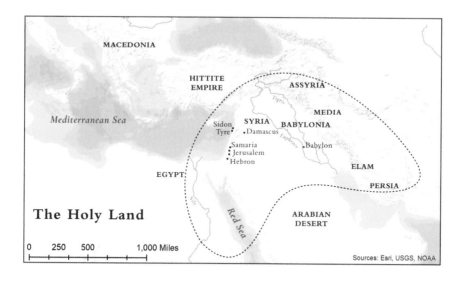

the Holy Land, contained a combination of climatic regions and special ecosystems that provided an intelligent, hard-working, creative people a "land of milk and honey."

Palestine, as defined by the ancient Greeks, had been settled by Canaanites prior to the arrival of the nomadic Hebrews led by Abraham. The Canaanites chose the well-watered valleys and lowlands, leaving the hills and mountains of the central backbone and core of this special land unsettled. The early Hebrews, initially nomadic herders, lived in tents and grazed their herds in watered sites in the hills and mountains initially. When they returned from Egypt, the Hebrews slowly evolved into subsistence farmers and livestock herders and settled permanently in small population clusters, then villages, towns, and cities. The earliest permanent settlements of the Israelites began in the Judean Negev, then they moved north and northeast into the hill areas and steppes, the unsettled frontier of the Trans-Jordan, next into the rock and forest-covered Judean hills, and eventually into the secluded lush valleys of Samaria, and finally in Galilee. The sparsely populated hills and low mountains of central Palestine were ideal for settlement and suitable for subsistence agricultural knowledge of the early Israelite settlers. Clearing the forests to plant life-sustaining seed plants and creating pastures for their live-stock, provided enormous quantities of wood. Wood became the natural resource needed to begin rudimental metal making, furniture fabrication, and farm implement-crafted industries.

Each of the basic agricultural products needed for a sound diet, e.g., grains, grape juice and wine, and olives, figs, and olive oil, were grown and flourished in the hill and low mountain land. Sheep, goats, and cattle products, along with figs, dates, and pomegranates, provided a sound Mediterranean-type diet. Israelites prospered and multiplied. Eventually 60 percent of the hill and low mountain country was covered by man-made terraces, water diversion ditches, small ponds, and cisterns. The hill country of semi-arid Israel, man-modified to a degree, was a natural haven from which its inhabitants eventually came down to conquer and occupy settlements in well-watered valleys and plains. Soon territorial contiguity and tribe linkage were achieved. Food was harvested every month of the year in ancient Israel. Mutual dependency and commerce between various regions led to the development of a complex road system. Groups of people specializing in specific items of exchange led to clusters as families bonded into villages, hamlets, towns, and cities. A well-defined settlement system pattern evolved. In time, the twelve tribes united into a nation, a king was selected, and a capital was chosen almost midway between the north and south and the east and west of the unified country – Jerusalem.

## THE BIBLE AS A DATA SOURCE

The Bible is a descriptive title derived from the Greek *ta biblia*, meaning "the books." The word "Bible" comes from a word-root designating the inner bark of the linden tree upon which ancient writers wrote their books. The application of the word "Bible" to the collected books of the Old and New Testaments can be traced back to the fifth century of our era. It included the Scriptures recording what was handed down as spoken by God, the Oracles and the Word that God spoke to humankind, the Testaments and Covenants or agreements of God with humans, and the Law or God's commandments as guidelines for humankind. The Bible is divided into sixty-six books: Thirty-nine in the Old Testament and twenty-seven in the New Testament. Twenty-two books are historical; five are political; eighteen are prophetical; and twenty-one are epistolary. Together, the Old and New Testaments include arguments, poetry, stories, parables, songs, hymns, biographies, fables, law, plus knowledge of geography, history, and anthropology. There are at least thirty-six different authors who wrote in three languages and seemingly every possible standpoint. Among those whose writings were included in the Bible were kings, scientists, lawyers, generals, farmers, mechanics, fishermen, a tax collector, a doctor, rich men, poor men, and nobles. They were born in rural places, villages, small towns, regional cities, and Jerusalem. The first book ever printed was the Bible, and more Bibles have been printed than any other book.

The Bible records events that Jewish, Christian, and Moslem communities look upon as a source of their beginnings. It also contains prescriptions and prohibitions by which people seek to regulate their lives and become good stewards of all that exists on earth. To millions of people on earth, the Bible contains a profusion of data touching upon basic concepts of regional and physical geography, human culture and history, concepts of time and space, incidents of environmental degradation, and socioeconomic change. Yi-Fu Tuan, a geography professor at the University of Wisconsin-Madison, once compared the phenomenon of the Hydrologic Cycle with "the wisdom of God."

## BOOK DESIGN

Volume III, *Geography of the Holy Land: Jerusalem, Regional Cities, Small Towns, and Rural Places*, was designed, written, and printed in response to requests from countless students of Bible geography nationally and internationally and in response for the acclaims of Volume I, *Geography of the Holy Land: Perspectives*, and Volume II, *Geography of the Holy Land: New Insight*. Book chapter authors are members of the Bible Geography Specialty Group (BGSG) of the Association of American

Geographers (AAG), and the chapters are based on papers presented in Bible Geography Specialty Group sessions at the AAG annual meetings. Members of the BGSG at the Annual Business Meeting in 2015 requested that: (1) A third volume of the Geography of the Holy Land series be published and be totally different in scope and content than volumes I and II. (2) William A. Dando would be the Senior Editor and Caroline Z. Dando and Jonathan J. Lu, Associate Editors. (3) Volume III would focus on the settlement geography of the Holy Land, particularly Jerusalem, regional cities, small towns, and rural places. (4) Bharath Ganesh Babu who had designed Volume I and Volume II's front and back covers would be the Graphics Editor. And (5) the book would be published by the Holy Light Theological Seminary Press. Jonathan J. Lu graciously volunteered to fund the publishing of the book.

Immediately upon returning to Terre Haute, Indiana, William A. Dando and Caroline Z. Dando did the following:

1. Prepared a list of every BGSG member who presented at an AAG annual meeting on an urban or settlement theme in the preceding five years.

2. Carefully reviewed the titles of their presentation topics and created a list of potential book chapter writers. Contacted all past and current members of the BGSG to determine if they had interest in contributing a chapter to Volume III.

3. Contacted Jonathan J. Lu in China and informed him of what was asked of us, and he responded positively, contacting individuals and organizations in South Asia and the Holy Light Theological Seminary Press.

4. Telephoned or e-mailed 40 potential authors to determine their intent in working with us on this new publication venture and providing potential titles for their book chapter or chapters.

5. Secured suggestions from BGSG members who were urban geographers or who had published on urban

themes for what should be included in our book that focused on urban and settlement geography.

6.  Designed a book tracing a "settlement continuum" from the first settlements mentioned in Genesis to the last mentioned in Revelation.

7.  Contacted potential authors of book chapters for a 19-chapter, 450/500-page book, received chapter confirmations, reworked our book plan, and prepared a draft Table of Contents.

8.  Edited, formatted, and entered selected manuscripts into a BC-based electronic format.

9.  Mocked up a book and backed-up the manuscript on a CD-R media.

10. Reviewed the entire manuscript, made corrections where needed, and sent the package to Bharath Ganesh Babu for final review. He then sent the manuscript electronically to the publisher in Taiwan.

Time required to complete the book exceeded three years. More than 35 people have been involved in the project.

## ACKNOWLEDGEMENTS

The editors of this book thank those who contributed in any way to the production of the book and are indebted to all who made completion of the project possible. Acknowledgements must be made to Bharath Ganesh Babu, Valparaiso University, IN; Lara Dando and Gregory Vandeberg, University of North Dakota; Ronald R. Boyce, Seattle Pacific University; Vijay Lulla, Indiana University-Purdue University; Suzanne Walters, Indiana State University; D. Kelly Ogden, Brigham Young University; Steve Harden, Indiana State University; Shelly Arvin, Indiana State University; Pastor Melvin Camp, Centenary United Methodist Church, Terre Haute, IN; Pastor David Rockhill, Maple Avenue United Methodist Church, Terre Haute, IN; Marion Dusenberry, Newell United Methodist Church, Newell, PA; Ken Dawes, University Lutheran Church, Grand Forks, ND; Bruce Bohlman, University Lutheran Church, Grand

Forks, ND; Pastor Tom Colenso, University Lutheran Church, Grand Forks, ND; and Joshua Bloomquist., University of Nebraska-Omaha. Special recognition must be made to Ms. Sandy Chang, Holy Light Theological Seminary Press, in serving as our liaison with the printer in Taiwan. We also thank the "Faith-Hope-Love Information, Art and Cultural Foundation" for their financial support.

# About the Editors and Contributors

## EDITORS

**William A. Dando** is Distinguished Professor and Chairperson Emeritus of the Department of Geography, Geology and Anthropology at Indiana State University, Terre Haute, IN. He also served as Chairperson of the Department of Geography and Director of the Weather Research Station at the University of North Dakota, Grand Forks, ND, and Director of the Senior Scholar Academy at Indiana State University. Dando has served as the Chairperson of the Bible Geography Specialty Group for approximately 30 years. He is the author or co-author of over 180 articles and more than 29 books, atlases, and monographs, including *Geography of the Holy Land: Perspectives,* Volume I (2005); *Climate Change and Variation: A Primer for Teachers,* Volumes I and II (2007); *Food and Famine in the 21ˢᵗ Century,* Volumes 1 and 2 (2012); and *Geography of the Holy Land: New Insights,* Volume II (2013).

**Caroline Zaporowsky Dando** is a specialist in Russian language, a professional editor, and co-author of six books including Geography of the Holy Land: Perspectives. Volume I (The Holy Light Theological Seminary Press, Taiwan, 2005); and Geography of the Holy Land: New Insights Volume II (2013). She taught in the English Department of the University of North Dakota and in the Foreign Language Department of Indiana State University. As a specialist in Russian culture, foods, and Russian women, she has traveled extensively in the former Soviet Union. She has taught periodically in the adult Bible study class at Centenary United Methodist Church in Terre Haute, IN and serves on committees of the Board of United Campus Ministries.

**Jonathan J. Lu is** Professor Emeritus at the University of Northern Iowa, Cedar Falls, Iowa; Professor Emeritus at Holy Light Theological Seminary, Kaohsiung, Taiwan; Visiting Professor of Biblical Geography, Biblical Seminary of the Philippines, Metro Manila, Philippines; and

Biblical Geography teacher in home churches in China. At the 1978 Annual Meeting of the Association of American Geographers, held in New Orleans, Louisiana, Jonathan first advocated research and teaching of Bible Geography as an academic subject. He was one of the founders of the Bible Geography Specialty Group of the Association of American Geographers and a co-editor of *Geography of the Holy Land: Perspectives*, Volume I (The Holy Light Theological Seminary Press, Taiwan, 2005); and *Geography of the Holy Land: New Insights*, Volume II (2013).

## GRAPHICS EDITOR AND BOOK COVER DESIGNER

**Bharath Ganesh Babu** is Associate Professor of Geography at Valparaiso University in northwest Indiana. His research interests lie in the use of remote sensing and geographic information systems to study the interactions between humans and the environment. Ganesh Babu is also interested in instructional design for applied geospatial education. He teaches classes in biogeography, environmental conservation, globalization, remote sensing, and GIS. He has published extensively with William A. Dando, most recently, *Food and Famine in the 21st Century (2012);* and *Geography of the Holy Land: New Insights*, Volume II (2013). Bharath also designed the covers for the books, *Climate Change and Variation: A Primer for Teachers*; *Geography of the Holy Land: Perspectives*, Volume I (2005); *Geography of the Holy Land: New Insights*, Volume II (2013); and *Geography of the Holy Land: Jerusalem, Regional Cities, Small Towns, and Rural Places*, Volume III (2019).

## CONTRIBUTORS

**Ronald R. Boyce** is Professor Emeritus and former Dean of the School of Social and Behavioral Sciences at Seattle Pacific University (SPU). He is also Professor at Large at Bakke Graduate University. He received his PhD in urban geography at the University of Washington, served as a professor there for over a decade, and has been active in the Bible Geography Specialty Group since its inception. Ron has served as a pastor, board member officer of several gospel missions, and as a Bible teacher. He is the author of numerous books and articles and has been listed in *Who's Who in America* for over a quarter century. Boyce has had two notable careers as a student of cities: the first, focusing on cities today, and a second, researching the role of cities in Scripture, particularly Jerusalem. He also co-authored with Edgar M. Horwood, a widely-acclaimed book, *Studies of the Central Business District and Urban Freeway Development* and *The Bases of Economic Geography*. After the death of his mentor, colleague, and friend, Edward L. Ullman in 1976, he compiled and edited the posthumous book, *Geography as Spatial Interaction*.

**Lara M. Dando** is an independent researcher, para-educator and special education teacher's assistant, and adult Bible study teacher at University Lutheran Church in Grand Forks, North Dakota. She received her Master's degree in Earth Sciences (with a geography emphasis) from Montana State University. Her recent research includes work on the published book series, *Food and Famine in the 21st Century*, Volumes 1 and 2, by Dr. William A. Dando, ed. (ABC-CLIO, 2012); she co-authored chapters in *Geography of the Holy Land: New Insights*, Volume II (2013). Her research interests include biblical geography, food crisis issues, and human historic and current impact on the environment.

**E. Nicole DePue** is an applied geographer who specializes in the Near East and North Africa. While studying in Israel to obtain her Master's degree in Historic Geography of the Middle East, she focused her research on the Second Temple period, with special interests devoted to the city of Hazor and the road network of northern Israel, the Patriarchal Highway, and a comparison of the Coastal Highway, Patriarchal Highway, and the King's Highway. Her research determined that the geography of ancient Israel's gateways had great influence on the historical events that impacted the Ancient Near East during the Second Temple period and Herod's contributions to the urbanization of Israel and a functioning road system. In the past she has been an adjunct professor of geography at Salem State University and Southern New Hampshire University. Expanding beyond academics, she currently is working on film projects which utilize her knowledge of historical geography in the

Middle East both with film corporations in Hollywood and the Near East. She also uses her geographic knowledge to continue teaching others in both private and public settings by giving lectures, tutoring, consulting, and assisting in the travel industry.

**Dorothy Drummond** was a geographer, author, world traveler, and lecturer. For her book, *Holy Land, Whose Land, Modern Dilemma, Ancient Roots*, now in its second edition, she was named the recipient of the Denis A. Baly Bible Scholar Geography Book Award by the Bible Geography Specialty Group of the Association of American Geographers. Drummond was the author or co-author of four world cultures textbooks. She wrote a chapter in *Geography of the Holy Land: Perspectives*, Volume I (2005) and two chapters in Geography of the Holy Land: New Insights, Volume II (2013). She retired as an adjunct Assistant Professor of Geography at Saint Mary-of-the-Woods College and Indiana State University. Dorothy served as president of the National Council for Geographic Education and was a founder of the Geography Educators Network of Indiana (GENI). Most recently she was the founder of the Terre Haute Chapter of Bread for the World as well as a civic activist in Terre Haute, IN. Regrettably, Dorothy Drummond died on November 30, 2018 as the result of an accident she had in China doing research for a class she was to teach in 2019.

**Gordon Franz** is a Bible teacher and an archaeologist who holds a MA in Biblical Studies from Columbia Biblical Seminary, SC. Since 1978, he has engaged in extensive field research, and he has participated in a number of excavations in and around Jerusalem, including Ketef Hinnom and Ramat Rachel as well as Lachish, Jezreel, Hazor, and Tel Zayit. Franz has taught geography of the Bible and led field trips in Israel for the Jerusalem Center for Biblical Studies, the Institute of Holy Land Studies, and the IBEX program of Master's College. He also taught in the Talbot School of Theology's Bible Lands Program. He wrote a chapter in the *Geography of the Holy Land: New Insights*, Volume II (2013). Gordon is on the staff of the Associates for Biblical Research.

**Perry Phillips** has a PhD in astrophysics from Cornell University; a MDiv from Biblical Theological Seminary in Hatfield, PA; and a MA in Hebrew from Jerusalem University College, Israel. He taught astronomy, geology, mathematics, and biblical studies at Pinebrook Junior College, Coopersburg, PA, before moving to the Boston area where he worked as a senior quality assurance engineer for a local software company. Phillips also taught calculus and biblical studies at Gordon College in Wenham, MA. Presently, he teaches part-time at Jerusalem University College in Israel where, together with his wife Elaine, he has taught historical geography of Israel to 70 groups over the years. Phillips has published numerous articles on the geography of Israel, including *Geography of the Holy Land: New Insights*, Volume II (2013).. He is also director of the Interdisciplinary Biblical Research Institute (www.ibri.org).

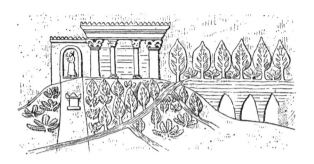

# PART ONE

## Prologue and Introduction

## Significance of Cities as Noted in the Bible

Cities are referred to more than 800 times in the Bible. According to Genesis, after the first humans were created, they lived in a rural site. They were given a command to multiply and they did. Albeit, they had developed a model to provide for their increasing numbers – a city. The earliest mention of a city in the Scriptures is that of Enoch, founded by Cain in c. 3870 B.C.E. (Genesis 4: 17). The last book of the Bible, Revelation, ends with a description of a "new age" when God's people will enter heavenly Jerusalem, a massive beautiful "city of God." There were many cities in Egypt before Abraham's entry into the Promised Land, and he came from Ur, one of the largest cities in the Middle East. When Abraham entered Canaan, he found many large and small cities, towns, and villages. An often-repeated Old Testament phrase was "cities and their suburbs" (Leviticus 25: 34; Joshua 21: 33).

The Prologue and Introduction for this book on settlements in ancient Palestine at the time of Roman occupation, Herod the Great's rule, and Jesus' ministry were written by Ronald R. Boyce. He outlines the nature of cities, comments on the "Where" questions in the Bible, and suggests a new theology of cities. William A. Dando and Lara M. Dando follow with an exploratory study of cities, towns, villages, and rural population clusters' names and meanings. E. Nicole DePue describes the growth of Herod's kingdom and his impact on city enhancement at the time of Jesus. This chapter is followed by one by Ronald R. Boyce who provides a word-portrait of Jerusalem's site and traces its history and significance. Finally, William A. Dando and Bharath Ganesh Babu identify Jesus' "Preacher Points" and "Miracle Sites" in the four Gospels, map them, analyze their patterns, and briefly describe each place. The first six chapters introduce readers to a well-defined, integrated human settlement system which evolved from carrying out the First Precept of the Bible (Genesis 1: 28).

# Prologue: The Nature of Cities

Ronald R. Boyce

Cities, as we know them today, were born on the banks of a few desert streams only six millennia ago. These seemingly insignificant city seeds have produced a tree, bearing fruits of many kinds and colors. Once cities began, innovation multiplied, commercialism grew, and wealth, power, and prestige dictated values. The rural environment became tamed; it was commercialized and controlled. Thereby, cities transformed and dominated the plants, animals, and resources of the planet. In turn, cities have been shaped by the areas with which they have interacted. Such transformation stemmed from necessity. Paradoxically, inherent dysgenic features of cities (food and demographic deficiencies) provided much of the motivation for domination, primarily their abilities to survive. Thereby, in carrying out the first precept of the Bible to "be fruitful and multiply, and replenish the earth, and have dominion . . . over every living thing" (Genesis 1: 28), cities have greatly increased the demographic carrying capacity of the planet. Thereby, cities are fruitful places. Nonetheless, some of their branches bear bitter fruit – e.g. conflict, injustice, pride, and pollution of the natural environment.

The antipodal nature of cities has enticed some to concentrate on one extreme or the other. For example, by using the tyranny of semantics, civilization itself (from the Latin word for city, *civis)* is the primary hallmark of cities. Without cities, presumably the world would be barbaric, chaotic, and pagan. Based on the Greek word for city, *polis,* it would be a place without police, politics, or progress. By focusing on another extreme, cities are cauldrons of unrest, injustice, exploitation, and catalysts for the fouling of Nature and the caging of wildlife. Christians are often among the fiercest of such city denigrators. However, careful examination of Scripture reveals the strong likelihood that cities are both a gift and a blessing. Even so, imperfect humans create imperfect cities, which they endow with all their failings – flawed and in need of betterment, even redemption. Consequently, many cities were designed in quasi-utopian fashion – e.g. Babylon and Peking. Utopian models range from Plato's Republic and More's Utopia, to Wright's Broadacre City. Seminal city planners such as Hippodamus, Hippocrates, and Vitruvius set the stage for much modern thinking about making cities better. Many have tried to minimize the negative and maximize the positive attributes of cities. Wilberforce's Clapham, Howard's Garden City, New Towns, and various Olmstead-influenced suburban complexes, were all designed to provide the ideal compromise settlement form between city and country. The ultimate planned balance between city and country will occur during the Millennium.

It should be noted that the study of the geography of the city in Scripture requires that one follows, insofar as possible, the same rules, techniques, concepts, and relationships as are applied in the study of cities in general. Of course, they must be examined within their right biblical, cultural, and spatial contexts. This requires knowledge of the Bible, the land of Israel, and other places outside Israel with which they interact. In fact, much of the Bible is devoted to treatment of other places in other lands. On-site understanding and investigation of the natural features are fruitful. In short, the Bible is the text, the city is the object for observation, and the land of Israel is the laboratory for understanding.

How should cities be evaluated? *Exegesis* provides a fruitful approach. It is a method of higher criticism employed by theologians to interpret the Bible. The general approach is to examine Bible texts within their historical and cultural contexts. This can be done at two scales or levels: the macro (large scale), and micro (small scale). At the macro level, cities are perceived as points. The placement patterns of cities and their relative sizes are examined over time. In so doing, a city's relationships with respect to other places, its position in the urban hierarchy, and even its economic base often can be determined. At the micro (neighborhood) levels, cities are viewed as areas, or sites, each having shape, density, height, and internal configuration of social, economic, and political features. Moreover, each pattern contains various associated spatial interactions. Investigation at the micro level usually requires on-site field observation.

For example, large American, Canadian, and many West European cities are composed of many communities; they are multicultural, not intercultural. Religious, ethnic, demographic, and economic features are segregated in self-selected enclaves, thereby providing a kaleidoscopic-like spatial pattern. Other components are Balkanized in bunker-like fashion – e.g. gated communities, restricted upper-income residential neighborhoods, guarded workplaces, and controlled compounds containing the homeless. It was not always the case. In ancient Greek cities, the *agora* was centrally situated and easily accessible to all social groups. Today, public space in cities is rapidly disappearing. The mélange of intercultural mixing afforded by the agora is gone. The modern towers of commerce are now the hallmarks of cities throughout the world. Today, economic and political considerations dominate the cityscape; the sacred and the social have been cast aside.

Cities are symphonies of moving parts, contrapuntal streams of commerce and culture. Cities never sleep; they are perpetual engines of spatial interaction. Such interaction is multifaceted – commuting to and from work, shopping, business services, recreation, and municipal "housekeeping;" these keep the transportation and communication routes humming. Even so, density of population within cities reverses between being at home at night and away from home during the day. Nonetheless, such constantly changing patterns do not expose any group to easy access or social interaction one to the other. People move about in cocoon-like fashion in locked vehicles. At each destination, they sequester themselves behind protective shields dictated by privilege and privacy: Homes are segregated in various ways; businesses are guarded; many functions are entered by payment only; and even schools, churches, and malls operate more as clubs than as places for public access offering unfettered intercultural interaction.

All societies write their values in the fabric of their cities. The placement of functions within cities reveals societal priorities and aspirations. Even the built-up area and density of urban places provide important clues. In America and elsewhere, centrality is the treasured prize. The function that wins the bidding war among competing contestants occupies the most prized sites. The highest bidders control the most accessible spaces, each in descending order of rent-paying ability. Public land use is provided primarily to serve the economic engine of cities. Parks, schools, and public services are distributed somewhat haphazardly over the urban landscape as the local governments see fit; governments are largely controlled, and make decisions, based on vested interests. Planning and zoning, while evident, are weak as contrasted with the power of business. In fact, planning is largely the handmaiden of business – e.g. to maintain land values, provide accessibility, and protect wanted areas from unwanted intrusion. As would be expected, the poor are pushed aside to the less desirable and more dangerous places. In fact, those forces responsible for the shaping and structuring of American cities apply at a grander level on a world scale.

Today, globalization provides another dimension for urban understanding. European colonization set the world stage for a global economy. Such colonization, coupled with mercantilism and capitalism, led to fierce competition for trade among a cadre of cities in Europe. This resulted in commercial rivalries among cities elsewhere. City rivalry is rampant throughout history – Babylon vs. Nineveh, Memphis vs. Thebes, Athens vs. Sparta, Rome vs. Carthage – but earlier rivalries were never of a strictly commercial nature. Today, industry and commerce have become the engines, and population size has become the *sine qua non* of success and significance.

The concept of "global cities" is becoming a conundrum of confusion. The rise of the internet and satellite-based communications has enticed countless cities to declare themselves to be "global cities" – a very dubious assertion. Communication among cities has greatly expanded, but this does not make all cities equally global. Even worse, some have mistakenly concluded that distance is now irrelevant and that the planet is now a level playing field for commercial competition. Neither is correct; distance is not annihilated, nor has the earth become less differentiated. Even minor features among places may now loom important in understanding areal differentiation. Simply put, a feature of the new spatial freedom is that it allows small differences to have big consequences.

Identifying the much-touted world city or *ecumenopoli*, is fraught with futility. It is apparent that a world city has not yet emerged. Even the nearly ubiquitous internet represents only one aspect of world urban interaction. The fiber optic network allows almost instantaneous transmittal of information, but little else. Material goods are still much affected by the tyrannies of distance, time, and cost. Container ships encircle much of the globe, but they move cargo slowly among designated ports. Air travel enables worldwide delivery of high valued cargo and people, but it also is distance-handicapped and port-controlled. The world is a somewhat interconnected commercial, financial, and quasi-governmental system, but it is still in embryonic form.

Nonetheless, the fruit of cities is omnipresent. Babylon is everywhere! Cities are the cockpits of control for the earth's people and its resources. They shape people's lives in countless ways – where they live, what they do, even how they think. We live in a world in which cities have triumphed. They play the dominant role in configuring and controlling the concourses of human affairs and assessing the earth's usability. The paramount paradox of cities is that very few understand them, and even fewer appreciate them.

# Preface to a New Theology of the City

Ronald R. Boyce

## INTRODUCTION

There have been many articles and books about cities in Scripture, some even claiming to be theologies of the city. (The word "city" here is used as a uni-plural noun, much as the word "man" is commonly used). Why do we need a new theology of the city? The first reason is that the study of cities in the past suffers from two biases: (1) The love of the country and (2) the hatred of the city. These prejudices have caused many to either conclude that the country (garden, rural, wilderness) provides the closest glimpses of God and/or that the city is evil, even cursed. A second reason a new treatment of the city is needed is that most studies and commentaries on cities lack a clear *thetic* or thesis of the city. "It is *thetic* that it [any systematic theology] follows a human devised thesis form and presents and verifies truth as *truth*" from that principle as grounded in Scripture (Chafer 1947: 6).

Please note the title of this chapter. It is simply meant as a preface or foundation for a new theology of cities in Scripture. Obviously, the complete theology of cities cannot be presented in this limited space. Therefore, this chapter might be considered as simply an extended outline for a new approach to the theology of the city. The word "new" in the title is to remind the reader that there have been other attempts to write a new theology of the city, which this author has concluded are deficient or wrong. To the best of this author's knowledge, the thetic in this chapter is original.

The rural bias in the treatment of the city in Scripture by many is evident. It has been well documented that most Americans were and are anti-city in attitude (Conn 1978: 28). Keith Martin maintains that "Biblical theologians have sometimes been guilty of reading scriptures in light of contemporary issues and attitudes (Martin 1977: 274). "Most Christians still read the Bible through rural lenses" (Bakke 1997: 14). The ancient Greeks imagined Heaven as modeled after the Elysian Fields. Many Christians also think Heaven is a bovine-like rural environment where the lion lies down with the lamb and where believers, like sheep, are brought to green pastures laden with still waters. They further conclude that Heaven is like a garden. Their reasoning is based on the origin of the human race in the Garden of Eden and its final restoration as a kind of Garden of Eden. It is usually stated something like this: "The human story begins in a garden. Paradise is lost in a garden. Redemption takes place in a garden. Death is defeated in a garden. And Paradise is restored as a garden" (Martin 2017: 2). The pitfall in such thinking is not in what is proclaimed but what is ignored, i.e. the prominent role of the city in biblical history and prophesy.

It is a logical progression from field to garden and then to the wilderness. In fact, attitudes toward the city have gone through several phases (Tuan 1974). Initially, Eden and the garden were considered the perfect ideal or sacred place; the country was considered as profane, the home of the barbarian. For a season, the composite or "Middle Landscape" was considered perfect. The city itself was labeled as profane and undesirable, not unlike the wilderness at the time. The ideal environment was deemed to be neither big city nor pristine country but an amalgamation of the best of each – brought to planning fruition as the Garden Cities movement. For a season, after World War II, suburbia became a new utopian Middle Landscape in the minds of some. That too passed and the common quip has been modified to say that God made the country, man made the city, the devil made suburbia, and none of these is Heaven-like.

Today, the utopian view is that the pristine wilderness brings one closest to God. Nature is the sacred ideal; it has become an environment even to be worshipped. It is an old attitude. Shakespeare described it in this way; "Are not these woods more free from peril than the envious court? Here feel we but the penalty of Adam. . . .And this our life exempt from public haunt, finds tongues in trees, books in running brooks, sermons in stones, and good in everything" (Shakespeare, *As You Like it,* Act II, Scene 1). This animism-like tendency to worship nature permeates the New Age Movement. Many Christians think they are getting closer to God by communing with nature. They forget that humans were created in the image of God, not pine trees and sunsets. It also includes religious Jews, such as Rabbi Mike Comins. He argues that "Religious Jews need the natural world. *Wilderness matters because it's an optimal place to work out a personal, unscripted, fresh relationship with divinity. . .*spirituality is alive in the wilderness and absent in the city. When he leaves the wilderness, he leaves his spiritual life behind" (Comins 2007: 6). Of course, it is fitting to worship God by his creation, but it is not proper to worship and serve the creation more than the Creator (Romans 1: 25). Paradoxically, secular city planners had a better grasp of Heaven, with a balance of country and city, than most theologians (Mackintosh and Forsberg 2013).

Hatred of the city is even stronger in interpreting the city in Scripture than the love of nature. It seems to be a matter accentuating the negative and eliminating the positive. Charges against the city are old and widespread. Rousseau claimed that "cities are the final pit of the human spirit" (Clapp 1986: 204). Williams Jennings Bryan in his famous "Cross of Gold" speech proclaimed: "Burn down your cities and leave your farms and your cities will grow again. But destroy your farms and the grass will grow in every city in the union. . . .You shall not press down upon the brow of labor this cross of thorns. You shall not crucify mankind upon a cross of gold," by which he meant the city (Critchfield 1991: 26). Henry George lamented the mournful condition of a population divorced from the genial influences of nature and concludes that the life in great cities is not natural. Under such conditions, the urban dweller must "deteriorate, physically, mentally, morally" (George 1968: 4). William Stead in his famous book, *If Christ Came to Chicago,* says that the city is "the *cloaca maxima* [great cesspool] of the world" (Stead 1894: 25).

Consequently, many Christians think that the Scriptures portray cities as evil, destructive to the human soul, and cursed by God. Ellen White, founder of the Seventh Day Adventist church, was certain that the Bible condemned cities. Her admonition to church members was to ". . . keep out of the cities. Build no sanitariums in cities. Educate our people to get out of the cities into the country, where they can obtain a small piece of land, and make a home for themselves and their children. Out of the cities! Out of the cities! This is the message the Lord has given me" (Oosterwal 1980: 20). In 1970, Jacque Ellul undertook a comprehensive examination of the city in Scripture and concluded that the city was both endemically evil and cursed by God. He argued that the city is the place where "slavery (is) tolerated. Human relations destroyed in the anonymity of the great city. . . . Man subject to man, instead of to nature" (Ellul 1970: 60-61). According to Bakke, with whom this author agrees, "Ellul misread the data. The Bible has many other city case studies he could have used to correct his rather depressing view" (Bakke 1997: 186). It is this author's contention that Ellul's view was both biased and fallacious.

The primary thesis of this author is that cities are necessary to achieve the purpose of God and that God provided cities. The seminal text for this thesis is Genesis 1: 28: "Be fruitful, and multiply, and replenish the earth, and subdue it: and have dominion over. . . every living thing that moves upon the earth." Each word needs to be studied carefully. For example, (1) "multiply" means to increase exponentially in number; (2) "replenish" is a geographical term meaning to fill-up or use fully; (3) "subdue" means to use cities as suggested here for positive purposes; "i.e., to acquire a knowledge of and mastery over his material environment, to bring its elements into the service of the human race" (Scofield 1998: 4); and (4) to have dominion as the viceroy and steward of God over his creation. To subdue the earth and have dominion over it suggests that humankind is to govern the earth and its inhabitants in a manner such that the earth will be made fruitful throughout and that the population will be multiplied peacefully. This means that four things are essential in good governance. It must: (1) fully utilize the earth's resources; (2)

evaluate their utility and redistribute them fairly; (3) provide moral authority and render justice to all God's creatures including humans, so as to produce the common good; and (4) understand and be a good steward of the physical environment. This is what cities should ideally do and is demonstrated by the classic secular definition of cities as "focal points in the occupation and utilization of the earth by man" (Harris and Ullman 1945: 7; for a detailed comparison of the First Precept and the definition of the city by Harris and Ullman, see Boyce 2013a: 31-36).

But first, what is theology as it might apply to cities? "Theology" is composed of two Greek words – *Theos* meaning "God" and *Logos* meaning "word." Therefore, theology is the discipline of trying to determine what God says in his word, the Bible, about a particular topic of scriptural importance. Traditionally, systematic (topical) theology has rightfully focused on a number of subjects such as soterology, Christology, anthropology, and eschatology. "However, since no consideration of God will be complete which does not contemplate his works and ways in the universe which he has created, as well as his person, theology may be extended properly to include all material and immaterial realities that exist and the facts concerning them and contained in them" (Chafer 1947: 3). That the city is a proper subject of inquiry in Scripture is undeniable. It has been examined by countless persons because it plays such a prominent role in the Scripture. There are more than one thousand references in the Bible to the word, and there are numerous mentions of specific cities.

This author explored the thesis that cities are necessary to fulfill the First Precept in a chapter in an earlier volume of this series which was commented on by several prominent scholars and theologians (Boyce 2013b). It was demonstrated that God provides the tools, people, and resources to accomplish his purposes and to enable the fulfillment of his precepts. It is also evident that he often makes these provisions or gifts in the most unexpected ways and through the most unlikely objects and persons. This was termed the *Jehovah Jirah* Principle as based on Abraham's naming the place where Abraham's son was to be sacrificed on Mount Moriah, after God provided a sacrifice as a substitute for Isaac (Genesis

22: 8). This principle is illustrated by the provision of God for fallen humankind, i.e. (1) the provision of an animal atonement for Adam and Eve: "The LORD God made coats of skins and clothed them" (Genesis 3: 21); (2) the provision of a ram for sacrifice; and (3) the consummate Christ on the Cross for the salvation of the human race (Romans 5: 6, 18). The First Precept could not be accomplished without cities. In fact, even when Christ sets up his Kingdom during the Millennium, Jerusalem will play a paramount role, and other cities will also be involved.

In this chapter, the author follows up on the application of the thesis by proof texts that God endowed specific cities or civilizations with seminal gifts which are appropriate and essential to the proper use of cities to aid in the fulfillment of the First Precept. These gifts were frustrated by humanity, but they will be perfectly applied when Jerusalem is redeemed. Despite their great gifts, cities polluted them in much the same way that humankind has corrupted its gifts. Therefore, the examination here is really a city-based perspective on the story of the human race. The cities or civilizations which best illustrate this giving of gifts include: (1) the cities of Cain; (2) Babel; (3) Sodom, Gomorrah, and other cities; (4) Tyre and other nearby sister cities; and (5) Nebuchadnezzar's Babylon.

## GOD'S GIFTS TO CITIES AND THEIR CORRUPTION OF THEM

Table 1 is a template for the presentation of the thesis. The focus is on the gifts of these cities as they relate to the First Precept (Genesis 1: 28). To emphasize this connection, key connective words have been placed in italics. Interestingly, five (the number of grace) cities are found that demonstrate these gifts most directly. (There may be others). Note that all are Gentile cities. This is no doubt significant and possibly acts as a counterpoise to the privileged place among cities by Jerusalem. Jerusalem, of course, was blessed, among other things, with the *axis mundi* (connection between Heaven and Earth) by the Temple (Eliade 1959: 41).

Also, note that in all cases, including Jerusalem, these gifts were perverted and corrupted. For example, inventions meant for peace and productivity were corrupted into instruments of war, fruitlessness, and violence. This corruption of a gift into one designed for evil has probably contributed to the idea that cities are cursed, and inventions are Satanic-inspired rather than God-gifted.

## CAIN'S CITIES – TOOLS

It is this author's belief that Cain may have invented the city, but that it was done by the hidden hand of God. Some insight into this is obtained by the study of the meaning of names in this passage (Genesis 4: 16-24). As students of Scripture know, names have meanings that often shed understanding on the context of what is being discussed, in this case Cain's cities. There are five generations mentioned in these verses. They begin with the gift of the initial city, Enoch. *Enoch* means "to initiate something and to teach." Thereby invention or initiation of something is the primary topic. We might expect to be presented with the pioneers or initiators of important inventions and skills essential for accomplishing specified purposes demanded by the First Precept.

Therefore, the gifts presented are seminal tools of enormous importance (Table 1). First, the greatest gift of God is the city itself, a subject which has been explored in some depth in an earlier volume in this series (Boyce 2013a). The word "city" (*'iyr)* refers to a protected, usually fortified place. Inasmuch as Cain was condemned to be a vagabond and a wanderer, this has led to much speculation, namely that this was a second rebellion of Cain. Even so, there is no evidence that Cain ever lived in the city he "invented." In fact, the city is given the complement (the geographical word is *complementarity* whereby spatial interaction occurs because of a specific supply and demand). The originator of the concept states that "In order to have interaction between two areas there must be a demand in one and a supply in the other. . . . Specific complementarity is required before interchange takes place. Complementarity is thus the first factor [requirement] in an interaction system …" (Ullman 1980: 13). The city is given its complement by the invention of Jabal who was the

## Table 1. God's Gifts to Selected Cites and Their Corruption

| City and Key Texts | God's Gifts | Corruption of God's Gifts |
|---|---|---|
| Cain's Cities (Gen. 4: 17-24) | Seminal inventions and skills – rural-urban *complementarity*, the arts, music, and metallurgy | Used inventions for violence and for moral depravity |
| Babel (Gen. 11: 1-9) | Unity and community. Ability to *multiply* in population and *replenish* the earth | Pride in self. Refusal to *replenish* the earth |
| Sodom (Gen. 13:10; Ezek. 16:49,50) | Eden-like physical environment, a *fruitful* economy and much wealth, *multiply* | Pride, self-service. Neglect of the poor. Perversion of persons and refusal to *multiply* |
| Tyre (Ezek. 27: 3, 25, 33; 28: 2,4, 12, 17, 18) | Ability to redistribute earth's resources, and *replenish* and *subdue* it positively | Perverted God's gifts of commerce to their own aggrandizements |
| Babylon (Dan. 4: 10-12,30; Jer. 51: 7; Isa. 13:19) | Given *dominion* over the earth by God. | King Nebuchadnezzar claims credit for God's gifts. Destroyed. |

pioneer of all who live in tents (nomadic) and raise cattle, presumably to supply commodities needed by city dwellers and initiated a system of spatial interaction. Thereby, a complementarity community between the country and the city was created. Continuing with the meaning of names, Jabal was the son of Adah whose name means "to advance an important need." She also bore Jubal, the one who invented music and the arts. His name means "stream," which might be interpreted in this context as the pioneer who continued the stream of advancements of the new unity between country and city. Hence, the city is "both a product of and an influence on the surrounding regions" (Harris and Ullman 1945: 7).

Zillah, the other wife of Lamech, in the fifth generation from Cain, was the mother of Tubal-cain. Tubal-cain was a craftsman who perfected the skills of metallurgy. (Note that this came late in the invention parade). Also it should be noted that metallurgy discovery and skills might be used primarily for products of peace and disfigured into weapons of war. Tubal-cain's sister was Naamah, whose name means "pleasant." Evidently, created items made city life pleasant, both practically and to the eye; a hedonistic lifestyle resulted.

These discoveries, probably inspired by God, provided the opportunities for improving the earth and its population in various ways. Some recognize that such inventions originated from spiritual sources, but reason that they are from the Devil and not from the Divine. This led Larkin to the counter-conclusion that "It is not likely that the Holy God imparted to the ungodly race of Cain the knowledge to invent things that would lead to the downfall of the race and help to bring on the Flood. Neither is to be supposed that a God of Love would impart to men the knowledge that would enable them to invent such hellish instruments of warfare as were used in the great European war" (Larkin 1920: 44). Unfortunately, they did not use these great advances in a positive manner but in a corrupted way. This is seen initially in the braggadocio and presumptiveness of Lamech. Lamech killed a boy who had threatened and hurt him in some fashion. We see the full corruption of these gifts in the end-product of violence on the earth. "And the earth was also corrupt before God, and the earth was filled with violence. . . .And (the earth) was corrupt, for all flesh had corrupted his way upon the earth" (Genesis 6: 11-13). Finally, the antediluvians had also corrupted their flesh to such an extent and in such a manner that that civilization was destroyed by the Flood. But Noah found grace and was "perfect in his generations" (Genesis 6: 9). There is much mystery in that phrase.

## BABEL – REPLENISH

There were two great provisions or gifts of God in the brief description of Babel (Genesis 11: 1-9). Both are linked to the First Precept. The first gift for accomplishing his purpose is generally just taken as a given. That is, that the people could all communicate with one another and were unified as a community. As the Lord said "the people is one, and they have all one language, and this they begin to do, and now nothing will be restrained from them, which they have imagined to do" (Genesis 11: 6). They had great power and opportunity to do God's will and thereby advance the First Precept.

Instead, they perverted their communal gift and his command to replenish (scatter throughout) the earth. They decided to concentrate in a single city of their design to give them independence from God and to glorify themselves. "Let us build a city, and a tower whose top may reach unto heaven; and let us make us a name lest we be scattered abroad upon the face of the whole earth" (Genesis 11: 4). This was rebellion against a direct command to replenish the earth, something which they viewed as making themselves vulnerable and unimportant.

Ironically, this rebellious act led God to give them a gift which they could not refuse; he confused their language. Nonetheless, few understand it in a positive way; they see it as punishment, not a gift. Actually, this is just another example of the Lord using a human failure to accomplish his will. The Scriptures couldn't be clearer on this. Note that the Lord did this to advance his command to replenish the earth: "so the LORD scattered them abroad from thence upon the face of all the earth" (Genesis 11: 9).

## SODOM – BE FRUITFUL AND MULTIPLY

"And Lot lifted up his eyes, and beheld all the plain of the Jordan, that it was well watered everywhere, before the LORD destroyed Sodom and Gomorrah, even as the Garden of the LORD" (Genesis 13: 10). This is the first mention of Sodom in Scripture. It is described as situated in a fruitful land, a beautiful land with green pastures, abundant water, and reminiscent of the Garden of Eden. No other land is referred to in this fruitful manner – not even Israel, described as a land "flowing with milk and honey," was equal to it. Sodom is positioned in a bountiful plain and was poised to be a material blessing to its cities and to others less naturally endowed.

Usually it is the city that makes the land fruitful. Even the theologian, Henry Drummond (1893) recognized this process. "The city is strategic. It makes towns, the towns make villages; the villages make the country. He who makes the city makes the world" (Mackintosh and Forsberg 2013: 741). But here the process appears to be reversed; the land is presented as a great gift to the city to make the city fruitful. And Sodom's material wealth and abundant food reflected this blessing from God, but the Sodomites were lacking in generosity and had a surfeit of stinginess. In short, the Sodomites corrupted their endowment of promise into a downward spiral of destruction, even to the perversion of the human body. In this context, they refused to "multiply" the population of the earth; homosexuality frustrated that possibility. Consequently, both the cities and their fertile fields were destroyed by fire and brimstone (Genesis 19: 24-25. They reached the pivotal point of no return; they became reprobate of mind and reprehensible in the misuse of their bodies.

They evidently followed a retrogressive path leading to destruction. It began with pride, reasoning that they were entitled to their wealth and productive land. Thereby, they simply labeled the poor and needy as undeserving, causing their own problems. They then pursued entertainment and hedonism, luxury living, and a love of idleness. This, in turn, evidently led to a process of behavior which rendered them fruitless with respect to procreation; they would not multiply (Ezekiel 16: 49-50). A similar progression, leading to the same sin, is described in Romans 1: 19-31.

Their destruction evidently was more than the corruption of a great gift gone sour. The destruction of Sodom, Gomorrah, and other cities in the plain, was "set forth as an example" to all who would follow in a similar refusal to multiply the population of the earth by 'giving themselves over to fornication and going after strange flesh'" (Jude 7).

## TYRE – SUBDUE

Tyre was given the gift of its location at the gateway to the seas and thereby to the world. It became the trading and transfer station for people of many places (Ezekiel 27: 3). Its great cargo ships made them wealthy: ". . . the ships of Tarshish did sing of thee in thy market: and thou was replenished, and made very glorious in the midst of the seas" (Ezekiel 27: 25). The consequence was that they used their blessings and riches selfishly, even deluding themselves that they had done these things because of their prowess and were invincible. "Because thou hast said, I am a God, I sit in the seat of God, in the midst of the seas; yet thou art a man and not God" (Ezekiel 28: 2). Tyre was in a position to redistribute resources around the globe fairly. They went on three-year voyages, thus, they could have fulfilled much of the commandment to subdue the earth, but they refused.

In fact, Tyre is in many ways the prototype of the prophesied Mystery Babylon in the book of Revelation. "How she hath glorified herself, and lived deliciously, so much torment and sorrow give her: for she saith in her heart, I sit a queen, and am no widow, and shall see no sorrow" (Revelation 18: 7). Her great wealth had deluded her into thinking she was invulnerable. But she was destined for destruction.

## BABYLON – DOMINION

Nebuchednezzar's Babylon was the epitome of blessings long lost. It was given dominion over the known world. And there is no doubt where its blessings originated. The Scriptures state clearly that they are from God, "for the God of heaven **hath given thee a kingdom, power, and strength, and glory**" (Daniel 2: 37; emphasis added by the author). Babylon is blessed with a restored dominion for even the animal kingdom: "the beasts of the field, and the fowls of the heaven hath he given into thine hand, and hath made thee ruler over them" (Daniel 2: 38).

No other city was blessed with dominion over all creatures. In fact, the dominion ability is generally believed by theologians to have been lost with the Fall. It is assumed that humans "lost sovereignty over the earth" (Scofield 1998: 3; Genesis 3: 17-19). Dominion is not even mentioned after the Flood when the reiteration of much of the First Precept was given to Noah. Instead, it is stated that "the fear of you and the dread of you shall be upon every beast of the earth and upon every fowl of the air, upon all that moves upon the earth, and upon all the fish of the sea" (Genesis 9: 1-2). This deliberate omission of a part of the First Precept is generally interpreted as evidence that dominion had been lost.

Therefore, the restoration of it to Nebuchadnezzar's Babylon is startling. Nebuchadnezzar had a vision of a great tree which Daniel interprets as follows:

> The tree that thou saw, which grew, and was strong, whose height reached unto the heaven, and the sight thereof to all the earth; whose leaves were fair, and their fruit thereof much, and in it was meat [food] for all; under which the beast of the field dwelt, and upon whose branches the fowls of the heaven had their habitation: It is thou, O king, that art grown and become strong: for thy greatness is grown, and reached the heaven, and thy dominion to the end of the earth (Daniel 4: 20-22).

But this kingdom and its great gift of dominion were destroyed "...that the living may know that the most High rules in the kingdom of men, and gives it to whomsoever he will, and sets up over it the basest of men" (Daniel 4: 17). The gift was not given because of any worthiness on the part of the recipient, but because God wills it (Exodus 33: 19)

## THE FIRST PRECEPT, PERFECTED – THE MILLENNIUM

According to most students of eschatology, the Millennium is a one-thousand-year period immediately following the Tribulation. It begins with the Second Coming of Christ with his touchdown on the

Mount of Olives (Zechariah 14: 4). There is an abundance of Scripture about it. In fact, "a larger body of prophetic scripture is devoted to the subject of the Millennium, developing its character and conditions, than any other subject. This millennial age, in which the purposes of God are fully realized on the earth, demands considerable attention" (Pentecost 1958: 476). However, for our purposes, the focus will be on those attributes that relate to the fulfilling of the First Precept.

First, it should be noted that the people in the Millennium are normal people, not resurrected people; they bear children and carry on agriculture and commerce. Government of the earth is pinnacled at Jerusalem, but is also administered from other cities. The Millennium is not Heaven, but a restored and regenerated present earth. Its geography, while modified, is recognizable.[1] Weather patterns, oceans, lakes, and rivers still persist. During this time, the First Precept will be perfectly applied. Therefore, an examination of these attributes within the context of the First Precept provides a good demonstration of how the gifts given to accomplish it should have been used.

Examination of the Millennium from the standpoint of the First Precept presents a knotty problem. Many of the mundane features – topography and water features – are supernaturally achieved in the Millennium. Also much is implied about various spatial interactions, but no details are provided. Routes, shipping vessels, and commodities are mentioned, but not specified geographically. War is eliminated and peace obtained, but the methods of accomplishing them are vague – probably based on an abundance of food and/or a fair distribution of resources worldwide. Justice is swift and miscreants are penalized. On the other hand, cadastral assignments to the land of Israel and other features are provided in considerable detail.

The perfect application demonstrates well how the gifts given to the cities above should have been applied and how they were misapplied. For example, metallurgy can be used to make weapons of war or for purposes of peace. In the Millennium, the people will beat their swords into plow shears and their swords into pruning hooks. Cities in the Millennium are the governance centers for all the earth, not just their own urban area. The city is to have been the container of the place of worship for all inhabitants of the planet.

## THE NEW RIVERS AND THE NEW LANDS – SUBDUED

> And it shall come to pass in that day, that the mountains shall drop down new wine, and the hills shall flow with milk, and all the rivers of Judah shall flow with waters, and a fountain shall come forth of the house of the LORD, and shall water the valley of Shittim [The Dead Sea area] (Joel 3: 18).

When Christ touches down on the Mount of Olives, a great earthquake will occur. It will split the Mount into two parts with an east-west valley running from Jerusalem to the Dead Sea. This valley will be traversed by a new river, which begins under the Temple in or near Shiloh. It will flow twelve miles southward to Jerusalem and then will split into two streams, one flowing westward to the Mediterranean Sea and one flowing through the new valley to the Dead Sea (Ezekiel 47: 1-12). Consequently, the Dead Sea will be rejuvenated and teem with fish much as is in the Mediterranean Sea.[2] In other words, the Dead Sea will still be salty, but it will contain fish such as are found in the salty waters of the oceans. Along the banks of that stream, fruit trees for food and leaves for medicine will grow (Ezekiel 47: 7, 12). In fact, because of abundant rainfall, springs and rivers will occur in the dry lands and ". . . waters shall break out, and [there will be] streams in the desert" (Isaiah 35: 6). Evidently, abundant rainfall will come in dry lands in their season in Gentile lands as well: "whoso will not come up of all the families of the earth unto Jerusalem to worship the King. . . even upon them shall be no rain" (Zechariah 14: 17).

This has great significance. First, with the refreshing, the Dead Sea will be made fruitful as well as most of the land about it. (The marshes will not be healed [Ezekiel 47: 11]). The shores of much of the Dead Sea will be as a fruitful plain much as in the Days of Sodom.[3] The second implication is that it is entirely appropriate to re-shape lands and rivers to aid in the replenishment of the earth. The earth is in need of improvement; it is imperfect physically and otherwise and is meant to be improved upon. The "Earth is no Garden of Eden – no perfect place, environmentally speaking. Great possibilities for improvement seemingly abound. Some areas are too wet, some too dry, some too high, some too cold, some too steep, others too flat and low" (Boyce 1982: 7). Unlike the view common today that treat pristine wilderness as sacred and untouchable, the changes of the land during the Millennium demonstrate that its physical features need reshaping in order to increase the fruitfulness of the earth. Therefore, the topography of Israel will be changed. Most of Israel will be flattened as a fertile plain; it will blossom as the rose and the fields will flow with milk and wines. Israel as a land will be redeemed (Isaiah 43: 1). Jerusalem will be raised in elevation and a parkway will run the twelve miles from Jerusalem to Shiloh along a ridge (Zechariah 14: 10).

## REDISTRIBUTION OF RESOURCES – SUBDUED AND REPLENISHED

The resources of the earth are distributed unequally for a purpose. If the excesses from some places are not redistributed to other places lacking them, the planet cannot be fully occupied (replenished). And, as today, many people starve in some areas, but people in other areas have more than enough to eat. In fact, there is more than enough food produced, even in the commercial tyranny of today, not only to feed the present population but billions more. However, the economic system and conflicts among nations do not allow this to happen. This author studied the question in some depth several decades ago and concluded the following:

> It is evident that the question of the adequacy of the food
> base of the Earth is contaminated appreciably by polit-

24

ical, economic, and even moral and ethical conditions. The issues appear to far overshadow the sheer physical production capacities of the Earth such as might relate to climate, soil, water, energy, fertilizer, and other factors of production such as farm size and field size. The earth is physically capable of feeding a vastly greater population than it currently does (Boyce 1982: 314).

During the Millennium, Israel will be the cornucopia of the continents. It will produce a prolific amount of food which will be shared with the world without cost or payment considerations. Likewise, various resources from distant lands will be redistributed to those lacking those items. "The kings of Tarshish [far westward and northward] shall bring presents [goods] to Jerusalem, and the kings of Sheba [eastern places] and Seba [southern places] shall offer gifts" (Psalms 72: 10) There will be no poor (see the Sermon on the Mount, Matthew 5: 1-12). "Thou [Israel] shall also suck the milk of the Gentiles, and shall suck the breast of kings, and thou shall know that I the LORD am thy Savior and thy Redeemer: the mighty One of Jacob. For brass I will bring gold, and for iron I will bring silver, and for wood brass, and for stones Iron; I will also make thy officers peace, and thine exactors righteousness (Isaiah 60: 16-17).

## THE NEW GOVERNANCE – REPLENISHED, SUBDUED, AND DOMINION RESTORED

The world will be governed by a theocracy and Jerusalem will be the supreme city. However, there will also be subservient cities to Jerusalem, ruling their respective territories (Matthew 19: 28). The world will be ruled with a "rod of iron." "In short, the eschatological city is planned" (Mackintosh and Forsberg 2013: 730). Consequently, the planet is not only governed from Jerusalem, with Israel as the head nation, but it will be orchestrated and planned. This is particularly evident in the planned complementarity between city and country. The city of Jerusalem will be laid out four square, nine miles on a side. Garden suburbs supplying food are laid-out adjacent to it.

The entire land of Israel is specified as to cadastral and administrative units, beginning with an expanded territory of Israel as described in the Palestinian Covenant (Genesis 15: 18). It will stretch from the Mediterranean Sea to the Euphrates River, and it will be about eight times larger than that formerly occupied by the twelve tribes at the time of David. Beginning with the tribe of Dan to the north to Gad in the south, each tribe is assigned a vast rectangular strip of land. The Holy oblation is laid out in the center of Israel. It is a square, encompassing 2,500 square miles. The Temple at Shiloh is located in the middle of the Holy territory (Ezekiel 40: 1 – 43: 27). The priestly square is adjacent to it on its north, and Jerusalem and its suburbs are on its south.

War and violence will be eliminated. Whether this is the result of the righteous replenishment and subduing of the earth or by government edict and enforcement, it is not known, possibly both. "The government will *deal summarily with any outbreak of* sin. Any overt act against the authority of the King will be punished with physical death" (Pentecost 1958: 503). War will be learned no more and weapons of war will be eliminated. All production and activities associated with war and violence will no longer exist. This absence alone would no doubt make the world several times richer than it is today.

> For the law shall go forth of Zion, and the word of the LORD from Jerusalem. And he shall judge among nations, and rebuke strong nations afar off [distance from Israel]; and they shall beat their swords into plow shears, and their swords into pruning hooks: nation shall not lift up a sword against nation, neither shall they learn war anymore (Micah 4: 3-5; Isaiah 2: 13).

But they shall sit, everyman under his vine and under his fig tree (Micah 4: 2-5). Agriculture will be a profession equal, if not superior, to governance, and craftsmanship. Evidently, agriculture will provide a built-in rest, peace, and joy. (As an aside, note that the five cities given the gifts above were at peace and could have utilized these gifts fruitfully in accordance with the First Precept).

"And there was given him [Christ] dominion, and glory, and a kingdom, that ALL people, nations, and languages, should serve him: his dominion is an everlasting dominion which shall not pass away, and his kingdom that which shall not be destroyed" (Daniel 7: 14; Revelation 5: 1-7). This text reminds the readers that the First Precept is not so much about humans as about the resurrected Christ. Adam lost his dominion, but the "last Adam" (1 Corinthians 15: 45) will exercise it again. In the Millennium, the wolf will lie down with the lamb, the cow will feed with the bear, and even the adder will not harm a child (Isaiah 11: 6-9). That is the restoration of dominion, a dominion that is supernaturally obtained, but which is partaken in by all. "The Millennium will be a time when the dominion given to Adam is recovered and perfectly applied by Christ. By virtue of his obedience unto death [Christ] is given universal dominion to replace that which Adam lost" (Pentecost 1958: 480).

## CONCLUSIONS

In this chapter, the author has attempted to demonstrate how certain cities were given gifts, calculated to aid in the advancement of the First Precept, but used improperly. None of the five cities at the time were encumbered by wars or other circumstances that would have interfered with their abilities to carry out their mission. Consequently, perhaps this demonstrates the fallen nature of humankind. The perversion of these gifts was voluntary, deliberate, and even rebellious. The Millennium, while consummating numerous things lost when Adam fell, also provides a powerful demonstration of how these seemingly mundane gifts could and should have been utilized to fulfill the overarching first command ever given to humankind by God.

Notably, the tools were provided to secular Gentiles cities, not to spiritual ones. The spiritual gifts were given to Jerusalem and Israel, something which they also corrupted. The means provided, beginning with the gift of the city itself, were practical, utilitarian, and necessary.

They were essential in order to fulfill the first commandment to: (1) be fruitful, (2) multiply, (3) replenish, (4), subdue, and (5) have dominion over the earth. Interestingly, these five gifts were given to five different cities, and five is the number of grace in Scripture.

## A REFLECTION BY THE AUTHOR

Permit me to share a feeling I had upon completing this work. I was surprised by joy – a spontaneous, inexplicable and fleeting feeling – which was followed immediately by the sensation of sadness. Joy cannot be anticipated, manipulated, or created. "Clamoring after joy leads only to fevered simulacra: an art of professional echoes and planned epiphanies. . . . (Wiman 2017: 434). My tandem of joy and sadness experience reminded me of a poem entitled "Joy" by the famed poet, Lisel Mueller, particularly the stanza:

> It's not about loss. It's about
> Two seemingly parallel lines
> Suddenly coming together
> Inside us, in some place
> That is still wilderness

(Wiman 2017: 43).

It is the "still wilderness" that captivates me. It has so many different but subtle meanings. While the arguments made above are deceptively simple, the end result is that, within my mind, a great unknown wilderness still reigns. Significant things are exposed, but before I could grasp fully the sensation of joy, it vanished into a fog-enclosed cloud of great uncertainty. I realized also that my thoughts on the theology of the city are but a wilderness of true truth and full understanding. There is much more, by much brighter minds than mine, of the unknown wilderness still to be explored. Finally, I have the nagging question as to whether scholars will follow-up on the foundation I have begun to lay.

# ENDNOTES

[1] I do not think the New Jerusalem described in Revelation 21 applies to the Millennium. There is considerable controversy about this interpretation and other end-time texts, but I am not going to argue the point. (See Pentecost 1958: 563-80). In this chapter, I will not discuss various theological interpretations such as pre-tribulations, post-tribulation, or a-millennialism, but will limit my attention and scriptural texts regarding the First Precept. In fact, I avoid hermeneutics as much as possible. The focus here is limited to descriptions of these texts which bear on the geographical, political, and economic features which may relate to Genesis 1: 28. This is not a Bible study in the plenary sense, but it is an inquiry into these texts as they pertain to the immediate subject at hand. In order to avoid esoteric arguments, I accept the text at face value and avoid as much as possible spiritual interpretations. Therefore, important features of the Millennium are deliberately omitted. Nonetheless, there are numerous Scriptures that make it abundantly clear that many events discussed are supernaturally orchestrated.

[2] There is much that is supernatural with respect to the river and the trees about it. It is a river and a tree which increase life. There was a river in the center of the Garden of Eden which flowed outward into four streams. The Tree of Life was in the center of the Garden (Genesis 2: 9-10). During the Millennium, we are told that "wherever the rivers shall come, shall live" (Ezekiel 47: 12). The river will begin in the Tabernacle and flow to Jerusalem, where it will be broken into two branches. Along its banks will be trees bearing different fruit for each month and having leaves for medicine. "Living waters will flow from Jerusalem" (Zechariah 14: 8). In the new earth, waters will flow from under the throne in the Holy City. Trees of Life will be found on both sides of the river, both for food and for the healing of nations (Revelation 22: 1).

[3] However, the marshes about the Dead Sea will not be healed. Perhaps this was the area formerly occupied by Sodom and Gomorrah and their neighboring cities in the Valley of Siddim (salt) (Genesis 14: 3).

# REFERENCES

Bakke, Ray. 1997. *A Theology as Big as the City*. Downers Grove, IL: InterVarsity Press.

Boyce, Ronald R. 1982. *Geographic Perspectives on Global Problems: An Introduction to Geography*. New York, NY: John Wiley and Sons.

Boyce, Ronald R. 2013a. "The First Precept: The Primary Purpose of Cities and the Provision of God," In William A. Dando, Caroline

Dando, and Jonathan J. Lu. Eds. *Geography of the Holy Land – New Insights*. Kaohsiung, Taiwan: Holy Light Theological Press, pp. 30-61.

Boyce, Ronald R. 2013b. "The First Precept: Implications for a New Theology of Cities. In William A. Dando, Caroline Dando, and Jonathan J. Lu. Eds. *Geography of the Holy Land – New Insights*. Kaohsiung, Taiwan: Holy Light Theological Press, pp. 62-107.

Chafer, Lewis Sperry. 1947. *Systematic Theology*. Dallas, TX: Dallas Seminary Press, Vol. I.

Clapp, James A. (Ed.). 1986. *The City: A Dictionary of Quotable Thought on Cities and Life*.

Comins, Rabbi Mike. 2007. *A Wild Faith: Jewish Ways into Wilderness, Wilderness Ways into Judaism*. Woodstock, VT. Jewish Lights Publishing.

Conn, Harvie M. 1978. *A Clarified Vision of Urban Mission: Dispelling the Urban Stereotypes*. Grand Rapids, MI: Zondervan.

Critchfield, Richard. 1991. *Trees, Why Do You Wait? America's Changing Rural Culture*. Washington, D.C.: Island Press.

Eliade, Mircea. 1959. *The Sacred and the Profane: The Nature of Religion*. New York, NY: Harcourt, Brace & World, Inc. (Translated from the French by Willard R. Trask).

Ellul, Jacques. 1970. *The Meaning of the City*. Grand Rapids, MI.: William B. Eardmans Publishing Co.

George, Henry. 1968. "City and Country". In Lyle W. Dorsett, Ed. *The Challenge of the City: 1860-1910*. Lexington, KY: D. C. Heath and Co.

Harris, Chauncy D. and Edward L. Ullman. 1945. "The Nature of Cities." *The Annals of the American Academy of Political and Social Science*, November, pp. 7-17.

Larkin, Clarence. 1920. *Dispensational Truth or God's Plan and Purpose in the Ages*. Philadelphia, PA: Rev. Clarence Larkin Est.

Mackintosh, Phillip and Clyde R. Forsberg Jr.: 2013. "Co-agent of the Millennium: City Planning and Christian Eschatology in the North American City, 1890 – 1920." *Annals of the Association of American Geographers*, May, pp. 727-47.

Martin, Daniel J. 2017. *2016-17: A Year of Celebration*. Seattle, WA: Seattle Pacific University.

Martin, Keith. 1977. "Perspectives on Urban Theology." *Center for Theology and Public Policy, Shalom Paper No. 3*.

Oosterwal, Gottfried. 1980. "How Shall We Work in Cities – From Within?" *Ministry*, June.

Pentecost, J. Dwight. 1958. T*hings to Come: A Study in Eschatology*. Grand Rapids, MI.: Zondervan Publishing House.

Scofield, C. I. 1998. *The New Scofield Study Bible*. New York, NY: Oxford University Press.

Stead, William T. 1894. *If Christ Came to Chicago*. Chicago, IL: Laird and Lee.

Tuan, Yi Fu. 1974. *Topophilia: A Study of Environmental Perceptions, Attitudes, and Values*. New York, NY: Prentice-Hall.

Ullman, Edward L. 1980. *Geography as Spatial Interaction*. Ronald R. Boyce, Ed. Seattle, WA: University of Washington Press.

Wiman, Christian. 2017. "Still Wilderness: What Are We Feeling When We Are Feeling Joy? And Where Inside Us Does That Feeling Reside?" *The American Scholar*. Washington, D.C.: Phi Beta Kappa, Autumn, pp. 36-50.

# Seeds on the Road to Sychar: Stunning Answers to "Where" Trigger Questions

Ronald R. Boyce

## INTRODUCTION

Sometimes seemingly simple questions result in surprising answers. Such questions in Scripture evoke a cascade of surprising, stunning, even shattering responses. Interestingly, the answers to six where-based questions provide a progressive road map of the nature, purposes, and provisions of God to enable a fallen human race to carry out his precepts and participate in his purposes. Six questions, based on the third of the well-known Six Interrogatives – who, what, **where**, when, why, and how – will be examined below:

1. Where is my Helpmate? (Genesis 2: 18-20)[1]
2. Adam, where are you? (Genesis 3: 9)
3. Where is your brother Abel? (Genesis 4: 9)
4. Where is my promised seed? (Genesis 15: 2)
5. Where is the lamb for the burnt-offering? (Genesis 22: 7)
6. Where is your cup and your cord for drawing water? (John 4: 11)

Pregnant questions based on the other interrogatives are also important. And all are necessary to understand anything comprehensively and in context. There are examples in the Bible which focus on each of them. The most important "when" and "what" questions occurred when Jesus' disciples asked him "**When** will these things be, and **what** shall be the sign of thy coming and the end of the age?" (Matthew 24: 3; emphasis added by author). The understanding of his response to that question is very complex and requires knowledge of eschatology. Possibly the most shocking and shattering answer to a "who" question occurred to the apostle Paul on the road to Damascus when he asked "**Who** are you Lord?" (Acts 9: 5; emphasis added). Paul was certainly startled to learn that Jesus, the one whom he had been persecuting, was YHWH, the Messiah. He was no doubt further shattered to learn that he was going to be sent to take this yet-to-be fully understood Gospel of Grace to the Gentiles, a people considered barbaric by the Jews. This too requires extensive study. Therefore, in this chapter, only a few of the most instructive where-based questions are examined.

The "where" trigger questions and the general stories related to them are well-known to the average Christian. However, the answers require deeper contemplation than is commonly provided.[2] Also, when these six questions are presented in this order, a progressive development of seminal themes in Scripture occurs. They begin in Genesis 1 and continue in general chronological order up to the Cross. Thereby, these are a set of "where" trigger questions. The pun of "where trigger" is deliberate in that it suggests a catalyst whereby a hair trigger, when pulled, detonates a fuselage of new revelations.

It will be evident that responses to these "where" trigger-based questions reveal not only the promises of God but the provisions of God (the YHWH-*jireh*, the Provision Principle) to fulfill his precepts. Some provide provisions for fulfilling the First Precept, which is to "be fruitful, multiply, replenish, and subdue the earth" (Genesis 1: 28). For example, in the first "where" question, Adam presumably asks God "Where is *my* helpmate?" we get the shocking solution to the command to "multiply." The second question was introduced by the Lord God, when he asked Adam "Where are you?" (Genesis 3: 9). This led to great insights about the nature and path of the promised Messiah.

In general, the third interrogative leads to more comprehensive and critical answers than most of the other interrogatives. "Where," may refer to place, situation (relative location or condition), position, or circumstances. In the six trigger questions below, often several dimensions of "where" are implied by the question and/or the answer. In some cases, the question posed is not directly stated in the biblical text, but it is strongly suggested by the context.

It is also important to pay attention to the "With whom?" feature. Who is asking and to whom is it being asked? This "seventh interrogative" was first discussed by Aristotle, but is usually used in police interrogations. Likewise, in biblical study, it is critical to an understanding of the context. Various combinations are used – e.g. Adam asking God, God asking Adam and Cain, Abraham asking God, Isaac asking Abraham, the woman at the well asking Jesus "Where is your cup for drawing water?" (John. 4: 11).

Finally, please note that various names for God in each case. When *God* is used it generally refers to *Elohim.* (the term *God* is used in a generic sense or as a surrogate for the more specific appellation being discussed). *Elohim* is the creator, the independent, the self-existent one. He is He that is who He is (Exodus 3: 14). He is the great "I AM." It is also a uni-plural noun which encompasses the godhead. The word LORD (all caps) is so sacred to the Jews that they refuse to speak it. The letters are YHWH, which many Christians pronounce as "Jehovah," or "Yahweh." However, the Jews pronounce it *Adonai.* This often refers to the covenant-making and covenant-keeping God. "Lord" refers to master and is generally used by believers such as Abraham or the woman taken in adultery. Finally, there are about a dozen compound words beginning with YHWH, or LORD. In most cases these compound names of God show him "as meeting every need of man from his lost state to the end" (Scofield Reference Bible 1998: 140). Therefore, they demonstrate the provisions of God. The most specific one for our purposes is "YHWH-*jirah*" (God will provide) which was first used when God provided a substitute sacrifice for Isaac who had already been placed on the altar (Genesis 22: 7).

## WHERE IS MY HELPMATE? (GENESIS 1: 26 – 2: 25)

This question was surely asked by Adam to YHWH-*Elohim* (LORD God). The Lord God had said earlier that it was not right that Adam should be alone – i.e. without a mate. The word "helpmate" in the Hebrew is best described by the English word "complement."[3] In other words, two separate but symbiotic components are necessary to function properly. Thereafter, the Lord God caused all the animals with their mates to parade in front of Adam who gave names to each species. And then the text says that no complement was found for Adam among them. Certainly, Adam surely wondered and probably asked, "Where is *my* helpmate? (Genesis 2: 18-20; emphasis added). Paradoxically, Adam was complete internally but alone externally.

It is important to realize that six significant events occurred in the life of Adam **before** woman appeared: (1) Adam was given the First Precept: "Be fruitful, multiply, replenish and subdue the earth" (Genesis 1: 28). (2) Elohim had sanctified the seventh or Sabbath day as a day of rest (Genesis 1: 2-3). (3) The Lord God (YHWH-Elohim)[4] commissioned Adam to till the ground (Genesis 2: 5, 15), a commandment that continued even after Adam and Eve were removed from the Garden of Eden (Genesis 2: 3). (4) Adam was placed in the Garden of Eden, and (5) commanded by the Lord God not to eat from the Tree of Knowledge of Good and Evil which stood in the center of the garden or he would die (Genesis 2: 17). Finally, (6) the animal pairs were paraded before Adam for their naming and to look for a complement (Genesis 2: 19).

Then God moved in a most surprising manner. He put Adam into a deep sleep,[5] then extracted an embryo-like substance from Adam's side from which he created a being (a complement) out of Adam who is called *woman*, meaning "from man." The female was embedded in Adam from the beginning. Otherwise, two saviors, not one, would be required: one for males and one for females. Of course, "God could have formed the woman out of the dust of the earth, as he had formed man; but had he done so, she must have appeared in his eyes as a distinct being, to which he had no natural relation. But God formed her out of <u>a part of the man</u> himself, he saw she was of the same nature, the same identical flesh and blood, and the same constitution in all respects, and consequently having equal power, faculties, and rights" (Clarke 1960: Vol. I, 45). Nonetheless, their relationship retained Adam as the champion (federal head) of the human race. They became one in marriage but maintained separate roles. As Boice says, "the woman was made *for* man; she was made *from* man; and she was given *to* man – the greatest of all God's gifts [and] she is named *by* man (Boice 1998: 130). Adam was overjoyed and proclaimed that she is "bone of my bone and flesh of my flesh," implying that more than a bone (rib) was extracted. Some have made much of the place from which the womb-like substance was removed from Adam. "She was not made out of head to rule over him, nor out of his feet to be trampled upon by him, but out of his side to be equal with him, under his arm to be protected, and near his heart to be beloved" (Henry 1972: Vol. I, 12).

Perhaps a few words should be said about the name for the female embryo (rib) extracted from the side of Adam and activated by God. *Woman* is an English word which means "out of man" and is composed of a compound of **wo** and **man**, which may mean more than out of man (Genesis 2: 23) but womb of man, a womb that was formerly embedded in Adam. The Hebrew word for "man" is *Ish* and the woman is *Ishshah*. The words "male" and "female" are similar, but few words describe the female without reference and deference to the male.

In today's terms, Adam before the "rib" was extracted was a hermaphrodite.[6] Therefore, when God states the First Precept to Adam (them), he was addressing them both (Feldig 2002: 41). This interpretation is consistent with the Scripture earlier. When God says "Let us" make man in our image, he is using a uni-plural pronoun. Therefore, "male and female He created them," a uni-plural pronoun (Genesis 1: 26-27).[7] However, only Adam, the male, was evident outwardly at that time. When activated by God from the complement within him – something which God had prepared in advance, the new creation could hardly have been closer, yet more different. The result was the she-man or the womb-man. From one uni-plural person, Adam, became two separate but interconnected beings. When united in marriage the two are re-united to form one flesh (Genesis 2: 24). Thereby, the creation of woman now made possible the first part of the First Precept (Genesis 1: 28): to "multiply."[8]

## ADAM, WHERE ARE YOU? (GENESIS 3: 9-21)

When God said to Adam, if you eat of the fruit of the Tree of Knowledge of good and evil, you will surely die, the outcome was fixed. Secondly, when Adam ate of the fruit the eyes of both Adam and his wife were opened. They knew that they were guilty and that judgment was deserved and eminent; they expected death. Thirdly, to understand the "death" administered, it is important to recognize that both God and man are composed of three parts. Just as God (*Elohim*) is a uni-plural noun (composed of God the Father, God the Son, and God the Holy Spirit), humans consist of three components: a body, a soul, and a spirit. The spirit provides the communication fellowship human beings had with God before they sinned. It became dead (inoperable) when they sinned, just as God declared. The soul also consists of a trinity of the mind, the will, and the emotions. The soul is instructed by the spirit. When Adam disobeyed, the soul was changed from a God-oriented nature to a sin-oriented nature. It became a wandering star, moved about by the fleshy demands of the body – touch, taste, smell, seeing, and hearing. These fleshly demands continue unabated as long as the natural man lives.[9] However, with Adam's sin, the body also began to die.[10] It was a slow process, taking hundreds of years at first.

Note that God did not say "Where are you, Adam and Woman?" The federal head of the human race was Adam alone; it was not a shared headship. Of course, there is no distinction in salvation, etc. (Galatians 3: 28). Adam and Christ are comparable in this respect, albeit Christ is vastly superior.[11] Scripture refers to Christ as the last Adam (1 Corinthians 15: 45). The first Adam was made a living soul, earthy, but the last Adam was made a life-giving spirit, heavenly. And of course, Christ is superior to Adam in that when he sinned "the power of death could be broken. This Christ did. 'He destroyed death and has brought life and immortality to light through the gospel' (2 Timothy 1: 10). By contrast, Christ's work cannot be undone" (Boice 1998: 211).

This "where" trigger question is followed by several facts: (1) Adam and his wife knew their plight. They were conscious of their guilt, afraid, hiding, and without hope. They were also ashamed of their nakedness and tried to cover it up with fig leaves. (2) The verdict and judgments of God would surely follow. The human race was found guilty and cursed; this was the *stare decisis* (stand on that decision) – an inviolate verdict which would stand as a precedent for all fallen future generations. Therefore, God continued his litany of curses and his necessary actions because of their disobedience. The woman's desire would be to her husband, but she would be delivered through childbirth – perhaps a reference to the promised seed. Adam would face a cursed soil and earn his existence by the sweat of his brow. And he and Eve would surely die physically. They were driven from the Garden so that they could not eat of the Tree of Life and live forever in their fallen state (Genesis 3: 5). (3) They were forcibly removed from the Garden of Eden. Interestingly, they were driven out to the east and the entrance – now heavily guarded – was on the east.[12]

It also resulted in provisions, the provisions shortly to be provided by grace of YHWH *Elohim*, one of the most stunning promises in the Bible, and (4) the evidence of belief and (5) the new beginning whereby the human race could continue, even though under the condemnation of sin. Little did they know that God is love and he was immediately going to provide for their highest interests. It began with the curse given the provocateur, the serpent (*nacash*, the most cunning of God's creatures, but whose end was here prophesied. However, in doing so, the most stunning of God's promises[13] was revealed: the seed of the woman would kill the serpent (Genesis 3: 15).

It was a shocking proclamation. The deliverer to come was buried inside the woman, much as Adam's helpmate was embedded within him. For her seed shall bruise (kill) Satan's head – the only place where a serpent can be killed. We now know that this seed was the promised deliverer and restorer of the fallen condition of the human race (Luke 1: 34-35). The inert seed will be activated, not by man, but by God. The promised seed of the woman is "by her alone, without concurrence of man" (Clarke 1960: Vol. I., 53).[14]

The promise of a savior by the seed of woman also provided the foundation for Adam to demonstrate renewed faith in God's word. This was manifest when Adam changed the name of woman to Eve, meaning the "mother of all humankind," not "mother of all living," as stated in the KJV. The mother of all living would have to include animals as wells as people (Hertz 1960: 12). Eve demonstrated her renewed faith with respect to the birth of Cain when she said "I have gotten a man from the LORD" (Genesis 4: 1). Immediately following Adam's profession of faith, the Lord God provided a way of redemption – a temporary covering or atonement.

Then God restored them in a most surprising way. Evidently, he killed an animal and covered them with its skin. Death of another innocent being was here first introduced as a substitution for Sin. We know from the book of Hebrews that an animal cannot permanently take away sin, but it can postpone punishment until the real and permanent redeemer arrives – i.e. Jesus. (Hebrews 9: 11-14). So this begins periodic blood sacrifice on the part of believers in order to remain under the protection of God. Evidently because of Adam and Eve's faith, God also "clothed them" (Genesis 3: 21). This is the righteousness of God imputed to humans: "he has clothed me with the robe of righteousness" (Isaiah 61: 10). It is made even more explicit in the New Testament with respect to Abraham: "Abraham believed God, and it was accounted to him as righteousness" (Galatians 3: 6; Genesis 15: 6).

Therefore, the seemingly simple question to Adam, "Where are you?" triggered an amazing cascade of change: place, condition, and hope. They entered the stage hiding, afraid, helpless, and without hope; they exited the stage confident, clothed with his righteousness and burgeoning hope. First, the death of the body was postponed, at least for a season. Second, Adam and Eve were promised progeny so as to begin fulfilling the multiply command of the First Precept, even though fallen and flawed creatures. Third, victory over Satan was promised by a coming seed of the woman. Fourth, Adam and Eve were provided continued good graces of God by periodic blood sacrifices of an animal, and fifthly, God's righteousness was imputed to them because they believed what God said.

## WHERE IS YOUR BROTHER, ABEL? (GENESIS 4: 9)

The basic story of Cain and Abel is one of the most familiar in the entire Bible. Even children can describe the narrative they learned in Sunday school. Cain and Abel brought offerings to the Lord. Abel, a keeper of sheep, brought his offering of a lamb and was accepted, but Cain, a tiller of the soil, brought his offering from his field and was rejected. This angered Cain so much that he killed Abel and buried him in his field. Afterward, God put a mark on Cain and exiled him to a life of wandering in the land of Nod. That simplistically stated story is wrong, incomplete, and misses the main point; it is therefore one of the most misunderstood stories in the Bible.

The parallel between the sin of Adam and that of Cain is summarized in Table 1 It shows a clear chronological parallel or path between Adam and Cain. Faith, protection, and provision are in that path. This parallelism provides insights into both. In fact, their journeys in this regard are strikingly similar in seven ways. Both disobeyed God by choosing their selfish desires over God's commands. Of course, the commands are different, but the result is similar. In both cases, the exposure of their guilt began with "where" trigger questions. Adam hid himself in shame, whereas Cain hid (buried) his brother Abel, whom he had killed and buried in his field. Both are then administered their sentences, but with opportunity for revealing their faith embedded within them. Adam showed his faith by changing his wife's name to Eve, Cain evidenced his faith in a way more difficult to pinpoint, but his guilt and nakedness were surely exposed by God's statement about the blood of Abel crying,

**Table 1. The Parallel Paths of Adam and Cain – From Sin and Guilt to New Beginnings**

| Chronological Path | Adam | Cain |
|---|---|---|
| Sin Documented | Disobeyed God – *But of the tree of good and evil you shall not eat* (Gen. 2: 17) | Disobeyed God – Refused to bring the required offering. *But unto Cain and to his offering he had no respect* (Gen. 4: 5) |
| Guilt Exposed | *Where are you?* (Gen. 3 :9) | *Where is Abel, your Brother?* (Gen. 4: 9) |
| Sentence Rendered | Soil cursed, but must till the ground by sweat of his brow until death (Gen. 3: 19) | Soil cursed to Cain for farming, but he must become a fugitive and a vagabond (Gen. 4: 12) |
| Faith Evidenced | God's sentence is accepted. Woman is renamed Eve by Adam (Gen. 3: 20) | God's sentence is accepted, but *my punishment is greater than I can bear* (Gen. 4: 13) |
| Nakedness Remedied | God *made coats of skins and clothed them* (Gen. 3: 21) | *The LORD set a mark* [of protection] *on Cain* (Gen. 4: 15) |
| Geography Changed | Relocated from the Garden of Eden to East Eden – *He drove man out of the Garden eastward in Eden* (Gen. 3: 24) | Relocated from East Eden to the Land of Nod – He drove Cain of Eden into *the land of Nod on the east of Eden* (Gen. 4: 16) |
| New Beginning Provided – birth of rural and urban endeavors and cultures | *And Adam knew Eve and she conceived and bore Cain and Abel* (later to be replaced by Seth) (Gen. 4: 1, 25) | *And Cain knew his wife and she conceived and bore Enoch* (Gen. 4: 17) |

probably for revenge, from Cain's field. Both were restored to serve God despite their fallen conditions. And both were physically removed from their places of original sin and pushed into lands with harsher conditions. Finally, both were provided with progeny to begin a new life whereby they could begin to fulfill the First Precept.

Even the common questions raised miss the main message. There are two main diversionary questions: (1) Why was Abel's offering accepted and Cain's rejected? (2) What was the mark of Cain? Both are important, but incidental to the primary point of the story, particularly the omission of the provision by the Lord of a new beginning (See Table 1, Row 7) because both of Adam's children, Seth and Cain, follow a somewhat similar chronology.

The reason Abel and his offering were accepted has to do with the faith evidenced by Abel in bringing the offering specified by God, a blood sacrifice. This principle had been established by the blood sacrifice of an animal to clothe Adam and Eve. Evidently, Cain was rejected because he disobeyed the Lord by bringing an offering produced by his own hands from a cursed ground. Therefore, Abel believed God and obeyed God, and Cain lacked faith and evidenced pride in himself.[15]

The next question generally turns to why Cain killed Abel. Most fallaciously assume that it was because Cain was jealous of Abel. The most likely reason is that Cain was angry at God for accepting Abel and thereby decided to destroy God's chosen one. This is known as the "Salieri Syndrome." It is "derived from the movie, *Amadeus* (meaning "God's beloved"). In the movie, Antonio Salieri had made a deal with God – at least in his own mind – that he would lead a pious, God-fearing life in exchange for God's providing to him the talent for producing fine music. However, his disdain for Amadeus, coupled with his 'heavenly music,' caused Salieri to vow to destroy the one that God evidently loves" (Boyce 2013: 42). Salieri was angry at God for favoring one that he considered inferior morally and otherwise. It is clearly the same kind of reasoning that Cain must have had about God when he decided to destroy Abel.

Even so, the pivot point in the story is triggered by the "where" trigger question: "Where is your brother, Abel?" God stopped Cain in his tracks. However, unlike Adam who knew his guilt, Cain is defiant, sarcastic ("Am I my brother's keeper?"), secure (not my problem), defensive, and delusional. Cain was confident that he had hidden his action from God by burying Abel. And he was delusional in thinking that he could frustrate the purpose of God by killing Abel.[16]

Cain is brought up short by the shocking revelation of God that Abel's blood cries out from the ground. Life is in the blood, and it causes Cain to realize that Abel is alive, at least in testimony against him. In fact, the soil was the source of Cain's pride; now it became the source of his undoing. Suddenly, Cain was sober, helpless (naked), inadequate, and afraid. Cain has become convicted; he believes God. Cain's evidence of faith has been stated by many. "According to Rabbis, Cain was a repentant sinner... God's mercy to the guilty who repents of his sin is infinitely greater than that of man" (Hertz 1960: 15). Rabbi Rashi[17] presents Cain's response as a rhetorical question: "Is my sin too great to be forgiven?" Obviously not.

Similar to the chronology of Adam, God continues with the sentence (Table 1, Row 3). First, the ground from which Cain took his pride now will no longer yield to him; he can no longer be a farmer. Second, he can't even herd sheep; instead, he is sentenced to become a wanderer and a vagabond. He has no occupation..

However, evidently based on Cain's faith in the word of the Lord, Cain accepts the sentence, but with fear of death.[18] Thereby, God puts a protective mark or sign on (or for) Cain. Contrary to popular opinion, this is **not** a punitive mark but a protective one. This mark or letter or sign given to him is not a scarlet letter of disgrace as was administered to Hester Prynne.[19] And despite the clear text of Scripture and the careful work of scholars that it is a mark of protection, the myth of condemnation continues.

One interpretation, based on the "mark" and its purposes in Ezekiel 9: 4-6, suggests that it is "a mark, lit. a *tau*, the last letter of the Hebrew alphabet, written at the time like a cross [possible predictive of Christ] . . . persons so marked would be spared. Similarly, God will mark the 144,000 during the tribulation period" (Revelation 7: 3-4; Ryrie 1994: 1196). In fact, throughout Scripture the mark is always used as a symbol of protection, not condemnation. Even the Antichrist uses his mark of the beast to protect his followers (Revelation 13: 16).

The mark is also evidence of repentance. Cain would have had to repent and believe God in order to receive the blessings. "Some of the doctors in the Talmud say that it was the letter ת *tau* marked on his forehead, which signified his contrition, as it is the first letter of the word *techubah*, **repentance**" (Clarke 1960: 61; emphasis added by the author). Of course, the common notion is that Cain received no blessings. As has already been solidly established, the mark was a blessing and an evidence of belief.

The end of the story of Adam and Cain is commonly omitted. In fact, new beginnings for both were provided. God has restored the fallen condition by providing a new birth of opportunities under more adverse conditions. In fact, Adam and Eve are the parents of two new endeavors and cultures, one through Abel and the other through Cain. "From the very face of this account it appears evident that Cain and Abel were *twins*.[20] Otherwise the acts of conceiving and bringing forth are mentioned to each child; here it is not: here it is *not* said that she *conceived* and brought forth Abel, but simply that *she simply added to bring forth Abel*, his brother" (Clarke 1960: Vol. I, 58). And we know that another took the place of Abel "for God has appointed me another seed [Seth] instead of Abel" (Genesis 4: 25). And of course, there are two genealogies in Scripture; one following Cain and one following Seth, whereby they represent two different cultures, one urban and one rural and one more spiritual. Cain's linage is more secular, more worldly-minded, more profane and highly inventive; this line of six great pioneers introduced the phenomena of cities and civilization itself. By contrast, the lineage of

## Table 2. Abram's Promised Seed and His Stunned Surprise

The Promise: "*I will make of thee [form] a great nation, and I will bless thee, and make thy name great; and thou (a nation and a seed) shall be a blessing: and I will bless them that bless thee, and curse them that curse thee: and in thee shall all the families of the earth be blessed.*" (Gen. 12: 2-3).

| Steps to the Promised Seed | Description |
|---|---|
| Abram's Promised Seed and the Promised Land is stated | After his promised seed was described as numerous as the sand of the sea, Abram built an altar in the Plain of Moreh, at Bethel, and at the Plain of Mamre (Hebron). (Gen. 12: 6, 8; 13: 15-18). All become sacred places in Israel. |
| **Not** by a Substitute Seed | Abram thought it might be Eliezer, but was told the seed would be out of his own bowels. Abram believed, as he understood it, and it was accounted to him by God as righteous (Gen. 15: 2-6) |
| **Not** by a Surrogate Seed | Sarai thought the seed would be a surrogate for her, through her handmaid, Hagar, but the child, Ishmael, was not the promised seed (Gen. 16: 10). |
| **Not** by man, but all of God – revealed *El Shaddai* (God Almighty), and as *El Elyon* (God, the Highest) | Abram's name was changed to Abraham (father of *many* nations), and Sarai's name was changed to Sarah (mother of nations, presumably *all* of them (Gen. 17: 4, 15-16; 18: 12). Will be by a female, not the male seed (Gen. 3: 15). Circumcision initiated as the covenant evidence. |
| **All** of Grace – Sarah's womb was activated; no longer was she barren (Gen. 21: 1-3). | Sarah laughed with dumfounded joy at the birth of Isaac, the promised seed (singular and plural) of Israel, and the promised seed (singular, in Christ and of Israel) of all families of the earth. (Gen. 21: 6-7; Lk. 24: 41). All was accomplished through the female, not the male (Gen. 3: 15). Isaac could be rightfully called "Abraham's seed" because, with marriage, Abraham and Sarah became *one flesh* (Gen. 2: 24). |

Seth is more sacred, more spiritual, and more prophetically rich. Enoch, the sixth from Adam, walked with God and never saw death.[21] Moreover, Enoch begat Methuselah, who lived longer than anyone before or since. And Noah, the son of Lamech,[22] was given grace, meaning he was by no means perfect, and he and his family were brought through the Flood in the Ark. Interestingly, Noah lived 777 years. Even so, there is evidence of God-mindedness in both genealogies – e.g. the *el* endings in Cain's line (Mehujael and Methusael) and in Seth's line (Mahalahel and Methuselah).[23] And the two groups evidently became entangled in symbiotic and intermarriage relationships (Genesis 6: 2). In fact, the whole population became violent and corrupt (Genesis 6: 11).

The next blessing, after his exit from Eden to Nod, given Cain is the city – it is a new beginning for Cain (Genesis 4: 17). In fact, *Enoch* means (Strong # 2585) to "initiate," "cause," "favor," and "show mercy"; thereby, the name implies a new beginning.[24] Therefore, Enoch signifies a new beginning for Cain. From the bowels of Enoch came a cascade of inventions and change. Each person mentioned is an originator of new things – in commerce, city-country interaction (Jabal); the arts, music, architecture (Jubal); metallurgy and craftsmanship (Tubal-cain); law and government (Lamech). Thus, the way was open for humankind to fulfill the full components of the First Precept: to multiply, replenish, and subdue the earth. Indeed, "the cultural mandate given at creation was a mandate to build the city. . . the common grace city has remedial benefits even in a fallen world. It becomes the drawing together of resources, strength, and talent no longer just for mutual complementation in the task of developing resources of the created world, but now a pooling of power for defense against attack, and as an administrative community of welfare for the relief of those destitute by reasons of the cursing of the ground" (Kline 2006: 162).

"From a secular history perspective, the major event between the Fall of Adam and the Flood is the founding of cities (Gen. 4: 17) and the consequent growth of population (Gen. 6: 1) [the birth of Babylon was probably the most seminal cultural event]" (Boyce 2013: 42). The link between the First Precept and the first cities is becoming more widely understood by Bible scholars. "It is widely understood that when God tells Adam and Eve to have dominion and fill the earth he is directing them to build a God-honoring civilization. They are to bring forth the riches that God put into creation by developing science, art, architecture, human society. . . . Therefore, God was calling Adam and Eve to be city builders" (Keller 2002). That may be a stretch. It is stunning to realize that such a fundamental provision by God was first administered in the genealogy of Cain. Of course, it was administered imperfectly and corruptly, even as a way to frustrate the purpose of God.[25]

## WHERE IS MY PROMISED SEED?

The calling and conversion of Abram are shocking. He lived in Ur, the largest city in the world at that time. It was only a few miles downstream on the Euphrates from the infamous Babylon, the place from which two hundred years earlier God scattered humankind to replenish the earth. And Abram was an idolater as was his entire family (Joshua 24: 2).

He was told by God to leave his father's house and from his home city and go to a land yet to be shown him, and if he did, God would make his name great, give him a great nation from his seed, and through his seed all the peoples of the earth would be blessed (Genesis 12: 1-3). To make from him a great nation required that the nation yet to come must contain many people. And a nation required a land and a leader. This great nation would be a blessing to the world. Abram believed and departed. He was at least fifty years old and his wife, Sarai, was barren.

We now know that Abram was being sent to the land of Canaan which at that time contained many cities. Interestingly, Jerusalem is directly west of Ur. To get to Canaan with a herd of cattle, one had to travel northwest on the Euphrates until they reached a departure point somewhere near what became Haran. Inasmuch as Abram's father, Terah, and other family members also went with him, he remained in Haran for about twenty-five years until his father died. Abram then was told to go southward into the land of Canaan where he grazed his cattle in the Plain of Moreh near Shechem. (Genesis 12: 6). There the Lord appeared again to Abram and told him that this land would be given to him. Abram then built an altar and made a sacrifice unto the Lord, probably at the foot of Mt. Gerizim. He then continued southward to Bethel where he made another altar. Because a famine was in the land of Canaan, he went to Egypt for a season. On his return from Egypt, he camped near Hebron. For a further understanding of these events, see the Postlogue.

All three of these places became sacred sites to Israel. Jacob's well was dug at Shechem, Joseph's bones brought back from Egypt are buried there, and this was the place where Jesus encountered the woman from Sychar (Shechem). It was here also that Josiah brought the Torah and read it to Israel (2 Kings 23: 15). At Bethel, Jacob had a dream (Genesis 28: 19) and named it "the house of God "(Bethel). And of course, Sarah, Abraham and others are buried at Hebron.

It should be noted that the seed and the land are tandem twins. The word "seed" in Genesis 12: 7 is plural when he said "unto thy seed I will give this land." Abram had questions about both. When he asked how he might know that he would receive the land, God went through the legal process for deeding the land. Even so, Abram continued to live the life of a nomad and grazed his herds only by permission of the Canaanite city dwellers. The perplexing question in Abram's mind was the matter of the promised seed. Sarai was barren. Therefore, Abram and Sarai began to wonder how God might fulfill his promise for a seed. First, Abram assumed that it would be by a substitute seed, his steward, Eliezer from Damascus (Genesis 15: 2). God said "No," and declared that it would be by his own bowels. Abram believed God, even though he did not understand how, and God accounted Abram righteous (Genesis 15: 6; Galatians 3: 6).

Sarai began to think that she was the encumbrance to fulfilling the promise and reasoned that she could provide her servant, Hagar, as her surrogate. Abram evidently thought it was a great idea and obliged. A son, Ishmael, was born, thereby demonstrating that Abram was virile. But God again corrected their fallacious reasoning and declared that there would be no surrogate. When Abram was 99 and Sarai was 89, God made it clear that Ishmael, then 13, was not the promised seed: "my covenant shall be established with Isaac, which Sarah shall bear unto you" (Genesis 17: 21). Sarai and Abram were stunned and stumped. Then God declared himself to be *El Shaddai* (God Almighty). Simply interpreted, this meant that God's actions are not dependent on human actions or even belief. Thereupon Abram's name was changed to Abraham (father of many nations), and Sarai's name was changed to Sarah (mother of *all* nations (Genesis 17: 4, 15-16). Thereupon, circumcision was demanded by God as evidence of the covenant made between God and his promises.

The conclusion is that it is all of grace (Table 2, Row 7). The miracle of the seed of the woman continued as the seed was activated (Genesis 3: 15 and Isaiah 54: 1a). Sarah laughed with great joy, not disbelief, but gleeful astonishment (cp. Luke 24: 41 with respect to the resurrection of Christ). "In this place [in the text] not in the sense of being incredulous, but to express such pleasure, or happiness, as almost suspends the reasoning of faculty for a time" (Clarke 1960: 133).

The theme of the barren female, whose seed is made alive, is a persistent pattern in biblical history. Man had nothing to do with any of this; it was all by the activated, formerly dead, seed of the woman. It only begins with Sarah (See Galatians 4: 27). It continues with Rachel who also was barren but became the mother of Joseph and Benjamin (Genesis 29: 31). Hannah became the mother of Samuel (1 Samuel 1: 5). Samson's mother was barren until her womb became alive with the birth of Samson (Judges 13: 24). Elizabeth, the mother of John the Baptist, was barren until her seed was activated (Luke 1: 7). And most wondrous of all, Mary had no earthly husband at all with respect of Jesus' birth; her womb was activated by the Holy Spirit. (Genesis 3: 15).

The key to understanding how this is consistent with "and I will make of thee a great nation" where it is declared that with marriage, the two persons – e.g. Abraham and Sarah – became one person: "and they shall be of one flesh" (Genesis 2: 24). Therefore, when the seed with Sarah was resurrected and bore the fruit, Isaac, Abraham also bore fruit. However, the promise fulfilled was all through Sarah, not Abraham. The sperm of Abraham was not part of the miracle, only the physical, natural act. In fact, Abraham had children before Isaac (Ishmael) and after (with Keturrah, Genesis 25).

## WHERE IS THE LAMB FOR THE BURNT-OFFERING?

After a brief *entracte*, the presentation continues. The focus of attention is on Isaac, but this act also has a surprising ending. The story begins with a statement, presumably giving the reason for the event: Abraham is "tempted" by God. The word "tempt" has caused much confusion because of the translation. The word "tempt" as used here is a different word than used in most other places. The word in the Hebrew is *nacah*, which means "to assay" or "prove." Just as an assayer examines a rock to reveal the precious mineral within it, so here Abraham is assayed so that his faith might be evidenced or proclaimed. In this sense, the story is designed to be a tribute to Abraham. In the Septuagint, the Greek word is *epeirase* which means "to be tried so as to display" or "shine forth." In this case, Abraham's faith is to be showcased and Abraham glorified in the outcome. Symmachus,[26] translated the Hebrew word as *nissah*, which is "to glorify by focusing light on it." (see also Exodus 17: 5 as applied to God). Thereby, according to Symmachus, "God put great honor on Abraham by giving him this opportunity of showing to all successive ages the nature and efficacy of an unshaken faith in the power, goodness, and truth of God" (Clarke 1960: Vol. I, 138). But this is only the prologue to the story.

The story begins with a "where" question from God to Abraham: "Where are you?" Abraham answered with "Here," signifying a readiness for duty. The orders of God were shocking: "Take now thy son, your only son [he also had fathered Ishmael] Isaac, whom thou love, and go to

51

the land of Moriah, and offer him there for a burnt-offering upon one of the mountains which I will tell you" (Genesis 22:2). Even the most devout person would likely experience weak-knees, guts-grabbing, and cross-eyed confusion. Therefore, the text should be full of emotional reactions. It contains none. Abraham said nothing when ordered to sacrifice his most loved son on an altar, particularly because human sacrifice was condemned in Scripture.[27] And Isaac, who was probably 33 years of age, offered no resistance when he found out he was to be the sacrifice.

No doubt Abraham was strengthened as he remembered that he had encountered Melchizedek, the priest of the Most High God (*El-Elyon)* at the foot of Mount Moriah (Genesis 14: 17-18). The name means "Almighty God," who is completely independent, capable of accomplishing his purposes perfectly without any assistance or counsel. Note also that a change of place – i.e. from Beersheba to Mount Moriah – was required. Therefore, Abraham left the next morning. He took with him, not only Isaac for the offering, but "two of his young men." Early *Targums* in Aramaic, and the *Midrash*, say that the two men were Eliezer and Ishmael.[28] (Clarke 1960: Vol. I, 139); if so, they clearly tie this story in with those presumed to be the promised seed described earlier.

This story is so shocking and so profound in its implications that it is commonly withheld from children. It was a test which would strengthen Abraham's faith. God knew Abraham would pass. Even so, it was a grim three-day trek from Beersheba to the mountains of Moriah (probably the Temple Mount).[29] The final ascent up the mountain was agonizing. Isaac was burdened with the wood for the burnt-offering, a task usually done by a servant. And Abraham knew when Isaac asked the question, "Where is the lamb for the burnt-offering?" that it would be Isaac himself. Therefore, Abraham answered as he had been told. Unknown to him, it was a prophetic statement, "God will provide," that "he spoke more than he knew" (Hertz 1960: 74). Or did he? We are told that Abraham offered up Isaac by faith, recognizing "that God was able to raise him up, even from the dead; from whence also he received him in a figure [a symbol of the real  thing]" (Hebrews 11: 19). It is very doubtful that Abraham knew that it was a fore type of the real thing. Abraham did know "that previously to the birth of Isaac both he and his wife were *dead* [not Abraham] to all purposes of procreation; that his birth was a kind of life from the dead" (Clark 1960: Vol. I, 139; emphasis added).

At any rate, at the place specified, they built an altar, laid the wood, and Isaac was bound and placed on it. Now the sacrifice had to be killed; its blood had to be shed. Abraham raised his knife for the kill, but he then received a stunning surprise. An angel of the Lord restrained him and a ram appeared in a nearby bramble thicket, provided there by God as a substitute for Isaac. Therefore, Abraham named the place YHWH-*jireh*, meaning "The LORD will provide."[30] In fact, this author calls it the *Provision Principle* in Scripture (Boyce 2013: 32-38). The Lord always provides the means and the method for fulfilling his precepts. However, in order to understand and illustrate the principle more cleanly, other synonymous words such as "make," "call," "send," and "give" are often used. For example, in this case, a ram was **given** (provided) as a substitute for Isaac. In Genesis 3: 21, the Lord God **made** coats of skins and clothed them. And in the Abrahamic Covenant, God said "I will **make** of thee a great nation. . . and in thee all the earth will be blessed" (Genesis 12: 2-3; emphasis added). And as discussed earlier in this chapter, God initiated cities as a mechanism for subduing the earth.

God then rehearsed the promises to Abraham and his descendents. His seed would be as numerous as the stars in the heaven and the sands on the seashore. And in thy seed (singular) all the peoples of the earth will be blessed (Genesis 22: 17-18). Obviously, this brings the reader back to the original covenant promise to Abraham in Genesis 12. The significance of this is lost on almost all Christian commentators. They recognize, of course, that the primary significance of the event is that there would be substitute atonement for the human race – a lamb that would take away the sins of the world, and that "lamb" would be Christ. The ram in the thicket offering as a sacrifice in place of Isaac was only a metaphor for the real sacrifice. They usually miss the point that Isaac is NOT the promised seed; Isaac is only one seed in the promised lineage of Christ. Just as Eliezer and Ishmael were rejected earlier, Isaac is rejected here. Isaac is not the promised seed either; he was sinfully stained and required atonement as well. Abraham was no doubt mystified and wondered just who and when the genuine promised seed would occur. Then, the text is startling in what it does NOT say. There is no mention of any celebration that Isaac was spared. There is no mention that he came down the mountain with Abraham. In fact, there is no further mention of Isaac until Eliezer was sent to Haran to seek a bride for Isaac (Genesis 23: 4).

The promise then ends with the perplexing phrase, "and thy seed shall possess the gate of his enemies" (Genesis 22: 17b). This refers to the gate of the city. If it is breached, the city is lost. According to this metaphor then, Abraham is given a promise that, though his enemies will try, they will "try in vain to destroy Abraham's descendents" [the Jews] (Hertz 1960: 75). The history of the Jews and attempts to destroy them are wrapped up in that promised provision of God. This also is a reminder of the covenant to Abraham (Genesis 12: 2-3). And we know from events which follow in Scripture that the seed in the lineage chain is protected and unbroken until procreation and continues the chain until the ultimate seed comes.

## WHERE IS YOUR CUP AND YOUR CORD FOR DRAWING WATER?

Many assume that Jesus simply used the place he was at as a prop to illustrate his points, but places are much more important than that. In fact, "The writings of prophets, apostles, and the Master Teacher Jesus himself may be fully understood only in the physical context and setting in which they were given" (Ogden 2013: 13). Nowhere is this more apparent and more essential for understanding than the encounter of Jesus with the woman from Sychar (formerly Shechem). Almost every aspect of the dialogue is based on the well and the geographical setting of three primary spatial components:

— Samaria and the Samarians
— Sychar and Vicinity
— Jacob's Well and Its Setting

The Samaritans were named after their capital city, Samaria (approximately a dozen miles northwest of Sychar). Samaria became the capital after the northern ten tribes followed Jeroboam, the son of Solomon, rather than Rehoboam. The ten tribes were commonly called "Israel," whereas the southern two tribes of Judah and Benjamin, were called "Judah." Samaria itself was composed of the tribes of Ephraim and Manasseh, the two sons of Joseph. Shechem (later called Sychar) was designated a City of Refuge (Joshua 20: 7) and the city placed under control of the Levitical priests (John 21: 21). Inasmuch as Joseph fathered these sons by Asenath, the daughter of Potipherah, the priest of the Egyptian sun god, *On*, they were of mixed race (Genesis 46: 20). This was compounded when in 727 B.C.E., the Assyrians captured Israel and carried off to Nineveh all but the lower elements of the population. They then sent colonists from Assyria into Israel, thereby mixing the race through marriage. Also, the already compromised worship of the Samaritans was bastardized even further. They had earlier constructed their own temple at Mount Gerizim and after their captivity, Shechem became the capital. Consequently, the southern Jews ostracized them. They would not worship with them, socialize with them, and certainly not share a common cup. Jesus initially commanded his disciples not even to enter Samaria, but to go only to the lost sheep of the house of Israel (Matthew 10: 5-6). In short, the Jews despised the Samaritans. Therefore, when Jesus said that he must go through Samaria on the way from Jerusalem to the Galilee, it raises a most perplexing question. Why?[31]

There were two other routes to Galilee: one along the Mediterranean coast and one up the Jordan valley. Jesus usually took the latter route. Certainly, Jesus was not intimidated by the hostile Pharisees such that he would avoid his customary route. His decision to go through Samaria, generally avoided territory and its hated people, was evidently a moral imperative, not a geographical convenience to save time or to avoid the

Pharisees. Some think that the Samaritans were the ones he was thinking about when he said "other sheep I have which are not of this fold" (John 10: 16), but there is much disagreement on the meaning of that phrase.[32]

Sychar was a place with great historical significance. It was situated in a valley between two mountains: Mount Ebal to the north and Mount Gerizim to the south. These famous mountains were designated by Moses, who never entered the Promised Land, to be mountains of choice: Mt. Ebal for choice that would bring curses and Mt. Gerizim that would generate blessings (Deuteronomy 11: 29). Joshua read the Torah to the Jews who entered Canaan in the valley between the mountains (Joshua 8: 33). He split the tribes in two groups, one on Mt. Ebal and one on Mt. Gerizim and admonished them to choose Mt. Gerizim on the south. Abraham first erected an altar there when he entered the land of Canaan. Jacob purchased land there where Joseph's body was buried. He also built an altar there, and evidently dug the famous well on which the event described here took place (Genesis 33: 1-20).

There is almost nothing said about Jacob's famous well of Sychar in Scripture. Presumably, Sychar was located on the lower slope adjacent to Mt. Ebal, and Jacob's well was situated about a half-mile to the southeast. Its prominence is primarily derived from this specific mention in John. 4: 9. The reason probably is that, in context of this story, the water in that well is natural or dead (vs. living or moving), and only temporarily satisfying.

The journey from Jerusalem to Sychar is over fifty miles and would take three days by foot. If Jesus and his disciples arrived at 6 p.m., it would be at the beginning of the fourth day.[33]

They evidently stopped at two other places before reaching Sychar, but there is no mention of them in the text. Obviously, the stop at Sychar was deliberate and significant. The nature of the place and its environs demonstrates why.

The story begins with Jesus sitting on the well. "This illustrates another important principle, the application of which is often of great aid to the understanding of a purpose, namely of noticing the place where a particular incident occurred. According to many, "the 'well' was a *figure of himself*, and its water was the emblem of *the solution* that is to be found in him" (Pink 1945: 163-64; emphasis added). There he speaks shocking words – to a Samaritan woman, no less. He requested from her a drink of water from the well. Jews were prohibited from drinking out of a cup used by a Samaritan. This question produced an amazing response from the woman. "I know that Jews have no dealings with Samaritans" (John 4: 10), so why do you ask when you have no cup (water pot) to hold water and no cord with which to lower it down into the deep well. But his request is even more disturbing to her than it might at first appear. When Jesus requested that she give him a drink, "he was making a demand on her with which, at the time, she was unable to comply … He was bringing her face to face with her helplessness" (Pink 1945: 176). Let's look at the situation even more bluntly: "From a woman's perspective, Jesus is clearly out of line. For her, there is a gender issue as well as a religious issue involved in his boldly asking her for a drink from the well. . . . she is in a sense doubly distant from Jesus, he is male, she is female. Her being taken aback by Jesus' request suggests that public exchanges between men and women were highly regulated by custom. Evidently, an unaccompanied man was not to speak to an unaccompanied woman. And even beyond the strict gender issue, Jesus is not just any man – he is a Jewish man speaking to a Samaritan woman. They likely would have avoided contact had they both been of the *same* sex; their being of opposite sexes accentuates the social tension" (Spina 1992: 147).

The presumed "where" trigger question of the woman was caused by the response Jesus gave to the woman when she rightly, according to custom, told him something that he obviously knew: that Jesus, as a Jew, must have no dealings with the Samaritans (John 4: 9). Jesus said, that if she knew the gift God had for her, she would ask him – an even more shocking thing – and he would give her "living water." (*what?*) It was then that the text implies that she asked him "Where is your cup and your cord with which to draw it [*how?*]?" Obviously, she was thinking about well water, because she asked him whether he thought he was greater than Jacob who dug the well and drank out of it. But Jesus was not thinking of well water. "By this expression, which was common to the inhabitants both of the east and of the west, is always meant *spring water* in opposition to *dead, stagnant water* contained in ponds, pools, tanks, or cisterns" (Clarke 1960: Vol. VI, 539). Jesus was not even thinking of spring water. He was talking about spiritual water: water that is within one, water by which one would never again thirst, and "a well of water springing up into everlasting life" (John 4: 14). Then the woman made a request of him for that living water so she wouldn't have to come to the well to draw water.[34] He agreed, provided she would bring her husband. Then she made a confession and Jesus revealed something she was trying to hide: she had had five husbands and was then living out of wedlock with another man.

The woman was startled by his prophetic prowess and changed the subject to *where* one should worship God; should it be on Mount Gerizim or at Jerusalem? Jesus made it clear that salvation was of the Jews (Jerusalem) and stated that soon (*when*) such worship at either place would end. God was no longer to be worshipped in a fleshly, external, earthly, and ceremonial system but heavenly in spirit and in truth. Worship would be a spiritual act and would be in truth, not tradition (*how?*) or place (*where?*). She then referenced the promised Messiah (*when?*) for the Samaritans believed the Pentateuch. Jesus gave the resounding response by saying (*who*) that "I am that is speaking to you" (author's paraphrase). This was a clear reference to Exodus 3: 14 where God described himself as the great "I AM." (There are eight such "I AM" presentations in the book of John). That did it! This was the apotheosis and the termination of a host of interrogatives. From the revelation of *who*, the *what, where, when, why,* and *how,* the results are obvious. She believed and several spatial shifts occurred:

— The disciples returned from the city, saw Jesus talking with the woman and were mystified, but said nothing.

- The woman left her water bucket and went to the city to proclaim Jesus was the Messiah to the men of the city.
- The men believed and went to the well where their beliefs were confirmed: "This is indeed the Christ, the Savior of the world" [not just the Jews] (John 4: 42).
- Jesus went with them back to the city where he stayed two days, and many more were converted.

Contrast this success among the mongrelized Samaritans with his reception in the synagogue when he returned to his own home city of Nazareth.[35]

When the woman made the statement, posed as a question, "Where is your cup and your cord to draw water?" she triggered a flow of rising waters that led to her recognition that Jesus was the promised Messiah. As such, he was the fount of living water and every blessing. She demonstrated her faith by risking even further her reputation by returning to Sychar and giving her testimony to the *men* of the city who likely had condemned her. Amazingly, they believed her and went to the well for the living water which the woman had found. They were not disappointed. "This is a unique instance in the Gospels of a true moral revival on a large scale produced by preaching apart from miracles. The Preachers were the Samaritan [woman] and the Messiah" (Williams 1971: 786).

## CONCLUSIONS

Hopefully, some of the things Christ may have explained to Cleopas and his friend on the road to Emmaus are discussed in this chapter. "Beginning with Moses [the first five books of the Bible] . . . he expounded unto them all the scriptures, the things concerning himself" (Luke 24: 15). Critical points along the path to Sychar have enriched our understanding on the progressive revelations to the promised seed, with periodically placed seeds, beginning with Adam and the woman embedded within him, and ends with the woman at the well.

The seed was initially embedded in a side pocket of Adam from which woman (womb of man) was created. Then the ultimate seed is promised through the seed of the woman on the long road to Mary, to whom was born God in the flesh. The pathway commonly is dependent on the miraculously activated "seeds" of formerly barren women. However, each seed in the unbroken chain is also attributed to the associated male – e.g. Adam, Seth, Enos, Cainan, Maleleal, Jared, Enoch, Mathusala, Lamech, Noah, Shem, etc. (Luke 3: 36-38).[36] And it is evident that there is a long line before Abraham is even reached. But each link in the chain to the Messiah is critical. However, only five were selected here, each activated by a "where" triggered question and each one resulting in a stunning answer. And each of the five "seeds" featured above are cumulative and connected to others. There is a general progression in the parade route to the ultimate promised seed, as revealed from the mouth of Jesus himself at Jacob's well which served Sychar. No doubt, there is an important story behind each link, but that is yet to be revealed. Even so, Adam is the "first man," and Christ is the "last Adam" (1 Corinthians 15: 45). With the last Adam, the full tree is produced from the promised seed of the woman, Mary.

The astute student of the Bible will notice that there are two lineages presented in the New Testament, one in Luke and one in Matthew. In Matthew, the seed line listed is for Joseph. In Mary's seed line from David (her lineage is listed back to Adam), it is entirely different. Both descended from David and are in the tribe of Judah, but Mary and Joseph's genealogy begin with the two different sons of David: Joseph's from Solomon, and Mary's from Nathan. Also note the different terminology in each scriptural account. In the genealogy of Mary, only males are listed, and there is a series of "begats." Then there is a clear statement that Joseph was not the father; he did <u>not</u> begat Jesus.

In fact, in the genealogy of Joseph in Matthew 1, Joseph is disqualified as the father (begetter) of Jesus, not only by the clear statement of Scripture. First, four women of shady character are listed, and three are violations of Mosaic law: (1) Tamar who also casts condemnation upon

Judah; (2) Rahab, a Canaanite and a prostitute; (3) Ruth, a Moabite; and (4) Bathsheba, possibly a Hittitite. These are not women listed in the genealogy of Christ, as is customarily stated, but jaded women in the genealogy of Joseph. Thereby, these may be more of a contamination of the line of Joseph – certainly stunning surprises. The clear disqualification of Joseph as the father of Jesus is found in this lineage related to Coniah. According to Scripture, Coniah broke the seed chain. For Scripture declares that "Coniah and his seed are cast out" because no man of his seed shall prosper, sitting upon the throne of David and ruling any more in Judah (Jeremiah 22: 30). Even so, Joseph was the legal or titular father. As almost everyone knows, the activator of the seed within Mary was the Holy Spirit, totally uncontaminated by any male.

At Sychar, the genuine, ultimate, bone-fide, and consummate seed, the promised Christ, was revealed directly to a woman, even a wicked, ostracized Samaritan woman. It is notable that the promise of the seed initiated with a woman, Eve, and terminated with a woman, both under sin and condemnation. Thereby, began the first great awakening and awareness of the Messiah. And the chief evangelist was a woman. Even the men in Sychar, who had rightfully condemned her, believed. After encountering Jesus directly, they also believed and gave a profound testimony: ". . . that this is indeed the Christ, the Savior of the world" (John 4: 42). He is savior of all people, not just the Jews. Jesus revealed himself to the woman at the well as the great I AM (the *Shema*) (YHWH) and evidently did the same to the men of Sychar. That message is proclaimed throughout the book of John by eight great I AMs. He is revealed as the Most High God (*El Elyon*), the true Melchizedek, the God of all. (Genesis 14: 18).

## ENDNOTES

[1] It will greatly aid understanding if the biblical references and the footnotes are read when cited before continuing.

[2] I am indebted to Harold Brodsky for the idea for this chapter. At a meeting of the AAG, Geography of the Bible Group, he presented a paper on the first "where" question

in Scripture. In particular, I wish to thank the following people for their special aid in the development of the topic: About a dozen people listened to my reasoning on these topics for several months, read the manuscript, and made helpful comments. Among these were Bill Birks, Bob Bisnett, Gary Durr, Franchot Fenske, Jim Guest, Paul Leaf, Al Lutz, John Marker, Les Minnig, Dave Randles, Richal Smith, Dick Terman, and John Vandekamp. I also want to thank my wife, Norma Rae, for her helpful comments throughout the project. Arden Snyder also read the manuscript and made valuable comments. Finally, I owe a tremendous debt to Bill Dando for reviewing the document for publication and making excellent suggestions for its improvement.

[3] According to Webster's Dictionary, *complement* means "to fill out" or "complete," "mutually supplying each other's lack." Complementary is required to supply a deficiency resident in the other. *Complementarity*, derived from "complement," is the primary prerequisite for all spatial interaction. For a definition and some applications of its importance, see Ullman 1980: 15-16.

[4] Some theologians, especially those subscribing to the German school of Higher Criticism, claim that at least two different authors wrote Genesis 1 and Genesis 2. They base this on the fact that the word for God, *Elohim*, is used in the first chapter and in the second chapter YHWH-*Elohim* is used. The translation of YHWH is unknown, but is commonly pronounced in the English as either Jehovah or Yahweh. The Jews treat it as sacred and substitute the pronunciation of Adonai. I agree with the general Jewish interpretation that "the nature of the context decides which Divine Name is employed. In the same way, different Divine Names in the Hebrew text do not argue for a diversity of writers, but simply that the Divine Name has each time been selected in accordance with the idea to be expressed" (Hertz 1960: 199).

[5] A deep sleep, as in XV, 12, the word implies that something mysterious and awe-inspiring was about to take place" (*ibid*, 9).

[6] *Hermaphrodite* is derived from the Greek myth about Hermaphrodites, a handsome son of the gods Hermes and Aphrodite. He fell in love with a nymph, and while bathing with her in the fountain of Salmacis, begged the gods to grant that she be completely united with him. The result was the formation of a being half-man and half-woman. Biologically, it is used to describe an individual having both male and female reproductive organs – i.e. a testis and an ovary. This appears to have been the condition of Adam between the time of his creation until the female complement containing both his flesh and bone was removed from his side or chest.

[7] In Genesis 1: 1, the word, God (*Elohim*) is a uni-plural noun.

[8] Given the fact that Adam was initially a hermaphrodite, it may have been possible for him, even without the excised woman, to have been able to procreate or multiply.

Inasmuch as this did not occur, this is conjectural.

[9] When one believes on the full redemptive work of Christ on the Cross, the inert spirit is reactivated.

[10] When a person today believes, the Holy Spirit of God re-activates the spirit within him much like a dead battery is re-generated. This, in turn, affects the soul which then affects the body. Nonetheless, the old fleshly nature continues until natural death.

[11] Adam is called a "pattern" when compared with the second Adam (Christ). Christ is superior to the first Adam in: (1) time, (2) effect, (3) number of people, and (4) territory of the affected (See Boice 1998: 211).

[12] The Garden of Eden was located on the east side of a territory called Eden. Evidently, Eden was a region encompassing the Promised Possession of Israel – i.e. from the River of Egypt to the Euphrates. The center of Eden would be Jerusalem. This reason has caused many scholars to conclude that "apparently [the Garden of Eden] is in Mesopotamia (modern Iraq), since two of the four rivers in its vicinity are the well-known Tigris (Hiddekel) and Euphrates, (kvs. 14)" (Ryrie 1994: 7). For a detailed discussion of this thesis, see Congdon. Scripture indicates that one moves away from God by going eastward. Cain was driven eastward into the land of Nod. Ur is directly east of Jerusalem and is the home city of Abraham. The Wise Men came from the east. And the Temple could only be entered from the east.

[13] The word *stunning* has several meanings. It may mean "shocking," but it may also mean "elegant" or "delightful." That is the meaning used here.

[14] The seed of woman is also stunning in that it reveals the omniscience and fore-planning of God. "Physiologically speaking,. . . there is none of the mother's blood that ever becomes part and parcel of the little baby. [the sin transference of Adam's transgression comes from the male] The blood comes from the father. . . Christ had to be born of a woman, but yet He had to be sinless. Now, since the ovum, or reproductive cells, do not carry the curse. . . Jesus could be born without that sin nature. . . (Feldig 2002: 172).

[15] This kind of argument has been entertained in depth by theologians. One of the most comprehensive in this regard and one that presents counter thesis is by Spina, "The Ground for Cain's Rejection." Spina argues that Cain's offering was rejected because it came from the cursed ground.

[16] Cain had probably never seen a dead human and assumed that they, like animals, were entirely dead when physically dead. However, as he found out, the soul lives on – a stunning shock to Cain and a conviction.

[17] Rashi (Shelmah Itzhaki, 1040-1105) "is the most famous of all commentators of Jewish history" (Fields 1990: 10).

[18] Another possible evidence of the faith of Cain may have been demonstrated when he named his son, Enoch (instructed, initiated, and dedicated). "It may be considered some proof of Cain's repentance, that he appears to have dedicated his son to God, who in his father's stead, might minister in the sacerdotal office, from which Cain was forever excluded" (Clarke 1960: 61-62).

[19] Hester Prynne was a character in Nathaniel Hawthorne's novel, *The Scarlet Letter*, in which the letter "A" was attached on Hester's dress as a mark of her condemnation as an adulterer. The plot for this might have been modeled after the presumed mark placed on Cain.

[20] This is reminiscent of Esau and Jacob. Esau, the elder of the two, is worldly and Jacob, the younger twin is composed of two stages: Jacob, the deceiver, and Israel, the lineage of promise. In a sense, Jacob is brought back from death to a new person. Similarly, Abel is brought back from the dead in the form of Seth, who carries on the promised spiritual lineage.

[21] It is important for the reader to understand the symbolism. Critical links in the genealogical chain are surely missing. Both the names and their meanings and symbolism in the names mentioned in these genealogies are selective, and facts associated with the length of lives is probably significant – e.g. Enoch lived 365 years, Noah lived 777 years, etc.

[22] Note also that there are two Lamechs in the two lines. Lamech is the sixth and last in the line of Cain. There is no further genealogy given. However, the Lamech in the lineage of Abel-Seth is but a new beginning inasmuch as Noah, Lamech's son, is the carrier of the torch of humankind.

[23] *El* is another name for God. Often it is used in a compound – e.g. Elohim (creator God) or *El Shaddai* (Almighty God) or *El Elyon* (The Most High God).

[24] It should be noted that two different Enochs are mentioned in the genealogies, one as the beginning of a cascade of pioneers in the advancement of civilization in Cain's lineage and one in the lineage of Seth. Both demonstrated great evidences of grace. The reader must be careful not to equate Enos with Enoch. *Enos* simply means "a mortal man who is created in the image of Adam."

[25] This was clearly so in the case of Babel (Genesis 11: 1-9), when the whole world decided to live in one city rather than replenish the earth as instructed. But God is never frustrated by the rebellion of humans; God caused humankind to change from one language of common communication, to many languages, causing confusion among them. Thereby, God scattered them and they began to fulfill the command to replenish the earth.

[26] Symmachus was a Samaritan who converted to Christianity about 200 C.E. and wrote his Targum of the text. His conclusions and translations were also published by Origen.

[27] Animal sacrifice was established from the beginning when Adam and Eve were covered by animal skins prepared by God (Genesis 3: 21). And of course, Abel was told to bring a lamb from his flock as a sacrifice (Genesis 4: 4). Abraham offered animal sacrifices regularly as he moved through the Promised Land. Therefore, the shock was NOT that an animal was sacrificed in place of Isaac. The question was: Why was Isaac placed there in the first place, and why wasn't he sacrificed, given what we now know, as commanded by God to Abraham.

[28] The Hebrew word, *Targum*, means "translation." The best known *Targum* is the Septuagint. *Midrash* is the Hebrew word for "explanation" or "commentary." If the two men Abraham took with him were Eliezer and Ishmael, who were rejected as the promised seed – either as a substitute or a surrogate – then Genesis 22 really resolves the question of Isaac as being or not being the promised seed.

[29] The three days is significant. Christ was three days and three nights in the tomb. Jesus travelled three days from Jerusalem to Sychar because Beersheba to Jerusalem is about the same distance as Jerusalem to Sychar. There are many other significant threes in the Bible.

[30] The implications of this are earth-changing. This was a fore view of the coming Christ as a substitute for fallen humankind. It was also a foreshadow of the real event, only signaled here, of God slaying his only begotten son as the ultimate and consummate burnt-offering on the Cross.

[31] The most obvious and certainly the most correct answer is that Jesus, as God, is sovereign; he does what he wants, when he wants, and how he wants, without any council. God doesn't have to give a reason or account for his actions (See also Pink 1968).

[32] The common view is that Jesus was referring to Gentiles. If so, they would not be proselytized and not directly by Jesus until after the Cross – see John 12: 20-25, when some Gentiles asked to see Jesus. He refused to see them and explained that that would only happen after his death, burial, and resurrection. Mormons believe that Jesus came to America during his three days in the grave and preached directly to the Nephite people, described in the Book of Mormon.

[33] It is amazing how so many otherwise astute biblical scholars are confused about the application of Hebrew time and Roman time in Scripture. To mix this up causes a scrambled understanding of why and when various events occurred, most of which are fully understood once the time problem is solved. The book of John "uses Roman time . . . just as is done today. However, the synoptic use Hebrew reckoning, beginning with

sunrise (i.e. 6 a.m., 7 a.m. being the first hour." For example, "our Lord was put on the cross at 9 a.m. (Third hour, Mark 15: 25); darkness was over the land from noon until 3 p.m. ('sixth' till the ninth hour' (Matthew 27: 45-46; Mark 15: 33-34; ; Luke 23: 44). Thus here [John 19: 14] the 'sixth hour' could not be Hebrew time (noon), but rather 6 a.m. 'when the morning was come'" (Matthew 27: 1-2; Scofield1998: 1353). Likewise, when in John 4: 6, it says "it was about the sixth hour," it had to be Roman time or 6 p. m. Stopping at noon to send his disciples into Sychar for food and then spend the night at Sychar makes no sense.

[34] The Jews rejected the fountain of living water during Christ's earthly ministry (Jeremiah 17: 13), but non-Jews, whenever encountered, recognized him and believed. At his second coming, a fountain of living water will be opened for sin for the Jews (Zechariah 13: 1).

[35] The Book of John presents Jesus as the Son of God. He was in the beginning with God, all things were made by him and for him, and he is very God. Yet his own (the Jews) did not recognize or receive him (John 1: 1-3). The Synoptic Gospels, particularly the Book of Mathew present him as the Son of Man. In John, Jesus is completely independent and portends himself as the great I AM. As such, all things will become new: new wine, new birth, new water, new worship, new manna, and new life. In the consummation, there will be a new heaven and a new earth and a new city (Revelation 21: 1-2).

[36] Note that there are two Lamechs and two Enochs. They are quite different: one belongs to a secular line and the other to a sequence in the promised seed. In this long litany of guides along the path, only a few are described. Much like in the story of Hansel and Gretel, these are but breadcrumbs showing the way to the final destination.

## REFERENCES

Boice, James Montgomery. 1998. *Genesis*. Vol. I. Grand Rapids, MI. Baker Books.

Boyce, Ronald R. 2013. "The First Precept (Genesis 1: 28), the Primary Purpose of Cities, and the Provision of God." In William A. Dando, Caroline Z. Dando, and Jonathan J. Lu (Eds.). *Geography of the Holy Land: New Insights*. Kaohsiung, Taiwan: Holy Light Theological Seminary Press, pp. 30-61.

Clarke, Adam. 1960. *The Holy Bible with a Commentary and Critical Notes*. 6 vols. New York, NY: Abingdon Press.

Congden, Christopher and Jonathan J. Lu. 2005. "Putting Eden on the

Map: An Attempt." In William A. Dando, (Eds.). *Geography of the Holy Land: Perspectives*. Kaohsiung, Taiwan: Holy Light Theological Seminary Press, pp. 92-105.

Feldig, Les. 2002. *Questions and Answers from the Bible.* Kinta, OK: Les Feldig Ministries.

Fields, Harvey J. 1990. *Volume One: Genesis.* New York, NY: UAHC Press.

Henry, Matthew. 1972. *Matthew Henry's Commentary.* Wilmington, DE: Sovereign Grace Publishers.

Hertz, J. H. 1960. *The Pentateuch and Haftorahs: Hebrew Text English Translation and Commentary.* London: Soncino Press.

Keller, Tim. 2002. "A Biblical Theology of the City," http://www.cityclassics.org/ A Biblical-Theology-of-the-City.

Kline, Meredith G. 2006. *Kingdom Prologue.* Eugene, OR: Wipf and Stock Publishers.

May, Herbert G. (Ed). 1974. *Oxford Bible Atlas.* Second Edition. London: Oxford University Press.

Ogden, D. Kelly. 2013. "Understanding Biblical Teachings in Their Geographical Context." In William A. Dando, Caroline Z. Dando, and Jonathan J. Lu (Eds.). *Geography of the Holy Land: New Insights.* Kaohsiung, Taiwan: Holy Light Theological Seminary Press, pp. 13-29.

Pink, Arthur W. 1945. *Exposition of the Gospel of John.* Grand Rapids, MI: Zondervan Publishing House.

Pink, Arthur W. 1968. *The Attributes of God.* Swengel, PA: Reiner Publications.

Ryrie, Charles Caldwell. 1994. *Ryrie Study Bible.* Chicago, IL: Moody Publishers.

Scofield, C. I. 1998. *The Scofield Study Bible.* New York, NY: Oxford University Press.

Shakespeare, William. 1994. *The Complete Works of Shakespeare.* New York, NY: Barnes and Noble.

Spina, Frank Anthony. 1992. "The Grounds for Cain's Rejection (Gen. 4) *'damah* in the text of Gen. 1: 11." *Zeitschrift fur die Alltte stamentliche Wissernschaft. #104, Band, Heft 3,* pp. 319-332.

Ullman, Edward L. 1980. *Geography as Spatial Interaction.* Seattle, WA:

University of Washington Press.

Williams, George. 1971. *The Student's Commentary on the Holy Scriptures: Analytical, Synoptical, and Synthetical.* Grand Rapids, MI: Kregel Publications.

# In Search of More Precise Name and Place Name Identifiers

William A. Dando and Bharath Ganesh Babu

## INTRODUCTION

In biblical times, names and place name identifiers had an importance that is unknown today (Bryant 1982). The name of a person, people, or place indicated a closeness, unity, bonding of like-minded individuals, or a strong linkage of common factors. For many Bible readers and classroom teachers today, place names are as important as the setting for biblical events (Figure 1). One of the simplest and oldest methods for making the connection between geography now and back then is by means of toponyms. Toponyms are site identification terms or a combination of terms originally applied to enable outsiders to gain insights into the character or significance of a place at a specific time in history or today. Long ago, it was recognized that words that were used to identify a place could enhance or degrade a site or people, reward heroes and commemorate events, encourage commerce or trade or repel weary merchants or travelers, and heal scars or leave scars that would never heal. In most cases, terms currently used came from the Bible (Table 1). However, many terms are misapplied, are not understood, or are not always interchangeable. Place name identifiers and terms used to describe where cultural groups resided or passed through are also associated with specific eras or time periods (Anonymous 2010).

Figure 1. The World as Known to the Hebrews

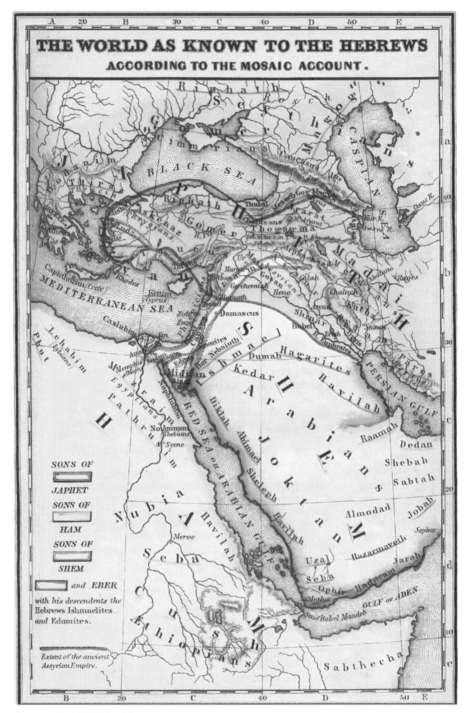

Source: *Smith Bible Atlas*

**Table 1. Sample of a Place Name Root Word in Ancient Israel:** *Beth* – meaning "house" or "habitation"

| | | | |
|---|---|---|---|
| *Beth* was the second letter of the Hebrew and PhotoSinatic alphabets. Its original form in the alphabet was a crude drawing of a Middle Eastern house. *Beth* is linked with another descriptive term to form a compound place name. | | | |
| **Place Name** | **Citation** | **Meaning** | **Significance** |
| Bethabara | John 1: 28 | "house of the ford" | John baptized here |
| Bethanath | Joshua 19: 38 | "house of echo" | A walled city |
| Beth'anoth | Joshua 15: 58 | "house of a reply" | A walled city |
| Bethany | Mark 11: 1 | "house of poverty" | Town of Jesus' last days |
| Beth-ar'abah | Joshua 15: 61 | "house of the desert" | One of six Arabah cities |
| Beth'aram | Joshua 13: 27 | "house of the height" | Town in Gad east of the Jordan |
| Beth-ar'bel | Hosea 10: 14 | "house of God's court" | Scene of Shalman's massacre |
| Beth-a'ven | Joshua 7: 2 | "house of idols" | Place on the mountains of Benjamin |
| Beth-az'maveth | Nehemiah 7: 28 | "house of Azma-veth" | Town in Benjamin |
| Beth-baal-meon | Joshua 13: 17 | "house of Baal-meon" | Town in Moab |
| Beth-bir'e-i | 1 Chronicles 4: 31 | "house of my creation" | Town in Simeon |
| Beth'-car | 1 Samuel 7: 11 | "house of the lamb" | Site of an Israelite/ Philistine battle |
| Beth-da-gon | Joshua 15: 41 | "house of the grain god" | City in Judah |
| Beth-diblatha'im | Jeremiah 48: 22 | "house of fig cakes" | Town in Moab |
| Beth'el | Genesis 12: 8 | "house of God" | Town in central Palestine |
| Beth-e-mek | Joshua 19: 27 | "house in a valley" | Town in Asher |
| Bethesda | John 5: 2 | "house of mercy/ water" | Site in suburban Jerusalem |
| Bethe'zel | Micah 1: 11 | "neighbor's house" | Town in Philistia |

| Table 1. Continued | | | |
|---|---|---|---|
| Place Name | Citation | Meaning | Significance |
| Beth-ga'der | 1 Chronicles 2: 51 | "house of the wall" | Important in genealogies? |
| Beth-ga'mul | Jeremiah 48: 23 | "camel-house" | Town in Moab |
| 21. Beth-gil'gal | Nehemiah 12: 29 | "a city of wheels" | Site of Passover in Canaan |
| Beth-hac'cerem | Nehemiah 3: 14 | "house of the vine" | Beacon station near Tekoa |
| Beth-ha-ran | Numbers 32: 36 | "house of the height" | Town in Gad |
| Beth-hog'la | Joshua 15: 6 | "partridge house" | Magnificent spring |
| Beth-ho'ron | Joshua 16: 3 | "house of caverns" | Town on the Philistine Plain |
| Beth-leb'aoth | Joshua 19: 6 | "house of the lionesses" | Town of Simeon |
| Beth'lehem | Ruth 1: 1 | "house of bread" | Birth town of Jesus |
| Beth-jesh'imoth | Numbers 33: 49 | "house of deserts" | Town in the Jordan Valley |
| Beth-ma'achak | Samuel 20: 4 | "house of oppression" | Place in the north of Palestine |
| Beth-nim'rah | Numbers 32: 36 | "house of leopards" | Walled city east of the Jordan |
| Beth-pa'let | Joshua 15: 27 | "house of flight" | Town in southern Judah |
| Beth-paz'zez | Joshua 19: 21 | "house of the dispersion" | Town in Issachar |
| Beth-pe'or | 2 Kings 15: 29 | "house of Peor" | Site in northern Palestine |

| Table 1. Continued | | | |
|---|---|---|---|
| Place Name | Citation | Meaning | Significance |
| Beth-mar'caboth | Joshua 19: 5 | "house of chariots" | Town in extreme southern Judah |
| Beth-me'on | Jeremiah 48: 23 | "house of Baal'meon" | Town in Reuben |
| Beth'-phage | Matthew 21: 1 | "house of figs" | Town on the Mount of Olives |
| Beth-rehob | Judges 18: 28 | "house of rehob" | Town near Laish |

| Table 1. Continued | | | |
|---|---|---|---|
| Place Name | Citation | Meaning | Significance |
| Bethsa'ida | John 12: 21 | "house of fish" | Home of Andrew, Peter, and Philip |
| Beth-she'an | 1 Chronicles 7: 29 | "house of rest" | Later called Scythopolis |
| Beth-she'mesh | Joshua 15: 10 | "house of the sun" | Town near Ekron |
| Beth-shit'tah | Judges 7: 22 | "house of acacia" | Gideon defeated Midianites here |
| Beth-tap'puah | Joshua 15: 52 | "house of apples" | Town near Hebron |
| Beth-zur | 2 Chronicles 11: 7 | "house of rock" | Town in Hebron Mountains |

## PLACE NAME CHANGES AND EVOLUTION

A result of its location, situated on a land bridge between four competing regional power centers and connecting three continents, the Holy Land was impacted by frequent invasions, affected by numerous relocations of households and clans, and exposed to new ideas and life-styles due to contact between people and place. Thus, the Holy Land experienced many name and place name identifier changes (Figure 2; Kent 1912). Most changes reflected the lingering influence of events, of invading or controlling groups, and of superior military or economic systems (Table 2). Ancient and biblical place names expressed coherence and continuity between the kingdoms of David and Solomon, of Israel and Judea, and of present-day Israel.

## IDENTIFIERS AND EXAMPLES

Name and place name identifiers that cause confusion and lead to descriptive or locational errors may be divided between two general classes, i.e., natural/descriptive and cultural/historical (Figure 3). Natural/descriptive place names mark some physical uniqueness of a site such as *Sharon* or plain, *Gibeah* or hill, and *Pisgah* or height (Smith 1884). Cultural/historical place names were given to honor ethnicity, individuals, or events such as *Enoch,* a city built to honor Enoch, and is mentioned in Genesis 4: 17. Place names of significance to students and teachers of the Bible are those related to the revelations of God to individuals such as Jacob (Genesis 28: 19 and 35: 15) and include Mahanaim (Genesis 32: 2) and Peniel (Genesis 32: 30). *Bethel* is a compound place name composed of *beth* or house and *el* or God. *Bethlehem* is composed of *beth* or house and *lakim* or bread, i.e., "house of bread." *Bethsaida* means "house of fishermen. *Mahanaim* is a compound place name signifying "two hosts" or "two camps."

*Peniel* identifies a site where the "face of God" was seen. *Kir* is the describer of a walled site or a fortress. *Kirjath* signifies a city, *en* identifies a spring or fountain, *beer* denotes a well, *able* notes a meadow, *tell* identifies a mound, *khirbet* is a ruin, *ma* pinpoints land, *galil* hints a circle or a district, *nain* means pleasant, *salem* is a special term purporting "peace," *tyropoleon* implies a place of cheesemakers, *negeb* implies dryness, *shur* connotes a wall or walled, and *baal* indicates "lord" (Figure 4).

The names of broad regions or countries are almost universally derived from the names of the first settlers, those who lived in the Promised Land before the arrival of Abraham, and those who conquered and occupied the Holy Land after the Exodus, and tribal areas named after the descendants of Shem, Ham, and Japeth (Genesis 10: 1-32), such as Canaan (Genesis 5: 9), Moab (Genesis 19: 37), and Ammon (Genesis 38; Miller *et al.* 1961). Preservation of place names of broad areas in the Promised Land has been constant since its early settlement and was a factor of the common Semitic background of its inhabitants and the significance of water, agriculture, trade, and religion (Aharoni 1979).

## TERMS THAT CAUSE CONFUSION

### Geographical Areas or Sites

**The Middle East** is an indefinite region stretching from the eastern Mediterranean Sea to the southwestern side of the Asian continent, including Egypt, the Arabian Peninsula, Israel, Jordan, Lebanon,

Table 2. Terms That Cause Confusion and Lead to Descriptive or Locational Errors and Identifiers

| I. Geographical Areas or Sites in the Holy Land | |
|---|---|
| 1.  Middle East | 7.  Israel |
| 2.  Levant | 8.  Judah |
| 3.  Holy Land | 9.  Judea |
| 4.  Fertile Crescent | 10. "Lukan Emmaus" |
| 5.  Promised Land | 11. Sodom |
| 6.  Canaan | 12. Zion |
| II. Cultural Groups in the Holy Land | |
| 1.  Semites | 7.  Phoenicians |
| 2.  Hebrews | 8.  Babylonians |
| 3.  Canaanites | 9.  Israelites |
| 4.  "The Chosen" | 10. Jews |
| 5.  Essenes | 11. Nabateans |
| 6.  Philistines | 12. Idumeans/Edomites |

Syria, Turkey, Iran, and Iraq. The Middle East is difficult to delimit and is an unofficial geographic term.

**Levant** is a French geographic term, meaning "rising", because to early French explorers the sun appeared to rise there. It is the term used to identify a beautiful and alluring region in the extreme eastern Mediterranean comprising modern-day Lebanon, Israel, portions of Syria, and southern Turkey.

**The Holy Land** is a land "separated" or "set apart from other lands." It is a wide crescent-shaped area that extends from the southern Nile River in Egypt, across the northern portion of the Arabian Peninsula to western Persia (Iran), and from the eastern Mediterranean Sea, across eastern Turkey through Assyria (Armenia) into eastern Persia (Iran). The geographic term implies a section of the world separated from all that is sinful, impure, or morally imperfect (Dando 2013).

**Fertile Crescent** is an often improperly delimited descriptive term coined by J. H. Brested in 1914 and meaning "great semicircle." The term describes an area of fertile land in the Middle East between the Mediterranean Sea and the deserts of Arabia, extending from southern Israel to the Persian Gulf, including the fertile Tigris and Euphrates river valleys in Iraq (Zeigler 2013).

**Promised Land** refers to the land God promised to Abram. Abram (Abraham), a righteous man, was "chosen" by God (Genesis 12: 19) to become the father-founder of a movement that would lead to the redemption of humankind. Abram was told by God to leave Ur and Haran and go to a land God promised him, a land that, at that time, was occupied by Canaanites. God made a covenant with Abram that He would make Abram the founder of a great nation and he and those who followed him would be a blessing to all. God also promised Abram and his descendants the land from the Nile River to the Euphrates River and from the Mediterranean Sea to the Trans-Jordan Highlands (Wigoder 1986).

**Canaan** initially was the "land of purple dye." It was settled by the descendants of Canaan, the fourth son of Ham (Genesis 10: 6). The Canaanites occupied the land west of the Jordan River and the Dead Sea, to the Mediterranean Sea, and from the northern Negeb to the foothills of Mt. Hermon (Dan). This land was promised to Abram by God because it was a "land of milk and honey."

**Israel** is the name given to Jacob after his wrestling with an angel at Peniel (Genesis 32: 28). Israel is sometimes translated to mean "the prince that prevails with God," or "God strives," or "soldier of God." It became the national name of the twelve tribes collectively, then later became the name applied to the ten northern tribes of the Kingdom of Israel (Davis 2010). The name *Israel* was also used to denote laymen, distinguishing them from priests, Levites, or other ministers (Ezra 6: 16; Nehemiah 11: 3).

# Figure 2. Palestine in the Time of Jesus

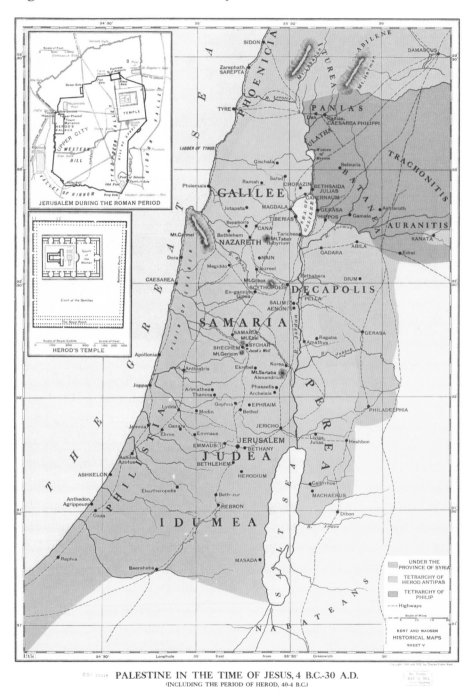

**PALESTINE IN THE TIME OF JESUS, 4 B.C.-30 A.D.**
(INCLUDING THE PERIOD OF HEROD, 40-4 B.C.)

Source: *Library of Congress, Geography and Map Divison.*

Figure 3. Natural and Descriptive Place Names Mark Sites' Physical Uniqueness

Source: Mount Tabor. Photo: Eli Zahavi, Kfar Tavor (PicWiki)

**Judah** (signifying "praise") was the name Leah gave to the fourth son of Jacob, and it became the name of one of the twelve tribes of Israel. From the name *Judah* came the descriptive term *Jew*. Judah also became the name of the Southern Kingdom of the divided monarchy once ruled as a unified country by Solomon. The division of Solomon's kingdom occurred in Shechem (meaning "back" or "shoulder") in 975 B.C.E. Ten tribes of Solomon's kingdom bonded together to form the Kingdom of Israel, and the remaining two tribes, Judah and Benjamin, united to form the Kingdom of Judah (1 Samuel 27: 6; Joshua 19: 1).

**Judea** was the name applied to the assigned area west of the Jordan River to those who had been taken into captivity and were permitted to return to their homes and land (Haggai 1: 1 and 14). Later, under Roman occupation and at the time of Christ, it was the designated title of the southernmost three divisions of Palestine (Matthew 2: 1 and 5). The Romans assigned Judea to be a political division of the province of Syria.

Figure 4. Word Roots Determine Material Cultural Items and Landscape Features

Source: Camels in a meadow. Photo: Shaker. Levah Rahat Center (PicWiki)

**Lukan Emmaus** (a town of "hot baths") refers to the village seven miles from Jerusalem to which two disciples were going when Jesus appeared to them. It was the day of Jesus' resurrection (Luke 24: 13-35). The two disciples were talking to each other about all the things that had occurred. When they arrived at Emmaus, Jesus ate with them and when he broke the bread, they recognized him. The site of Emmaus remains yet to be identified (Lu 2013).

**Sodom** (possibly "hot" or "simmer") was a city rampant with moral corruption and evil. It was destroyed by God along with the city of Gomorrah (Genesis 19). It is believed that Sodom stood on the northern end of the Dead Sea. No trace of it or of the other cities in the same locale have been discovered, so complete was their destruction. The wickedness and corruption of Sodom and its total destruction are held up as a warning in many passages of the Old and New Testaments (Mark 6: 11; 2 Peter 2: 6).

**Zion** (probably "fortress" or "citadel") refers to one of the high standing physical features and pronounced defensive positions upon which the city of Jerusalem was built. It was the southeastern hill of Jerusalem separated from Mt. Moriah by the Tyropoeon Valley and approximately 105 feet (32 meters) lower in elevation. Zion was a formidable natural Jesubite stronghold (Judges 19: 11). David captured Zion and built a citadel and his palace upon it. It became "the city of David (1 Kings 8: 1). David was buried there" (1 Kings 2: 10).

## CULTURAL GROUPS IN THE HOLY LAND

**Semites** refer to the descendants of Noah's second son Shem (Genesis 9: 18-19). From their home area in northwestern Arabia, they migrated north and west into the Fertile Crescent and beyond. They constituted a linguistic unit but not a racial unit and included the Canaanites, Aramaeans, Akkadians, Arabs, Ethiopians, and Hebrews. It has been said by many biblical scholars that "the tent of the Semitic patriarch was the starting point of mankind's religious progress." *Semite* is not a biblical term.

**Hebrews** (means "to pass over") were the sons of Shem. Allegedly they were an Aramaean branch of the large Semitic family who migrated west out of Arabia (Genesis 10: 21). They were primarily nomadic shepherds grazing their flocks at the semiarid eastern edge of the Fertile Crescent (Genesis 11). The Hebrews were a composite race (Deuteronomy 26: 5). They maintained close and long-lasting relations with their northern kin. Abram (Abraham) and Jacob sought wives from kin living near Haran and from Padan-aram (Genesis 24: 10; Genesis 28 and 29). Abraham was regarded by the Hebrews as their progenitor (Genesis 11: 27-32). The Hebraic ethnic groups included the Hebrews, Edomites, Moabites, and Ammonites. Distinctions must be made between the words "Hebrew," "Israelite," and "Jew."

**Canaanites** (possibly meaning "lowlanders") may have been migrants from northwestern Arabia sometime before 3,000 B.C.E.

Canaanites were described to be strong, excellent farmers and herders, and creative city builders. Astute evaluators of agricultural land, they settled the rich coastal lowlands west of the central mountain range of the "Promised Land" and the lush Jordan Valley (Genesis 10: 18-20). Canaanites gave name to the land west of the Jordan River and the Dead Sea, and between the Mediterranean Sea and the deserts of Arabia. Living in a land of "milk and honey," the Canaanites prospered, were numerous, and eventually divided into six different sub-groups or tribes (Exodus 13: 5).

"The Chosen" (Hebrew from *Bahar*, Greek from *eklektos*) is a term that means "singled out from others for some special service or position." Examples include Hebrew warriors selected for hazardous military assignments because of recognized and respected skills (Exodus 15: 14; Judges 20: 16). Abraham was chosen by God for a very important assignment because God recognized in him a pure heart and unwavering faith. Abraham was chosen and his descendants multiplied, assumed the assignment given to Abraham, and they became "the chosen people." The Hebrews, the chosen people, after many, many generations, begat Jesus Christ whom Christians believe is the Son of God (Psalms 105: 43; Deuteronomy 7: 67; Isaiah 42: 1).

Essenes (possibly meaning "the silent") came from ascetic Jewish communities of men who developed the first organized and structured monasteries worshiping the true God in the Mediterranean world. There were rigid procedures required and years of testing before a man was accepted into the monastery and the order. Major monasteries were near the northern end of the Dead Sea. The origin of the Essenes is obscure. Josephus first mentioned them in Ant. 13.5.9. Nothing is known of the Essenes after the destruction of Jerusalem in 70 C.E. – they simply disappeared from the literature.

Philistines (probably meaning "immigrants") were uncircumcised Aryans who migrated from Crete (Amos 9: 7), settled in Egypt, and moved northeast along the coast of the Mediterranean Sea. They were well established in the land of Canaan before the time of Abraham (Genesis 21: 32, 34, 26: 1). The territory of the Philistines was part of the Promised Land and was assigned to the tribe of Judah. Small Philistia's ability to remain a threat to Israel was largely due to its control of the important coastal trade routes between Egypt and Mesopotamia and their effective political organization based on a league of great cities including: Gaza, Ashkelon, Ashdod, Ekron, and Joppa. No portion of Philistia was conquered in the time of Joshua (Joshua 13: 2). Eventually Saul defeated them and after many years of warfare, the Philistines were included into Solomon's empire.

**Phoenicians** (possibly meaning "date palm growers" or "reddish purple dye") were Semitic inhabitants of Phoenicia, a long narrow Mediterranean Sea coastland-nation famous for its commercial activities and its international ports of Tyre, Sidon, and Byblos (Unger 1966). They were Canaanites, descendants of Canaan, a grandson of Noah, from which Canaan was named. The Phoenicians were one of the most distinguished seafaring people in history. Phoenician commercial colonies were founded on the shores and on the islands of the Mediterranean Sea as far west as Spain. Men of Byblos were famous for shipbuilding (Ezekiel 27: 9) and Sidonians for timber felling (1 Kings 5: 6). Jeremiah forecast the downfall of the Phoenicians and the destruction of Sidon and Tyre (Jeremiah 25: 19-26).

**Babylonians** (probably meaning "confusion," Genesis 11: 9) referred to Semitic inhabitants of what was called Shinar, later Chaldea or the land of the Chaldeans (Jeremiah 24: 5; Ezekiel 12: 13). They were descendants of Cush and followers of Nimrod (Genesis 10: 8-10). Originally from lands conquered by the Assyrians, the Babylonians were planted colonists in the delta land of the Tigris and Euphrates rivers (Ezra 4: 9). These colonists were creative and their accomplishments were many, including the development of the wedge-shaped cuneiform script and the formulation of a vast Babylonian Empire. They were polytheistic. Their king, Nebuchadnezzar (605-562 B.C.E.) was a brilliant military leader. He captured and destroyed Jerusalem. Nebuchadnezzar also made the city of Babylon one of the largest and most splendid ancient cities of the world (Genesis 11: 9).

**Israelites** (possibly meaning "having power with God"; Genesis 32: 28) initially signified the descendants of Jacob and then the whole people of Israel, that is, the twelve tribes (Joshua 3: 17, 7: 25; Judges 8: 27). With the division of Solomon's kingdom in 922 B.C.E., the name was given to those who resided in the Northern Kingdom in contrast to Judah or the Jews who resided in the Southern Kingdom (2 Samuel 2: 9-10, 17, 28; 1 Kings 12: 1). After the Babylonian captivity, the name *Israel* was assumed as designating the entire reborn nation. Israelites were those God chose to be the repository of ethical monotheism, i.e., the chosen people (Deuteronomy 7: 6-8; Exodus 19: 25, 24: 7). Much later in history, *Israel* would be the name given to the Jewish state on May 5, 1948.

**Jews** (men of Judea) is the name attributed to the descendants of Judah and a name identifying members of the Kingdom of Judah after its formation and the separation of the ten Northern tribes (2 Kings 16: 6). After the people returned from exile in Babylon, the term *Jew* received a greater meaning (Ezra 4: 12): (1) From the predominance of members of the old Kingdom of Judah who returned to Palestine from Babylon. (2) From the identification of Judah with Jerusalem and the Temple. (3) From the hopes and religious ideals of the returned exiles. (4) From the determination of rebuilding a temple and a strong and unified God-based nation. Three descriptive terms have been utilized to identify the "chosen" people: (1) Hebrews or the descendants of Abraham; (2) Israelites or the descendants of Jacob; and (3) Jews who were the descendants of Judah.

**Nabatean** is the term describing a citizen of a remarkable and dynamic Arabian kingdom inhabited by very creative people. The terms *Nabatea* and *Nabatean* are not mentioned in the Bible. Nevertheless, these people were quite pivotal in Hebrew history. Nabateans were originally Arabians who expanded their lands and seized Edom and Moab. They took control of one of the great caravan trade routes in the Middle East. In

Jesus' day, Nabatea included the Sinai Peninsula, the Gulf of Aqaba, Petra, the lands east of the Dead Sea, the Negeb to the Mediterranean, south to Gaza, and the eastern Fertile Crescent to the Euphrates River. Nabateans controlled Damascus when Paul entered the city (2 Corinthians 11: 32). They were exceptional "water engineers," astute traders, and extraordinary architects. The capital of Nabatea was Petra (Crew 2005).

**Idumean** is a Greek term referring to a person of Edom/Idumea (Isaiah 34: 5). Edom was named for Esau (Genesis 32: 3). Idumeans were Semites, closely related in blood and language to the Hebrews. The Idumeans/Edomites controlled the land from the rough hills of northern Arabah, extending from the head of the Gulf of Akabah and the Gulf of Elat, to the southern tip of the Dead Sea (1 Kings 9: 26). The land of the Edomites contracted and expanded with their national fortunes. It basically was a wild and rugged land including mountains, fertile plateaus, and fruitful valleys. The Kings Highway crossed the eastern length of Edom. There was almost constant strife between the Edomites and the Israelites/Jews. King Herod was a Idumean – not one of the Herods was a Jew by blood.

## UNDERSTANDING HOLY PLACES, PEOPLES, AND CONTROVERSIES

### The Hebrew-Israelite Era

It is important for a student of the geography of the Holy Land to understand the descriptive terms applied to those who lived there or are living there today, and to understand that the names of villages, cities, and archaeological sites have socioeconomic meaning. In many instances, they preserve a long tradition of the name. Many descriptive terms and place names that had Hebrew, Greek, or Roman origin have been altered but are preserved in Arabic. However, there are many ways to determine the original basis for the natural/descriptive name of a site or place and the cultural/historical reason for a word or a compound word applied to a people or where those people lived. These include geoarchaeological research and field work, the pronounced physical characteristics of a site, vegetation growing at the site, or of work tasks or acts performed on the site. In search of more precise early Hebrew place names and physiogeographic site names, an understanding of the early settlement pattern is required. The Hebrews were initially nomadic and herded their flocks on the margins of the mountainous central core of Canaan. In the last stage of the Bronze Age (fourteenth to thirteenth centuries B.C.E.), there were only a few fortified towns and scattered unfortified hamlets on the ridges of the Central Mountain (or highland) core. Towns and settlements that were there at the time were along the main north-south highway that runs along the crest.

Most Hebrews who dwelled in the void of Canaanite settlements were tent dwellers whose main livelihood depended on pasture for their livestock. The Patriarchs of Genesis dwelled in hamlets or on sites in the hill country of Judah, Ephraim, and Gilead, plus the Negev. As the settlement pattern of the Hebrews in the hill country expanded, developed sites seemingly were selected for water and by the settlers' sense of national-religious destiny. They were permanent agricultural, commercial, transportation, or governmental central places (Menashe 2005).

## The Grecian Era

Up to the fourth pre-Christian century, the influences which helped to shape place names in the Promised Land had their origins within or in the margins of the Fertile Crescent. It was in the later time period that the Persian power center had its beginnings. The Persian Empire conquered the Promised Land, spread to Egypt in the west and across the Hellespoint into Thrace (Greece). One of the European countries that Xerxes crossed was Macedonia. This little country remained unimportant until 359 B.C.E. when its throne was seized by an able leader named Philip. By reorganizing the Macedonian army, perfecting the celebrated Macedonian phalanx, Philip was able to bring all of Greece into his kingdom. He was assassinated in 336 B.C.E. and was succeeded by his twenty-year old son, Alexander. Alexander was educated by Aristotle, was trained as a ruler, and was taught military tactics by the best in Greece. In 334 B.C.E., Alexander crossed into Asia with 30,000 foot soldiers and 5,000 cavalry. He defeated Darius III near Tarsus, subdued Tyre, captured Gaza, occupied Jerusalem, and was welcomed into Egypt. He founded Alexandria and conquered the Persians. He took ill in Babylon and died at the age of 32. After Alexander's death, his empire was divided and Ptolemy I claimed the kingdom of Egypt which eventually included Judah (the Promise Land's Greek name). Ptolemy was a benevolent king and a supporter of Jewish culture. Greek was the common language in Alexander's divided empire, and as such it had a profound effect upon those who lived in Greek Judah. Antiochus Epiphanes, a Greek prince, became King of Syria (which included Judah), and he attempted to force Grecian thought and the Grecian way of life upon the Jews. Terrors of religious persecution enveloped Jerusalem and all other Jewish communities. The religious indignities instituted by Antiochus Epiphanes led to the revolt of the Maccabees. The 250-year control of Palestine by the Greeks was enormous. Most significant were the region and the Greek cities of the Decapolis. The Decapolis cities were Damascus, Dium, Abila, Capitolias, Gerasa, Philadelphia, Hippos, Gadara, Pella, and Scythopolis. They were situated along the King's Highway from Damascus to Aqaba (Drummond 2005). Most of the Greek place names and city names were modified or changed by the Maccabeans and later by the Romans.

**The Roman Era**

Roman leaders, who had great interest and a covetous eye on the land bridge between Egypt and Mesopotamia for a century and a half, began their drive to Jerusalem in 66 B.C.E. Pompey, the great Roman general, captured Syria and Damascus and ordered the occupation of Jerusalem. In the fall of 63 B.C.E., all resistance to the Romans ended in Palestine. Judaea then became a vassal to Rome. The Romans appointed Antipater, an Idumean, as their agent in resolving Jewish quarreling, and he became the administrator/procurator of Judaea. Antipater appointed his son Herod tetrarch of Galilee. Herod served the Romans well and eventually, by decree of the Roman Senate, he was named King of Judaea.

Herod was a great builder and he utilized Roman planners, architects, and designers, as well as others, to beautify initially Judaea, but later Samaria, Galilee, and Decapolis. His greatest achievements included the construction of the Fortress of Antonia, his magnificent palace, and the Jerusalem Temple. Twenty miles south of Mt. Carmel, he built the seaport of Caesarea, rebuilt the city of Samaria, renaming it Sebaste, along with several other cities, including Sepphoris, in his domain. Herod's throne was secure only if he would supply Rome with tax money to support Rome's mighty military complex and with food for the city of Rome.

Palestine in the time of Christ was a major food producer and a major source of food for Rome. To get the food to Rome, the Romans constructed a network of interconnected roads, assisted Herod to build Caesarea, the main port for food export, built cities and towns to serve as central places for food storage and transshipment, and devised irrigation networks or aqueducts, and water courses. Herod's sons constructed Caesarea Philippi at the base of Mt. Harmon and Tiberias along the shores of the Sea of Galilee. Rome and the individuals Rome appointed to rule Palestine until c. 93 C.E. placed a tremendous imprint on the landscape and place names in the land between Egypt and Mesopotamia and upon the birth country of the three major religions of the world.

## SIGNIFICANCE OF PLACE NAMES IN RESOLVING ISSUES AND CLAIMS IN THE HOLY LAND, TODAY

The significance of place names in Palestine and Israel, today, lies in the potential to legitimize the land claims of the involved parties and all who use geohistorical archeology, archeology, ancient and modern maps, and place names as proof of their claims (Figure 5). Indigenous people's "geographic knowledge systems," that is, culturally appropriate site descriptors combining indigenous linguistics, landscape concepts, and place identifier technology in place name root-word selection, were found significant. Also, indigenous people's recognition and knowledge of earth features, soils, food crops, water sites, and food sources, i.e., "ethnophysiography" of places, had become almost indelible facets of a place (Mark

Figure 5. Place Names Assist in Resolving Land Claims and Mapping Issues, Today

Source: Black Obelisk of Shalmaneser III, plaster cast of original in the British Museum, 827 BC — Oriental Institute Museum, University of Chicago (Wikimedia).

*et al* 2007). In some instances, there appeared to be a silencing of the voices of indigenous people and as cover-up of the existence of people's claim to land through cartographic employment of blank spaces and even contrived place names – a form of cartographic "cultural and territorial erasure" (Harley 1992; Johnson *et al* 2006).

The importance of geographical site naming or "toponymy" was first recognized by the British in the late nineteenth century. Palestinian place names are primarily Arabized ancient Semitic names or newer Arabic terms or compound terms. Since the founding of Israel in 1948, place names have also been Hebrewized or are known by their biblical names. Place name changes made by successive empires that have ruled the land bridge between Egypt and Mesopotamia and crossroads between Europe, Asia, and Africa were common. For example, biblical Sapphoris was initially a small agricultural unnamed village in Galilee four miles north of Nazareth, located in a beautiful setting. The Greeks, recognizing the value of the site, built a beautiful city and called it "Sepphoris." The Romans and Herod the Great added to the beauty of the city and called the city "Diocaesaria." When the Arabs and Islamic rulers controlled the city, they named it "Saffuriya." Today, the city is known as Tzippori. With the Arab expansion into most of Palestine, Greek and Latin place names were reverted to pre-classical Semitic names, and for new settlements established during this period, Arabic names were coined.

Data from geographical map-making expeditions in Palestine in the late nineteenth century by the Palestine Exploration Fund (PEF) and other Western biblical geographers contributed to the shape of the borders delineated for the British Mandate in Palestine, and eventually the boundaries between the new Israel and Arab Palestine in 1948. In 1992, Cohen and Kliot made a strong case for the role of place names in nation building, state formation, and the clash within and between the Israelis and Arabs over historic rights for land possession. They stress that until peace comes, place names will play a key role in the resolution of the conflict over territory that is central to the Arab-Israeli dispute (Cohen and Kliot 1992).

## MODERN CARTOGRAPHIC ERRORS AND MISREPRESENTATIONS

Along with place names, maps have contributed much to the delineation of nations and to the shape of borders. Holy Land maps in the collection of Eva and Gimpel Wajntraub and members of the Israeli Map Collectors Society offer an excellent source of place names and economic, social, and political administrative regions in the Holy Land (Wajntraub and Wajntraub 2005). Maps are a synthesis of spatial knowledge at a time and a reflection of the geopolitics of a region. It was once said that maps contain geographic truths, and most maps do. However, care must be taken in the use of maps and atlases to determine the boundaries of a modern nation state. Errors abound on ancient maps, and errors are purposely made on modern maps. Modern inconceivable and unjustifiable cartographic misinformation maps and atlases include those recently printed by HarperCollins, Rand McNally, and Google Maps.

HarperCollins, one of the world's largest publishing houses, sells English language atlases to schools in the Middle East. In recent editions, the editors have omitted Israel (Figure 6). The Middle East atlases show Jordan and Syria extending to the Mediterranean Sea. The atlases were printed for distribution in the United Arab Emirates and neighboring Arab countries. The management of HarperCollins has stated that including Israel on the map would not have been acceptable to their customers in the Persian Gulf region. This is a shocking example of "cultural-cartographic erasure." It nullifies the value of the atlases, negates in the minds of atlas readers the claim for Israel's existence, and undermines the basic rules of atlas publishers' ethics (HarperCollins 2015).

In a Rand McNally world atlas published in 1989, the states of North Dakota, South Dakota, and Oklahoma were left out. Rand McNally officials, when confronted by Oklahoma Governor Henry Bellmon, publicly stated that the three states were omitted from the new atlas' regional maps and photographs because of "space limitations" (Rand McNally/*Los Angeles Times* 1989). In 2010, an embarrassing Google Maps cartographic error was blamed for Nicaragua's accidental invasion of Costa Rica. Nicaraguan troops crossed the inaccurately drawn international border, removed the Costa Rican flag, and raised their own flag on Costa Rican land. Costa Rica's President Laura Chinchilla fumed and said "Costa Rica is seeing its dignity smeared and there is a sense of great national urgency." In that same year, Google Maps cartographers misrepresented the Thai-Cambodian border and also completely misplaced the Florida town of Sunrise, infuriating local council members and town business leaders (Brown 2010).

The internationally most inflammatory Google Maps misrepresentations were noted in 2014. Their maps showed the Crimean border differently on maps distributed in Russia from maps distributed in the United States and Western Europe. As reported by the National Public Radio's Corey Flintoff, "If you check Google maps from the United States, you'll see Crimea portrayed as part of the Ukraine. If you check from Russia, you'll see an international boundary drawn between Ukraine and the Black Sea peninsula, indicating that Crimea is part of Russia"

**Figure 6. An Example of "Cultural-Cartographic Erasure"**

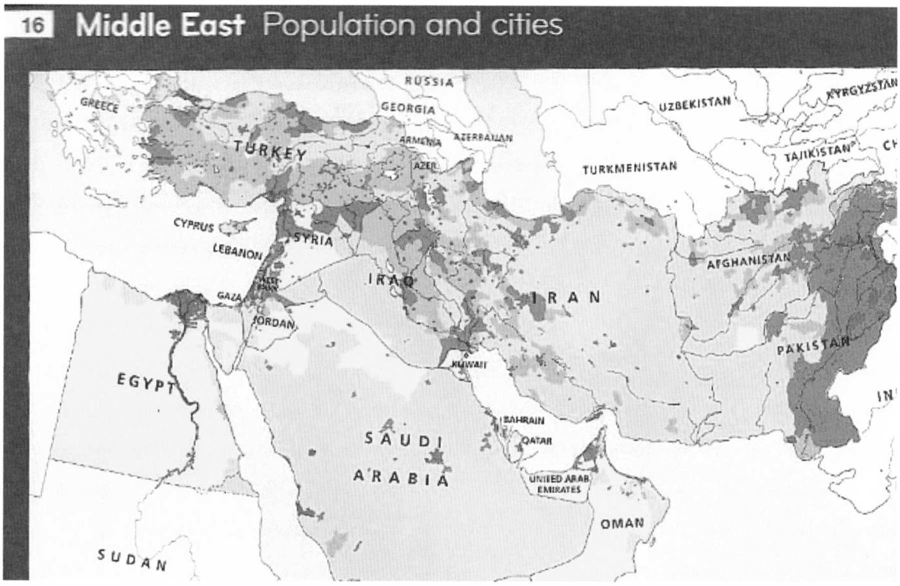

Source: Erasure of Israel from a map in an atlas by Harper Collins for English speaking schools in the Persian Gulf. *Tribune Review*, Greensburg, PA. Vol.126, No. 333, January 7, 2015, p. A2.

(Flintoff 2014). Americans see the Crimea as "occupied territory," and they and their allies refuse to accept the incorporation of the Crimea into Russia. Sensitivities over how countries, borders, and territories are depicted on maps are both old and real. A map is supposedly an accurate and verified drawing of the earth's surface or part of it. That which is included on a map is given importance or prominence to a place or object. Accuracy is the hallmark of a good map or atlas. Yet politics, religion, and economics have perverted maps since the first one was drawn. Dishonest maps are a powerful tool in de-legitimizing a people and a nation. It can lead to confusion rather than clarity, to mistrust, and to war.

LAST WORD

In the Bible, names were very important. Names were given to demonstrate what a person or place is or professed to do or be. So significant is a name that Adam is commanded by God to name the animals to reveal their being. In Genesis 2: 19, it is stated "...the Lord God formed every beast of the field and every bird in the air and brought them to the man to see what he would call them; and whatever the man called every living creature, that was its name." Why was naming so important in the ancient world? Simply stated, to know a person, place, or object's name meant some knowledge of the object or item of reference. When one knew the name, one could determine what the entity was to do, hoped to do, or did. Names had power and names carried a message – even place names. For example, Magdala, the largest and most important city on the Sea of Galilee during the time of Jesus' missionary work, was called *Taricheae*, Greek for "city of salted, smoked, or dried fish" (Zapata-Meza and Sanz-Rincón 2017).

In our twenty-first century world, those events that we have no control over seem chaotic, unpredictable, and insecure. We seek leaders of our governments who establish tranquility, beauty, security, and justice, as did the people of Israel, from the time they entered the Promised Land until the fall of Jerusalem in 70 C.E. However, Israel was constantly surrounded, occupied, and/or dominated by larger and more ruthless nations. From 587 B.C.E. onward, with the exception of the Maccabean period in c. 144-63 B.C.E., God's people were under the rule of foreign emperors. Their lives were lived in difficult circumstances, but they survived, cleared land, built houses, established towns and cities, and connected these abodes of life by trails, paths, and roads. As caretakers of that which was created by their God, they named their communities on the basis of what was done or produced in their environs (Hopko 2010).

## REFERENCES

### I. Books, Dictionaries, and Reviews
Aharoni, Yohanan. 1979. *The Land of the Bible*. Philadelphia: Cansdale, p. 111.
Bryant, T. A. 1982. *Today's Dictionary of the Bible*. Minneapolis: Bethany House Publishers, p. 442.
Davis, Philip R. 2010. "The Origins of Biblical Israel." A review by

Norman K. Gottwald in *Bible Interpretation*. Vol. 187, pp. 60-63.

Hopko, Thomas. 2010. *The Names of Jesus*. Chesterton, IN: Ancient Faith Publishing, p. 11.

Miller, Madeleine S. and J. Lane Miller. 1961. *Harper's Bible Dictionary*. New York: Harper & Row, Publishers, pp. 477-478.

Smith, William. 1884. *A Dictionary of the Bible*. Philadelphia: The John C. Winston Company, pp. 431-432.

Unger, Merrill F. 1966. *The New Unger's Bible Dictionary*. Chicago: Moody Press, pp. 903-904.

Wigoder, Geoffrey. 1986. *Illustrated Dictionary & Concordance of the Bible*. Jerusalem: G. G. The Jerusalem Publishing House, pp. 22-23.

**II. Articles, Book Chapters, and Newspapers**

Anonymous. 2010. "Site Names and Their Meanings." *Near Eastern Archaeology*. Vol. 794, pp. 216-217.

Brown, Mark. 2010. "Nicaraguan Invasion? Blame Google Maps." *Permalink*, November 8. http://www.wired.com/2010/11/google-maps-error-blamed-for-nicaraguan-invasion/.

Cohen, Saul B. and Nurit Kliot. 1992. "Place Names in Israel's Ideological Struggle over the Administrative Territories." *Annals of the Association of American Geographers*. Vol. 82, No. 4, December, pp. 653-680.

Crew, Bruce R. 2005. "Geographical Dimensions of the Nabateans and the Birth of Early Christianity in the Ancient Near East." In William A. Dando, Caroline Z. Dando, and Jonathan J. Lu, Eds. *Geography of the Holy Land: Perspectives*. Kaohsiung, Taiwan: Holy Light Theological Seminary Press, pp. 374-405.

Dando, William A. 2013. "The Holy Land." In William A. Dando, Caroline Z. Dando, and Jonathan J. Lu, Eds. *Geography of the Holy Land: New Insights*. Kaohsiung, Taiwan: Holy Light Theological Seminary Press, p 1.

Drummond, Dorothy. 2005. "The Decapolis: Ancient Sites, Current Situations." In William A. Dando, Caroline Z. Dando, and Jonathan J. Lu, Eds. *Geography of the Holy Land: Perspectives*. Kaohsiung, Taiwan: Holy Light Theological Seminary Press, pp.

264-281.

Flintoff, Corey. 2014. "Google Maps Display Crimean Border Differently in Russia, U.S." National Public Radio, April 12. http://www.npr. org/blogs/thetwo-way/2014/04/12/302337754/google-maps-displays-crimean-border-differentl.../

Harley, B. J. 1992. "Rereading the Maps of the Columbian Encounter." *Annals of the Association of American Geographers*. Vol. 82, pp. 522-536.

HarperCollins Publishing Company. 2015. *Tribune Review*. Greensburg, PA., Vol. 126, No. 333, January 7, p. A2.

Johnson, J. T., Louis, R. P., and Pramono. 2006. "Facing the Future: Encouraging Critical Cartographic Literacies in Indigenous Communities." *ACME: An International Journal for Critical Geographies.* Vol. 4, No. 1, pp. 80-98.

Lu, Jonathan J. 2013. "Searching for the Real Lukan Emmaus." In William A. Dando, Caroline Z. Dando, and Jonathan J. Lu, Eds. *Geography of the Holy Land: New Insights.* Kaohsiung, Taiwan: Holy Light Theological Seminary, pp. 216-235.

Mark, D. M., Turk, A. G., and Stea, D. 2007. "Progress on Yindjibarnodi ethnophysiography." *LNCS*. No. 4736, pp. 1-19.

Menashe, Har-El. 2005. "Dwellers of the Mountain." In William A. Dando, Caroline Z. Dando, and Jonathan J. Lu, Eds. Ge*ography of the Holy Land: Perspectives.* Kaohsiung, Taiwan: Holy Light Theological Seminary, pp. 187-196.

Rand McNally. 1989. "Incomplete Atlas Has Official Fuming." *Los Angeles Times,* Los Angeles, CA, October 7, http://articles. latimes.com/1989-10-07/news/mn-640_1_incomplete-atlas/.

Wajntraub, Eva and Gimpel. 2005. "Christian Pilgrims and Travelers and Their Influence on the Cartography of the Holy Land: 1619-1749." In William A. Dando, Caroline Z. Dando, and Jonathan J. Lu, Eds. *Geography of the Holy Land: Perspectives.* Kaohsiung, Taiwan: Holy Light Theological Seminary, pp. 121-134.

Zapata-Meza, Marcela and Rosaura Sanz-Rincón. 2017. "Excavating Mary Magdaline'sHometown." *Biblical Archaeology Review.* May-June, Vol. 43, No. 3, pp. 20, 27-42.

Zeigler, Donald J. 2013. "The Fertile Crescent: From Ur to Haran to Hebron." In William A. Dando, Caroline Z. Dando, and Jonathan J. Lu, Eds. *Geography of the Holy Land: New Insights.* Kaohsiung, Taiwan: Holy Light Theological Seminary, pp. 247-258.

**III. Maps**

Kent, C. F. 1912. Palestine in the time of Jesus, 4 B.C. - 30 A.D.: including the period of Herod, 40--4 B.C. [S.l.: s.n] [Map] Retrieved from the Library of Congress, https://www.loc.gov/item/2009579463/.

# The Growth of Herod's Kingdom

E. Nicole DePue

## INTRODUCTION

### Herod's Rise to Power

As biblical historian Anson Rainey so elegantly puts it, "Herod's rise to power occurred against the backdrop of the decline of the Hasmonean dynasty and the emergence of two intertwined rivalries: one domestic and one international" (Rainey 2006: 334). The "domestic rivalry" which Rainey mentions was a dispute between two of the sons of Alexander Jannaeus, namely John Hyrcanus II and Judas Aristobulus II. They both wanted the position of high priest. However, their mother, Alexandra Salome, designated her succession to Hyrcanus. Aristobulus rebelled against this notion and usurped the position from Hyrcanus (*ibid.*). After Salome's death in 67 B.C.E., war raged between the two brothers over the high priesthood in Jerusalem (Wright 2008: 126). When Pompey went to Jerusalem, he was able to stop the four-year long fraternal squabble between Aristobulus and Hyrcanus by ultimately throwing Aristobulus in jail in Rome and giving the throne of high priesthood to Hyrcanus (*ibid.*). But the tension created within Judea still had impact. Meanwhile, the "international" rivalry which Rainey speaks of erupted between Pompey and Julius Caesar. Rome became the leading empire of the world when Pompey came on the scene. However, shortly after Pompey's rise to power, there was a civil war between Pompey and Julius Caesar. Caesar not only won the war by killing Pompey in a battle in Egypt in 46 B.C.E., but he also won the territories which Pompey had taken over from the Greeks (*ibid.*). Although the world as Herod knew it was wrought with turmoil at this time, Herod himself was gaining power through the efforts of his father, Antipater.

After Pompey's death, both Antipater and Hyrcanus played their cards to win the favor of Julius Caesar (Rainey 2006: 337). Caesar responded by allowing Hyrcanus to continue his position as high priest and granting Antipater the new position as Procurator (or Chief Financial Officer) over Judea (Wright 2008: 126). Antipater's position played the main role in granting Herod the opportunity to become king of Judea. Later Antipater abused this position and placed both of his sons, Phasael and Herod, as governors over Jerusalem and Galilee respectively (Rainey 2006: 337). Due to Herod being of Idumean descent, he was not well received in Galilee. He acted unjustly by executing without trial before the Sanhedrin a group of Galileans who had resisted Roman rule (*ibid.*). Many actions that Herod did during his reign made him disliked by the Jews, especially the fact that he himself was not a Jew but Idumean.

**Turmoil Ensues**

Shortly after Herod's appointment as governor in Galilee, Antigonus, the son of Aristobulus II, returned to Judea to try to usurp the throne (Rainey 2006: 337). At this time (40 B.C.E.) the Parthians joined Antigonus and invaded the land under the leadership of Pacorus, son of Orodes, king of the Parthians (Carta 2002: 162; Figure 1). Antigonus, with his assistant Marion, marched into Galilee and took three of Herod's fortresses there (Antiquities 1999: 14: 298). Herod fought back against Antigonus and drove him out of the country. Antigonus' three fortresses in Galilee were left in Tyrian hands, but they were eventually recovered by Herod (Rainey 2006: 337). Because of his victory over Antigonus, Herod was greeted warmly in Jerusalem. Hyrcanus, seeing the common threat of Antigonus, allowed Herod to marry his granddaughter Mariamme, a Hasmonean (*ibid.*). Herod saw this as a way to gain support from the Hasmoneans and further his power although he had not yet officially been given the throne by Rome. Around this time, Pacorus came up to

Figure 1. Parthian Invasion with Antigonus

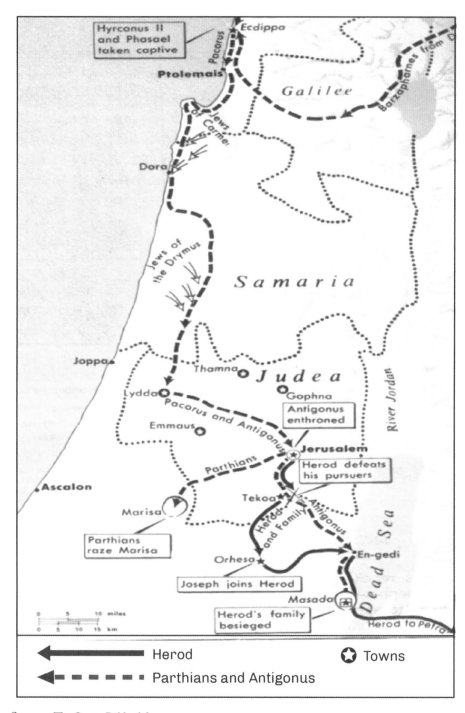

Source: *The Carta Bible Atlas*

Jerusalem and was joined by the Jews of Carmel, as well as the Jews of the forest in the Sharon plain, and together they revolted against Phasael and Herod (Carta 2002: 162). The Parthian legion, led by Barzapharnes from Damascus, imprisoned Phasael and Hyrcanus, but Herod and his family escaped to the south. Herod was able to avoid capture by the Parthians. He fled to Rome to relate the misfortunes that had befallen him in Judea to Mark Antony, the new Caesar after Julius' death (Antiquities 1999:14: 379). Herod was officially granted the position as King of Judea in 40 B.C.E. (Rainey 2006: 338). Antigonus, however, was considered a rebellious person by Antony and declared an enemy of Rome (Antiquities 1999: 14: 382).

## Gaining His Kingdom

Although Herod was officially declared King over Judea, he had much work to do in order to actually secure the territory of his kingdom. The land was in the midst of a Parthian war. With the entitlement of kingship, Herod gained the possessions of Hyrcanus including Joppa, eastern Idumea, Perea, Galilee and the Jezreel valley (Rainey 2006: 338). However, Herod had to regain this land from the Parthians before truly having rule over it (Figure 2).

Thus, a mere seven days after attaining the official title as king, Herod departed from Italy to face the charges of atrocities he had committed at home (Antiquities 1999: 14: 387). Herod sailed out from Italy to Ptolemais on the Mediterranean coast of the Levant, near Acco. In the winter of 39 B.C.E. after arriving at Ptolemais, Herod acted quickly to establish his rule, starting out in Galilee, moving from there to Joppa on the coast, and continuing on to Masada (Carta 2002: 164). Along the way, Herod gained quite a large army of those who joined in his efforts against Antigonus (Antiquities 1999:14: 395). With a strong army at his side, Herod was able to free his family members who were under siege of Antigonus' troops at Masada (*ibid.* 14: 399-400). After these efforts, the coastal regions and Idumea were now under Herod's control. He decided to ascend into the hill country through Idumea due

# Figure 2. Herod's Battle for His Kingdom

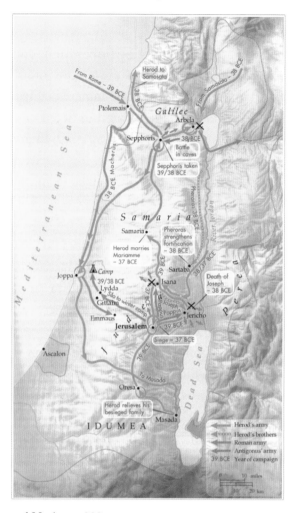

Source: Rainey and Notley, p. 339.

to hostile forces in the Judean hill country (Rainey 2006: 338). Herod set up a garrison at the Idumean fortress of Oresa and began his approach to Jerusalem by 39 B.C.E. (*ibid.*). Herod marched up to Jerusalem with his many troops, including those led by Silo who was appointed by Rome to assist Herod, and pitched his camp to the west of the city (Antiquities 1999: 14: 400). As Herod was pitching his tent there, a battle broke out between his troops and the soldiers guarding that part of the city (Antiquities 1999: 14: 401-402). Herod pleaded with the soldiers and citizens of Jerusalem that he came for the good of the people and for preservation of the city (*ibid.*). However, Antigonus declared that Herod had no right to rule as he was only a half-Jew and Idumean (*ibid.* 14: 403). During the winter months, the Roman army under Silo was dismissed and sent to camp at Lydda after accepting bribes from Antigonus (39/38 B.C.E.), but Herod used this time to remove Antigonus' sympathizers in the districts surrounding his territory: Idumea, Galilee, and Samaria (Rainey 2006: 338). Herod was able to capture Sepphoris as a result of Antigonus' garrison surrendering (*ibid.*). At Arbel, Herod faced many who were steadfast in opposition to his rule. He overcame the opposition and was victorious in securing all of Galilee (Antiquities 1999: 14: 415-417).

At this time the Parthians were defeated in Syria at Pacorus' death (Rainey 2006: 338). In the summer of 38, Machaeras was sent with two legions to assist Herod. Herod had appealed to Antony, informing him of Machaeras taking bribes. Herod then headed to Samosata and returned shortly after with aid from Sossius, the new governor of Syria (*ibid.* 389). While he was gone, Herod's brother Joseph was killed, and rebels to Herod's reign in Galilee revolted and drowned Joseph's troops in the lake (*ibid.*). In anger, Herod marched through Galilee subduing any resistance and got revenge for his brother's death at Jericho by executing Antigonus' troops there (*ibid.*). Herod came back to Jerusalem and sought to overtake the city with the assistance of Sossius and his troops. There was opposition from Antigonus' troops and from the Jews living within the city walls (Antiquities 1999: 14: 468-470). Herod was able to take the city by first capturing the lower city and the outer court of the Temple and then taking over the upper city and the rest of the Temple and its environs (Antiquities 1999: 14: 476-480). Jewish historian Josephus describes the Roman siege of Jerusalem under Herod as a blood-bath with many dying, as the Jews on Herod's side continued to kill their fellow Jews who were adversaries in this fight (*ibid.* 14: 480). Although Sossius took Antigonus captive and imprisoned him under Antony's authority, Herod bribed Antony to have Antigonus killed. Antigonus was killed, thus bringing an end to the Hasmonean government and family rule and leaving all to Herod, "the son of Antipater, who was of no more than a vulgar family,

Figure 3. Growth of Herod's Kingdom

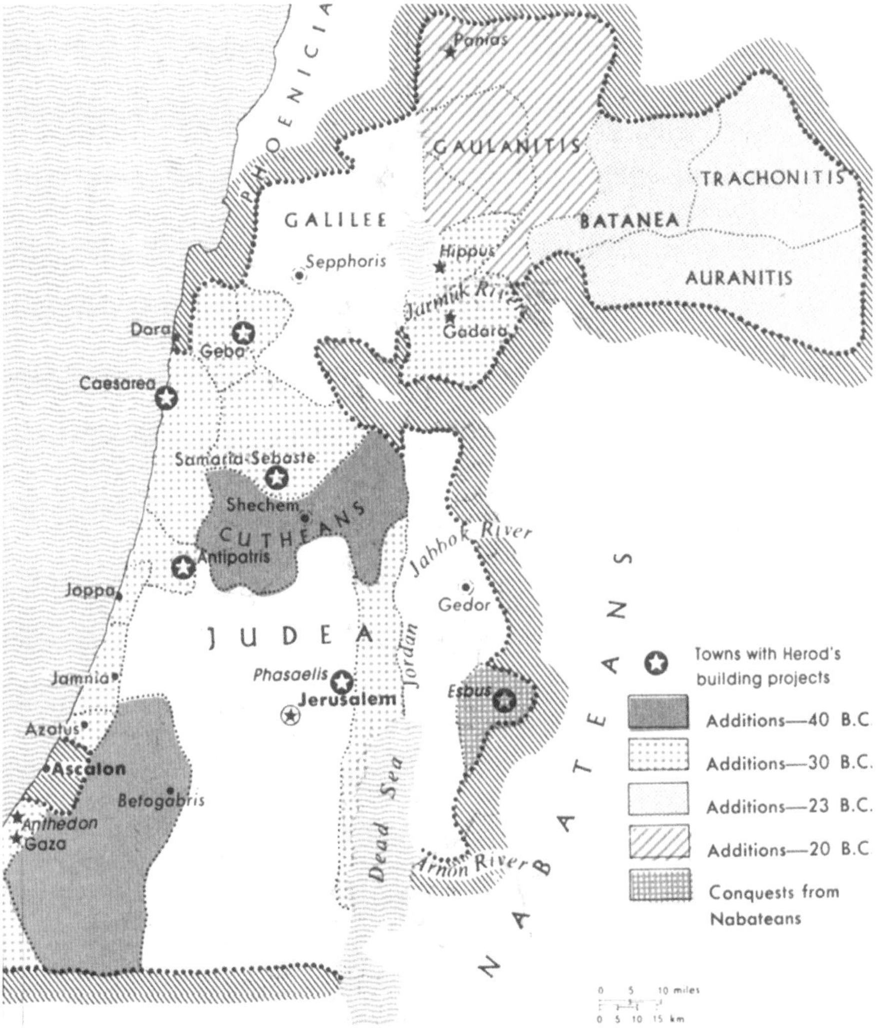

Source: *The Carta Bible Atlas*, p. 164.

and of no eminent extraction, but one that was subject to other kings"
(Antiquities 1999: 14: 490).

## Herod's Greatness and Subsequent Demise

After Herod finally gained control of his domain, he set forth
to build up his kingdom into a glorious and thriving country (Figure

3). Upon the death of Antony in 31 B.C.E. at the hand of Octavian who thereby gained rule of the Roman Empire and new title as Caesar Augustus, Herod succeeded at winning the favor of his new king (Carta 2002: 164). Augustus granted Herod more land for his kingdom including Gaza and the coastal cities as well as Gadara and Hippos in Galilee (*ibid.*). Over the years of his reign, Herod's kingdom continued to grow as he expanded it by defeating Batanea, Trachonitis and Aruranitis in 23 B.C.E. and gaining that land as well as Panias and Gaulinitis in 20 B.C.E. (*ibid.*). Overall, Herod's kingdom included a large expansion of territory administered by Judea.

Herod tried to gain the favor of the Jewish people under his rule. Much effort was focused on enhancing their Holy City, Jerusalem, and their Holy Temple in Jerusalem. Herod's architectural contributions to the city of Jerusalem were magnanimous and left a remarkable imprint on the shape of the city still to this day (Rainey 2006: 346). Altogether, Herod made the Temple more glorious than Solomon's. He fortified Jerusalem and built a magnificent palace in the Upper City with three strong towers (one of which still stands today), along with a theater and a stadium (Carta 2002: 165).

Outside of Jerusalem, Herod's efforts did not go unnoticed either (Figure 4). He had the impossible artificial harbor of Caesarea constructed on the coast as well as a beautiful palace, theater, hippodrome, and amphitheater there which had access to fresh water via an aqueduct to the north of the city (Rainey 2006: 345). Herod also built up Samaria, Jericho, Masada, and many other towns, villages, and cities throughout his territory. Herod had the self-entitled Herodium constructed – the largest and most impressive of his palaces. It is still being excavated by geohistorical archaeologists today to determine the extent of its environs, its vastness, and its beauty (*ibid.* 346).

Although Herod was able to accomplish such amazing architectural feats, he was never able to overcome his ethnic background which caused him to be constantly suspicious of everyone, even his wife and

# Figure 4. Herod's Caesarea

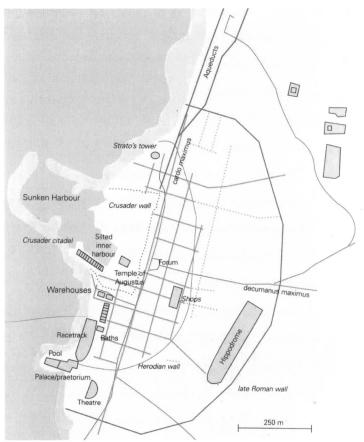

Source: http://www.kermitrose.com/images/family/VermesHerod005mapCaesarea.jpg

mother-in-law. Herod was controlled by his fear of unacceptance as a Jew and struggled to straddle the line between the Jews and Rome as he himself belonged to neither. Through this struggle, Herod killed his beloved wife Mariamme in 29 B.C.E. and his mother-in-law Alexandra shortly after (Antiquities 1999: 15: 232-247). This created tension between Herod and his sons Alexander and Aristobulus, the two sons born of Mariamme (Rainey 2006: 347). While battling the crux between the Jews and the Romans, Herod's health began to decline as well as his relations with his family. Just a mere five days before his own death, Herod had his oldest son Antipater executed (*ibid.* 348). According to Josephus (Antiquities 1999: 17: 174-175), Herod's last efforts to gain some sort of honor was to forcibly cause all the nation to mourn his death by instructing that the leaders of the country be killed upon his death. However, Herod's last order was rescinded and when Herod died in 4 B.C.E., he was not mourned by the Jews. Herod's kingdom was divided among his three surviving sons. His building efforts are the only remnants of his power that remain today and are respected by historians and archaeologists alike.

## SOURCES

Much is known about Herod, his actions and his building accomplishments due in great part to Josephus, a Jewish historian who lived during the first century C.E. Josephus' writings such as *Antiquities* and the *Jewish War* give much of the information that we have about Herod, his predecessors and successors, as well as details of his gaining his kingdom and building projects thereafter. In addition to Josephus' writings, we are able to use writings of Manetho, who was a contemporary of Josephus. Manetho was an Egyptian historian who sought to write his people's history from the very beginning up until his time, the time of Cleopatra. While Manetho does a wonderful service to us in relating the history of Egypt, he does not touch much on the world outside of Egypt throughout history or during his own time. In addition to Jewish and Egyptian historians, Greek historians such as Herodotus are also beneficial to the quest of finding historical data. Herodotus was a Greek historian living during the fifth century B.C.E. and therefore yielded extensive information on the Persian Empire, as he was contemporary with that time. However, Herodotus gives only the Greek perspective of the history of the Greco-Persian wars as well as his personal knowledge and opinion of the Persian kings such as Cyrus, Cambyses, Darius, and Xerxes.

It is feasible to say that without ancient historians such as Josephus, Manetho, and Herodotus, not much would be known of the history of the Ancient Near East. However, as every historian has their own presuppositions that influence their writing, they must be understood alongside archaeological evidence. While it is great to have archaeological evidence that supports historical accounts, it does not happen all the time.

Fortunately, there are ancient texts that have survived since the Persian period and the time of Herod for archaeologists to find during excavation and investigate thereafter, such as the Cyrus Cylinder. Although finds such as these give an excellent first-hand account, they must be taken lightly as they too can have presuppositions and are told only from the viewpoint of the royalty and only from one side of whatever situation they may be explaining.

## REFERENCES

Aharoni, Yohanan., Michael Avi-Yonah, Anson F. Rainey and Ze'ev Safrai,. 2002. *The Carta Bible Atlas*. Jerusalem: Carta (cited as Carta).

Bright, John. 2000. *A History of Israel*. London, England: Westminster John Knox Press.

*Holy Bible: NIV Study Bible*. 2000. Grand Rapids, MI: Zondervan Publishing House.

Josephus, Flavius. 1999. *The New Complete Works of Josephus*. Grand Rapids, MI: Kregel. Publications. Translated by William Whiston (Cited by text used, book number and line number. Ex: Antiquities 14: 386).

Rainey, Anson F. and R. Steven Notley, 2006. *The Sacred Bridge*. Jerusalem: Carta, (Cited as Rainey).

Rasmussen, Carl G. 1989. *Zondervan NIV Atlas of the Bible*, Grand Rapids, MI: Zondervan Publishing House.

Stern, Ephraim. 2001. *Archaeology of the Land of the Bible*. Volume II. New York, NY: Doubleday.

Wright, Paul. 2008. *Greatness, Grace and Glory: Carta's Atlas of Biblical Biography*, Jerusalem: Carta.

# Jerusalem – The Superlative City

Ronald R. Boyce

## INTRODUCTION

What? Jerusalem is the Supreme City of the World? Preposterous! It lacks all the qualifications for greatness or even a super city. To the world, Jerusalem seems little more than a mere periodic blip buried among the pomp-colored spikes in the parade of mighty cities – cities such as Babylon, Rome, London, or New York.

On the basis of its site and situation, it strikes out. It lacks the essential attributes of greatness as defined by urban geographers (Ullman 1980: 171-83). It has no direct access to the seas, no productive hinterland, and it is not at the crossroads of Israel. Its hinterland is drought-ridden and resource-deficient. Fertile fields are rare, and then on rock-laden steep gradients. Jerusalem itself is located on a handicapped site composed of several rocky and steep hills and interspersed ravines. It is a city embedded as a dwarf among nations. Its population is minuscule compared with great cities. In the past, it often fared even worse. Neither is Jerusalem a "Primate City." (Jefferson 1939). To qualify for such a title, the largest city of a nation would have to be at least twice the population of the next largest city. Except for a few decades of King Solomon's reign, it was not outstanding. Based on the area within the city walls of Jerusalem compared with other cities in Israel, Jerusalem probably contained fewer people than several other cities at any given time. Just as is the case today, Jerusalem is not even the largest city in Israel.[1]

Jerusalem, as almost everyone knows, is the quintessence of a sacred city. Therefore, it is venerated by Jews. David Ben-Gurion proclaimed that "no city in the world, not even Athens or Rome, ever played as great a role in the life of a nation for so long a time, as Jerusalem has done in the life of the Jewish people" (Ben-Gurion 1947). Kolleck, the former mayor of Jerusalem, well expressed the place of Jerusalem in the mind of the Jews when he noted that "for three thousand years Jerusalem has been the center of Jewish hope and longing. No other city has played such a dominant role in history, culture, religion and consciousness of a people as has Jerusalem in the life of Jewry and Judaism" (1990: 19-20). Throughout the Diaspora, the dictum has been "next year in Jerusalem." And every Jew is admonished to "pray for the peace of Jerusalem" (Psalm 122: 6). To the Jew, Jerusalem is the link between God and man. Jerusalem may also be the North Star, the cynosure of world history. Montefiore argues that "it is impossible to write a history of the city without acknowledging that Jerusalem is also a theme, a fulcrum, a spine even, of world history" (2012: xxii).[2] Yet the Jews of today are primarily secularists. They practice the Law, but are blinded to Jesus as the Messiah (Romans 11: 25). They think generally that they're being in the news daily is not because of the hidden hand of God, but of mundane worldly affairs:

> Israel is often the centre [sic] of world attention. This is seldom for her achievements, which are considerable, or for the quality of life which she has created, and which is the envy of many nations. It is Israel's wars, her political and social divisions, her conflict with her neighbor and with the Palestinians, and the stark intrusion of acts of terror into daily life, that make its locations and its leaders internationally recognized (Gilbert 1998: 619).

Even so, one has the nagging feeling that something about the significance of Jerusalem has been missed, that there is a transcendental significance that is not captured by the usual measures of value. Perhaps Protagoras was wrong when he proclaimed that man is the measure of all things. God is. Everything is evident except the essential element of why.

Why is Jerusalem, a seemingly insignificant city prominent on the world stage? Why is it really in the news almost daily? Why is it viewed as a kind of tinder box of not only the Middle East but the world? Why does the United Nations spend such inordinate time and issue so many edicts about Jerusalem, a city dubbed by them as a "World Heritage" (Boyce 2005b: 289). No one is allowed to remove any evidence of its cultural heritage. Why does peace in the Middle East rest so much on Jerusalem and why does the problem seem to be so insoluble? Paradoxically Jerusalem's place among cities is as a pariah, more a hindrance to peace in the Middle East than a helper; more like a fly in the soup, making peace unpalatable, even impossible. Why does the fall of great nations in history correlate with their treatment of the Jews and Jerusalem, e.g., Nineveh, Babylon, Rome, and London? The answer lies in the Bible itself. It cannot be obtained from secular sources or geographical analysis of its earthly features. "That which belongs to the physical realm is finite. Everything that is physical is limited" (Cahn 2016: 9). The first mention of Jerusalem in Scripture is mystical, supernatural, and fleeting, yet essential for its understanding throughout time. The biblical presentations of its protection are miraculous and mind-boggling, even requiring the movement of the sun. The record of its destructions and rebirths are Phoenix-like in their nature; Jerusalem is reborn from its ashes and rises in pristine glory, thereby becoming the very emblem of immortality. In between, in the long march of Jerusalem's history, its protection, destruction, and restoration on several occasions will be examined.

In this chapter, information will be provided from the Bible, ranging from its inception to its glorious consummation. The following presentation is chronological and covers the time of the first mention of Jerusalem in Scripture until its final glorification. It will be examined primarily from its geographical, economic, and political attributes as described in the Bible. Spiritual and theological questions and arguments will, as much as possible, be avoided. Even so, the Scriptures will be accepted at face value. Symbolism, metaphors, and nuances will be clarified as needed. The chapter is subdivided into five sections as follows: (1) the mystery of Melchizedek and the first mention of Jerusalem, (2) the preservation of Jebusite Jerusalem from Joshua to David, (3) the initial Jewish occupation and birth of Jerusalem, (4) Jerusalem during the Times of the Gentiles, and (5) the glorification of Jerusalem at the Second Coming.

## THE MYSTERY OF MELCHIZEDEK AND SALEM (JERUSALEM?)

According to most Bible scholars, the first mention of Jerusalem in Scripture is with respect to the mysterious appearance of Melchizedek, the King of Salem, *circa* 2000 B.C.E. (Genesis 14: 18). It is commonly assumed that the similarity of the names of Salem and Jerusalem proves that they are the same. The standard accepted argument is that "there is an apparent connection between the name-title *Shalem* and *Salem*, where Melchizedek, a prince of peace, reigned as king in a city called 'Peace.' The toponym [place name] Salem seems to be a short form of the later Jerusalem" (Galbraith, Ogden, and Skinner 1996: 26). However, there is no clear semantic connection between Salem and Jerusalem; "the etymology of the name is not certain" (Unger 1970: 576).

It is certainly true that Salem was located at the same site – Mount Moriah – as was Jerusalem later. But was Salem an actual earthly city or was it an ethereal, symbolic fore view of the future city of the "King of Salem"? If so, it would be in the same category as the Transfiguration of Christ (Matthew 17: 1-3) before he appeared permanently in his glory after his ascension (Acts 9: 3; Revelation 1: 12-16). In fact, there is no mention of a possible city on that site until several hundred years later. The name, *Urusalim*, meaning "city of peace," first appears in the Tell el-Amarna tablets about 1370 B.C.E. The British School of Archeology in Jerusalem shows that a walled tower existed on the site as early as 1800 B.C.E. (Encyclopedia Britannica 1966: 1007). However, there is no other historical mention of either Melchizedek or Salem after their initial appearance, either in the Bible or in the secular record. The first time in Scripture the place is called Jerusalem is at the time of Joshua, *circa* 1500 B.C.E. when it was a Jebusite city.

Therefore, there is considerable doubt about whether Salem truly existed at the time as a material city. It is known that the future Jerusalem was built on the same hill as Salem because "In Salem also is his [God's] tabernacle and his dwelling place in Zion" (Psalm 76: 2). But there is no evidence or mention in Scripture that Abraham ever looked for a city on Mount Moriah. When Abraham was told by God while he was in Beersheba to make the three-day journey to offer Isaac on Mount Moriah, he neither expected nor is there any report of a previous city there. To the contrary, Abraham "looked for a city which has foundations, whose builder and maker is God" (Hebrews 11: 10). He looked forward to a heavenly city, not an earthly one.

The historical facts of the capture of Lot and his rescue by Abraham provide an important background to the event (Boyce 2013b: 111-15). The story is straightforward and understandable. Here is a digest of Scripture on the matter. Abraham with his wife Sarah and nephew Lot entered the land of Canaan from Haran. Canaan contained a considerable number of cities from ten different tribes. Abraham was a nomadic herdsman. He maintained good relationships with the city dwellers and carried on a productive trade with them. In fact, he was dependent upon the various kings for permission to graze his flocks in their hinterlands. Even so, Abraham and his group deliberately kept themselves spatially separate from the cities.

After a few years, a famine occurred and Abraham and his family migrated to Egypt, a materially rich and bountiful country. Then, after Abraham lied about his wife being his sister, and she was brought into Pharaoh's harem, Pharaoh and his family were sent a plague from God, (Genesis 12: 17) whereby it was revealed to him that Sarah was Abraham's wife, not his sister. Therefore, he unceremoniously sent Abraham with his goods back to Canaan: "the Pharaoh commanded his men concerning him: and they sent him away, and his wife, and all he had" (Genesis 12: 20).

Soon, there was a conflict between the herdsmen of Lot and those of Abraham because of their large flocks. Abraham determined it was best to divide the limited grazing area and gave Lot the choice of going east or west. Lot "lifted up his eyes, and beheld all the plain of Jordan and it was well watered everywhere; and Lot journeyed east: and they separated themselves the one from the other" (Genesis 13: 10-11). Lot chose the productive hinterlands of Sodom and other great cities, evidently situated near the Dead Sea. Shortly, Lot abandoned his life as a nomadic herdsman and became a prominent resident of Sodom (Genesis 19: 1).

Lot's life became complicated when Amraphel, the king of Babylon with three other kings in Mesopotamia, invaded Sodom and the other companion cities in the alley of Siddim. They had been paying tribute to the kings of Mesopotamia for twelve years, presumably for protection, but suddenly refused. The armies from Mesopotamia attacked Sodom and the other cities. A battle occurred in the Valley of Siddim (salt) near the Dead Sea and the Mesopotamian kings won handily. "They took all the goods of Sodom and Gomorrah, and their victuals [food supplies] and went their way" (Genesis 14: 11). They also took Lot and his goods with them. However, the kings of Sodom and Gomorrah escaped capture by fleeing to the nearby mountains.

When Abraham learned of this, he was grazing his herd in the Plain of Mamre (fat) a few miles from Hebron. He immediately commandeered 318 of his trained servants and pursued the victors. After about a six-day trip, they engaged them at Hobah, near Damascus. Although only scanty details of the battle are provided, Abraham defeated them and "recovered all the goods, and also brought back Lot and his goods as well as all the captured women and children" (Genesis 14: 16). This was an amazing accomplishment and involved the intervention of God.

Thereafter, the matter of Melchizedek and the city of Salem became mysterious and supernatural. The Bible states the matter lucidly and perfectly in Genesis 14: 17-20 as follows:

And the king of Sodom went out to meet him after his return from the slaughter of Chedorlaomer, and the kings that were with him, at the valley of Shaveh, which is the king's dale. And Melchizedek king of Salem brought forth bread and wine: and he was the priest of the most high God [*El Elyon*]. And he blessed him, and said, Blessed be Abram of the most high God, possessor of heaven and earth: and blessed be the most high God, which has delivered thine enemies into thy hand. And he gave him tithes of all.

Based on later statements of Scripture, the city of Salem and Melchizedek portend Christ and thereby provide a preview of the future heavenly city. Christ is the "Prince of Peace [literally, Salem] (Isaiah 9: 6). The Lord is "a priest forever after the order of Melchizedek" (Psalm 110: 4; Hebrews 5: 6). This implies that Melchizedek was not a human being, but a theophany of Christ. [John Walvoord, the former president of Dallas Theological Seminary, defines a theophany as "a manifestation of God in visible and bodily form before the incarnation. Usually the term *theophany* is limited to appearances of God in the form of man or angels" (Chafer 1948: 310]. In other words, he had no earthly genealogy, no descendents, and was eternal, both in nature and in position: he "abides as a priest continually" (Hebrews 7: 3).

And why did Abraham give tithes, a tenth of his wealth, to Melchizedek (Genesis 14: 20)? The Mosaic Law, mandating the tithe was not mentioned for another five hundred years. Moreover, what is the significance of the bread and wine provided in the Valley of Shaveh, the King's dale? This was a valley adjacent to Mount Moriah or Zion, which some believe may have been the Kidron Valley. This valley is well-known and is mentioned with respect to the pillar of longevity which Absalom erected there over one thousand years later (2 Samuel 18: 18). Also, bread and wine were introduced at the Lord's Supper and with regard to Communion, today (1 Corinthians 11: 23-34). Melchizedek, like Christ, provided the elements (Matthew 26: 26-28). Jesus also gave the interpretation of the bread representing his body to be broken and the wine representing his blood to be shed on the Cross. Abraham surely had no knowledge that the event was a shadow or fore type of the coming Messiah and the New Covenant. Another clue to the interpretation is that Melchizedek was the high priest of "the Most High God" (*El Elyon)*. The Most High God is not just the God of Israel, but the universal God, the God of both the Jews and the Gentiles. This same appellation is applied the true God by Daniel and Nebuchadnezzar (Daniel. 2: 47; 5: 18).

The critical clue to the mystery of the city of Salem is provided by the Bible itself. "Howbeit that was not the first which is spiritual, but that which is natural; and afterward that which is spiritual" (1 Corinthians 15: 46). The example provided in Scripture notes that Adam, who was of earth, earthy, is contrasted with the second man, Christ, who was the Lord from Heaven. The first man was earthy, natural, mundane, and profane; the second man is sacred, spiritual, and heavenly. This rule appears applicable to many important things in Scripture. It is very evident pertaining to personages, e.g., first Cain, then Abel; first Ishmael, then Isaac; first Esau, then Jacob; first King Saul, then King David. It also applies to other features such as first Law, then Grace. It is also quite evident in the rise of cities, first the profane, then the spiritual. Babylon was the first earthly city – profane and destined for destruction. Babylon has become the generic name for the profane city throughout Scripture. It is contrasted with the heavenly city to come. The earthly will be superseded by the New Jerusalem which will "be beautiful for situation. the joy of the whole earth, is Mount Zion on the side of the North, the city of the great king (Psalm 48: 2). It will then be given a new name, JHWH *shammah*, meaning the Lord is there (Ezekiel 48: 35).

In fact, the contrast between the two cities is one of the major themes in the entire Bible. "When the Holy City is examined in this manner, it appears to be the exact opposite of Babylon (Boyce 2005a: 231). James Boice likewise concludes that "as far as cities go, the major contrast is between Babylon, the representative city of the world, and Jerusalem, which is God's city" (Boice 1996: 47). Therefore, Salem is the spiritual antipodes of the pagan city of Babylon.

The crux of the matter is that Mount Moriah is a sacred site super-seding all others in Israel. If the earthly and natural always precede the holy and heavenly, how could a material, physical, earthly city of Salem precede secular Jerusalem? It couldn't or this would violate the general principle of Scripture. Therefore, the Jebusites, who occupied Jerusalem (also called Jebus) for almost one thousand years, must have built the first actual (real, earthly) city on that site. The actual real, heavenly city will finally occur only when Christ, the true Melchizedek, establishes his Kingdom in Jerusalem at his Second Coming. Therefore, the city of Salem and Melchizedek of Genesis 14, as is evident in Hebrews, serves as "the example and shadow of heavenly things …" (Hebrews 8: 5).

## JEBUSITE JERUSALEM – FROM JOSHUA TO SAUL

American marines are constantly reminded before going into battle to ask the question, "What is the mission?" The Hebrews were given a specific mission. They were to enter the land as warriors and commanded by God to act as his hammer to destroy the Canaanites and their cities completely. Genocide was demanded. "But of the cities of these people, which the LORD thy God doth give thee for an inheri-tance, thou shall save alive nothing that breaths: but you shall utterly destroy them; namely, the Hittites, and the Amorites, the Canaanites, and the Perizzites, the Hivites, and the Jebusites [the prime city of which was Jerusalem, or Jebus], as the LORD thy God has commanded thee" (Deuteronomy 20: 16-17). The reason for this was primarily to fulfill the promises of God: "Not for your righteousness, or for the uprightness of thine heart, dost thou go to possess their land: but for the wickedness of these nations the LORD thy God does drive them out from before thee, and that he may perform the word which the LORD sware unto thy fathers, Abraham, Isaac, and Jacob" (Deuteronomy 9: 5).

Although dozens of large, fortified cities in Canaan were destroyed by the Hebrews under Joshua, the Jebusite city of Jerusalem escaped unscathed until the time of King David some 500 years later. They certainly had opportunity to destroy it. Why didn't Israel make its destruction a high priority? It is now known that this is the most sacred site in Israel – the place where Abraham took Isaac for sacrifice and God provided a substitute-- the *YHWH Jirah*, or Provision Principle (Boyce 2013a: 36-38). It is evident, by omission, that the invading Hebrews showed little interest in finding and protecting places where theophanies occurred; they focused on their mission, which was to destroy the Canaanites and their cities. Maybe the full sacred significance of Mount Moriah was not made known to the Jews until the time of David when the "LORD stood by the threshing floor of Ornan the Jebusite" (1 Chronicles 21: 15) and later, when Solomon recognized this as the place where the Temple was to stand (2 Chronicles 3: 1). But can any further insights be gained into why Jerusalem was not destroyed when Israel entered the land?

**The Invasion**

First, the place of Jerusalem is mentioned several times and is associated with some of the greatest miracles in Scripture. The entire matter of Jerusalem was triggered by a treaty between Israel and the deceptive Gibeonites (Joshua 9: 1-15). When Adoni-zedek (meaning Lord of righteousness), king of Jerusalem, learned of this, he panicked, formed an alliance with the kings of Jarmuth, Lachish, Eglon, and Hebron then led an army to destroy Gibeon (Joshua 10: 3). This demonstrates that at the time, "Jerusalem exerted more less a dominating influence in the land of Palestine, for not only was it [whose] king took the lead in this movement, but his city was to be the gathering centre for the others" (Pink 1964: 268). The Gibeonites, based on their treaty with Israel, called upon them for help to defend the Gibeonites. Joshua and his troops raced from their encampment at Gilgal to Gibeon. Then God intervened miraculously to defeat Adoni-zedek and the kings with him. "And the LORD discomfited them before Israel, and slew them with a great slaughter at Gibeon" (Joshua 10: 10) and [as they fled down the steep slope of Beth-horon], "the LORD cast down great stones from heaven upon them and they died: they were more which died with hailstones than they whom the children of Israel slew with the sword" (Joshua 10: 11; Aharoni 1968: 44). And a gigantic miracle occurred. Joshua asked the Lord to have the sun stand still "and the sun stood still, and the moon stayed, until the people had avenged themselves upon their enemies "(Joshua 10: 13). Then the kings were slain at the cave of Makkedah and hanged. The way was wide open to Israel for carrying out the mission of destruction given it. Its king was killed and its army eradicated. But Joshua did not follow-up with Jerusalem. To the contrary, Joshua continued his seven-year campaign of destruction northward, not southward toward Jerusalem (Wiersbe 2007: 412). Only at the end of his life did he move his army southward to the Shephelah (lowlands) when he captured and destroyed Yarmuth, Lachish, Eglon, Libnah, Hebron and other cities, but not Jerusalem. (Joshua 10: 40; Aharoni 1968: 45).

But note the contrary, but parenthetical verse of Judges 1: 8: "Now the children of Judah had fought against Jerusalem, and had taken it, and smitten it with the edge of the sword, and set the city on fire." How can this be? Evidently, the city surrendered but the people were not killed and were allowed to remain in Jerusalem. "It is possible that the Jebusites who had been discomfited by Joshua, had again become sufficiently strong to possess themselves of Jerusalem ... of their stronghold on Mount Zion …" (Clarke 1831: 104). If so, it was temporary. Moreover, it is evident that Judah had undertaken a badly botched mission. This is very perplexing.

So why wasn't Jerusalem destroyed under Joshua? There are three possible explanations. The most common one is that Jerusalem (Jebus) was too highly fortified, especially the southern portion or Millo (mound). Neither the tribe of Judah or Benjamin could drive out the Jebusites at Jerusalem (Joshua 15: 63; Judges 1: 21). It certainly was well-fortified but so were almost all other cities in Canaan, e.g., Jericho, but they were destroyed miraculously by the hidden hand of God. Therefore, the standard explanation does not pass the test of common sense.

The second reason that Jerusalem was not destroyed was presumably because of a lack of faith by the Hebrews. This also is true as far as it goes. But Joshua certainly had faith. And there is no scriptural evidence that this is not true with respect to Jerusalem. All the other large, fortified cities in the Judean Mountains were taken and their population destroyed, e.g., Hebron, Debir, and Lachish. It was the cities of the plains, such as those of the Philistines, which remained intact.

Jerusalem surely appeared to be ripe for the picking, but remained untouched. Why? The answer rests on the treaty between Israel and the Gibeonites: "you shall make no league with the inhabitants of this land [the Gibeonites]; you shall throw down their altars: but you have not obeyed my voice: why have you done this? Wherefore I also said, I will not drive them out from before you; but they shall be as thorns in your sides, and their gods shall be a snare unto you" (Judges 2: 2-3). Despite the miraculous works of God, the Israelites failed miserably to take much of Canaan. The Philistines on the coast went largely unscathed, as were the cities of Phoenicia. The Jews primarily occupied the higher hill lands running north-south down the spine of Israel, from Mt. Carmel to Beer-sheba, plus the Transjordan (Baly 1971: 112; Aharoni 1968: 50). Jerusalem stood about in the middle, as a thorn in Israel's side, and an effrontery and a perennial frustration to Israel but it remained undisturbed.

A deeper reason that Jerusalem was not destroyed seems to be that God did not allow it. This principle was first revealed with respect to an earlier prophesy given to Abraham regarding the length of Israel's coming captivity in Egypt: "But in the fourth generation they [Israel] shall come hither again: for [the reason] the iniquity of the Amorites [Canaanites] is not yet full" (Genesis 15: 16). The same idea is stated with respect to the Church, the Body of Christ, and its future termination "that blindness in part has happened to Israel until the fullness of the Gentiles be come in" (Romans 11: 25). This might be known as the "ripeness principle." Just as one does not pick fruit from a tree until it is ripe, a city may not be ripe for picking (destruction), even if logic suggests the contrary. It surely seemed that Jerusalem was ripe for destruction at the time of Joshua, but evidently it was not. When it comes to the history of Jerusalem, all must be done exactly according to God's timetable, the purpose of which may be concealed until much later. The same principle is stated with respect to the birth of Christ: "But when the fullness of the time was come, [God's timetable] God sent forth his Son, made of a woman, made under the law" (Galatians 4: 4). The principle is seen even more clearly in the case of the protection of Jerusalem at the time of King Hezekiah.[3]

## Contamination of Israel

The book of Judges covers a period of over three hundred years. Jerusalem is not mentioned once with respect to a judge, and only mentioned once in passing with respect to a Levi priest. However, the one mention is heady with insights about the condition of Israel and the nature of its relationship with Jebusite Jerusalem at the end of the period. In fact, the non-mention of Jerusalem is reminiscent of the story in Arthur Conan Doyle's *Silver Blaze* about the dog that didn't bark. "Is there any point to which you would wish to draw my attention?' 'To the curious incident of the dog [Jebusite Jerusalem,] in the night-time.' 'The dog did nothing in the night-time.' 'That was the curious incident,' remarked Sherlock Holmes" (Doyle 1892). The silence about Jerusalem during this long period is the critical clue to the mystery. The story concerns the Lord's (Colonel Ross) trusted servant (Straker) who had been contaminated, but was known to the dogs, who consequently did not bark when he took Silver Blaze. The mystery is easily solved by applying it as a metaphor to Israel (contaminated) and Jerusalem (Silver Blaze) and the dogs that didn't bark (the prophets) and give warning. There were no warnings on the wall – the Jews presumptively exploited their privileged relationship with the Lord and neglected to carry out their mission because they were dead in trespasses and sins (See for cp. Ephesians 2: 1).

After Joshua's death, Israel was composed of twelve tribes, each having their own territories and cities. There was no titular head, except the periodic reign of various judges. There was usually one judge at a time, eventually one from each tribe. These judges were mightily used of the Lord to rid their respective areas of Jewish enemies, often from outside the land. Among the most prominent of these enemies were the Midian-ites, the Amorites, the Moabites, and of course, the persistent Philistines.

It was the story of descending gyro-like circles couched in compounding cycles of sin, each one deeper than the former. First, Israel adopted the gods of Canaan. They were then enslaved and tormented by outsiders. They then cried out in desperation to the Lord and he sent a judge to their rescue. After Israel was delivered – usually in a miraculous manner – they served the Lord again for a few years during a time of peace. Then the cycle was repeated. With each occurrence, Israel's disobe-dience grew.

The tragic pattern continued for about three hundred years, beginning with Othniel, the first judge appointed by God, but Jerusalem remained under the control of the Jebusites. As noted, it was not once mentioned with respect to a judge, and only once in passing with respect to a Levite priest. However, this event demonstrates the utter degrada-tion of the Hebrews and the corrupt nature even of the priests. It was the catalyst for a fratricide among the tribes, one that almost destroyed the tribe of Benjamin. It demonstrated that Israel had sunk to almost unbe-lievable depths. The story is presented in detail in Judges 19. A priest, who resided at Mount Ephraim, had a concubine from Bethlehem who played the whore and returned home to her father. After four months, the priest went to Bethlehem to retrieve her. They left at dusk and shortly came to Jebus (Jerusalem). His servant tried to get the priest to stay overnight at Jebus. "And when they were by Jebus, the day was far spent; and the servant said unto his master, come I pray thee, and let us turn in unto this city of the Jebusites and lodge in it" (Judges 19: 11). But the priest did not want to lodge in a Gentile city, although he could have done so, but pressed on a few more miles to Gibeah, a city of the tribe of Benjamin. There, they lodged with an old man and were soon pressed by a group of homosexuals to come out. "The men of the city, certain sons of Belial, [worthless men; sons of Satan (2 Corinthians 6: 15)] beset the house round about, and beat at the door, and spoke to the master of the house, the old man, saying, bring forth the man that came into your house, that we may know him" (Judges 19: 22). It is almost the identical thing said to Lot when he had angelic visitors in Sodom (Genesis 19: 5). The priest sent out his concubine, which they abused all night, and who lay clawing at his door the next morning. The Levite put his dead concubine on his donkey, returned to Mount Ephraim, and cut up his concubine's body in twelve pieces and sent one piece to each of the tribes, calling for revenge on Gibeah. The tribes came to Gibeah and demanded that the sons of Belial be delivered to them. The citizens of Gibeah refused, and fratricide resulted. The tribe of Benjamin was nearly destroyed. This event demonstrates the wicked state of the Hebrews, their relationship with Gentile cities, particularly Jerusalem, and the wickedness of the priests.

Interestingly, the people demanded a king because of the wickedness of Judge Samuel's sons (1 Samuel 8: 3). Saul "was the last of the judges and the first of Israel's kings" (Aharoni 1968: 61). He was from the tribe of Benjamin and a great warrior who destroyed many of Israel's enemies, especially at the battles of Jabesh-gilead and Michmash (1 Samuel 11; 13: 1-8). Although his capital was at Gibeah – an ignominious choice – and within five miles of Jebus, and within the tribal territory of Benjamin, Saul made "no attempt to impose his rule over various Canaanite enclaves, even pagan Jebus" (Aharoni 1968: 61). Seemingly, Jebusite Jerusalem was being protected by God.

In summary, the Jews did not drive out the Canaanites as they were commanded to do. And as God stated in the reason for the genocide, they had become a snare to their faith and a thorn in Israel's administration. They also acted as a test and evidence of the rebellion of Israel against God. By the end of Judges, five hundred years after Joshua, the Jews had accommodated the Gentiles, even integrated them. Jebus, containing the most sacred site in the land, remained entirely under the control of the Jebusites. The Jews had been completely contaminated, having adopted their gods of Baal (male) and Ashtoreth (female) and intermixing them in an unholy manner with the Lord. As the matter of Gibeah demonstrates, the Hebrews even tolerated homosexuality. That sin almost proved fatal to the tribe of Benjamin. In *The Second Coming*,

Yeats's writing about the awfulness of World War I is eerily applicable to the deteriorated state of Israel during this period of time. In order to lead the reader in this uncanny similarity, this author has provided in brackets some helpful interpretations of the poem. Even so, Yeats states the matter much more eloquently and more encompassing.

*Turning and turning in the widening gyre*
[With each increasing circle, more pagan practices occur]

*The falcon cannot hear the falconer;*
[The Hebrews cannot hear the word of the Lord as the circle widens]

*Things fall apart; the centre cannot hold*
[They become disoriented, their faith is weakened]

*Mere anarchy is loosed upon the world,*
[Everybody does his own thing, and it spreads]

*The blood-dimmed tide is loosed, and everywhere*
[The flood of violence dims understanding of truth]

*The ceremony of innocence is drowned;*
[The act of innocence is extinguished]

*The best lack all conviction, while the worst*
[Anything goes. Wickedness grows]

*Are full of passionate intensity (Yeats 1917).*
[The immoral have become fiercely violent]

## JEWISH JERUSALEM – ITS SECULAR AND SACRED ROOTS

The Jewish roots of Jerusalem began when David planted the flag of eternal ownership within its boundaries, and declared it the capital city of Israel. The sacred roots were planted by his son Solomon, forty years later when he completed the Temple on Mount Moriah. David reigned as King in Jerusalem for thirty-three years, and Solomon's temple required seven years to build. These two roots – one secular and one sacred – laid a firm foundation for Jerusalem as the supreme city of the world.

David became famous as a teenager when he killed Goliath. And he killed many other enemies of Israel, so much so that Saul became insanely jealous and chased David all over Israel for over a decade. After Saul's tragic death at Mount Gilboah, (2 Samuel 1: 1-24), David began his *de facto*[4] reign as king of Judah from his capital at Hebron. When he became king of all Israel, he decided to move the capital to Jerusalem, then occupied by the Jebusites. This was one of the most momentous decisions in the Bible. Almost all geographers think that "David's move from Hebron to Jerusalem is probably the single most important event – geographically – in the Bible" (Galbraith *et al.* 1996: 41-42).

Therefore, the silence of the Bible as to why David selected Jerusalem is astounding. There is no scriptural evidence that he was advised to do so and no reasons are provided. In fact, Jerusalem wasn't even within the tribal territory of Judah, but was assigned to the tribe of Benjamin. Yet, there now is abounding scriptural evidence that Jerusalem was, and is, God's chosen city. Consequently, commentators, knowing after-the-fact that this was the right decision, attributed to David's great strategic and spiritual insights, e.g., well-fortified, reliable spring, etc. The most common reason given is that Jebus (Jerusalem) was well-situated within Israel and was controlled by no Jewish tribe, thereby making it somewhat neutral. This bolsters the deterministic dictum that geography is destiny.

So what did David know about Jerusalem from God's perspective, and when did he know it? David was an unlettered shepherd who became a fierce and bloody warrior. Evidently, he did not know the Scriptures regarding the past happenings on Mount Moriah, so this could not have had anything to do with his decision to move the capital of Israel from Hebron to Jerusalem. (Remember that the synagogues had not yet been established wherein the Torah was studied by the everyday Jew). The primary revelation of the will of God to David and the population was through the prophets. Yet, there is no indication that David consulted the prophets with respect to his invasion of the fortress of Jebus. Of course, David was a solid believer and was periodically enlightened in various ways. And of course, David was also a prophet himself, as is evident by the Psalms and as stated in Acts 2: 30.

In fact, the capture and occupation of Jebus focused entirely on the fort, "the stronghold of Zion," later to be dubbed the "City of David" (2 Samuel 5: 7). This heavily fortified place was a small, peninsula-like promontory sloping downward on the south of Mount Moriah. It seemed impenetrable. It was sheltered on its east, south, and west by steep slopes and the deep valleys of the Kidron, Hinnon, and Tyrotopeon. The Hinnon valley is also called Gehenna, where human sacrifices were dedicated to Molech and where rubbish was continuously burned. Thereby, it became another name for Hell. On its higher north side, it was protected by a fortress and a great earthen work called the Millo, meaning "mound." This fort became a symbol for reliance on self rather than God.

Solomon was selected as king by David. In fact, he was anointed twice; once without much public proclamation when he rode from the Mount of Olives to the Gihon spring on the back of a donkey, and once when he was anointed formally and with great acclaim. Massive sacrifices and offerings were made for all Israel "and they made Solomon the son of David, King the second time and anointed him unto the LORD… then Solomon sat on the throne of the LORD as king" (1 Chronicles 29: 21-23). [5]

The manner in which King David learned that Mount Moriah was the most sacred site of Israel is paradoxical. The significance of the site was caused by David's failing, not his faith. Obviously, the significance of the place was previously unknown to David. The story is shocking, not only because it was the consequence of a great sin of David, but because of the role of Satan. And the frightening event was caused by what appears to the casual reader as a simple census of Israel.

David evidently was incited by Satan: "and Satan stood up against Israel and provoked David to number Israel" (1 Chronicles. 21: 1). Even though David was warned by Joab not to do so, he did so anyway. "David's census was to gratify his pride in the great strength of his army and consequent military power. He was also putting more trust in his forces than in his God. He was taking credit for his victories by the building of his great army." (MacArthur 2005: 487). David's seer was then sent by the Lord to David and told that because of his disobedience, God sent famine and pestilence upon Israel. Seventy-thousand died. Then came the final judgment -- Jerusalem itself was to be destroyed. "And the angel of the LORD stood by the threshing floor of Ornan the Jebusite. And David lifted up his eyes and saw the angel of the LORD stand between the earth and the heaven, having a drawn sword stretched out over Jerusalem" (1 Chronicles 21: 15-16). (Possibly, the destruction of Jerusalem was the underlying reason for Satan's influence over David). The same kind of pretentious sin and the same satanic connection is also evident in Solomon's paramount sin). But David repented, and the Lord instructed Gad to tell David to set up an altar in the threshing floor of Ornan the Jebusite (Araunah is his Jebusite name). He did so, and then somehow realized that this place on Mount Moriah was a sacred place of the highest order). Ironically, it was revealed to David that this was the most sacred site in Israel, if not the world. Therefore, he vowed to retrieve the Ark of the Covenant from the high place at Gibeon, and to assemble the materials so that Solomon could build a house for the Lord (the Temple) on that site (1 Chronicles 21: 28-30; 22: 5).

The Temple was awesome in its planning, its construction, its detailed décor, and its overpowering glory and richness. Its planning began when David, after the revelation above, fetched the Ark of the Covenant and placed it in the City of David, or Zion. Solomon at the beginning of his reign retrieved the Tabernacle and many temple utensils and priestly accompaniments from the high place at Gibeon. He then engaged Hiram, the king of Tyre to supply timber, highly skilled craftsmen, and builders for the Temple. In return, Solomon gave Hiram 20,000 baths (a bath is over eight gallons) of wheat, barley, wine, oil and other products from Israel, which had become a cornucopia of agricultural production – the bread basket of the region (2 Chronicles 2: 10). He then conscripted the aliens in the land to undertake various other tasks. Evidently, the Canaanites had become an indispensable workforce for

Israel. All was done in accordance with specific instructions (2 Chronicles 3: 1). It is now understood that all its features signify Jesus in his resurrected glory when he establishes his capital at Jerusalem.[6]

After a seven-year construction period and a seven-day ceremony, the Temple was formally commissioned. Elaborate ceremonies were performed, Solomon gave a magnificent public prayer to the Lord, and the Ark was brought up from the City of David and placed in the Holy of Holies in the Temple. As confirmation, the Temple was suddenly engulfed "in the glory of the LORD [when] the fire came down from heaven, and consumed the burnt-offering and the sacrifices; and the glory of the LORD filled the house" (2 Chronicles 7: 1).

After the completion of his castle near the Temple, probably outside the Millo, "The LORD appeared to Solomon the second time, as he had appeared to him at Gibeon" (1 Kings 9: 2). The Lord said to Solomon: "I have hallowed this house which you have built [the Temple and the palace] to put my name there forever; and my eyes and my heart shall be there perpetually" (1 Kings 9: 3). This second time was futuristic and prophetic. (This will be discussed in detail in the last section of this chapter). It was also conditional as far as Solomon's time was concerned, but eternal as far as God's promises were concerned.

At the first appearance at Gibeon, Solomon petitioned the Lord for "an understanding heart to judge thy people, [so] that I may discern between good and bad" (1 Kings 3: 9). This prayer was answered fully, as Solomon's fame and wisdom spread through the world. "All the kings of the earth sought the presence of Solomon to hear his wisdom that God had put in his heart. And they brought every man his present, vessels of silver, and vessels of gold, and raiment, harness [armor], and spices, horses, and mules, a rate [certain amount] every year" (2 Chronicles 9: 23-24). Among these worldly leaders was the Queen of Sheba (2 Chronicles 9: 1-12). He, in tandem with King Hiram, launched great ships on three year journeys to the east and west. From such far-away places as Ophir, he obtained gold, peacocks, ivory, apes, and other items. There is much speculation about where these places were, but with little avail:

> Most authorities interpret both the visit and the voyages
> as indicative of an alliance between Sheba and Solomon
> to break or bypass an Egyptian grip on the Red Sea trade.
> Nor would this necessarily preclude voyaging beyond an
> Arabian Ophir into wider seas as Crauford, Berkowitz,
> Boyce and others have severally proposed. Careful prepa-
> ration, Phoenician help, three-year expeditions, exotic
> products, and an accumulative of evidence that there had
> been long contact between Middle Eastern and Indian
> cultures have all been invoked to sustain the argument
> that Solomon's ships may have sailed much farther than
> southern Arabia (Lewthwaite 1987: 62).

The point is: Solomon became uniquely rich and powerful. His
cedar-laden castle was indescribably elaborate. His throne was of solid
ivory overlaid with gold. Even his footstool was of solid gold, as were the
steps to his throne, and it was book-cased by lions of solid gold. "And the
King made silver in Jerusalem [as common] as stones, and cedar trees
made he as sycamore that are in the low places in abundance" (2 Chronicles 9: 27). In summary, his kingdom was in many ways a prototype of the
promised kingdom of the coming Messiah. It was to Solomon's glorious
kingdom that Jesus' disciples after his resurrection asked "Lord will you at
this time restore again the kingdom to Israel" (Acts 1: 6).

But the last twenty years of Solomon's forty-year reign demonstrated his fallen and frail humanity, his shortcomings, and his pride.
He was ensnared by his own self-glorified wisdom, by wealth, women,
and weapons – the three deadly Ws so perfectly predicted, and which
were prohibited by God, for Israel's kings (Deuteronomy 17: 14-20). He
relied upon his chariot cities, 12,000 mounted cavalry, and his fortified
structures, rather than on God. In this regard, his self-reliance on his
armies is similar to that of David when he took his census and provoked
God to threaten to destroy Jerusalem. And of course, he neglected to

read and study the Torah as also was commanded. He married seven hundred foreign wives and three hundred concubines (1 Kings 11: 3). Presumably he did this to maintain his dominance and prominence with foreign nations. And he erected altars to their gods and even worshiped them, particularly on the Mount of Olives. He built altars to Ashtoreth, Chemosh, Milcom, Molech and others (1 Kings 10: 5-8). These altars so contaminated the Mount that it became known even three hundred years later at the time of King Josiah, as "The Mount of Corruption." (2 Kings 23: 13).

It is shocking to see the similarities between the fall of Satan and the fall of Solomon. Both were contaminated by their riches and wisdom. Satan was:

> . . .full of wisdom and perfect in beauty. . . . You were perfect in your ways from the day that you were created, until iniquity was found in you. . . . By the multitude of your <u>merchandise</u>, they have filled the midst of you with <u>violence</u>, and you have sinned. . . . Your heart was lifted up because of your <u>brightness</u>, you have corrupted your <u>wisdom</u> by reason of your brightness. . . . You have <u>defiled your sanctuaries</u> by the multitude of your iniquities, by the iniquity of your <u>traffic</u> [merchandise]. . . (Ezekiel 28: 12,14, 15, 17, 18; underlining added for emphasis by the author).

It is clear that Solomon's beauty and wisdom were used for his glory and gain, not God's. Solomon was not only a master monarch but a master merchant and a master man (see Ecclesiastes and the Song of Solomon). He ruled the most glorious kingdom ever known, before or since. But he used his wealth to build up weapons of war and to fortify places. He defiled the holy places with altars to other gods. Despite his wisdom, wealth, war machines, and politically connected wives, he became paranoid (Shades of King Saul after his fall from grace). Such extreme paranoia was finally evidenced when he further fortified the old fort, "the stronghold of Zion" by rebuilding the Millo. Note that Solomon's castle was north of the City of David near the Temple. The strengthening of the fort and the building of Millo to greater strength evidenced the last ditch stand that Solomon feared might come from his enemies.

Solomon's further fortification of the Millo proved fatal for the continued unification of all Israel. Solomon was removed as the last king of a unified Israel because of his fortification of the Millo. This is surprising, given Solomon's many other sins, but this one act of his reliance on self rather than God -- "And this was the cause that he [Jeroboam] lifted up his hand against the king: Solomon built Millo, and repaired the breaches of the city of David his father" (1 Kings 11: 27). Thereby the prophet Ahijah, rent the new garment of Jeroboam in twelve pieces and "he said to Jeroboam, Take thee ten pieces [Israel] for thus saith the LORD, the God of Israel, Behold, I will rend the kingdom out of the hand of Solomon and will give ten tribes to thee: But he shall have one tribe for my servant David's sake, and for Jerusalem's sake, the city which I have chosen out of all the tribes of Israel" (1 Kings 11: 31-32).

## JERUSALEM DURING THE TIMES OF THE GENTILES

In 605 B.C.E., Babylon occupied Jerusalem. They set-up their own government, pierced out the eyes of the Jewish King Zedekiah and brought him under chains to Babylon (2 Kings 25: 7). The population was sorted and a few of the brighter children, such as Daniel, were conscripted to serve Nebuchadnezzar in his palace as eunuchs. Thereby began the "Times of the Gentiles," a time when Jerusalem would be "trodden down of the Gentiles" (Luke 21: 24). "This period began with the Babylonian captivity when Jerusalem fell into the hands of Gentiles. It has continued unto the present time and will continue through the tribulation period, in which era the Gentile powers will be judged. The dominion of the Gentiles ends at the second advent of the Messiah to the earth" (Pentecost 1958: 315). This period of subservience to foreign nations continued until the present time, or at least it did until 1976 when Israel liberated Jerusalem from Jordan.

During this twenty-five-hundred year period, Jerusalem was completely destroyed twice – in 586 B.C.E. by Babylon and in 70 C.E. by Rome, and it is destined for destruction at the mid-point of the Tribulation.[7] It has been rebuilt once and is in the process of rebuilding today. It will finally and permanently be restored and glorified at the time of the Second Coming. The reasons for its destructions and rebuilding are God-based and are explained in Scripture. The perfect timing of these events in accordance with prophecy is carefully detailed. God is orchestrating the history of Jerusalem, but the world is not aware of this (Anderson 1969). The gaps of Jewish exile and diasporas from the land are periods when the land was desolate. At each destruction and rebuilding process, Jerusalem had deteriorated morally and spiritually. Outwardly however, with each rebuilding, it became more splendid, luxurious, materialistic, and technologically advanced.

In some respects, the demise and re-rise of Jerusalem is like the tale of the Phoenix bird. The Phoenix, according to Egyptian religion was brought back to life by the sun god. "The fabled bird lived about five hundred years, and then was consumed by fire by its own act, and rose to youthful freshness from its own ashes. Hence it is often an emblem of immortality" (Webster's New Collegiate Dictionary). However, the 1965 movie, "The Flight of the Phoenix," more fittingly describes the regenerations of Jerusalem. With each re-rise, it is weaker as a sacred city than formerly, but more impressive outwardly and worldly. Like the story of the re-constructed airplane in the movie, Jerusalem spiritually is only a shadow of its former time. However, in its final restoration by Christ, it will be eternal and glorious.

Like the Phoenix, Jerusalem has gone through much of two cycles, and it is destined for a final third cycle. And like the presentation of the Cross, each "Phoenix Phenomenon" cycle begins with death, not with birth. And the cycle is in three parts: (1) death, (2) burial, and (3) resurrection (Table 1). The death of Jerusalem is the result of sin, thereby bringing about its destruction. Its "burial" is evidenced by a time of silence, Jerusalem is deadly desolate, and the Jews are dispersed to foreign lands.

(When Jews are outside of Israel, the Bible often refers to them as dead, e.g., Ezekiel 37: 13). After years of such burial, Jerusalem returns to life, often in stages (See Table 1).

### The Initial Cycle

The destruction of Jerusalem after its first occupation occurred in 586 B.C.E. It was a clean sweep. The city and the palace were burned to the ground. Hunger, cruelty, and depravity ruled. "The Temple was destroyed, its gold and silver vessels plundered, and the Ark of the Covenant vanished forever. 'They have cast fire into thy Sanctuary' recounted Psalm 74. The priests were killed before Nebuchadnezzar" (Montefiore 2012: 49). And the people were exiled to Babylon as slaves. The city was devoid of life and the land left desolate. Trees were felled, farms destroyed, and wells ruined. The causes of the judgment were: (1) the continued idolatry of the people, and (2) the failure to keep the seven-year Sabbath (Jeremiah 25: 11; 2 Chronicles 36: 21).

Jerusalem sat vacant, much as a widow abandoned. Jeremiah describes its condition in poetic terms, each stanza beginning with a different Hebrew letter. (See the Tanakh for details). Here are some of his laments:

> How doth the city sit solitary that was full of people! How is she become as a widow! She that was great among the nations, and princes among the provinces, how is she become tributary [a vassal]! ... The Lord has trodden under foot all my mighty men in the midst of me: he has called an assembly against me to crush my young men: the Lord has trodden the virgin, the daughter of Judah, as in a winepress. ... The Lord has accomplished his fury, he has poured out his fierce anger, and has kindled a fire in Zion [Jerusalem], and it has devoured the foundations thereof (Lamentations 1: 1-15; 4: 11).

Table 1. The Phoenix Phenomenon of Jerusalem: Cycles of "Death," "Burial," and "Resurrection"

| Cycle Name | "Death" – Judgment, Destruction, Desolation | "Burial" – Jerusalem destroyed and desolate. The people dispersed | "Resurrection" – Jerusalem rebuilt, Temple restored, people returned |
|---|---|---|---|
| Initial<br><br>605 B.C.E. – 70 C.E. | Destroyed by Babylon 605-586 B.C E. Sins of idolatry and violation of 7 yr. sabbatical | Duration: 70 years. Exiled into Babylon | Edict to return in 536 B.C.E. by King Cyrus. Temple rebuilt, city repaired, but made magnificent by King Herod 300 years later |
| B. Penultimate<br><br>70 – 20?? C.E | Destroyed by Rome, 66-70 C.E. Sin of rejecting their Messiah and Holy Spirit | Duration: Still extant. The Great Diaspora to all nations | Zionism, Israel a nation, Jerusalem re-taken. Prophetic future: (1) Prince comes with victory, (2) peace treaty made, (3) Temple rebuilt, (4) city flourishes |
| C. Ultimate<br>(All prophetic future) | At mid-point of the Tribulation: Antichrist revealed, treaty broken, Temple desecrated, city destroyed | Jews again scattered, but a remnant escapes to the mountains. Majority of world's pop. dies | Armageddon. Christ returns: (1) geography changed, (2) remnant believes, (3) nations judged, (4) Temple and city glorified, (5) Earth governed from Jerusalem |

The exile in Babylon lasted seventy years. The Jews had not kept the Law of Moses which required a seven-year Sabbath or rest of the land for four hundred and ninety years, thereby missing seventy of them. In Babylon, the people were discouraged, despondent, and desperate. They were forced for the entertainment of their captors to sing the joyous songs of Israel. They longed for Jerusalem. "By the rivers of Babylon, there we sat down, yea, we wept, when we remembered Zion. ... How shall we sing the Lord's song in a strange land? If I forget thee, O Jerusalem, let my right hand forget her cunning" (Psalm 137: 1, 4, 5).

In fact, the exile was a period of great learning for the Jews. They were cured of idolatry, they recognized more fully the sacred significance of worshipping the one true God, and they gained some understanding of the pinnacled place of Jerusalem among cities. "Babylon, forced into the presence of objects associated with other deities, captive Jews confronted how different their own notion of the divine had become. Their visceral refusal even to acknowledge the pagan gods, much less bow before them, was a first clear demonstration that they had become monotheists – believing not just that their God was alone to be worshiped, but that their God alone was real" (Carroll 2011: 59).

The beginning of the rebuilding of Jerusalem after the seventy years of desolation was piecemeal, slow, and for decades most unimpressive. After the edict of King Cyrus of Medo-Persia in 538 B.C.E. that the Jews could return, few responded. In fact, by 515 B.C.E. only the foundation of the Temple had been completed. When it was completed in 458 B.C.E., it was so shabby in comparison to Solomon's Temple, that many of the people wept (Ezra 3: 13). When Nehemiah arrived, he found that Jerusalem still lay in shambles (Nehemiah 2: 17). This was almost a century and one-half after the initial return. Jerusalem showed signs of life, but it was only a skeleton of its former self.

However, by the time of Christ, the Temple Mount, much of the city, and a most impressive Temple had been built by King Herod the Great. In fact, "Herod pulled down the Second Temple and built a wonder of the world in its place. ... the Holy of Holies was ready in two years, but the entire complex was not completed for eighty years" (Montefiore 2012: 90). "It was said that whoever had not seen the Temple of Herod had never seen a beautiful building in his life ... Although the architectural glories of Herod's Temple far surpassed those of Solomon's Temple, Herod's Temple had little of its predecessor's spiritual atmosphere" (Galbraith 1996: 186). So at the time of Christ, the Temple was resurrected, at least physically. The Phoenix phenomena continued – from death and dust, to life and outward glory. But spiritually, Jerusalem was on a downward spiral.

The reason for the return to Jerusalem and its reconstruction clearly was because of the promised coming to Israel of their Messiah. In fact, the nature and purpose of all three cycles is about Christ. Christ came precisely on the specified day to fulfill or confirm the covenant promises made to Israel (Romans 15: 8). "But when the fullness of time was come, God sent forth his son ... to redeem them that were under the law" (Galatians 4: 4-5). Likewise, the reason for its destruction in 70 C.E. was because of the Jew's rejection of Christ. Not only was Jerusalem again swept clean and the Temple destroyed, but the Jews were dispersed throughout the world in what is known as the Diaspora.

Many Christians believe that the rejection of Christ was the cause. "He came unto his own, and his own received him not" (John 1: 11). Christ's lament over Jerusalem and its coming destruction is chilling. "O Jerusalem, Jerusalem, which killest the prophets, and stonest them that are sent unto thee how often would I have gathered thy children together, as a hen does gather her brood, under her wings, and you would not! Behold, your house [Jerusalem] is left unto you desolate" (Luke 13: 34-35). Even after his crucifixion and resurrection, Israel continued to reject him by refusing the Holy Spirit. Seemingly, here is a paradox of paradoxes, that through the fall of Israel, the Gentiles are being blessed, but their eventual belief will be like life from the dead (Romans 11: 15-20). Now, during the great Diaspora of the Jews, the Age of Grace has been presented to the Gentiles.

The Penultimate Cycle

The destruction of Jerusalem in 70 C.E. by Rome has been well-documented and was horrendous, and even more severe than its earlier destruction. "The war lasted from A.D. 66 to 70 – five years of devastation, destruction, horrendous massacres, loss of hundreds of thousands of Jews and Romans, urban famine, the Temple burned to the ground, and Jerusalem completely destroyed. The 'Jewish War' ended in an inferno and a military tragedy unparalleled in history" (Dando 2013: 148). The Romans not only desecrated the city and removed the Jews from their land, they added insult to injury. "On top of these desolate and cheerless ruins, on which neither Jews nor Christians were allowed to set foot on pain of death, the Emperor Hadrian built a new Roman colony – the Aelia Capitolina. . . . A statue of Jupiter was enthroned above the ruins of the Jewish Temple as if in derision, and on the site of the Holy Sepulcher, strangers climbed the terraced steps to do homage at a shrine of the pagan goddess Venus" (Keller 1956: 406).

And the land of Israel remained dead and desolate until the beginning of the twentieth century. It remained so because of earthquakes, malaria, drought, and other physical conditions which rendered it practically uninhabitable. Note Mark Twain's description of the land in 1869:

> The further we went the hotter the sun got, and the more rocky and bare, repulsive and dreary the landscape became … there was hardly a tree or shrub anywhere. Even the olive and the cactus, those fast friends of a worthless soil, had almost deserted the country. No landscape exists that is more tiresome to the eye than that which bounds the approaches to Jerusalem. … Decked on its eternal hills, white and domed and solid, massed together and hooped with high gray walls, the venerable city gleamed in the sun. So small! Why, it was no larger than an American village of four thousand inhabitants (Twain 1869).

In the Diaspora, against all odds, the Jews maintained their identity. Even so they were spiritually blinded because of their unbelief in Christ (Romans 11: 25). They continued to observe kosher laws and the various Feast Days. And their constant dictum, particularly at Passover, was "next year in Jerusalem." So what, aside from the paradox of opening the way to the Church, is the purpose of the Diaspora? Certainly, the world doesn't feel blessed by them. In fact, they have been viciously persecuted, the German Holocaust being the most horrendous recent example.

> Since the destruction of the Second Temple by the Romans in A.D. 70, the Jews, who were dispersed all over the Roman Empire, had prayed for a return to Zion. ... Everywhere Jews learned to adapt to the nations within whose borders they lived. Frequent expulsion to other lands made a new adaptation necessary, and this was done [but] since the early sixteenth century, [it] was possible for only a few [to return to the land] (Gilbert 1998: 3)

The first Jews began to trickle back to the Land in the seventeenth century. However, it began more earnestly with the rise of Zionism in the late nineteenth century. Even so, the road back to life for the land and Jerusalem has been slow. The rise of the current return of the Jews and the rebirth of Israel as a nation began with the arguments made by Theodore Hertzl in *The Jewish State* in 1896. He argued that "Once the Jews were 'fixed in their own land', Herzl wrote, it would no longer be possible to scatter them all over the world. 'The Diaspora cannot take place again,' he added, 'unless the civilization of the whole earth shall collapse, the idea must make its way unto the most miserable holes where our people dwell. They will awaken from gloomy brooding, for into their lives will come a new significance" (Gilbert 1998: 11-12).

Their recent history is well-known. In 1917, the British made their famous Balfour Declaration that gave the nod to Israel for a homeland. After the horrible holocaust, the United Nations in 1947 made Israel official. In 1948, the returnees declared themselves an independent state.

The Land began to blossom and the military victories over the enemies of Israel became legendary, the most significant being the Six Days War in 1967 when Jerusalem was liberated.

Despite the obvious hand of God in the affairs of Jerusalem and Israel, neither the world nor the Jews recognize it. Even after the miraculous Six Days War when Jerusalem, for the first time in almost two thousand years, was occupied by Jews, the Jews neither understood the significance nor the cause of their victory. For example, secularist Yitzhak Rabin said with respect to it "Of course we were proud, and we had every right to be – not because we were 'invincible' and not because our adversaries were tin soldiers, but because the IDF [Israel Defense Force] had earned the praise being showered upon it by its professionalism, creativity and sheer obstinacy. We had earned the right to feel confident in our military prowess and without denigrating the virtues of our adversaries or falling into the trap of arrogance" (Gilbert 1998: 395).

Henceforth, now enter into the ethereal arena of the prophetic future, a place where there are many opinions and erudite books, but few, if any, agreed upon conclusions. This is odd in view of the fact that over one-third of the Bible provides information on future events. Fortunately, one's attention is focused on geographic, economic, and political matters where there is less controversy than on most others, e.g., the 144,000, the mark of the beast, resurrections, the identification of the two witnesses and Antichrist. The primary questions are on the when and the what, not on the usual spiritual and theological questions.

In the presentation below, this author will simple provide a coherent story based on the understanding of such happenings. Counter-arguments will not be discussed not only because space does not permit it, but it would be more confusing than enlightening. Instead, references will be provided to explain the scenario. Therefore, the reader is advised that this presentation of the chronology may be flawed in places. Even so, that does not negate the validity of the events themselves. Finally, as an essential aid, it will be very helpful for the reader, not only to carefully examine the biblical texts as they are provided, but to consult Table 1 frequently.

When the Prince (actually the Antichrist) comes (Daniel 9: 27), he will deceive the Jews. This was prophesized by Jesus when he said "I am come in my Father's name, and you [Israel] believe me not: if another [the Antichrist] shall come in his own name, him you will receive" (John 5: 43). "Because they rejected the true Son of God who came in his Father's name, they would one day accept a false messiah, the Antichrist, who would come in his own name" (Wiersbe 2007: 247). The Antichrist "who's coming is after the working of Satan with all power and signs and lying wonders. And with all deceivableness of unrighteousness in them that perish; because they received not the love of the truth, that they might be saved. And for this cause God shall send them [those in the Tribulation] strong delusion, that they should believe a lie" (2 Thessalonians 2: 9-11). The counterfeit Christ will be a great charismatic leader of the Western World, presumably out of the revived Roman Empire, and probably from the eastern side (Anderson 1969: 190-95; Richardson 2012: 15-33). But how might this happen?

Why might the Jews and the Moslems trust such a person? The answer is that he will fit perfectly their expectations of a coming Messiah. Strikingly, "the biblical descriptions regarding the coming of Jesus the Jewish Messiah bear many striking resemblances to the coming Antichrist of Islam, who Muslims refer to as the *al-maseeh al-dfajjaal* ... Second, the Bible's Antichrist bears numerous striking commonalities with the primary messiah figure of Islam, who Muslims call the Mahadi" (Richardson 2012: iv}. Three events provide the reasons for the Jews being deceived into believing the Antichrist is the Messiah: (1) The miraculous defeat of Israel's adjacent Moslem neighbors as reported in Ezekiel 38 and 39. They will be attacked by a cadre led by Russia. Israel will be unfortified (Ezekiel 38: 11). Why had Israel removed its defense system? It appears that the Prince may have had something to do with it. This war required a seven-year clean-up period by Israel and therefore must have occurred before the formal start of the Tribulation (Ezekiel 39: 9). (2) The

Prince will accomplish the long-awaited peace treaty between Israel and its remaining Moslem nation neighbors (Daniel 9: 27). Evidently, this treaty will grant Israel permission to rebuild their Temple on the Temple Mount and to begin worship and sacrifice.

## JERUSALEM GLORIFIED

The ultimate or final cycle of Jerusalem is all future and prophetic (Table 1). Israel is destined to go through a third cycle, from burial to resurrection. However, in all cases, the events are much more prominent than previous counterparts. As Jesus said with respect to the Tribulation, that unless these days are brought to their conclusions on time, no one would survive (Matthew 24: 22). It is a time of colossal suffering and judgment, not only for Israel, but for the entire world. Even so, the redemption (resurrection) will be glorious, thereby providing a capstone to the drama of the human race, from its fall in the Garden of Eden to its regeneration.

The ultimate cycle actually begins at the mid-point of the Tribulation when the Prince that comes will be revealed as the Antichrist. "In the midst of the week [seven year tribulation, or seventy week] he shall cause the sacrifice and the oblation to cease, for the overspreading of abominations he shall make it [Temple and Jerusalem] even until the consummation" (Daniel 9: 27). This revelation occurs when he commits the sin of "the abomination of desolation," i.e., when he enters the Holy of Holies in the Temple and proclaims himself to be God (2 Thessalonians 1: 4; Matthew 24: 15). At this signal, a remnant of Jews will flee in frantic fear to gain protection in the mountains (Matthew 24: 15). This is expressed symbolically as follows: "And to the woman [remnant Israel] were given two wings of a great eagle [the same symbolism is used in Exodus 19: 4] that she might fly into the wilderness, into her place, where she is nourished for a time, and times, and half a time, [three and one-half years] from the face [wrath] of the serpent" (Revelation 12: 14). Secondly, the treaty will be broken and the Jews will be persecuted, not only in Jerusalem and Israel, but throughout the world.

It will be "the time of Jacob's trouble" to the Jews (Jeremiah 30: 7), and to the unbelieving world, the dreaded "Day of the Lord" (1 Thessalonians 5: 2). It will be the great hour of judgment (Revelation 14: 7). There will be wars, plagues, famine, and great earthquakes. The red, black, and pale horses of the Apocalypse will occur. "And I looked, and behold a pale horse: and his name that sat on him was Death, and Hell followed with him. And power was given unto them over the fourth part of the earth, to kill with sword, and with hunger, and with death, and with the beasts of the earth" (Revelation 6: 8). The majority of the population of the earth will die. In the finale, Armageddon will finally arrive. "And he [God] gathered them [the armies of the earth] into a place called in Hebrew tongue Armageddon" (Revelation 16: 16). Then the great world city (Mystery, Babylon, The Great) of greed, commerce, luxury, and corruption shall be burned with fire (Revelation 17-18). There will be great mourning on earth, but celebration in Heaven. This is desolation and "burial" magnified. It would be hard to believe if the Scriptures didn't declare it so clearly and so profusely. In fact, there is more Scripture on the Tribulation events than those prophesying the first coming of Christ. Each of those prophesies happened exactly as stated. Why wouldn't these?

At his Second Coming, the earth will be regenerated to a condition strikingly similar to the Garden of Eden, but where Jerusalem will be the primate city of the world. The physical geography will be changed. For example, almost all Israel will be like the Arabah, a plain. There will be new streams in the desert (Isaiah 35: 6). The land will blossom as the rose (Isaiah 35: 1). Even the Dead Sea will be made alive with fish. (Ezekiel 47: 8-10).

The economy will be decidedly agricultural and it will be bountifully blessed productively (Ezekiel 34: 13-15). Each person will sit under their own fig tree (Isaiah 36: 16). There will be no war and nations will grind their weapons into pruning hooks. All will live in perfect peace (Isaiah 26: 3).

And the biology will be changed to Garden of Eden conditions.

Animals will no longer be carnivorous, including humans, but will follow a vegan diet similar to Adam and Eve – plants, seeds, vegetables, fruit. Fish might be an exception inasmuch as there are fishermen on the shores to the regenerated Dead Sea (Ezekiel 47: 10). Moreover, the lion and the lamb will lie down together as the lion will eat grass like the ox (Isaiah 11: 6-8). Even the serpent world will be harmless. And long life will be restored.

Therefore, some have concluded, evidently without consulting the Scriptures that cities will have been rendered superfluous, even destructive. There was no city in the Garden of Eden. So why does one need cities, even Jerusalem, in the Millennium? The foremost reason is that the redemption and the occupation of David's throne in Zion is the fulfillments of the Davidic Covenant. Evidently, David also wanted to build a house for the Lord, i.e., the Temple. David was then living in a grandiose cedar-laden mansion. But God, through Nathan, corrected him by reminding David that the Lord does not live in a building made with hands and had never asked that a house be built for him. Instead, "And the LORD told thee [David] that he will make you a house" (2 Samuel 7: 11). This was the Davidic Covenant that a seed of David (could not be Solomon, but only Christ) "He shall build a house for my name, and I will establish the throne of his kingdom forever" (2 Samuel 7: 13).

The second reason that a city is needed is because of the commandment in the First Precept: to "be fruitful, multiply, replenish and subdue the earth, and have dominion ... over every living thing that moves upon the earth" (Genesis 1: 28). Remember that those entering the Millennium are non-resurrected flesh and blood individuals. They were given entrance, not by expressed faith in the Messiah, but because during the Tribulation they have aided the Jews, even with a drink of water (Matthew 25: 34-40). They will live long, have many children, and will be tempted in all sins common to the fallen human race. Also, remember that in the Garden of Eden Adam and Eve had not yet fallen, yet they sinned. A perfect environment does not produce a perfect person or society. Therefore, the city is needed for the administration and maintenance of justice

– he will rule them [the nations] with a rod of iron (Revelation 2: 27); it will be a theocracy, not a democracy. Even worship will be mandatory. Serving God and making treks periodically to Jerusalem to worship will not be a choice, but a requirement. Justice will be immediate. If they do not worship at the Feast of Tabernacles, they will be punished. Those in dry land will receive no rain, those in oasis-like conditions or along exotic streams, like Egypt, will receive plagues (Zechariah 14: 16-19). Obviously, control of such a population is required. Moreover, those who sin will not receive mercy but immediate justice. Administration will be established. For example, the apostles of Jesus were promised that "in the regeneration [Millennium] when the Son of man shall sit in the throne of his glory [on David's throne in Jerusalem] you will sit upon twelve thrones judging the tribes of Israel" (Matthew 19: 28). And all commerce will be orchestrated from Jerusalem so as to redistribute the earth's resources fairly, thereby fully replenishing the earth (Isaiah 60: 9; 66: 20).

Could it be that Jerusalem is the antipodes of Sodom? If so, it is another evidence of the necessity of the city during the Millennium. Sodom was situated in a Garden of Eden-like environment: "it was well watered everywhere … even as the Garden of the LORD" (Genesis 13: 10). It had abundant food resources and every opportunity to honor and serve God. But it corrupted its opportunity to do so, and chose evil. Thereby, it was the antithesis of Jerusalem in an Edenic-like environment during the Millennium. Sodom demonstrates the fallen nature of humankind and the perversion of blessings into a downward death spiral. Note this descent to doom as pertained to Sodom: It had the advantages and the possibilities for good, but it used its cornucopia-like environment for evil. "Behold, this was the iniquity of thy [Jerusalem without Christ] sister Sodom, pride, fullness of bread, and abundance of idleness's was in her and in her daughters, neither did she strengthen the hand of the poor and needy. And they were haughty, and committed fornication before me [God]: therefore I took them away as I saw good" (Ezekiel 16: 49-50). The spiral of destruction appears to be a seven-fold process:

1. **Selfishness**--self-seeking aggrandizement, rather than seeking the good of others. They were only interested in making themselves great (Cp. Genesis 11: 4 with respect to Babel).

2. **Negligence**--callousness, even unawareness, with respect to the needs of others.

3. **Self-indulgence**--sumptuous living, wallowing in luxury, focus on leisure and entertainment. (Cp. Mighty Babylon in Revelation 18: 3, 16).

4. **Pridefulness**--taking credit for their good fortune, puffed up in self-importance.

5. **Haughtiness**--esteeming themselves better than others; noble, lofty, considering themselves superior and blaming the needy as undeserving.

6. **Abominable sins**--perversion of nature itself (Cp. Romans 1: 19-26).

7. **Destruction**--by fire and brimstone (Genesis 19: 24).

Modern cities contain traits of Babylon and Sodom. They are monuments to greed, jungle-like containers for the survival of the fittest. They are in a constant state of change, thereby causing confusion and hardship. Commerce is focused on their own aggrandizement. The modern city often is offensive to the senses. They are ugly to the eye, a cacophony of noise to the ear, a stench to the nose of justice, and destructive to those who touch and taste it. Their inhabitants are primarily there by necessity, not by free choice. Therefore, many people detest cities for good reasons. Nonetheless, cities perform critical and God-based services. There is a city of Heaven and a city of Hell, and both are the same city (Jones 1966: 1). Therefore, every city is a container of conflicts and contrasts. To a choice few, it is a counterfeit Heaven; to most it is a treadmill, a place of torment, and a predicate to Hell.

Jerusalem at its glorification will have all the virtues and none of the vices. Jerusalem will be redeemed (Isaiah 52: 9). The Temple and the city will be built anew. "And the LORD shall be king over all the earth:

in that day shall there be one LORD, and his name one. All the land [of Israel] shall be turned as a plain … south of Jerusalem: and it [Jerusalem] shall be lifted up" (Zechariah 14: 9-10).

Redeemed Jerusalem will serve several different purposes: (1) It will bring glory to God. In fact, its name will be called YHWH *Shammah*, meaning "the Lord is there" (Ezekiel 48: 35). (2) It will administer law and justice throughout the earth. (3) It will be the place of worship for the earth. And (4) it will fulfill perfectly the First Precept (Genesis 1: 28; Boyce 2013a). As such it will redistribute resources, enable the entire earth to be occupied, end war, and enable people to live peaceable, long, and fruitful lives. Thereby, the population will greatly increase, possibly even exceeding the present population of the planet. The earth will be filled with righteousness and peace. Satan will be removed from the scene, thereby opening gigantic possibilities for great achievements of the human race – physically, intellectually, morally, and spiritually than any other time in human history. And Jerusalem will be the crowned jewel among cities, encased in a golden Garden of Eden.

## CONCLUSIONS

The significance of Jerusalem began in a seemingly insignificant, fleeting, and mystical manner with Melchizedek, the king of the Most High God and Priest of Salem. Even so, "though thy beginning was small, yet thy latter end should greatly increase" (Job 8: 7). "Its name begins with the smallest of Hebrew letters, the *yad* (י). The yad begins the greatest and most sacred of Hebrew words: the sacred name of God, YHWH, begins with a yad and the land of God, Israel, begins with a yad. The city of God, Jerusalem, begins with a yad" (Cahn 2016: 7). But Jerusalem will be redeemed as the holy and sovereign city of the earth. The Scriptures sum up Jerusalem's consummate destiny perfectly: "The mountain of the LORD's house shall be established in the top of the mountains, and shall be exalted above the hills, and all nations shall flow into it" (Isaiah 2: 2). ("Mountain" and "hills" used here are metaphors for nations). Therefore, Jerusalem is described as triumphant, transcendent, superlative, glorious, and eternal; as the city of cities and the supreme city of all the earth.

There is no other city in the world, past, present, or future, that possesses such a persistent and pertinent place in world affairs or a more epic history. Other great cities are but dust in the ash cans of the past; they once were VIPs (very important places), but are now, if they exist at all, WIPs (were important places). When it comes to Jerusalem, God is supersensitive, super protective, and super prescriptive. His sovereignty reigns. **Jerusalem is God's chosen city**!

## ENDNOTES

[1] It is strongly recommended that the reader meticulously read this chapter with at least two sources constantly at his side: (1) a good Bible atlas and (2) the King James translation of the Bible. The location of places and their spatial relationships often provide critical insights to the reader about the matter being discussed. All Bible references should be looked-up and read when referenced. These provide fuller understanding of the context. Because of space limitations, quotations are kept to a minimum. Other translations will also prove useful. I recommend the Jewish *Tanakh* for the Old Testament. Finally, I have referenced other articles, especially by the Geography of the Bible scholars which are found in Volumes I and II of this series. These provide useful background information.

[2] I have drawn heavily in this paragraph from my previous work (Boyce 2013b; 108-109), entitled "Jerusalem: A City for all Seasons."

[3] King Hezekiah was one of the good kings of Judah. He ruled about three hundred years after King David and about one hundred years before Jerusalem was destroyed by the Babylonians. But Babylon was God's hammer, (Jeremiah 50: 23) particularly as pertained to Jerusalem, not Nineveh. When it comes to Jerusalem, God is supersensitive, super-protective, and super- prescriptive. Jerusalem is his city.

The key verse for understanding is 2 Kings 20:6: "And I will add unto thy days fifteen years; and I will deliver thee and this city out of the hand of the king of Assyria; and I will defend this city **for mine own sake and for my servant David's sake**" (emphasis added). It was not done because of any goodness in Hezekiah or because of the things he had done or would do. In fact, he failed colossally both before and after the event. However, this was the fallacious assumption of the prayer made by Hezekiah in his plea for the deliverance of Jerusalem and himself: "I beseech thee, O LORD, remember now how I have walked before thee in truth and with a perfect heart, and have done that which is good in thy sight" (2 Kings 20: 3). But there is a Divine Principle with regard to answered prayer and to the preservation of Jerusalem. "The Divine Principle, that God forgives sin for Christ's sake, and not because of any worthiness discernible in the sinner ... Not because of any moral beauty in Hezekiah did God deliver Jerusalem, but for his own sake and for David's sake, i.e. the true David, Christ" (Williams 1971: 217).

[4] David was anointed as a mere child by Samuel at Bethlehem to be king. He was the king *de jure* for at least a decade, but did not assume the throne until about 2010 when he became King of Judah and ruled from Hebron.

[5] In fact, Solomon at the acme of his rule mirrored somewhat the Second Coming of Christ when he will set up his throne in Jerusalem from which he will govern the entire earth. "The Temple of Solomon was a fore-picture of the millennial glory of Christ as Melchizedek, whilst the Tabernacle in the Wilderness set out his grace as a Savior. But structures were minutely designed by God" (Williams 1971: 241).

[6] "Thus, Solomon and the Temple together picture Christ's glorious kingdom over the earth. Solomon in his glory, riches, and wisdom, rests on the person of Christ. The Temple symbolizes the nature of Christ – gold prefiguring His Deity, Cedar his humanity; but all has Grace in Atonement as its foundation; for this palace of glory was built upon the threshing floor of Ornan the Jebusite" (Williams 1971: 241). There is a profound spiritual application of this comparison of the first and second coming of Christ, but our attention is focused on the geographical, economic, and political aspects of Jerusalem as the supreme city of the world.

[7] The Tribulation is the seven-year period of time between the Rapture of the Church and the beginning of the Millennial Kingdom of Christ. It is known by a variety of names in Scriptures. Some of these include the Tribulation (Deuteronomy 4:30; Matthew 24: 15-28), the seventh week of Daniel (Daniel 9: 25), the time of Jacob's trouble (Jeremiah 30: 7), The Day of the Lord (1 Thessalonians 5: 2), the wrath to come (1 Thessalonians 1: 10), the hour of judgment (Revelation 14: 7), and the day of vengeance (Isaiah 61: 2).

## REFERENCES

Aharoni, Johanan and Michael Avi-yonah. 1968. *The Macmillan Bible Atlas*. New York, NY: Macmillan Publishing Co., Inc.

Anderson, Robert. 1969. *The Coming Prince: The Marvelous Prophecy of Daniel's Seventy Weeks Concerning the Antichrist*. Grand Rapids, MI: Kregel Publications

Baly, Denis and A.D. Tushingham. 1971. *Atlas of the Biblical World*. New York, NY: The World Publishing Co.

Ben-Gurion, David. 1947. "Speech Before the Knesset," In *History of Jerusalem* in Wikipedia, FN 5. http://en.wikipedia.org/wiki/Jerusalem.

Boice, James Montgomery. 1996. *Foundations of God's City: Christians in a Crumbling Culture.* Downers Grove, IL: Intervarsity Press.

Boyce, Ronald R. 2005a. "Exploring the Spatial Antipodes of the Holy City." In William A. Dando, Caroline Z. Dando, and Jonathan J. Lu, Eds. *Geography of the Holy Land: Perspectives.* Kaohsiung, Taiwan: Holy Light Theological Seminary Press, pp. 229-45.

Boyce, Ronald R. 2005b. "Why Jerusalem Is Special: An Examination of Sacred Space from Biblical and Geographical Perspectives." In William A. Dando, Caroline Z. Dando, and Jonathan J. Lu, Eds. *Geography of the Holy Land: Perspectives.* Kaohsiung, Taiwan: Holy Light Theological Seminary Press, pp. 282-96.

Boyce, Ronald R. 2013a. "The First Precept: The Primary Purpose of Cities and the Provision of God," In William A. Dando, Caroline Dando, and Jonathan J. Lu. Eds. *Geography of the Holy Land: New Insights.* Kaohsiung, Taiwan: Holy Light Theological Press, pp. 30-61.

Boyce, Ronald R. 2013b. "Jerusalem – A City for All Seasons," In William A. Dando, Caroline Z. Dando, and Jonathan J. Lu, Eds. *Geography of the Holy Land: New Insights.* Kaohsiung, Taiwan: Holy Light Theological Press, pp. 108-42.

Cahn, Jonathan. 2016. *The Book of Mysteries.* Lake Mary, FL: Front Line, Charisma Media.

Carrroll, James. 2011. *Jerusalem, Jerusalem: How the Ancient City Ignited Our Modern World.* New York, NY: Houghton Mifflin Harcourt.

Chafer, Lewis Sperry. 1948. *Systematic Theology.* Dallas, TX: Dallas Seminary Press, Vol. V.

Clarke, Adam. 1831. *Clarke's Commentary.* Nashville, KY: Abington Press, Vol. II.

Dando, William A. 2013. "The Jerusalem Famine of A.D. 70: A Horrible Tribute to Human Failings." In William A. Dando, Caroline Z. Dando, and Jonathan J. Lu, Eds. *Geography of the Holy Land: New Insights.* Kaohsiung, Taiwan: Holy Light Theological Press, pp.

143-58.

Doyle, Arthur Conan. 1892. *Silver Blaze.* http://holmes.es/stories/pdf/a4/1sided/silv.pdf

*Encyclopedia Britannica.* 1966. Chicago, IL: Vol. XII.

Galbraith, David B., D. Kelly Ogden, and Andrew C. Skinner. 1996. *Jerusalem: The Eternal City.* Salt Lake City, UT: Deseret Book Co.

Gilbert, Martin. 1998. *Israel: A History.* New York, NY: William Morrow and Co. Inc.

Jefferson, Mark. 1939. "The Law of the Primate City," *Geographical Review,* April, pp. 226-32.

Jones, Emrys. 1966. *Towns and Cities.* New York, NY: Oxford University Press.

Keller, Werner. 1956. *The Bible as History: A Confirmation of the Book of Books.* New York, NY: William Morrow and Co. Translated by William Neil.

Kolleck, Teddy. 1990. *Jerusalem.* Washington, DC: Washington Institute for Near East Policy.

Lewthwaite, Gordon, R. 1987. "The Geographical Horizons of the Early Israelites: The Table of Nations Revisited," Vol. XXVII, *The California Geographer,* pp. 39-74.

MacArthur, John. 2005. *The MacArthur Bible Commentary.* Nashville, TN: Thomas Nelson.

Montefiore, Simon Sebag. 2012. *Jerusalem: The Biography.* New York, NY: Vintage Books, a Division of Random House Inc.

Pentecost, J. Dwight. 1958. *Things to Come: A Study in Bible Eschatology.* Grand Rapids, MI: Zondervan Publishing House.

Pink, Arthur W. 1964. *Gleanings in Joshua.* Chicago, IL: Moody Press.

Richardson, Joel. 2012. *Mideast Beast.* New York, NY: WND Books.

Twain, Mark. 1869. *The Innocents Abroad.* San Francisco, CA: Bancroft and Co. (www.Gutenburg.org).

Ullman, Edward L. 1980. *Geography as Spatial Interaction.* Seattle, WA. University of Washington Press. Edited by Ronald R. Boyce.

Unger, Merrill F. 1970. *Unger's Bible Dictionary.* Chicago, IL: Moody Press.

*Webster's Collegiate Dictionary.*

Wiersbe, Warren W. 2007. *The Wiersbe Bible Commentary*. Colorado Springs, CO: David C. Cook. Vol. I.

Williams, George. 1971. *The Student's Commentary of the Holy Scriptures*. Grand Rapids, MI: Kregel Publications.

Yeats, William Butler. 1919. *The Second Coming*. http://www.potw.org

# A Cartographic Analysis and Brief Description of "Preacher Point" and "Miracle Site" Cities, Towns, Villages, and Rural Places Cited in the Four Gospels

William A. Dando and Bharath Ganesh Babu

## ADDRESSING A NEED

The Gospels of Matthew, Mark, Luke, and John were written to meet the needs of the expanding Christian Church. There were no written gospels (*gospel* meaning "good news" or "good story" from medieval English) in the early days of the Church. Those who became members depended entirely on word-of-mouth testimony of the Apostles and their converts (Table 1). All the gospels bear a common theme: the life, work, message, and death of Jesus Christ. There are differences in the accounts of these events, Jesus' teachings, and his miracles. It has been suggested that Matthew's Gospel was a product of Christians in Jerusalem, including Peter, James, and John. Luke, a friend of Paul, researched and wrote his account by firsthand investigation. He was deeply interested in the "humane" aspects of Jesus' ministry. Mark gleaned material for his gospel from Peter while John's Gospel is different from the other three. His gospel was written more than forty years after the other three gospels, and it was intended to declare that Jesus was the son of God and that he brought God into the life of humankind. Matthew, Mark, and Luke are called the "Synoptic Gospels" because they give a basic identical portrait of Jesus. The Synoptic Gospels describe a Galilean ministry and then a final journey to Jerusalem. John's Gospel differs in that he describes Jesus

## Table 1. Spreading the Gospel by a Chosen Few

| | |
|---|---|
| 1. | **Andrew** – preached in Asia Minor, Greece, and Scythia (martyred in Patrae, Archia by crucifixion). |
| 2. | **Bartholomew (Nathaniel)** – preached in Parthia, Armenia, and India (martyred in Armenia; flayed alive and crucified head-downward). |
| 3. | **James** (brother of Jesus) – preached in Palestine and was a church administrator in Jerusalem; taught in Egypt (martyred by stoning in 62 C.E.). |
| 4. | **James** – preached in Palestine (beheaded by Herod Agrippa in 44 C.E.). |
| 5. | **John** – preached in Asia Minor, Macedonia, Corinth, Ephesus, seven churches in Asia, Samaria, and Patmos Island (died in Ephesus). |
| 6. | **Matthew** – preached in Palestine and taught in neighboring foreign countries including Greece (he was beheaded – the first disciple martyred). |
| 7. | **Paul** – preached in Cyprus, Rhodes, Asia Minor, Asia, Bithynia, Macedonia, Greece, Rome, Italy, Eastern Europe, and Spain (was martyred by beheading in 66 C.E. in Rome on orders from Nero). |
| 8. | **Peter** – preached in Jerusalem, throughout Palestine, Babylon, and Rome (martyred by Nero in Rome). |
| 9. | **Phillip** – preached in Phrygia, Caesarea, and Samaria (martyred in Hieropolis, Phrygia). |
| 10. | **Thaddeus** – preached in Edessa, Syria, Arabia, Mesopotamia, Armenia, and Iran (martyred by being speared repeatedly and then stoned). |
| 11. | **Thomas** – preached in Syria, Parthia, and India (martyred by a lance). |
| 12. | **Simon** – a zealot and member of the Kaneweak sect; preached in Armenia and Iran (stoned to death and then sawn into pieces). |

Source: *Geography of the Holy Land: New Insights.* 2013, p. 361

going back and forth between all regions of the Holy Land and Jerusalem (Tables 2 through 5).

The **Gospel of Mark** was written by John whose surname was Mark. Mark was the shortest of the four gospels and was the basis for Matthew and Luke's gospels. Mark, whose name means "large hammer," was a Jerusalem Jew, son of Mary, kinsman of Barnabus, an early supporter of Jesus' ministry, and one of the original disciples. Mark had unique insights into the life and teachings of Jesus Christ. His mother's home was the secret meeting place of the disciples, and it is believed to have been the site of the Last Supper and other Christian gatherings.

Mark's Gospel was the earliest record of Jesus' life, and it was written and distributed in Rome in c. 66-70 C.E (Scholz 2013; Rockhill 2018). Earlier, in 50 C.E., he wrote a brief sketch of Jesus' life. His gospel was written for Greek-speaking Romans and Gentile Christians. Mark focused his book on the wonder-working son of God, living, teaching, and healing while in human form. Mark was a companion of the two great missionaries, his cousin Barnabus and Paul in their travels from Antioch to Cyprus and Perga in Pamphylia. It is believed that a critical source of information and insights was Peter's discourses and personal discussions. There are no references to Judaic law in Mark's Gospel and only two quotes from the Old Testament. Mark concentrated on Jesus' wondrous deeds and life-exalting work in the cities, towns, and places of Galilee where many Roman and Greek inhabitants lived and in Jerusalem (Figure 1, Table 2).

The **Gospel of Matthew** was written by Matthew, one of the original twelve disciples. Unlike the fishermen whom Jesus had already selected as disciples, Matthew, whose name means "gift of the Lord," was a wealthy Jewish tax and toll collector in Capernaum for the Roman government. Tax collectors and toll collectors were despised as traitors and sinners by the Jews. Matthew was a faithful disciple. After Jesus' ascension, he met with the other disciples in the Upper Room where they selected the man who would replace Judas Iscariot as the twelfth disciple.

Matthew wrote his gospel for the Christian Jews of Antioch, Syria in c. 80-85 C.E. (Scholz 2013). Employing a "ladder of evidence" approach, he begins with an account of the genealogy of Jesus. Then Matthew builds a narrative of events around six of Jesus' discourses, i.e., the Sermon on the Mount, the missionary charge to his disciples, the parables, the instructions given to his disciples, the denunciation of the Pharisees, and his discussion on the destruction of Jerusalem and the world. Jesus Christ is presented as the expected Messiah in whom the sacred books of the Old Testament are fulfilled. Matthew provides the most authoritative and comprehensive record of Jesus' life and teachings. He focuses his record of Jesus' life and missionary activities throughout

**Table 2. Cities, Towns, Villages, and Rural Places Mentioned in Mark's Gospel**

| Place | Verse |
|---|---|
| 1. Bethany | 11: 1; 14: 3l |
| 2. Bethphage | 11: 1 |
| 3. Bethsaida | 6: 45; 8: 22 |
| 4. Caesarea Philippi | 8: 27 |
| 5. Capernaum | 1: 21; 2: 1; 9: 33 |
| 6. Cyrene (in Libya) | 14: 21 |
| 7. Dalmanutha (Magdala?) | 8: 10 |
| 8. Decapolis | 5: 20; 7: 31 |
| 9. Jericho | 10: 46 |
| 10. Jerusalem | 1: 4; 3: 8; 3: 22; 10: 32-33; 11: 1; 11: 27; 15: 41 |
| 11. Nazareth | 1: 9; 1: 24; 14: 67; 16: 6 |
| 12. Tyre | 3: 8 |
| 13. Sidon | 3: 8 |

Source: *Good News Bible*. 1976. New York, NY: American Bible Society.

Roman Palestine and in Jerusalem. Also, he mentions the non-Jewish cities of Sidon, Cyrene, Nineveh, and Babylon (Figure 2, Table 3).

The **Gospel of Luke** was written by Luke, a Greek born in Antioch, a physician, and companion of Paul. Luke, whose name means "light" or "bright," was the only non-Jewish author of a New Testament Gospel. He traveled with Paul from Troas to Philippi and later to Jerusalem. Luke was with Paul when he made his final voyage to Rome. His gospel and the Acts of the Apostles reveal his knowledge of geography, nautical and medical basics, and the political and historical events of the time. He relied heavily on Mark's Gospel and augmented his gospel from his own sources. Luke wrote his book in c. 89-90 C.E. (Scholz 2013) for a Roman official and for intelligent seeking Gentiles outside the growing Christian Church. The universality and vitality of the Christian faith are strongly emphasized in this book. He shows particular attention to Jesus' concern for the poor and defenseless, the efficacy of prayer, and Jesus as the universal savior. Luke focuses on Jesus' ministry in Galilee and on an

# Figure 1. Places Mentioned in the Gospel of Mark

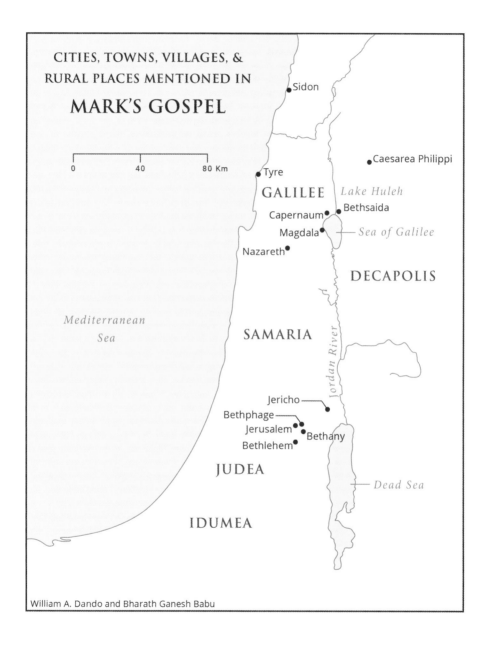

CITIES, TOWNS, VILLAGES, &
RURAL PLACES MENTIONED IN
**MARK'S GOSPEL**

0    40    80 Km

Sidon

Caesarea Philippi

Tyre

GALILEE    *Lake Huleh*

Capernaum    Bethsaida
Magdala    *Sea of Galilee*
Nazareth

DECAPOLIS

*Mediterranean
Sea*

SAMARIA

*Jordan River*

Jericho
Bethphage
Jerusalem
Bethlehem    Bethany

JUDEA

*Dead Sea*

IDUMEA

William A. Dando and Bharath Ganesh Babu

**Table 3. Cities, Towns, Villages, and Rural Places Mentioned in Matthew's Gospel**

| Place | Verse |
|---|---|
| 1. Babylon | 1: 12; 1: 17 |
| 2. Bethany | 21: 17; 26: 6 |
| 3. Bethlehem | 2: 1; 2: 5; 2: 8; 2: 16 |
| 4. Bethphage | 21: 1 |
| 5. Bethsaida | 11: 21 |
| 6. Caesarea Philippi | 16: 13 |
| 7. Capernaum | 2: 13; 8: 5; 11: 33; 17: 24 |
| 8. Chorazin | 11: 21 |
| 9. Cyrene (in Libya) | 22: 32 |
| 10. Decapois | 4: 25 |
| 11. Gomorrah | 33: 15 |
| 12. Jericho | 20: 29 |
| 13. Jerusalem | 2: 1; 2: 3; 3: 5; 4: 25; 16: 21; 20: 17; 20: 18; 21: 1; 21: 10; 23: 37 |
| 14. Magadan/Dalmanutha | 15: 39 |
| 15. Nazareth | 2: 23: 4: 13; 21: 11 |
| 16. Nineveh, Assyria | 12: 41 |
| 17. Ramah | 2: 18 |
| 18. Sidon (Zidon) | 15: 21 |
| 19. Sodom | 11: 23; 11: 24: 33: 15 |
| 20. Tyre | 11: 21; 15: 21 |

Source: *Good News Bible.* 1976. New York, NY: American Bible Society.

itinerary culminating in Jesus' entry into Jerusalem. Jerusalem occupies a central place in Luke's Gospel as well as the passion of Jesus, his resurrection, and his ascension into Heaven. Some scholars advocate that Luke's Gospel was a defense of Christianity and of Paul's apostleship (Figure 3, Table 4).

The **Gospel of John** was written by John, the son of Salome who was the sister of Jesus' mother, Mary. John, whose name means "the Lord has been gracious," grew up in Bethsaida, became a wealthy Galilean fisherman, and was one of the original twelve disciples. John had the

Figure 2. Places Mentioned in the Gospel of Mathew

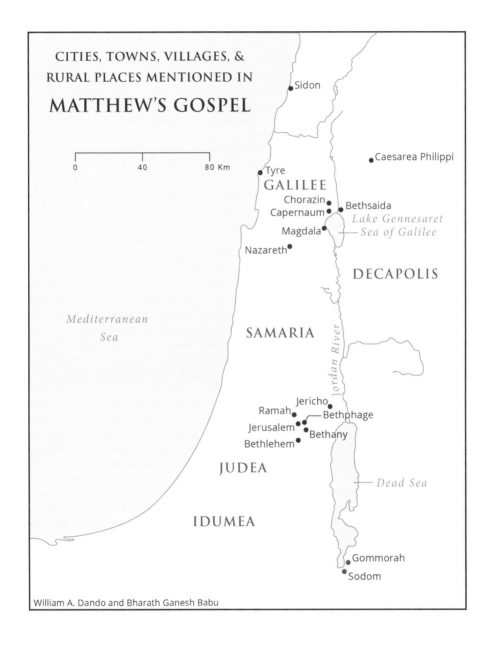

CITIES, TOWNS, VILLAGES, &
RURAL PLACES MENTIONED IN
MATTHEW'S GOSPEL

Sidon

Caesarea Philippi

0     40     80 Km

Tyre
GALILEE
Chorazin
Capernaum     Bethsaida
Lake Gennesaret
Magdala     Sea of Galilee
Nazareth

DECAPOLIS

Mediterranean
Sea

SAMARIA

Jordan River

Jericho
Ramah     Bethphage
Jerusalem     Bethany
Bethlehem

JUDEA

Dead Sea

IDUMEA

Gommorah
Sodom

William A. Dando and Bharath Ganesh Babu

159

**Table 4. Cities, Towns, Villages, and Rural Places Mentioned in Luke's Gospel**

| Place | Verse |
|---|---|
| 1. Arimathea | 23: 51 |
| 2. Bethany | 19: 29; 24: 50 |
| 3. Bethlehem | 2: 4; 2: 15 |
| 4. Bethphage | 19: 29 |
| 5. Bethsaida | 9: 10; 10: 13 |
| 6. Capernaum | 4: 31; 4: 34; 7: 1; 9: 51; 9: 53; 10: 15 |
| 7. Chorazin | 10: 13 |
| 8. Cyrene (in Libya) | 23: 26 |
| 9. Emmaus | 24: 13 |
| 10. Jericho | 10: 30; 18: 35; 19: 1 |
| 11. Jerusalem | 2: 22; 2: 25; 2: 41; 2: 43; 2: 45; 4: 9; 5: 17; 6: 17; 9: 51; 10: 30; 13: 4; 13: 22; 13: 34; 17: 11; 19: 11; 19: 28; 21: 20; 21: 24; 23: 6; 23: 28; 4: 47; 24: 52 |
| 12. Nain | 7: 11 |
| 13. Nazareth | 1: 26; 2: 4; 2: 39; 2: 51; 4: 16; 24: 19 |
| 14. Nineveh, Assyria | 11: 32 |
| 15. Sidon | 10: 13; 10: 14 |
| 16. Sodom | 17: 29 |
| 17. Tyre | 10: 13; 10: 14 |

Source: *Good News Bible*. 1976. New York, NY: American Bible Society.

distinction of being the disciple whom Jesus loved. Along with Peter and James, he was a member of the inner-most circle of Jesus' friends. John's Gospel was written between c. 90 and 100 C.E. (Scholz 2013) in Ephesus, primarily for all Christians and other Gentiles who had an interest in Christianity but knew little about the life and teachings of Jesus Christ. This gospel interpreted Christianity in terms of a new age and a turn of the century Mediterranean world setting. John combined historic fact with religious interpretation, dramatic narrative, and theological unity. Most of the subject matter contained in the Gospel of John came from Mark's writing and some from Matthew's and Luke's. A large part of this gospel is devoted to Jesus' pronouncements and discourses,

Figure 3. Places Mentioned in the Gospel of Luke

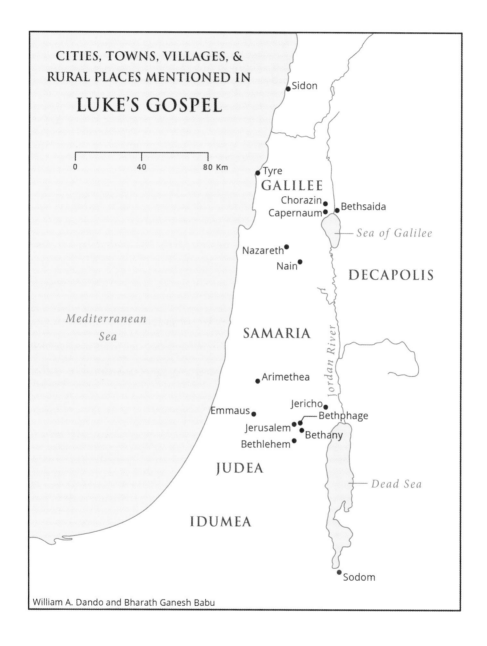

CITIES, TOWNS, VILLAGES, &
RURAL PLACES MENTIONED IN
LUKE'S GOSPEL

0    40    80 Km

Sidon

Tyre
GALILEE
Chorazin
Capernaum • Bethsaida

Sea of Galilee

Nazareth
Nain

DECAPOLIS

Mediterranean
Sea

SAMARIA

Jordan River

Arimethea

Jericho
Emmaus    Bethphage
Jerusalem    Bethany
Bethlehem

JUDEA

Dead Sea

IDUMEA

Sodom

William A. Dando and Bharath Ganesh Babu

Table 5. Cities, Towns, Villages, and Rural Places Mentioned in John's Gospel

| Place | Verse |
|---|---|
| 1. Aenon | 3: 23 |
| 2. Bethany | 1: 23; 11: 11; 11: 18 |
| 3. Bethlehem | 7: 42 |
| 4. Bethsaida | 1: 44; 12: 21 |
| 5. Cana | 2: 1; 2: 11; 4: 46; 21: 12 |
| 6. Capernaum | 2: 12; 4: 46; 6: 17; 6: 24; 6: 59 |
| 7. Ephraim | 11: 54 |
| 8. Jerusalem | 1: 19; 1: 23; 2: 23; 4: 20; 4: 21; 4: 45; 5: 1; 5: 2; 10: 22;   11: 18; 11: 55; 12: 12; |
| 9. Nazareth | 1: 45; 1: 46; 19: 19 |
| 10. Salim | 3: 23 |
| 11. Sychar | 4: 5 |
| 12. Tiberias | 6: 23 |

Source: *Good News Bible*. 1976. New York, NY: American Bible Society..

the relationship between Jesus and God, and the concept of eternal life. In matters of chronology and geography, there are considerable differences from Matthew, Mark, and Luke. John concentrates on the acts and activities of Jesus, specifically his repeated journeys to and from Galilee and Jerusalem. The First, Second, and Third Letters of John are closely related to the Gospel of John. The cities, small towns, and rural places cited in this gospel are evenly dispersed from Bethlehem to Capernaum, i.e., in the western sectors of Judea, Samaria, and Galilee. Jerusalem and Capernaum are the two most cited cities (Figure 4, Table 5).

## MAP COMPARISON

A comparison of the four maps locating the cities, towns, villages, and rural places mentioned in the gospels of Mark, Matthew, Luke, and John visually shows the spatial dimensions of each writer's theme, societal focus, and distinctive emphasis. There is unity in the dissimilarity of sites mentioned, and the disparity displayed reflects each author's background and Jesus' wisdom when he selected his disciples. Moreover, the selection

Figure 4. Places Mentioned in the Gospel of John.

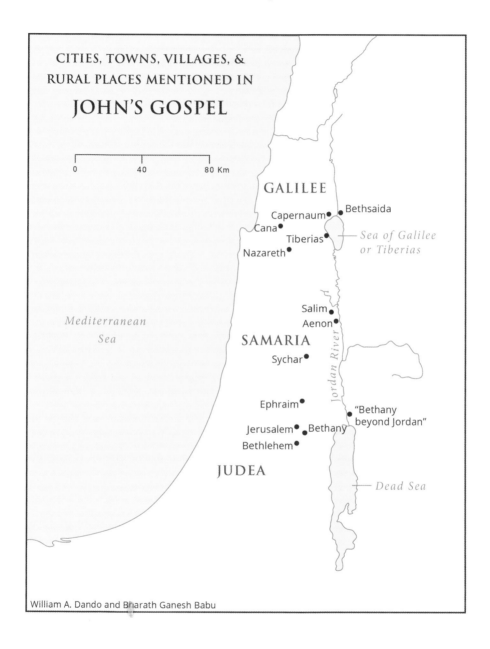

CITIES, TOWNS, VILLAGES, &
RURAL PLACES MENTIONED IN
JOHN'S GOSPEL

GALILEE

Capernaum • • Bethsaida
Cana •
Tiberias • *Sea of Galilee or Tiberias*
Nazareth •

*Mediterranean Sea*

Salim •
Aenon •

SAMARIA
Sychar •

*Jordan River*

Ephraim •
Jerusalem • • Bethany
Bethlehem •

"Bethany beyond Jordan"

JUDEA

— *Dead Sea*

William A. Dando and Bharath Ganesh Babu

163

**Table 6. Listing of Preacher Points and Miracle Sites of the Four Gospels**

| Cities | Towns | Villages | Rural Places |
|---|---|---|---|
| Babylon | Arimathea | Bethany | Aenon |
| Capernaum | Bethlehem | Bethphage | |
| Chorazin | Caesarea Philippi | Bethsaida | |
| Cyrene (in Libya) | Ephraim | Cana | |
| Decapolis | Nazareth | Dalmanutha/Magadan (Magdala?) | |
| Gomorrah | | Emmaus | |
| Jericho | | Nain | |
| Jerusalem | | Salim | |
| Nineveh | | Sychar | |
| Ramah | | | |
| Sidon | | | |
| Sodom | | | |
| Tiberias | | | |
| Tyre | | | |

Source: *Good News Bible*. 1976. New York, NY: American Bible Society.

Note: Classification into cities, towns, villages, and rural places was by their population, form, function, site, situation, Biblical classification, and/or governmental decree. Jesus' "preacher points" and "miracle sites" were located primarily in cities, suburbs of cities, on major transportation routes, or where events of religious significance occurred.

of the four Gospels provided those who wished to learn more of Jesus' message the scope, connections, diversity, and universality of the message to all humankind (Figure 5, Table 6).

# Figure 5. A Comparison of the Four Maps

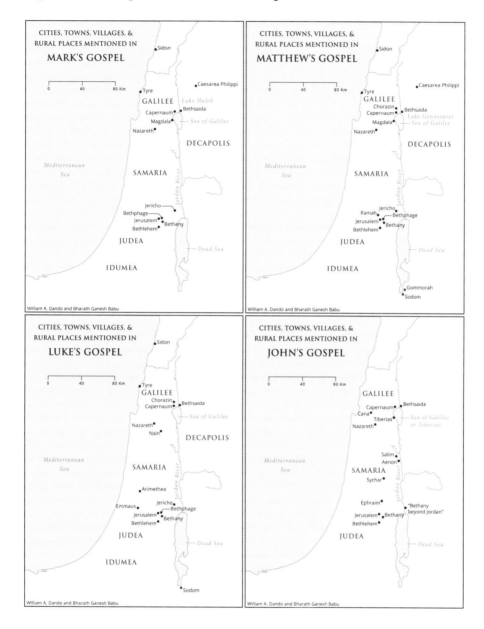

# Primate City, Regional Cities, Small Towns, Villages, and Rural Places of Special Interest, Preacher Points, and Miracle Sites in New Testament Times

## PRIMATE CITY

The term, *Jerusalem*, has had many meanings, such as "City of God," "City of Peace," at times "Salem," "Ariel," "Jebus," the "City of Judah," and the "Possession of Peace." Jerusalem was built on the tops of two mountains, Zion and Moriah. The mountains were approximately 2,450 feet above sea level, and the city was encompassed on the south and west by deep ravines. Centrally located in the Promised Land, it was 32 miles from the Mediterranean Sea, 18 miles from the Jordan River, 20 miles from Hebron, 36 miles from Samaria, and 133 miles from Damascus. First mentioned in c. 2200 B.C.E., the city was the home of Melchizedek and was visited by Abraham. It was called Salem but became Jerusalem when Adon-zedek was king. David captured the city in 1046 B.C.E. from the Jebusites and established his palace and governmental buildings on Mount Zion. He called the site of his palace "the City of Zion." David built an altar on the threshing floor of Araunah the Jebusite and made Jerusalem the capital of his kingdom. Solomon, David's son, enhanced the City of Zion and constructed a magnificent Temple of the Lord on Mount Moriah. Jerusalem became the capital of the Twelve Tribes from c. 1000 to 922 B.C.E. After the death of Solomon, the kingdom was divided into Israel and Judah, and Jerusalem became the capital of Judah. Besieged more than 17 times, the city was captured, pillaged, and eventually destroyed by King Nebuchadnezzar of Babylon in 586 B.C.E.

The site of Jerusalem was abandoned in 582 B.C.E. and remained uninhabited for approximately 50 years. King Cyrus authorized the return of the captured Jews and the rebuilding of the city and Temple in 538 B.C.E. The restored Kingdom of the Jews remained for about 200 years under the control of Persia, i.e., until 332 B.C.E. when the Kingdom and

Jerusalem were captured by Alexander the Great. Greek rule lasted until c. 63 B.C.E. when Pompey captured Palestine and Jerusalem. The Romans eventually appointed Herod as king and he restored the Temple. Upon the death of Herod, Roman procurators took residence in Jerusalem and occupied the fortress of Antonia. The Romans, as the result of a Jewish rebellion and war in 65-70 C.E., recaptured Jerusalem and destroyed the Temple and city in 70 C.E. Jerusalem slowly began to be rebuilt and in 131 C.E., Emperor Hadrian directed the city to be totally rebuilt and fortified. The city was again destroyed in 135 C.E. as the result of the Bar-Kochba revolt. It was rebuilt and renamed "Aelia Capitolina" until 325 C.E. At that time, Emperor Constantine proclaimed Christianity a lawful religion and Jerusalem became a Christian city. Roman Palestine was captured by the Persians in 614 C.E., and the city's name was changed to "al Khuds," i.e., "the holy." It was taken by the Crusaders in 1099 and then retaken by Saladin in 1189. Since then, Jerusalem basically remained under the control of the Ottomans and Moslems until the United Nations created the country of Israel in 1947.

## REGIONAL CITIES

### Babylon

*Babylon*, meaning "confusion" and "Gate of God," was the capital city of Chaldea and the administrative, cultural, and educational center of the Chaldeans. Founded in 2100 B.C.E., the city eventually covered more than 100 square miles and was in area nearly five times the size of London during the reign of Nebuchadnezzar. It was located on both sides of the Euphrates River, not far from the Tigris River in a region called Mesopotamia, i.e., "the land between two rivers." In the years of its greatest power, Babylonia dominated much of the Middle East. Babylon, a planned city, became one of the most beautiful cities in the world during Nebuchadnezzar's prosperous reign. It was famous for its massive defense walls, jewel-studded Ishtar Gate, broad Procession Street, lush Hanging Gardens, and tall Tower of Babel, for its time, an architectural wonder. Babylon influenced Hebrew life and religion more than any other city except Jerusalem. Abraham began his journey to the Promised Land from Ur in Babylon. The cultural and socioeconomic lives of Hebrews were disrupted and remolded by Babylonian armies. The plundering of Jerusalem and the Temple and the exile of the Jewish leaders to Babylon had a formative influence on Hebrew worship, business, science, and culture. The possible site of the Garden of Eden was within Babylonia.

## Bethsaida

*Bethsaida*, meaning "house of fish," was the home of Andrew, Peter, and Philip. A river-sea fishing port on the northeast side of the Sea of Galilee, two miles north of where the Jordan River flows into the sea, Bethsaida was the village that offered Jesus shelter in the fearsome days following the arrest of John the Baptist. The village sat just inside Gaulonitis in an area ruled by Tetrarch Philip, safely beyond the reach of Herod Antipas who had John the Baptist murdered and sought to find and kill his followers. It was near Bethsaida that the townspeople brought a blind man to Jesus and Jesus restored his sight. Also, according to Luke, Jesus fed the five thousand near Bethsaida (Luke 9: 10; Rockhill 2018). Jesus was treated with respect here and he visited often. Built on a beautiful site, it was upgraded and expanded by Philip and renamed Bethsaida-Julias after the Roman Emperor's daughter.

## Capernaum

*Capernaum*, meaning "Nahum's Town," was a port city on the northwestern shore of the Sea of Galilee, approximately three miles west of where the Jordan River flows into the sea. Not mentioned in the Old Testament, it was frequently cited in documents describing aspects of the adult life and the preaching of Jesus Christ. Capernaum was a central place located in one of the most populated, most prosperous, and most dynamic areas in Roman Palestine. It was a land and sea transportation hub linking land-locked Damascus and Jerusalem to the agricultural products of Galilee, fish from the Sea of Galilee, and the international markets of Acco (Acre) and the Mediterranean lands via Tyre. Also, the city was the site of a large custom station and an important Roman military post that facilitated commerce between Damascus and Capernaum, to Tyre, and to Jerusalem. Known as "Jesus' Town," Jesus based his ministry, recruited his disciples and followers, and performed many miracles there. Capernaum's location and its transportation links facilitated the spread of Jesus' message in and beyond Roman Palestine.

## Chorazin

*Chorazin*, along with Bethsaida and Capernaum, was a Galilean city where Jesus did many deeds of great power and love, but its inhabitants did not repent. All three cities were denounced by Jesus and their inhabitants condemned to be sent down to Hades on the Day of Judgement (Matthew 11: 20-24). Chorazin was situated on the northern coastal plain of the Sea of Galilee, up the Wadi Kerazin, two miles north of Capernaum. The ruins of Chorazin and remnants of a black basalt stone synagogue have been found along with the synagogue's "Moses Seat."

## Cyrene

*Cyrene* was a prosperous city in Cyrenaica, a portion of North Africa now known as Libya, and settled by Greeks. It was a port city lying on the southern coast of the Mediterranean Sea between Carthage and Egypt. Greek colonization of this part of Africa began in 631 B.C.E. Jews settled there in large numbers during the time of Alexander the Great. Cyrene became a Roman province in 75 B.C.E. Jewish settlers from Cyrene were in Jerusalem at Pentecost, and Simon who was a native of Cyrene, carried Jesus' cross at his crucifixion. A synagogue in Jerusalem was named for Cyrene. Christian converts from Cyrene contributed greatly to the first Gentile church in Antioch. They were very active and contributed much to the spread of Christianity to lands on the shores of the Mediterranean Sea.

## Decapolis

The term, *Decapolis*, means "ten cities," a Greek settlement coalition on the east and south sides of the Sea of Galilee. The coalition included portions of Bashan and Gilead. It was settled by the Greeks after Alexander the Great's capture of Palestine in the fourth century B.C.E. and his generals needed retirement communities for members of his legions. The original Greek cities were Scythopolis, Pella, Dion, Canatha, Raphana, Hippos, Gadara, Philadelphia, Damascus, and Gerasa. At the peak of Greek settlement, the Hellenistic city-league expanded to eighteen cities. Scythopolis (city of Scythians) was the only Greek-founded city west of the Jordan River. When the Romans conquered Syria in 65 B.C.E., they rebuilt and gave these cities special privileges and named them "Decapolis." Jesus knew and preached in a number of these cities; multitudes of Decapolis residents followed him; and many Christians fled and were welcomed here prior to the destruction of Jerusalem by Titus.

## Jericho

*Jericho* is one of the oldest inhabited city-sites in the Holy Land and possibly in the world. The term means "place of fragrance" and it also was known as the "moon city." First settled in c. 3,100 B.C.E., it was situated in a very fertile and well-watered site, 825 feet below sea level, seventeen miles west of the Jericho Road, and downhill from Jerusalem which is located at 2,550 feet above sea level. Also, Jericho lies seven miles west of the northern tip of the Dead Sea and five miles west of the Jordan River in the deepest "rift valley" on the earth's surface. A beautiful walled city in a vast orchard of palm trees, it was an important site that served as the fortress that guarded the entrance into the land of Canaan from the east. Destroyed and rebuilt after destruction by military sieges, earthquakes, and other natural catastrophes, Jericho was captured and destroyed by Joshua and his men in a remarkable manner and with the help of Rahab, spies, and walls that came tumbling down. Only the silver and gold and vessels of brass and iron were saved and put into the treasury of the house of Jehovah. In New Testament times, Jericho was rebuilt, was rich and flourishing, and a center of commerce and trade. It was visited by Jesus often on his journeys to and from Galilee, and to Jerusalem; it was the place of Jesus' parable of the Good Samaritan.

## Nineveh

The term, *Nineveh*, means "abode of Ninus," (an Assyrian deity). It was the capital of the ancient kingdom and empire of Assyria. The city was located on the eastern bank of the Tigris River, about 500 miles from where the river joins the Euphrates River and 250 miles north of Babylon. Known to the Jews as the land of Nimrod, Assyria was first called a kingdom in 770 B.C.E. The city has been mentioned in 2 Kings and Isaiah. The last mention of Nineveh was in 606 B.C.E. It was captured, plundered, and destroyed, and its inhabitants scattered or made slaves. Ruins have been excavated near modern Mosul, Iraq. Geohistorical archaeological research attests to the great size of a once flourishing city and the large number of inhabitants who lived there. The kings of Nineveh ruled an empire from the Caucasus and the Caspian Sea to the Persian Gulf, and the Tigris River to Egypt for more than 600 years. Its destruction was strange and sudden (Isaiah 10: 5-19). Known for ruling with hideous tyranny and violence, the city's destruction was foretold by Zephaniah and Nahum, and the city forgotten in the Scriptures until mentioned in Matthew and Luke.

## Ramah

*Ramah*, meaning "height," is an old regional city in the land allocated to the tribe of Benjamin. It was located on the border between Israel and Judah, five miles north of Jerusalem, near Gibeah. Noted as a town of Benjamin by Joshua and mentioned in Jeremiah, it was a defensive fort in the battle between the kings of Israel and Judah. Ramah was famous for the palm tree Deborah, a judge and prophetess, sat beneath when she held court and settled disputes. Jeremiah was held captive in Ramah when Jerusalem was captured by Nebuchadnezzar. Ramah's inhabitants also were forcibly taken to Babylon. They survived captivity and returned to Ramah after being released. Samuel, the prophet, was born and lived in Ramah. His father had been an exiled Jew who had returned to Ramah. Samuel lived in Ramah and when he died, he was buried in his own house; thus, the home became his tomb and a venerated site. It is said that Rachel, the wife of Jacob, buried close to Bethlehem, appeared from the dead and cried in Ramah for the children of the area slaughtered by Herod's troops in their attempt to kill the infant Jesus. For a small city, Ramah had a remarkable history.

## Sidon

The term, *Sidon*, means "fishery," the Greek form of the Phoenician name *Zidon*. It is an ancient and prosperous port city of Phoenicia, located on the southwest coast of the Mediterranean Sea, twenty-five miles north of Tyre and fifty miles from Nazareth. The city's height of wealth and importance was during a period of Persian dominance. The Sidonians revolted against the Persians and lost the battle for control of the city. A suicidal fire destroyed most of the residential sections of the city and killed 40,000 inhabitants. The port facilities were not destroyed and gradually the city recovered and flourished. King Solomon considered the Sidonians to be the best cutters of fine timber. Regionally known for their zealous enthusiasm for the worship of Baal and Ashtoreth created problems at times between them and the Israelites. Jezebel, daughter of Ethbaal, the king of Sidon, married and had much influence on Ahab, the king of Israel. Sidon is the most northern city mentioned in connection with Jesus' preaching journey. Jesus commented on Sidonian wickedness. Paul visited there on his way to Rome as a prisoner. Successful Christian missionary efforts led to the city becoming the seat of Bishop Theodorus who attended the Council of Nicaea. Historically, Sidon was famous for its commerce, manufacturing, arts, and science.

## Sodom and Gomorrah

Sodom and Gomorrah were two ancient cities commonly mentioned as the "twin cities of infamy," destroyed by an earthquake and fire in c. 1900 B.C.E. *Sodom*, meaning "burning," and *Gomorrah*, meaning "submersion," were the chief cities in a settled complex of cities and small towns believed to be located on the northern shore of the Dead Sea, near where the Jordan River flows into the sea. Their locations are presently unknown. Presumably their destruction was an example to all who live in impiety and wickedness. Comments made in the Book of Genesis seem to indicate that Sodom and Gomorrah were very wealthy and prosperous cities in a fertile and lush area called the "Vale of Siddim." Lot, Abraham's nephew, recognized the beauty and natural richness of this vale and the lower Jordan Valley and settled in Sodom. Lot's evaluation of the area as a Garden of Eden has been substantiated by geohistorical archaeologists. Sometime later, four Mesopotamian kings, led by Chedorlaomer, attacked Sodom and Gomorrah and captured Lot. They plundered the cities and took much loot, for the cities were wealthy. Abraham saved Lot and his family, but the wickedness of the Sodomites was proverbial. The Lord destroyed the cities and all life; no one was saved (Genesis 19: 24-26). So complete was their destruction, no traces of Sodom and Gomorrah have been found.

## Tiberias

*Tiberias*, a city on the Sea of Galilee, was built by Herod Antipas and named by him to honor Emperor Tiberius. It became the capital of Galilee from the time of its dedication until the reign of Herod Agrippa. Tiberias was located on a choice site, twelve miles south of where the Jordan River flows into the Sea of Galilee and six miles north of the Jordan River's exit from the sea, at an elevation of 681 feet below sea level. In Jesus' time, the city was shunned by pious Jews. Jesus did not enter Tiberias. It was noted as a beautiful city with a Hellenistic atmosphere and famous hot mineral baths. After Titus destroyed Jerusalem, Tiberias became a center of rabbinical learning.

## Tyre

Tyre was a famous commercial city and international port of Phoenicia. The term *Tyre,* means "a rock." Located on the border of the land given to the tribe of Asher on the southeast coast of the Mediterranean Sea, it was situated halfway between Beirut and Mount Carmel, about 23 miles north of Acre and 25 miles south of Sidon. Founded as a daughter port of Sidon on the mainland, Tyre spread to a nearby rocky island for defense. It was never a part of Israel, but its kings worked hand-in-hand with King David and King Solomon. King Hiram sent cedar wood and skilled workers to King David to assist him in building his palace. King Hiram also provided assistance to King Solomon when he was constructing the Jerusalem Temple. King Solomon supplied King Hiram with wheat, olives, wine, and oil. Later in history, King Ahab married Jezebel, the daughter of Ithobal, the king of Tyre. Tyre's wealth and fame attracted many pirates and invaders, but its strong fortifications and island setting resisted capture, including a thirteen-year siege by King Nebuchadnezzar. When Jesus visited Tyre, it was a magnificent port city with a population greater than Jerusalem. It was the largest city that Jesus ever visited, crowded with glass shops, dyeing and weaving facilities, glass and rock engravers, and polishers of precious stones. Jesus was well received in Tyre. Paul visited this city-port for seven days. It was the seat of an early Christian bishopric. The Moslems, in 1291, captured and plundered the city, then destroyed everything of value. Tyre never recovered.

## SMALL TOWNS

### Bethlehem

The term *Bethlehem* means "House of Bread." It was one of the oldest hill country towns in the land promised to Abraham and known at the time of Jacob. In the literature, Bethlehem was called "the city of David" and remembered as the place where Rachel, one of Jacob's wives and mother of Joseph, died and was buried. In the valley to the east of

Bethlehem was the site where Ruth, a Moabite, gleaned wheat when she and Naomi, her mother-in-law, returned to Bethlehem after Naomi's husband died in the land of Moab. David was born and was anointed king by Samuel in Bethlehem. From a well here, three followers of David risked their lives and brought water to him when he was hiding in the cave of Adullam. Jesus the Christ was born in Bethlehem. The town is located five miles south of Jerusalem, at an elevation of 2,550 feet, which is 100 feet higher than the city of Jerusalem. Constantine the Great (330 C.E.) built a church over the stable-cave where it was believed Jesus was born. This site is considered the oldest, active Christian Church in the world.

## Caesarea Philippi

*Caesarea Philippi* was a Canaanite sanctuary for Baal-worshippers, and it was named Baal-gad and/or Baal-hermon. Here, King Herod built a temple which he dedicated to Augustus Caesar. The town was expanded and embellished by his son, Herod Philip and renamed by him, Caesarea Philippi. The reconstructed Gentile city was built on a limestone terrace in a beautiful valley at the base of Mount Hermon. It is located 120 miles north of Jerusalem and 20 miles north of the Sea of Galilee at the site of the upper source of the Jordan River. Only mentioned in Matthew and Mark, the town was not mentioned in the Old Testament. Caesarea Philippi was the northern-most limit to Jesus' ministry and was renowned for its fantastic limestone caverns, caves, grottos, and springs, and as a place for worshipping the Greek and Roman nature god, Pan. It was the site of the Apostle Peter's pronouncement that Jesus was "the Christ, the son of the living God."

## Dalmanutha (Magdala?)

Dalmanutha (Magdala?), meaning "a tower," located on the west shore of the Sea of Galilee, about three miles northwest of Tiberias, was called the "city of color." An industrial district of Magdala, it was noted for its towers of cloth dryers and of dyed-cloth racks. Surrounding the city on the west were fields where indigo plants were cultivated. Christ came to Magdala by boat, across the Sea of Galilee, after feeding 4,000 on a gentle slope of a mountain on the eastern side. Mary Magdalene came from this town. She was an unmarried, wealthy, independently spirited woman who had an infirmity. It is said that Jesus cleansed her of evil spirits and her infirmity, and in gratitude, she provided financial aid to Jesus. She became one of his most loyal followers. She was present when Jesus was crucified, and she was the first to see Jesus rise from the dead. Her name, Mary Magdalene, signified that she was Mary born in Magdala.

## Ephraim

*Ephraim*, a small town in that portion of Canaan named after Joseph's second son, was situated in a tribal area of great riches and strong security. Located on a very fertile plain with well-watered valleys, it could only be reached by ascent through steep and narrow ravines. Jesus, feeling threatened by the chief priests and the Pharisees and no longer able to walk openly among the Jews, went to Ephraim with his disciples to an inaccessible area for safety. The Passover was approaching, and Jewish authorities in Jerusalem were looking for Jesus so that they might arrest him (John 11: 54-57).

## Nazareth

*Nazareth*, meaning "the guarded one" and/or "the watchtower," was a secluded small town in lower Galilee. It is not mentioned in the Old Testament. Its fame is derived from its connection with the history of Jesus Christ, and it shares with Bethlehem and Jerusalem the regard and esteem of Christians. Nazareth is located high on the slope of a valley in the southern Lebanon Mountains at the edge of the Plain of Esdraelon. From Nazareth could be seen lush agricultural fields, busy military highways, and farm roads from a distance of thirty or more miles in Jesus' time. Nazareth was the home of Joseph and Mary and the childhood home of Jesus. After Jesus' baptism by John the Baptist and after he was tempted by the Devil, he returned to Nazareth to preach in the synagogue. He was violently rejected and a mob tried to throw him over a cliff near the town. Jesus escaped the mob, fled to Capernaum, and made Capernaum his new home and headquarters. Nevertheless, Nazareth continued to be attached to his name, i.e., Jesus of Nazareth, by both his supporters and his foes.

## VILLAGES AND RURAL PLACES OF SPECIAL INTEREST

### Aenon

*Aenon*, meaning "springs," was the site near Salim, noted for its abundant fresh pure water, and where both John the Baptist and Jesus baptized. The site was located about twenty-five miles south of Tiberias and eight miles south of Scythopolis on the west side of the Jordan River (John 3: 23). Aenon was mentioned in the Bible only one time – in the Gospel of John.

### Arimathea

The term, *Arimathea,* means "heights" and it was also called "a city of Jews." It was the birthplace of Joseph of Arimathea. He was a rich, good, and upright man who was a member of the Council in Jerusalem. A secret follower of Jesus, Joseph of Arimathea asked Pontius Pilate for Jesus' body after he was executed (crucified). He took Jesus' body from the cross, wrapped it in linen cloth, and placed it in a tomb cut into the rock, one in which no one had been laid. This sepulcher was to be Joseph's own burial place. The town was sometimes called Ramah, the home of Samuel the prophet. No definite location site has been identified. It is believed to lie a few miles northwest of Jerusalem.

### Bethany

*Bethany* was located on the eastern slope of the Mount of Olives, about two miles from Jerusalem, on or near the road from Jericho to Jerusalem, and west of Bethphage. The term means "house of dates." Bethany and Bethphage are, at times, mentioned together. Bethany was the home of sisters Mary and Martha, and their brother, Lazarus. This village has been infrequently mentioned in the Bible, but when mentioned, it is related to the memorable acts and events of Jesus' visits and the last days before his crucifixion. At the time of Christ, Bethany was a beautiful rural village, founded upon an excellent location, somewhat secluded, and very peaceful. Jesus visited Bethany often because he was welcomed there, treated with love and respect, and it was restful. In Jesus' time, the route from Bethany to Jerusalem was a footpath, and on this footpath, the triumphant Palm Sunday procession began.

## Bethphage

*Bethphage* was a rural place on the base of the Mount of Olives, along the road between Jericho and Jerusalem. Its name means "house of figs." Situated near Bethany, it was the site where Jesus sent disciples to locate and bring to him a colt for him to ride in his triumphal entry into Jerusalem. Bethphage was the limit specified of a Sabbath day's journey to Jerusalem, i.e., 3,000 feet. Jesus, remembering the verses in the book of Zechariah, of how the king of restored Israel entered and was welcomed into Jerusalem, had rode into Jerusalem through the Valley Gate "triumphant and victorious," fulfilled Zechariah's prophecy.

## Cana

The term, *Cana,* means "place of reeds." It was a small Galilean village, approximately five miles northwest of Nazareth and about twelve miles northeast of Capernaum. Cana was the birthplace of the apostle Nathanael (his name appears only in the Gospel of John). It was the site of Jesus' first miracle where he was attending a wedding and changed water into wine (John 2: 1, 11), and a subsequent one, healing at-a-distance, a royal official's son who was dying in Capernaum. Cana is not mentioned in the Old Testament.

## Emmaus

*Emmaus,* meaning "warm baths," was located about seven miles northwest of Jerusalem (reported in the Book of Luke). Historian Josephus confirmed Luke's calculations, yet the site of Emmaus is still to be determined. It was reportedly a spa and recreational village, frequented by inhabitants of Jerusalem and the site where Titus stationed his troops during his siege of Jerusalem. Emmaus is important to Christians because it was the goal of Jesus' walk on the first Easter afternoon (Luke 24: 13-32). On the road to Emmaus, Jesus met and had a lengthy interview with two of his followers. His followers did not recognize him at first, but when they did, Jesus disappeared from their sight.

## Nain

*Nain* was a village in Galilee, believed to be located on or near a hill, approximately 1,600 feet in height and called "Little Hermon." Its name means "beauty." Nain was near the Plain of Esdraelon, about six miles south of Nazareth and approximately 30 miles north of Samaria. The hill upon which Nain was situated is composed of limestone and has many caves. Jesus raised a young man from the dead at the town's gate as his body was being carried to the cemetery. The young man restored to life was the only son of a widow (Luke 7: 11-15). This miracle was Jesus' first raising of the dead, and it astonished the residents of Nain and all of Jesus' followers.

## Salim

*Salim*, meaning "peaceful," was a village near Aenon, where John the Baptist conducted his last baptisms. It was a well-known village, noted for its fountains and an abundance of fresh water. Salim was located seven miles south of the Wadi Farah and Aenon and two miles west of the Jordan River near the northern boundary of Judea. Jesus and his disciples also baptized in the same area but at Salim. It was at this site that John, in a discussion with a rabbi, was asked about Jesus. John replied to the rabbi that he was not the Messiah, but was sent ahead of him to prepare the way (John 3: 22-30).

## Sychar

*Sychar*, meaning "liar," was a village in Samaria, near Mount Gerizim and adjacent to Jacob's Well. It is known for its location near the parcel of ground Jacob gave to his son Joseph (John 4: 5). It was here that Jesus was sitting by a well and a Samaritan woman came to draw water. Jesus asked her to give him a drink of water and when she questioned his request, he replied that she could refresh his thirst but he could provide "living water."

## REFERENCES

_____. 1976. *Good News Bible.* New York: American Bible Society.

_____. 2007. *Hammond Atlas of the Bible Lands.* Canada: Langenscheidt Publishing Group.

_____. 1989. *Holy Bible.* New Revised Standard Edition. Oxford, England: Oxford University Press.

_____. 1952. *The Interpreter's Bible.* Vol. VI and VIII. New York, NY: Abington Press.

_____. 1972. *Merriam-Webster's Geographical Dictionary.* Springfield, MA: Merriam-Webster, Inc.

_____. 1996. *Nelson's Complete Book of Bible Maps and Charts.* Nashville, TN: Thomas Nelson Publishers.

Bryant, T. A. 1982. *Today's Dictionary of the Bible.* Minneapolis, MN: Bethany House Publishers.

Dando, William A., Caroline Z. Dando, and Jonathan J. Lu., eds. 2013. *Geography of the Holy Land: Perspectives.* Kaohsiung, Taiwan: Holy Light Theological Seminary Press.

Isbouts, J. P. 2016. *Archaeology of the Bible.* Washington, D.C.: National Geographic Society.

Isbouts, J. P. 2012. *In the Footsteps of Jesus.* Washington, D.C.: National Geographic Society.

Isbouts, J. P. 2008. *Young Jesus.* New York, NY: Sterling Publishing Co., Inc.

Josephus. 1988. *Complete Works.* Translated by W. Whiston. Grand Rapids, MI: Kregel.

Miller, Madeleine and J. Lane Miller. 1961. *Harper's Bible Dictionary.* New York, NY: Harper and Rowe.

Ogden, D. Kelly. 1991. *Where Jesus Walked.* Salt Lake City, UT: Deseret Book Co.

Peloubet, F. N. and M. A. Peloubet. 1884. *A Dictionary of the Bible.* Philadelphia: The John C. Winston Co.

Rockhill, Rev. David. 2018. Personal Correspondence. August.

Shanks, Hershel. 2010. *Ancient Israel.* Washington, D.C.: Biblical Archaeology Society.

Scholz, Daniel. 2013. *Jesus in the Gospels and Acts.* Winona, MN: Christian Brothers Publication.

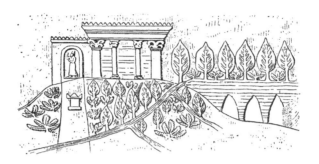

# PART TWO

## Urban Planning and Connectivity

The earliest settlements in the Promised Land were along the Mediterranean Sea coast and in the Jordan River Valley. There was very little formal urban planning initially. Population clusters, villages, towns, and cities slowly evolved. At the time of Jesus' ministry, they could be classified by their location, form, and function. For example, settlements could be classified as cities of coastal Phoenicia, cities of the Canaanites, cities of the plain, cities of the Decapolis, transportation cities, food-processing cities, storage and community reserve cities, chariot cities, Levitical cities, etc. Cities of consequence had stout stone walls, well-designed gateways, spaces for public assembly, places of worship, governmental and civic administrative buildings, numerous water wells and cisterns, narrow streets, small houses, food markets, shops, animal markets, food stalls, inns, and metal molding and woodworking facilities.

E. Nicole DePue introduces Part Two with a discussion of the various gateways to Herod's kingdom and the significance of transportation and linkages. Gordon Franz reports on current geohistorical archaeological discoveries on the Temple Mount in Jerusalem. Dorothy Drummond provides insights on the Decapolis cities and Jesus' work there, and she notes the findings at the newly excavated sites of Hippos and Susita. Drummond then concludes Part Two with an examination of political and socioeconomic relations between Israel and Phoenicia with emphasis upon Tyre and Sidon. The earliest description of a city in some detail was that of Sodom (Genesis 19: 1-22), and the first description of cities destroyed by natural forces was that of Sodom and Gomorrah.

# Damascus, Hazor, and Bashan: Northern Gateways of the Land of Israel

E. Nicole DePue

## INTRODUCTION

The Damascus, Hazor, and Bashan gateways were the northern-most gateways into and out of the "Land Between" (Israel) throughout the biblical period of history. Each gateway played a major role in the historical geography of the Bible as they not only were physically inter-connected, but also allowed the Israelites to connect with other people beyond their borders. This chapter examines how the physical geography of these gateways has influenced the historic events which greatly impacted the Ancient Near East during the Second Temple Period of Israel in particular, but other parts of ancient historical periods in general as well (Figure 1).

## HAZOR GATEWAY'S PHYSICAL GEOGRAPHY

The Hazor Gateway is named after the thriving Canaanite urban center in the midst of the Huleh Basin (also known as the Huleh Valley). The Huleh Basin is the northernmost part of the Rift Valley system in the land of Israel (Rasmussen 1989: 31). This basin extends from the northern shore of the Sea of Galilee (also referred to as Lake Kinesseret in biblical texts) all the way up to the site of ancient Dan, home of the Danites and the northernmost boundary city of the territory of biblical Israel. The Hazor Gateway route transverses this valley from the New

Figure 1. Northern Galilee, Philistia, and Phoenicia

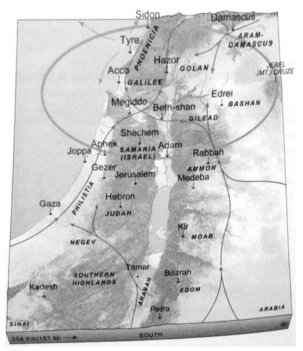

Source: Monson, James M. *Regions on the Ran: Introductory Map Studies in the Land of the Bible*. Rockford, IL: Biblical Backgrounds, 1998. p. 10.

Testament city of Capernaum on the northern coast of the Sea of Galilee, through the vast Canaanite city of Hazor, through the ancient site of Dan and onwards north into modern day Lebanon and the ancient-day areas of the Hittites and other lesser known peoples. The Hazor Gateway is a connecting point between Hazor and Damascus via Dan, as well as between Hazor and the Jezreel Valley via Capernaum and lower Galilee (Figure 2).

## HAZOR GATEWAY'S DIVERSE TOPOGRAPHY

The topography of this route is very diverse, extending through a variety of terrains. Starting on the Gateway at Capernaum, the route goes northwards toward Hazor, leaving behind the low sea level elevation of the Sea of Galilee and traveling through the elevated and rugged Rosh Pina Sill. Rosh Pina Sill, meaning "head of corner" in the original

Figure 2. Hazor Gateway's Diverse Topography

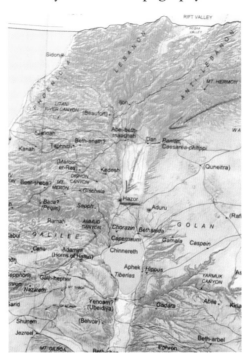

Source: Monson, J. M. "Regions on the Run Map Set: The Land Between" (marked by author).

Hebrew, is a basalt rock ridge. The basalt that forms this sill is merely a small section of the type of rock which is abundant in the area east of the Huleh Basin. These ridges were formed over time as volcanic activity caused outflows of lava to settle and harden as it cooled. Although here in the Rosh Pina Sill, the terrain is the most rugged part of the Hazor Gateway, yet these basalt ridges are not the most rugged basalt ridges that exist in Israel. In fact, parts of these ridges are rather flat terrain with mere rugged outflows and boulders which can create difficulties when traveling through (Monson 2008). Although this basalt rock can be a rugged terrain to transverse, it does, in fact, provide some rich soil that can be used for agriculture in certain areas and for herding in other areas. Due to the abundance of the basalt rocks in and around the Hazor Gateway, the inhabitants of the towns along this route made use of the rock and cut building stones and cultural implements out of the material.

After passing through the somewhat difficult Rosh Pina Sill, the next physical feature along the Hazor Gateway is a low valley that surrounds the tell of Hazor and stretches up to the main part of the Huleh Basin. The valley around Hazor is part of what helped this site become a major Canaanite city as the rich valley soil provided an excellent agricultural base for those who settled there. The rich soil is due in part to the geology of this area specifically Cenomanian limestone. Cenomanian limestone produces a rich terra rosa soil with natural bedding that allows terraced farming well suited for almonds, olives and grapes (*ibid*). Hard bedded limestone also served as a good source of building materials and for stone implements. A combination of factors further aided in enhancing Hazor's agricultural base throughout the city's history (*ibid*).

Another factor which impacted the good economic base for Hazor and other settlements in the Huleh Basin was the basalt rock surrounding the Cenomanian limestone. Part of the Huleh Basin southeast of Hazor is a plug of basalt which flowed down from the area of Bashan and filled this part of the Rift Valley to the Sea of Galilee, including the western part known as the Rosh Pina Sill. Here, the waters of the Jordan River were able to collect and form a medium-sized lake known as Lake Huleh, also known as Lake Semechonitis by Josephus (Rasmussen 1989: 31). Eventually the Jordan River, which flowed from the headwaters at Dan in the north down towards the Sea of Galilee, was able to break through this basalt plug and continue on to the Dead Sea. However, in making this cut through the basalt rock, the river drops approximately 900 feet over a short distance of 10 miles, creating the steepest gradient of the entire Jordan River (*ibid*). Regardless of the cut of the river, the wetness of the terrain north of this plug caused this section of the Huleh Basin to be a swamp through which travelers had to make their way as they continued north on the Hazor Gateway route. The abundance of water provided a stable source of water for agricultural needs of this area and thus, economic stability and growth. The climate of this area also provided Hazor with an environment that supported cane and papyrus which grew along the lake and throughout the swampland to the north of the city (*ibid*). In addition to the excellent agricultural environment and resources of cane and papyrus, this area was able to support an ample supply of edible fowl, fish, and animals (*ibid*).

Although the damp terrain of the Huleh Basin may be muddy to transverse, it is a much easier path to take than the steep cliffs of the eastern part of what is referred to as Upper Galilee which lay to the west of the Huleh Basin. After traveling through this swampy basin, the Hazor Gateway route continues north to the site of Dan where the headwaters of the Jordan River flow. The city of Dan marked the traditional northern boundary of Israel during Old Testament times. Because of this geographical location, Dan played a major role as a city on the Hazor Gateway route as it controlled traffic coming in and out of the land of Israel. Dan is situated on the northern tip of a valley of Cenomanian limestone. To the north of Dan, the terrain becomes rugged and is composed of basalt rock. The Hazor Gateway splits here at Dan with one route going through the basalt terrain to the north and onward to the Beqaa Valley in Lebanon and beyond. The other route going out from Dan is the road which leads to Damascus traveling northeast of Dan through Jurassic rocks. These Jurassic rocks are composed of limestones, sandstones, metamorphic and igneous rocks (Monson 2008). The route from Dan is where the Hazor Gateway turns into the Damascus Gateway (Figure 3).

## DAMASCUS GATEWAY'S PHYSICAL GEOGRAPHY

The Damascus Gateway is named after the city of Damascus in modern-day Syria. Multiple routes converge at Damascus and lead off in various directions. The route which connects the Damascus Gateway and the Hazor Gateway is one which travels southwest from Damascus to the city of Dan. Another route connects Damascus south to the desert and the King's Highway through Trans-Jordan (also known as the Trans-Jordanian Highway). While these two routes lead from Damascus into Israel, two more routes lead from Damascus off to Anatolia and Mesopotamia, one going mostly north and the other going mostly east. The connection of all of these routes at Damascus made the city an important

Figure 3. The Huleh Basin

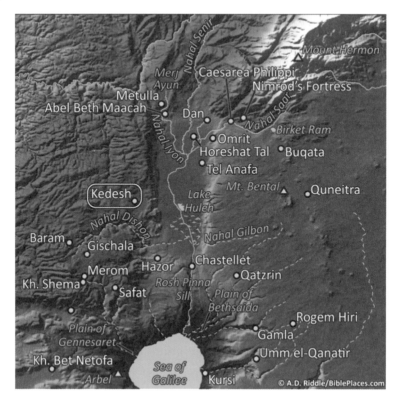

Source: Bolen, Todd. "The Pool of Siloam Revealed." Bible Places.com. Aug. 8, 2005. *http:/www.bibleplaces.com//poolofsiloam.htm*

gateway for trade and military campaigns throughout history (Figure 4).

## DAMASCUS GATEWAY'S UNIQUE TERRAINS

Each route leading out of the city of Damascus has its own unique type of terrain. The four routes which lead out of the city will be referred to here as: Dan to Damascus, northwest out of Damascus, northeast out of Damascus, and south from Damascus. The route which connects to the Hazor Gateway is the Dan to Damascus route which will be most highlighted in this section for the purposes of this chapter. However, each route's terrain will be explained for a thorough understanding of the importance of Damascus to historic events in this region.

## Figure 4. The Damascus Gateway

Source: "Regions on the Run Map Set" (marked by author).

## Figure 5. Dan to Damascus Route

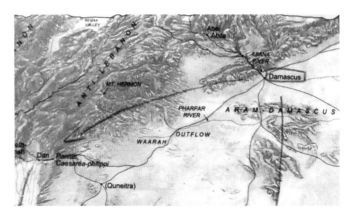

Source: "Regions on the Run Map Set: The Land Between" (marked by author).

## DAN TO DAMASCUS

The route which runs northeast from the Hazor Gateway from the city of Dan continues to connect with the city of Damascus. Leaving Dan, this route travels northeast through some Jurassic rock which forms the Anti-Lebanon Range (Figure 5). In the Anti-Lebanon Range, there are also deep beds of ancient limestone which rise to great heights and can be covered by snow even during summer months (*ibid*: 2). Fortunately, this route skirts between the Jurassic rock and the basalt rock of Upper Golan, giving a somewhat easier terrain to transverse. Continuing northeast on this route, the terrain changes as the route makes its way through the Waarah Flow that contains mountains that rise to an elevation of 3,136 feet. This basaltic area of the route leading from Dan to Damascus is rugged with boulders strewn throughout, as well as springs and pools which provide a stable water source for travelers. The route continues turning slightly more to the north and crosses an area of Eocene marl, a type of marine sedimentary rock (*ibid*: 12-13).

This rock, when it breaks down, provides the town of Qantana, which lies off this route to the north, only semi-productive soils and weak springs for a water source. Traversing this area would be quite easy along the edge, but the route goes through the middle of the Eocene marl as a more direct route to Damascus. After crossing the Eocene marl, the route transverses over a thin line of basalt rock again before it comes to the Damascus Plateau on which lies the city of Damascus. Entering Damascus, the route travels along the Abana River. It originates from tributaries of the Anti-Lebanon Mountains and runs through Damascus and then eastward through the fertile basin, providing the city and the basin with a good water source (DeVries 1997: 59).

The Damascus Plateau is a wide plateau composed of Lissan and other deposits. Lissan is the base of soils surrounding Damascus, and it comes from marine deposits of what was once an inland sea of which only the Dead Sea remains (Monson 2008: 12-13). The city of Damascus developed historically and grew large because of its location and its fertile

Figure 6. The Route through the Anti-Lebanon Mountain Range to Aleppo from Damascus

Source: Rainey, Anson F. and R. Steven Notley 2006. *The Sacred Bridge: Carta's Atlas of the Biblical World*. Jerusalem: Carta, p. 322.

soil and plentiful water supply. Both the Abana and Pharpar rivers provide clear cool water which, combined with the fertile soil, created a large and productive oasis. The inhabitants of Damascus were able to maintain a stable and diverse food supply through gardening, farming, cultivation of fruit orchards and cattle raising. However, the economy of this vast city was not limited to these agricultural and cattle base industries (DeVries 1997: 60). Because of its location, situated at a crossroads of routes, Damascus became a city that thrived as a caravan center for trade. Here at Damascus, the caravan travelers had options on which route to continue.

## NORTHWEST OUT OF DAMASCUS

Leaving Damascus to the northwest, this route travels through the Anti-Lebanon mountain range with its rugged terrain and into the Beqaa Valley (Monson 1998: 15). After reaching the low rich soil of the Beqaa Valley which lies between the Lebanon and Anti-Lebanon ranges,

Figure 7. The Route from Damascus to the Cities of Mesopotamia

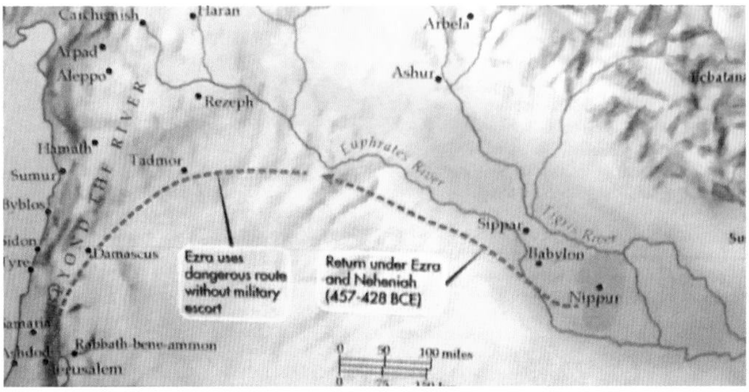

Source: Rainey, Anson F. and R. Steven Notley. 2006. *The Sacred Bridge: Carta's Atlas of the Biblical World*. Jerusalem: Carta, p. 290.

the route continues north through Hamath and eventually to Aleppo where it meets another crossroads (Figure 6).

## NORTHEAST OUT OF DAMASCUS

Leaving Damascus to the northeast, this route transverses along the edge of the Damascus Plateau and eventually goes through some areas of Eocene and other deposits. It also travels along a Cenomanian limestone ridge before reaching Tadmor. At the town of Tadmor, the route turns east and continues to Mari, a major city that lies on the edge of the Euphrates River. This connection to the land of Mesopotamia was very important for Damascus as a trade center and a city on military routes as invaders traveled east to west taking over territories such as Israel (Figure 7).

## SOUTH FROM DAMASCUS

The route leading south from Damascus starts out by easily traveling through the Damascus Plateau until it reaches an area of basalt rock which is higher in elevation and rougher in terrain. The route goes up and over this basalt and down into the Pharpar River, crossing it at an elevation of 2,300 feet. After crossing the river, the route comes to another area of basalt rock that spans the rest of the journey. This route reaches the

## Figure 8. The Damascus to Helam Route

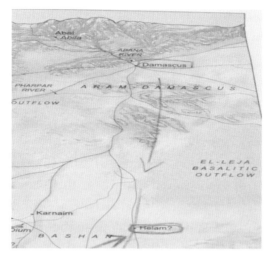

Source: "Regions on the Run Map Set: The Land Between" (marked by author).

## Figure 9. The Damascus — Red Sea Route

Source: Modified from Rainey, et al. 2006. *The Sacred Bridge: Carta's Atlas of the Biblical World*, p. 15.

region of Bashan and turns into three different routes. The two eastern routes continue south through Bashan and eventually to Ramoth-Gilead. These routes connect the Damascus Gateway with the Bashan Gateway (Figures 8 and 9).

## BASHAN GATEWAY

The Bashan Gateway connects the area of Bashan to other areas of Israel using multiple routes (Figure 10). The Bashan area is a high basalt plateau east of Galilee. The flatness of this plateau is broken up by extinct volcanoes. They have conical shapes, are comprised of basalt, and form a north-northeast downward slope to the south-southwest. The Bashan area is split into two parts by the Yarmuk (Yarmouk) river which runs through it and down into the Jordan River (Rasmussen 1989: 29). North of the Yarmuk River, the Bashan area is covered with volcanic rocks and soils. This northern section can again be split into two areas by the cut of the Nahal Raqqad.

To the west of Nahal, the land receives about 40 inches of precipitation per year. The abundance of precipitation, in combination with volcanic soils, makes this area a rich, lush agricultural region. This area was also excellent for cattle raising and was known as a place of fattened animals during the biblical period. South of the Yarmuk, the Bashan area consists of soft chalky limestone deposits that extend into the region of Gilead. The entire Bashan area was conducive to such crops as wheat and barley as well as cattle herding (Rasmussen 1989: 29). Some of the towns which lay in the region of Bashan are: Caesarea Philippi, Hippus (Hippos), Karnaim, Ashteroth, Edrei, Aphek, and Dium. These towns thrived along the strong Bashan Gateway routes which connected the region to the rest of Israel and beyond.

## THE BASHAN ROUTES

The Bashan Gateway routes connect the region of Bashan to the Mediterranean coast, to Arabia and Sinai, as well as all parts of Israel

Figure 10. The Bashan Gateway

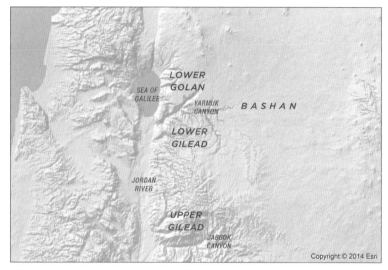

Source: Modified from Monson, James M. 1998. *Regions on the Run: Introductory Map Studies in the Land of the Bible*. Rockford, IL: Biblical Backgrounds, p. 11.

Figure 11. The Bashan Gateway's Major Routes

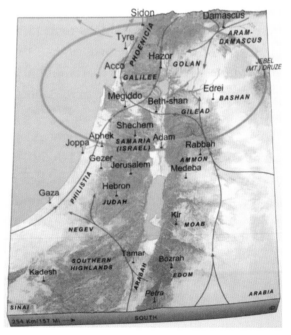

Source: Monson, James M. *Regions on the Run: Introductory Map Studies in the Land of the Bible*. Rockford, IL Biblical Backgrounds, p. 16.

Figure 12. Major Routes on the Trans-Jordanian Highway

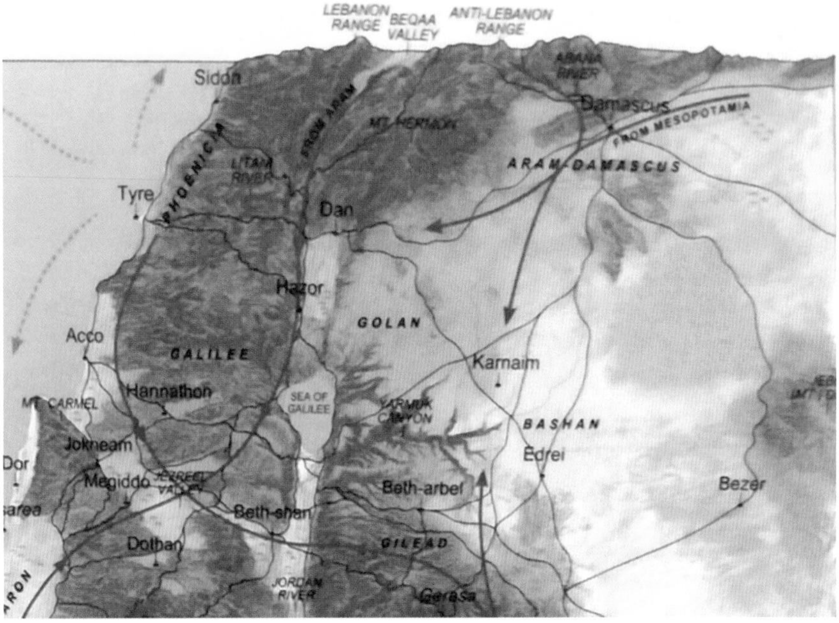

Source: Monson, James M. 1998. *Regions on the Run: Introductory Map Studies in the Land of the Bible*. Rockford, IL: Biblical Backgrounds, p. 17.

(Figure 11). These routes connect to all other routes throughout Israel. The three major routes of the Bashan Gateway are two routes which connect the region to the Mediterranean coast and one group of routes that transverses the land through Trans-Jordan to Arabia and Sinai.

Both coastal-bound routes go to the city of Acco, a port city on the Mediterranean Sea, south of modern day Tel-Aviv. The more popular of the two coastal routes was one which passed through the Bashan city of Aphek. This route leads south out of Damascus to the Bashan region. It follows west through Nahal Raqqad, varies greatly in elevation, and travels through rugged basaltic terrain. Eventually the route comes to Aphek in the basaltic hills to the east of the Sea of Galilee. The elevation of the basalt hills near Aphek is 1,217 feet. From Aphek, the route turns south, passing by the city of Hippus and entering a brief section of Eocene limestone (Figure 12). Continuing south the route goes through another small area of basalt rock and then reaches the plain of the Yarmuk

Figure 13. Crossing the Jordan River and the Jordan Valley

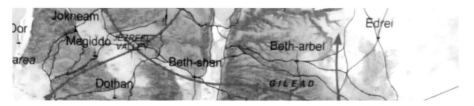

Source: Monson, James M. 1998. *Regions on the Run: Introductory Map Studies in the Land of the Bible*. Rockford, IL: Biblical Backgrounds, p. 17.

river. This flat low plain is where the Yarmuk River flows into the Jordan River. The area has very fertile soil and made this part of the route easy to transverse. The route turns abruptly west, cutting south of the Sea of Galilee, across the valley to the Jordan River at a city called Yenoam. At Yenoam, the route splits into many routes, interconnecting Bashan to Beth-shean, Acco, and Jezreel, and throughout the land of Israel to beyond her borders.

The second coastal route from Bashan connects Edrei with Beth-Shean. This route turns west at Edrei which is situated at a crossroads on rugged basalt terrain. The route goes south-southwest from Edrei following a ridge line through chalky Eocene limestone toward the town of Ramoth-Gilead (Monson 2008). The road increases in elevation to 2,487 feet and reaches Ramoth-Gilead. The city is situated on a high point and appropriately named "high point of Gilead" in Hebrew. From Ramoth-Gilead, the route follows west through an area of less-rugged terrain comprised of various deposits of rock types and connects to Beth-Arbel which is another crossroads city. From this city, which is on the eastern side of a block of Eocene limestone, the route follows west and south to the town of Ephron. The trek on this part of the route is easier as it starts sloping down in elevation through the Eocene limestone passing through Ephron and eventually to the eastern edge of the Jordan River valley. The route crosses the fertile Jordan Valley and the Jordan River before rising in elevation to the city of Beth-Shean (Figure 13). Here at Beth-Shean, the route yet again comes to a crossroads of routes which lead in all directions throughout the land of Israel all the way to the coast.

Figure 14. The Trans-Jordanian Highway

Source: Modified from Rainey, Anson F. and R. Steven Notley. 2006. *The Sacred Bridge: Carta's Atlas of the Biblical World*. Jerusalem: Carta, p. 15.

The last route of the Bashan Gateway and possibly the most traveled is part of the Trans-Jordanian Highway that travels through the Bashan area (Figure 14). This route is referred to as one route although it technically is comprised of two branches. The eastern branch of this route travels down through Edrei and Ramoth-Gilead and then back west. The western branch passes through Karnaim, Ashtaroth, and Dium, and then back toward the east. While both Karnaim and Ashtaroth are situated fairly deep into the basalt rock block of the Bashan, Dium sits on the basalt rock at the edge of Eocene limestone formations. Dium also is located at the end of a branch of the Yarmuk River which provides a good water source for the inhabitants of the city. Continuing south on the route it travels through these Eocene formations to Ramoth-Gilead where it meets with the eastern branch of the Trans-Jordanian Highway. After the two branches join again at Ramoth-Gilead, the route continues south down to the Gulf of Aqaba where it splits west to Egypt and east through Arabia. This route is the main route through the land east of the Jordan River. It is very important in connecting not only between the peoples who dwelled east of Jordan but also between them and other peoples such as the Israelites west of the Jordan, the Midianites in Arabia, the Egyptians west of Aqaba and the many people north and east of Damascus. The central importance of this route and its many connections gave importance to the area of Bashan throughout history.

## HISTORIC IMPORTANCE OF THE GATEWAYS

It is no mystery that these gateways to the land of Israel helped connect the ancient people of Israel to all other peoples throughout the Ancient Near East. Both biblical and extra-biblical texts testify to the many historic events which occurred on these routes and bear witness to the fact that those events were influenced by the physical geography and the location of the routes. To show the vast evidence of the importance of these routes, two lists are given below of the biblical and extra-biblical references to events which were influenced by the physical geography and location of these routes. However, for the purposes of this chapter, only a few events will be explored fully, and those will be focused on the events which occurred during the Second Temple Period.

**Biblical Evidence:**
— Genesis: Abraham passed through the Damascus Gateway
— Joshua 11: Canaanite King Jabin and Joshua fought at the "waters of Merom" northwest of Hazor
— 2 Kings 13: 17-19: Jehoash used the Bashan and Damascus gateways for his conquests
— Amos 4: The cattle of the Bashan are mentioned as an insult to

the character of the Israelites

— Amos 6: 13: Jehoash used the Bashan Gateway, battling the Arameans at Lo-Debar and Karnaim
— 2 Kings 14: 25: Jeroboam II restored Israel's boundaries past Damascus to Lebo-Hamath
— Psalm 22: 12: David lamented that the "bulls of Bashan encircle" him
— Ezra and Nehemiah: Jews returned from exile in Babylon and Persia (539 – 330 B.C.E.)
— Gospels: Jesus traveled through the Decapolis, using the Bashan Gateway
— Acts 9: 1-9: Conversion of Saul to Paul was on the "Road to Damascus"
— Missions: The Apostles traveled out of Israel, including to the north and east

**Extra-Biblical Evidence:**
— Egyptian texts: Merneptah traveled through Hazor and Bashan gateways on campaigns
— Ramesseum: Engraved battle scenes depicted the battle of Kadesh, north of Galilee
— Ramses II's Third Syrian Campaign: Egyptian Army marched on Hesbon, Damascus, on to Kumidi, and finally recaptured Upi (the land around Damascus)
— Babylonian Chronicle: Days of Nabupolassar, King of Babylon (650 – 610 B.C.E.)
— Diadorus 19: 95-97 Alexander the Great/ Ptolemy and Seleucus (315 – 306 B.C.E.)
— Zenon Papyri: Zenon of Canus traveled to Israel (259 – 258 B.C.E.)
— Josephus' *Antiquities and War*: Events taking place in all three gateways are mentioned

**Second Temple Period Events (530 B.C.E. – 70 C.E.)**
— Ezra and Nehemiah: Jews returned from exile in Babylon and

# Figure 15. The Damascus to Hazor Route and the Return of the Jews from Babylon

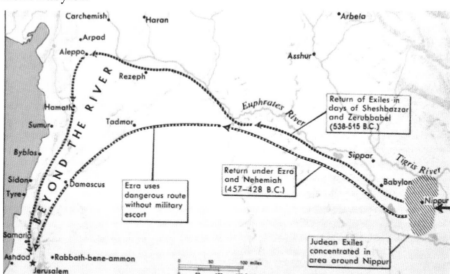

Source: Aharoni, Yohanan. 2002. *The Carta Bible Atlas*. Jerusalem: Carta, p. 128.

# Figure 16. The Damascus to Hazor Route and the Return of the Jews from Persian Rule

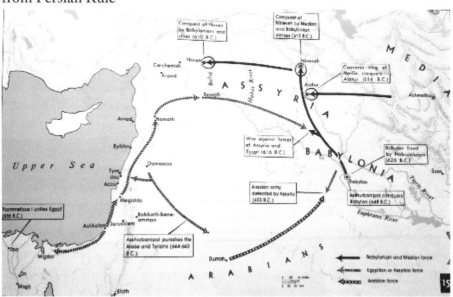

Source: Aharoni, Yohanan. 2002. *The Carta Bible Atlas*. Jerusalem: Carta, p. 121.

Persia (539 – 330 B.C.E.)
— Alexander the Great/ Ptolemy and Seleucus (315 – 306 B.C.E.)
— Zenon Papyri: Zenon of Canus traveled to Israel (259 – 258 B.C.E.)
— Josephus' *Antiquities and War*: Events taking place in all three gateways are mentioned
— Gospels: Jesus traveled through the Decapolis, using the Bashan Gateway
— Acts 9: 1-9: Conversion of Saul to Paul was on the "Road to Damascus"
— Missions: The Apostles traveled out of Israel, including to the north and east

While it would be beneficial to fully read and understand each of the events listed, that would be a long and arduous process. For this purpose, a particular time period is focused here to show the interconnectedness of these routes and their influence on history, highlighting their importance to Israel and her surroundings during the Second Temple Period.

## THE JEWS' RETURN FROM EXILE

One of the major historic events which took place on the Damascus and Hazor routes was the return of the Jews from exile in Babylon. This happened first from 538 – 515 B.C.E. under Sheshbazzar and Zerubbabel (Figure 15). The second occurrence was during the time of Ezra and Nehemiah from 457 – 428 B.C.E., as the Jews returned from captivity under Persian rule (Figure 16). Both events are depicted on the maps. Each was very significant to the people of that time, not just in Israel as the Israelites were able to return home, but for all the peoples of the Ancient Near East. These routes were established ways to get into and out of Israel. The exiled returned home to establish a new temple, a unified place of worship to their God and no longer requiring worship to the foreign gods of their captors.

Figure 17. Alexander the Great's Use of Gateway Routes

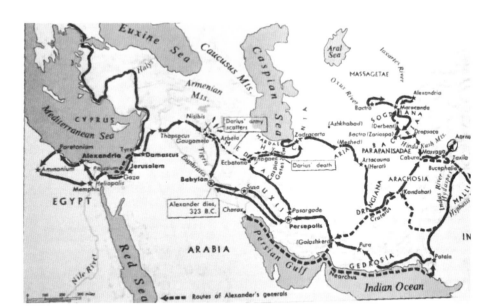

Source: Aharoni, Yohanan. 2002. *The Carta Bible Atlas.* Jerusalem: Carta, p. 134.


Figure 18. Alexander the Great's Damascus to Gaza Invasion Route
(Inset to Figure 17)

## Figure 19. Zenon's Travels in Ancient Palestine

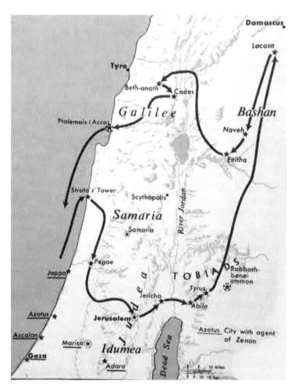

Source: Aharoni, Yohanan. 2002. *The Carta Bible Atlas*. Jerusalem: Carta, p. 135.

## ALEXANDER THE GREAT'S LATER CAMPAIGNS

For extra-biblical evidence to the significance of these routes during the Second Temple Period and later, there are the accounts of Alexander the Great's campaigns which showcase the use of these routes and their integral importance to historic events during this great empire. In his later campaigns (331-323 B.C.E.), Alexander traversed numerous routes leading to the Far East and into Europe, as he conquered a vast array of lands and peoples, establishing his grand empire and stamping his footprint as one of the greatest of all military geniuses. During these later campaigns, Alexander the Great was known for passing through Israel and utilizing the northern gateways, especially the Damascus and Hazor gateways. As shown in the maps below (Figures 17 and 18), it is apparent that Alexander trekked along these pre-established routes which allowed him to easily travel throughout the Ancient Near East. Thus, he was able to successfully gain control of regions not possible if these gateway routes were not readily available.

## ZENON PAPYRI

Under the Ptolemies, agents of the royal monopolies traveled to the far corners in search of goods needed in Egypt. Zenon of Canus was one of those agents who was sent to the land of Israel under Ptolemy II. Today there is evidence and accounts of his travels in the papyri which are titled after their author, Zenon Papyri. The events recorded on these papyri occurred between 259 and 258 B.C.E. Zenon's archives were discovered in Philadelphia in Egypt. According to the records, Zenon traveled to Israel from 259 – 258 B.C.E., landing at Strato's Tower in what is known as Herod's Caesarea on the Mediterranean coast. The papyri tell the story of how he proceeded from the coast to Jerusalem. After visiting Jerusalem, Zenon then went to Jericho and to Abila beyond the Jordan River. He visited Tyrus and reached Lacasa (Kisweh, near Damascus). To travel this way, Zenon took the Bashan Gateway up to Damascus. After arriving at Damascus, Zenon then went back down into the Bashan Gateway to Eeitha, and then through the basalt ridge to the northern part of the Hazor route near Dan before finding his way back to the coast of Acco. Zennon wrote explicit notes on how he traveled and what the routes were like. This information gives heed to the importance of these routes. They were well known at that time and commonly traversed by travelers of all types, including the agents who were sent by foreign rulers to seek goods and to spy on their neighbors (Figure 19).

## MENTIONED BY JOSEPHUS

In addition to biblical and other extra-biblical texts which mention these routes, there is a plethora of texts and accounts of events for which these routes played a significant role. Josephus mentioned these routes in his many writings of events during his time. The list below gives an exhaustive notation of how often these routes were referred to in his

Figure 20. The Battle of Hazor

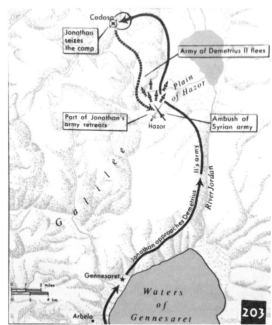

Source: Aharoni, Yohanan. 2002. *The Carta Bible Atlas*. Jerusalem: Carta, p. 151.

accounts, but only a few need to be explained to highlight the importance of these routes.

— Josephus mentions events taking place in all three gateways in his *Antiquities and War*:
— Maccabees (164 – 141 B.C.E.)
— Jonathan in Coele – Syria (150 B.C.E.)
— Battle of Hazor (144 B.C.E.)
— Tryphon against Jonathan (143 – 142 B.C.E.)
— Hamath Campaign (143 B.C.E.)
— Aristobulus Conquers Upper Galilee (104 – 103 B.C.E.)
— Alexander Janneaus' Kingdom (103 – 76 B.C.E.)
— Pompey's Campaign (63 B.C.E.)
— Parthian Invasion (40 B.C.E.)
— Herod vs Antigonus (39 C.E.)

Figure 21. Jesus' Trek along the Bashan Route

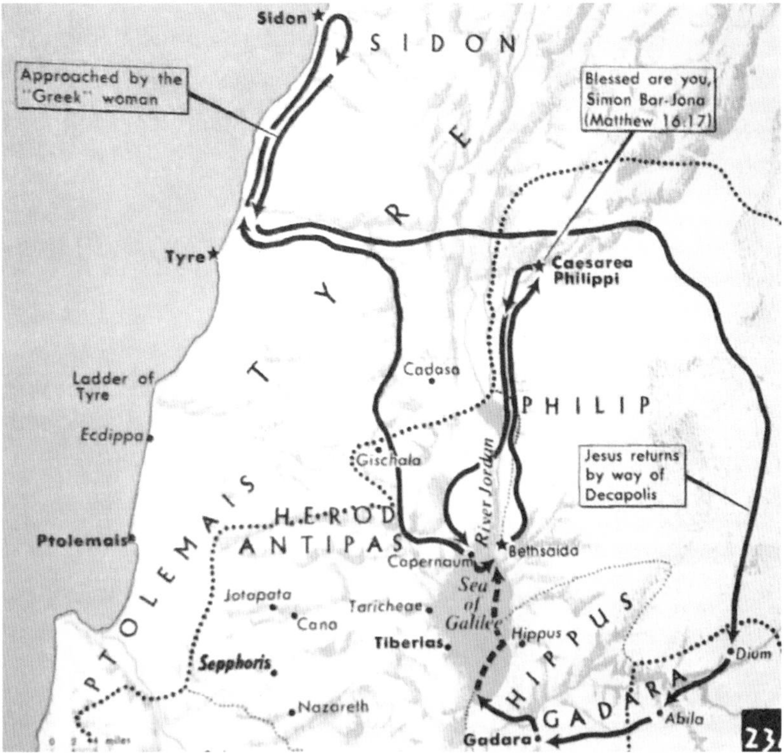

Source: Aharoni, Yohanan. 2002. *The Carta Bible Atlas. Jerusalem*: Carta, p. 173.

## A DETAILED BATTLE PLAN OF HAZOR

During Maccabean rule, circa 144 B.C.E., there was a great battle near the thriving town of Hazor, resting along the Hazor route. Josephus wrote a descriptive account of the events of this battle which is appropriately titled, "The Battle of Hazor" (Figure 20). According to Josephus' account, Demitrius' commanders were suspicious of Jonathan as they believed he was acting for their rival, Antiochus VI. In order to slow down Jonathan's activities in Coele-Syria, Demitrius' troops advanced past Damascus and camped at Cadasa on the boundary of Galilee. Jonathan then left Gennesaret (Galilee) and went up to the plain of Hazor. Meanwhile, Demetrius leaving part of his army in the hills of Cadasa attacked Jonathan and his forces from the rear, after he joined battle with the main force. In the end, surprisingly Jonathan and his two generals and their forces defeated the enemy and chased them back to Casada and then captured their camp there. This is recounted in 1 Maccabees 11: 63-74 and *Antiquities and War* 13: 158-162. Josephus, being the most well-known historian of his time, recorded this event since it was important to the Maccabean rule and the conflict occurring throughout Israel at that time.

## BIBLICAL REFERENCES DURING THE SECOND TEMPLE PERIOD

While it is important to take into account the multitude of extra-biblical references to these routes throughout history and specifically during the Second Temple Period, it is also just as important to understand the significance of these routes to biblical writers during that period. These routes are mentioned many times throughout the Bible. Two very significant accounts occurred during the Second Temple Period, namely, Jesus traveling along the Bashan route and Saul having his conversion to Christianity on the road to Damascus.

Jesus' trek along the Bashan route is referenced in the Gospel of Mark 7: 31 as it states, "Again He went out from the region of Tyre and came through Sidon to the Sea of Galilee, within the region of Decapolis…" (NASB; Figure 21).

The account of Saul's (Paul's) conversion from Judaism to Christianity along the road to Damascus can be found in Acts 9: 1-8:

> Now Saul, still breathing threats and murder against the disciples of the Lord, went to the high priest, and asked for letters from him to the synagogues at Damascus, so that if he found any belonging to the Way, both men and women, he might bring them bound to Jerusalem. As he was traveling, it happened that he was approaching Damascus, and suddenly a light from heaven flashed around him…. Saul got up from the ground, and though his eyes were open,

# Figure 22. Paul's "Conversion" Route from Jerusalem to Damascus

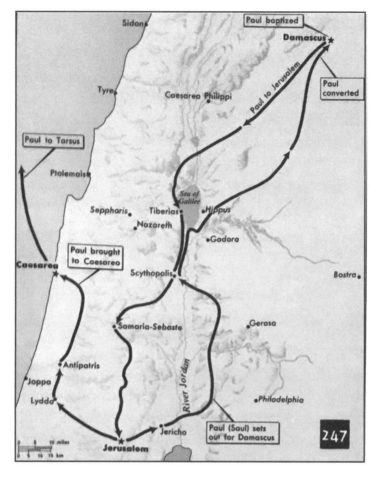

Aharoni, Yohanan. 2002. *The Carta Bible Atlas*. Jerusalem: Carta, p. 182.

he could see nothing; and leading him by the hand, they brought him into Damascus (NASB; Figure 22).

Both events are significant to Christianity – Jesus the Messiah traveling through the Bashan region for the purposes of his ministry and Saul converting to Christianity and becoming the foremost Christian minister of his time who went on to write the majority of the New Testament. Paul became the main spokesperson for the Christian faith and to this day, followers continue to learn from his teachings and mold ministry after ministry to the ways of his teachings.

## CONCLUSION

The gateways of Hazor, Damascus, and Bashan each hold an integral place in shaping the geographical, historical, and literary records of the Bible. The geography of these gateways influenced the paths on which significant routes were formed. The history of these gateways holds the key to understanding the past events that occurred in and around them. The literary records referring to these gateways bring insight and allusion to the texts in which they are mentioned. Each gateway is unique and distinct from every other, but all are important and are integral to connections between routes, lands, and people.

## REFERENCES

Aharoni, Yohanan. 1979. *The Land of the Bible*. London, England: Burns and Oates.

Aharoni, Yohanan. Anson F. Rainey, Michael Avi-Yonah, and Ze'ev Safrai. 2002. *The Carta Bible Atlas*, Jerusalem: Carta.

Bolen, Todd. 2005. "The Pool of Siloam Revealed." BiblePlaces.com. 8 August. <http://www.bibleplaces.com/poolofsiloam.htm>.

DePue, E. Nicole. 2009-2011. Physical Settings Class Notes (Both from class sessions and in-field research), Jerusalem University College.

DePue, E. Nicole. 2009. Physical Settings Foundation Map. Jerusalem University College.

DeVries, LaMoine F. 1997. *Cities of the Biblical World*. Peabody, MA: Hendrickson Publishers, Inc.

_____. 2000. *Holy Bible: NIV Study Bible*. Grand Rapids, MI: Zondervan Publishing House.

Monson, James M. 2008. *Geobasics in the Land of the Bible*. Rockford, IL: Biblical Backgrounds, Inc.

Monson, James M. 1983. *The Land Between: A Regional Study Guide to the Land of the Bible*, Jerusalem.

Monson, James M. 1998. *Regions on the Run*. Rockford, IL: Biblical Backgrounds, Inc.

Monson James M. 1998. "Regions on the Run Map Set: The Land

Between." Rockford, IL: Biblical Backgrounds, Inc.

Murphy-O'Connor, Jerome. 1998. *The Holy Land*. Oxford, England: Oxford University Press.

_____ 2000. *NASB Compact Reference Bible: New American Standard Bible*. Grand Rapids, MI: Zondervan Publishing House.

Rainey, Anson F., and R. Steven. Notley. 2006. *The Sacred Bridge: Carta's Atlas of the Biblical World*. Jerusalem: Carta.

Rasmussen, Carl G. 1989. *Zondervan NIV Atlas of the Bible*, Grand Rapids, MI: Zondervan Publishing House.

# Were Solomon and Herod's Temples in the City of David Over the Gihon Spring?

Gordon Franz

## INTRODUCTION

Robert Cornuke has written a book claiming that the temples of King Solomon and Herod the Great were never located on the historical Temple Mount, contrary to two thousand years of history. Claiming "amazing new discoveries" that he has observed, the book title states: *Temple: Amazing New Discoveries that Change Everything About the Location of Solomon's Temple* (2014). Later he reformatted the book and added an appendix by William Welty (2017: 205-236), but he did not change any of the mistakes pointed out in the original review of the book by this author/reviewer.

Mr. Cornuke is following his long-standing pattern of moving biblical sites to a different location – such as moving Moses' Mt. Sinai out of the Sinai Peninsula and into Saudi Arabia; shifting Noah's Ark out of the "Mountains of Ararat" (cf. Genesis 8: 4) into Iran; and wrecking Paul's ship in a different bay on Malta – which enables him to promote them as new "discoveries." So far, he has produced no credible historical, geographical, archaeological, geological, or biblical evidence for any of his alleged discoveries. How will he fare with these "new" discoveries?

Robert Cornuke has now relocated the temples of Solomon and Herod off the historical Temple Mount in Jerusalem. He bases this latest twist on the old theories of Dr. Ernest Martin in the latter's book, *The Temples that Jerusalem Forgot* (2000; cf. Cornuke 2014: 10; 2017: 4). However, Cornuke inconsistently locates his Temple enclosure/platform either about 900 feet or 1,700 feet farther south than the historical location on the Temple Mount, but he does not seem to be aware of the gross discrepancy (see pink and red squares in Figure 1). Cornuke's Temple enclosure/platform is inconsistent in size as well. He appears to be unable to decide whether it is only about 300 feet square or the approximate 860 feet square as attested in the ancient sources, and he seems utterly unaware of this problem (again see Figure 1).

Mr. Cornuke argues that it is a "legend" that the temples of King Solomon and Herod the Great were ever thought to be located on the historical Temple Mount in Jerusalem (2014: 9; 2017:3), even though the vast majority of people – Jews, Christians, and Moslems – through the ages understood that the temples were on the Temple Mount. His books instead argue that the temples were to the south of the historical Temple Mount, in the City of David, and over the Gihon Spring. It is also repeatedly stated in the books that the Antonia Fortress covered the entire Temple Mount enclosure, which was built by Herod the Great to guard his Temple.

In the appendix of the second edition of the book, William Welty takes aim at Dr. Randall Price and this author/reviewer for our critique of Bob Cornuke's views on the location of the temples. Our names were not cited in the appendix, but they appear on Welty's Internet blog from which the appendix was taken. He states that our negative criticism "consists not of the presentation of cogent and convincing arguments in rebuttal of the man's views, but rather in the presentation of sophomoric *ad hominem* attacks against the man personally." He goes on to say, "the actual scholarly content of most – if not all – of these criticisms fall far short of the rigorous academic criteria that should characterize a cogent search for truth" (2017: 206). Let the reader decide if this chapter is scholarly in nature and if *ad hominem* attacks are used on Cornuke and Welty. In actual fact, it is Mr. Welty who uses personal *ad hominem* attacks

Figure 1. Cornuke's Temple Mount as Shown on Ordnance Survey
Map of Jerusalem

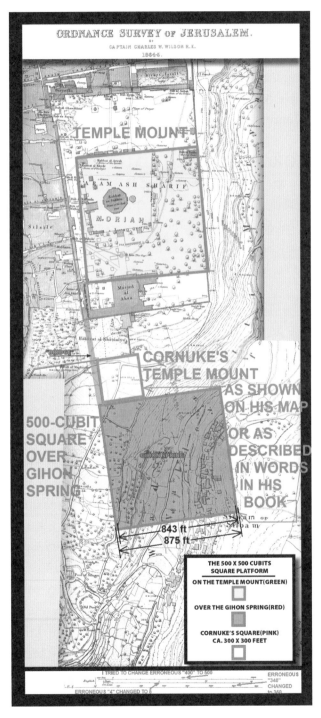

on this author/reviewer when he reprinted an article by Paul M. Feinberg which contained libelous falsehoods (2017: 230-233; Fienberg 2016: 14).

The following critique will be concerned with facts and whether the facts led to a correct conclusion. Do Cornuke's books present a credible, compelling case for re-locating the temples to the south of the historical Temple Mount with only the Antonia Fortress on the present-day Temple Mount?

## THE AUTHOR/REVIEWER AND HIS GOALS

This author/reviewer has lived, studied, led field trips, and worked on archaeological excavations in Jerusalem – on and off – for almost forty years. He is well familiar with the literary sources, history, archaeology, topography, geology, and geography of this city.

It is not this author/reviewer's intention to write a full-length book discussing Mr. Cornuke's (or Ernest Martin's) ideas about the location of Solomon's and Herod's temples, although a book could be written refuting these claims because there is so much erroneous information as well as faulty logic used in these two books. This author/reviewer will first deal with Cornuke's two main arguments.

First, according to the books, Solomon's Temple stood upon Zion and Zion was in the City of David; and second, that the temples stood over the Gihon Spring. Then some examples will be selected---these will by no means be exhaustive – of where Mr. Cornuke got his facts wrong and how he produced the "*greatest archaeological blunder of all times*" (cf. Cornuke 2014: 35; 2017: 31) by moving the temples of Solomon and Herod from the historical Temple Mount to the City of David. It will also be demonstrated that these books were not carefully researched. The facts are that the literary sources and archaeological records confirm the location of Solomon's and Herod's temples on the historical Temple Mount and not above the Gihon Spring in the City of David as claimed in Cornuke's books.

One resource this author/reviewer found particularly helpful concerning the topic is the excellent book by Dr. Leen Ritmeyer entitled, *The Quest. Revealing the Temple Mount in Jerusalem* (2006). Dr. Ritmeyer is probably the leading scholar on the topic of the temples on the Temple Mount. This book, drawn from his PhD dissertation at the University of Manchester in England, is carefully researched, clearly written, well documented, and profusely illustrated with detailed pictures, maps, and diagrams. It is a must-read for anyone interested in the location, history, and development of Solomon's and Herod's temples. Ritmeyer also worked in Jerusalem as the architect for Professor Benjamin Mazar, the director of the Southern Wall of the Temple Mount Excavation, south and west of the Temple Mount. It is interesting to note, the books under review do not interact with nor discuss Ritmeyer's scholarly work. In fact, it is not even mentioned in the bibliography. Mr. Cornuke should have first consulted this exhaustive resource before research was begun on his book.

All quotations from Josephus in this essay will be from the scholarly Loeb Classical Library (LCL) edition, unless otherwise noted. All Scripture quotes are from the *New King James Bible (*NKJV).

## WHERE ARE ZION AND THE CITY OF DAVID?

Mr. Cornuke's book repeatedly quotes 2 Samuel 5: 7 as if it proves his case, but take careful note of the exact wording in the Bible: "Nevertheless David took the **Stronghold of Zion** (that is, the **City of David**)" (NKJV, emphasis added by this reviewer). He claims this is proof that the Temple was in **Zion** and that Zion was the **City of David** (Cornuke 2014: 65, 69, 71, 74, 76, 77, 79, 113, 115, 122, 136; 2017: 63, 68, 69, 74, 76, 77, 79, 117, 119, 127, 140; emphasis added), but the Stronghold of Zion was not the same thing as the much broader city of Zion, which did expand in size over time until it did encompass the historical Temple Mount. The Stronghold of Zion never encompassed the Temple or the historical Temple Mount. The City of David began as identical to the Stronghold of Zion, and though it did expand in size, it never grew so far as to encompass Mount Zion where the historical Temple Mount/Temple resided.

As one examines the use of the word "Zion," it will be shown that the location of Zion did expand beyond the Stronghold of Zion/City of David, and eventually came to include the historical Temple Mount, hence this is no proof for Mr. Cornuke's anti-Temple Mount assertions. The word "Zion" is used 154 times in the Hebrew Scriptures:

> 2 Samuel 5: 7; 1 Kings 8: 1; 2 Kings 19: 21, 31; 1 Chronicles 11: 5; 2 Chronicles 5: 2; Psalms 2: 6; 9: 11, 14; 14: 7; 20: 2; 48: 2, 11, 12; 50: 2; 51: 18; 53: 6; 65: 1; 69: 35; 74: 2; 76: 2; 78: 68; 84: 7; 87: 2, 5; 97: 8; 99: 2; 102: 13, 16, 21; 110: 2; 125: 1; 126: 1; 128: 5; 129: 5; 132: 13; 133: 3; 134: 3; 135: 21; 137: 1, 3; 146: 10; 147: 12; 149: 2; Song of Songs 3: 11; Isaiah 1: 8, 27; 2: 3; 3: 16, 17; 4: 3, 4, 5; 8: 18; 10: 12, 24, 32; 12: 6; 14: 32; 16: 1; 18: 7; 24: 23; 28: 16; 29: 8; 30: 19; 31: 4, 9; 33: 5, 14, 20; 34: 8; 35: 10; 37: 22, 32; 40: 9; 41: 27; 46: 13; 49: 14; 51: 3, 11, 16; 52: 1, 2, 7, 8; 59: 20; 60: 14; 61: 3; 62: 1, 11; 64: 10; 66: 8; Jeremiah 3: 14; 4: 6, 31; 6: 2, 23; 8: 19; 9: 19; 14: 19; 26: 18; 30: 17; 31: 6, 12; 50: 5, 28; 51: 10, 24, 35; Lamentations 1: 4, 6, 17; 2: 1, 4, 6, 8, 10, 13, 18; 4: 2, 11, 22; 5: 11, 18; Joel 2: 1, 15, 23, 32; 3: 16, 17, 21; Amos 1: 2; 6: 1; Obadiah 1: 17, 21; Micah 1: 13; 3: 10, 12; 4: 2, 7, 8, 10, 11, 13; Zephaniah 3: 14, 16; Zechariah. 1: 14, 17; 2: 7, 10; 8: 2, 3; 9: 9, 13.

Zion is used with different modifiers, such as "Mount Zion": 1 Kings 19: 31; Psalms. 2: 6; 48: 2, 11; 74: 2; 78: 68; 125: 1; Isaiah 4: 5; 8: 18; 10: 12; 18: 7; 24: 23; 29: 8; 31: 4; 37: 32; Lamentations 5: 18; Joel 2: 32; 3: 17; Obadiah 1: 17, 21; Micah 4: 7.

Zion came to be synonymous with the city of Jerusalem and hence, again, inclusive of the Temple Mount. In Hebrew poetry, there is a literary device called "parallelism." Professor C. Hassell Bullock of

Wheaton College described this literary device as follows: "The heart of Hebrew poetry is a device called *parallelism*. It is a literary pattern that states an idea in one line and focuses more closely on the same idea in the following line, either repeating the thought in different terms or focusing on the thought more specifically" (2001: 36, highlighted italics in original). A good example of Hebrew parallelism for the study of the location of Zion is found in the words of Isaiah the prophet when he wrote in the eighth century B.C.E.: "For out of Zion shall go forth the Law [Torah], and the Word of the LORD from Jerusalem" (2: 3). In this verse, there are two parallel thoughts: Zion and Jerusalem are literally synonymous places from which the Torah/Word of the LORD goes forth. Law and Word are another set of synonymous terms. The eighth century B.C.E. prophet Micah repeated these two parallel thoughts in his book (4: 2). The psalmists also use the Zion/Jerusalem parallels in their poetry (51: 18; 76: 2; 102: 21; 128: 5; 135: 21; 147: 12).

This parallelism concerning Zion appears at least 40 times in the Hebrew Scriptures. The list is in chronological order and divided by the centuries:

> Date not known – Psalms. 51: 18; 76: 2; 102: 21; 128: 5; 135: 21; 147: 12
>
> Ninth Century B.C.E. – Joel 2: 32; 3: 16, 17
>
> Eighth Century B.C.E. – Isaiah 2: 3; 4: 3, 4; 10: 12, 32; 24: 23; 30: 19; 31: 4; 33: 20; 37: 22, 32; 40: 9; 41: 27; 52: 1, 2; 62: 1; 64: 10; Amos 1: 2; Micah 3: 10, 12; 4: 2, 8
>
> Seventh Century B.C.E. – Jeremiah 26: 18; Zephaniah 3: 14, 16
>
> Sixth Century B.C.E. – Lamentations 2: 10, 13
>
> Fifth Century B.C.E. – Zechariah 1: 14, 17; 8: 3; 9: 9

Zion and Jerusalem are recognized to be synonymous and literal places in Hebrew poetry. It is then important to determine *when* to apply the specific size and location of the city of Jerusalem in the different time periods of the First Temple Period and the beginning of the Second

Temple Period. Doing so will determine how the different psalmists and prophets use the word "Zion." It will be shown that the term is not limited to the City of David, but also included the historical Temple Mount.

The initial city, the core city, of Jerusalem was the ancient city of Jebus, that 13-acre area between the Kidron Valley and the Central Valley and slightly north of the Stepped Stone Structure (SSS). This was the early city conquered by King David.

The meaning of the name and also the location of the "City of David" (in Hebrew *'ir dawid*), like Zion, change throughout the history of Jerusalem. In a recent and important article by Dr. Jurg Hutzli of the College of France in Paris entitled, "The Meaning of the Term *'ir dawid* in Samuel and Kings" (2011), he shows that the term "City of David" expands beyond the southeastern hill of Jerusalem (i.e. the 13 acres between the Kidron Valley and the Central Valley). He summarizes Othmar Keel's views thus:

> . . . whenever the term [City of David] is mentioned in Samuel and Kings [2 Samuel 5: 7, 9; 6: 10, 12, 16; 1 Kings 3: 1; 9: 24] it relates to the *pre*-Davidic stronghold [i.e. the Stronghold of Zion], which is said to have been conquered by David (2 Samuel 5: 7). He outlines his views only briefly in a few lines: After its capture the stronghold served as a residence for David and then also for the daughter of the pharaoh. The ark was placed here before its transfer to the Temple. The residence [palace] also served as a burial place for the kings. It was only later, in the Book of Chronicles, that the term began to refer to the entire southeastern hill. Keel. . . also takes into account the suggestion by some scholars. . . who tentatively identify the Stepped Stone Structure and the assumed building it retains with the biblical 'stronghold of Zion' (Hutzli 2011: 167-178).

Note that this author/reviewer does not share Hutzli's view that the royals' tombs were in the stronghold (cf. Nehemiah 3: 16; Ritmeyer and Ritmeyer 2005). Also note that the Palace is not the Temple. They are two different structures. The early City of David on the Stepped Stone Structure is the Palace/Stronghold of Zion area.

Professor Nadav Na'aman, a biblical historian and geographer from Tel Aviv University. concurs with Dr. Hutzli's article that the term "City of David" is limited to the area around the Stepped Stone Structure in the tenth century B.C.E. He goes on to affirm that: "the 'City of David' referred to in 2 Samuel 5: 7, 9 overlaps the area of the conquered Stronghold of Zion, and in this limited scope it appears in the cycle stories of David and Solomon and the burials of the Judahite kings prior to Hezekiah" (2012b: 96). He then goes on to demonstrate that the term "City of David" in Isaiah 22: 9-11a, dated to the end of the eighth century B.C.E., was the entire southeastern hill, and not limited to the area around the Stepped Stone Structure. Thus, the term "City of David" encompasses different areas at different times.

Dr. Eilat Mazar excavated a monumental tenth century B.C.E. building just above the Stepped Stone Structure which she called the "Large Stone Structure" and identified it as the Palace of King David (Mazar 2009: 43-65). Whether that is the Palace of King David or a building within the "stronghold of Zion" is a matter of scholarly debate, but the pottery associated with the building is clearly tenth century B.C.E. The palace complex would have been somewhere in this general area.

David bought the threshing floor of Araunah the Jebusite, which will be shown to be above and to the north of the City of David, above the Stepped Stone Structure. David was not allowed to build the Temple because he was a man of war and bloodshed (1 Chronicles 28: 3) so his son Solomon built it in the tenth century B.C.E. on what is now known as the *Temple Mount*, or biblical *Mount Zion/Moriah*. This is separate and distinct from the Palace. In the recent on-going Temple Mount Sifting Project, archaeological remains of the tenth century B.C.E. have been found indicating human occupation on the top of the hill (Mount Moriah) during this period (Barkay and Zweig 2007: 37-41; Barkay and Dvira 2015: 16-20). During the Bronze Age (third-second millennium B.C.E.), temples were generally located on the acropolises, situated on the highest part of cities. The Temple Mount area would be the new acropolis for Jerusalem as it was the highest part of the city during Solomon's reign.

By the eighth century B.C.E. the city of Jerusalem had expanded to the Western Hill, which included the Tyropean Valley, the area that is called "Mount Zion" today to the south of Zion Gate and the Old City walls, the Jewish Quarter, the Armenian Quarter, and also the area of Jaffa Gate (Barkay 1985). In the seventh century B.C.E. the city still included the area of the Western Hill, but it also expanded to the north of the Iron Age wall, creating extramural suburbs outside the wall of the city. These suburbs included the areas of today's Christian and Muslim quarters (cf. Jeremiah 31: 38-40; Zephaniah 1: 10-11; Barkay 1985: 45-62, XI*; Avigad 1980: 58). Thus, the location of Zion changed over the centuries. Initially Zion was located in the City of David ("Large Stone Structure"), but then included the southeastern hill, as the hill of Zion or Mount Zion. With the expansion to the west in the eighth century, the entire Western Hill is considered Zion as well. In the eighth and seventh centuries "Zion" was more than just the Stronghold of Zion or the City of David.

The latter part of Psalm 48 is twice quoted in Cornuke's book (2014: 78, 114; 2017: 78, 118-119) but the first part of the psalm is not mentioned at all. One of the sons of Korah composed this psalm at the end of the eighth century B.C.E., and in this reviewer's opinion, during the Assyrian invasion of Judah by Sennacherib: "Great is the LORD, and greatly to be praised in the City of our God, in His holy mountain. **Beautiful in elevation**, the joy of the whole earth, is Mount Zion on the sides of the north, the City of the Great King." (48: 1-2; emphasis added). The psalmist apparently lived in the southeastern hill of the City of David and knew from first-hand, eye-witness experience of the elevation change walking from the City of David (at this time it covered the entire southeastern hill; see above) **up** to Mount Zion, the historical Temple Mount, where the Lord resided between the cherubim that protected the Ark of the Covenant in the Temple. It is also important to notice that Mount Zion is on the north side of Jerusalem. These two geographical indicators fit well with Solomon's Temple being on the historical Temple Mount.

King Solomon had brought the Ark of the Covenant **up** from the City of David where King David had placed it near his palace in the area of the Stepped Stone Structure (2 Chronicles 8: 11). "Now Solomon assembled the elders of Israel and all the heads of the tribes, the chief fathers of the children of Israel, in Jerusalem, that they might bring the Ark of the Covenant of the LORD *up from* the City of David, which is Zion" (2 Chronicles 5: 2; emphasis added). It is important to note that King Solomon brought the Ark up from the city of David, which is Zion, to a place *outside* the City of David; that place would be called Mount Zion, the area of the Temple Mount today. (Contra Cornuke 2014: 107; 2017: 111).

The point of this section is to demonstrate that the words "Zion" and "City of David" encompass different areas at different time periods. They are not limited to one specific place on the map. The historical context determines the locations of "Zion" and the "City of David" within Jerusalem.

## WHERE WAS THE THRESHING FLOOR OF ARAUNAH THE JEBUSITE?

King David bought a threshing floor from Araunah (Ornan) the Jebusite (2 Samuel 24: 18-25; cf. 1 Chronicles 21: 18-30). His son, King Solomon, built the First Temple on that threshing floor. "Now Solomon began to build the house of the LORD at Jerusalem on Mount Moriah, where the Lord had appeared to his father David, at the place that David had prepared on the threshing floor of Ornan the Jebusite" (2 Chronicles 3: 1).

Where are threshing floors located? And where, specifically, was the threshing floor of Araunah the Jebusite? In the book, it is dogmatically stated: "So there is absolutely no doubt that David bought the threshing floor as a site to build a future temple and it was in the strict confines of the ancient outline walls of the City of David – which the Bible clearly refers to as the stronghold of Zion" (Cornuke 2014: 79; 2017: 79, see also 2014: 66; 2017: 64). Is this a factually true statement?

Dr. Oded Borowski, an Israeli archaeologist, wrote his doctoral dissertation on agriculture in Iron Age Israel. In this important work, he described the location of the threshing floor (*goren* in Hebrew) thus:

> The *goren* [threshing floor] was *located outside the city* where the prevalent west wind could be used for winnowing (Hos. 13: 3). The exact location of the threshing floor was determined by the local topography. Sometimes it was close to the city gate (Jer. 15: 7), and at times it was situated in an area somewhat lower than the city itself (Ruth 3: 3). There is no direct statement in the Old Testament concerning the ownership of the threshing floor, but the story of Ruth (chap. 3) implies the existence of private threshing floors. Because it was a large open space, the threshing floors were publically owned. The use of threshing floors was most likely directed by the village authorities.
>
> *Being outside the city*, the site of the threshing floor could not be defended in case of attack, and thus we find Gideon threshing wheat in the *gat*, 'winepress' (Judges 6:11), inside the city, as a precaution against the Midianites. The same problem is illustrated by the attack of the Philistines on the threshing floor of Qe'ila (1 Samuel 23: 1; Borowski 1987: 62-63; emphasis added).

It will be observed that after Ruth spent the night at the threshing floor with Boaz, she went into the city (Ruth 3:15). The Bible placed the threshing floor of Boaz *outside* the city of Bethlehem. It will also be noted that Ruth went down to the threshing floor from Bethlehem because the city is set on top of a hill (Ruth 3: 3, 6). Boaz went up to Bethlehem from the threshing floor (Ruth 4: 1).

While the threshing floors were always outside the city, they were not necessarily on the tops of hills. They are placed where they can get the gentle westerly breeze in the evening hours. One of the exceptions, Bethlehem, has already been noted from the biblical text. Another one, el-Jib, sits at the base of ancient Gideon on the western side of the city to catch the westerly breeze across the Central Benjamin Plateau.

The threshing floor of Araunah the Jebusite would have been *outside* the City of David. In the book, the mistake that the threshing floor was *inside* the walls of the City of David was repeatedly made (Cornuke 2014: 66, 75, 77, 79, 80, 113; 2017: 64, 75, 77, 79, 80, 117). The Bible gives clues as to where the threshing floor of Araunah the Jebusite was, but it was not inside the city, but rather, outside the city, atop the open hill of Moriah.

There are two accounts of David numbering the people with the Lord sending a plague against Israel (2 Samuel 24; 1 Chronicles 21). During the plague, the Lord instructed the prophet Gad to inform David to "**Go up**, erect an altar to the LORD on the threshing floor of Araunah the Jebusite" (2 Samuel 24: 18; cf. 1 Chronicles 21: 18). Presumably David is in his palace in the City of David above the Stepped Stone Structure when he receives these instructions and he is to **go up the hill** to the threshing floor. When Solomon brought the Ark of the Covenant to the threshing floor from the City of David we read: "Now Solomon assembled the elders of Israel and all the heads of the tribes, the chief fathers of the children of Israel, in Jerusalem, that they might bring the Ark of the Covenant of the LORD **up** from the City of David, which is Zion" (2 Chronicles 5: 2; emphasis added).

The writer of the Book of Kings essentially says the same thing:

"Now Solomon assembled the elders of Israel and all the heads of the tribes, the chief fathers of the children of Israel, to King Solomon in Jerusalem, that they might bring **up** the ark of the covenant of the LORD from the City of David, which is Zion" (1 Kings 8: 1; Welty repeatedly and incorrectly said "2 Kings 8: 1" Cornuke 2017:228-230). Hutzli correctly observed on this verse that "it seems appropriate to assume that the term *'ir dawid* refers to a building or a complex of buildings: since the destination of the ark is a concrete place (the Temple), one expects a similarly concrete indication for the former location of the holy object" (2011: 170). The topographical points should be noted that the Ark was taken **uphill** from out of the City of David, just above the Stepped Stone Structure. The threshing floor could only be on the historical Temple Mount!

Dr. Leen Ritmeyer has suggested a more precise location on the Temple Mount. He wrote: "Araunah's threshing floor was located 21.6 feet (6.6 m) east of the Dome of the Chain. This was the place where David built an altar. The Angel who appeared to David probably stood on the Rock (Sakhra), where the Ark of the Covenant was later placed" (1992: 24-45, 64-65; 2006: 315; see also 2006: 7, 244, 312-314).

Another clue as to the location of the threshing floor is found in 2 Chronicles 3: 1. It stated that the House of the LORD (Temple) was built on Mount Moriah where the threshing floor was located. In the book, Mr. Cornuke never identified where Mount Moriah was located, (since it would upset his theory) nor does he even mention Mount Moriah in the book, which is astonishing.

The only passage where Mount Moriah is mentioned in the Bible is 2 Chronicles 3: 1. (*The mountains in the land of Moriah* are what are mentioned in Genesis 22: 2). Interestingly, Cornuke quotes 2 Chronicles 3: 1 three times in the book (2014: 66, 75, 113; 2017: 64, 75, 117), and cites the passage four times (2014: 70, 77, 80, 113; 2017: 68, 77, 80, 117), but he still insisted that the Temple was located near the Gihon Spring (2014: 66, 113; 2017: 64, 117). Yet every time he quoted the verse he had an ellipsis (three dots "…") in the middle of the passage. The ellipsis means that a word or words are omitted from the passage. What are the words that he deleted from this verse, 2 Chronicles 3: 1? Each time the Scripture verse is quoted, the words: "*on Mount Moriah, where the LORD has appeared to his father David*" is left out. Four of the quotes or citations of this passage are found in the chapter of the book entitled, "What Does the Bible Say?" The author should have let the "Bible Say" what it says and not left out any of the highly relevant words here. Quoting the whole Bible passage would have clearly identified where the Temple was located. "Now Solomon began to build the House of the LORD at Jerusalem on Mount Moriah, where the Lord had appeared to his father David, at the place that David had prepared on the threshing floor of Ornan the Jebusite." The biblical text is clear: The Temple and the threshing floor were **up** on Mount Moriah and not down in the area of the Gihon Spring in the Kidron Valley.

At the end of his section on threshing floors, Dr. Welty says: "Consider, if you would please, the photograph we've listed of a modern-day threshing, above. It depicts a threshing floor in the foreground, the agricultural fields leading off into the background. Both the fields and the threshing floor are distinctively *not* on the apex of a hill. Furthermore, the threshing floor depicted is located near Bethlehem, Israel, not more than a kilometer or two from the old City of David! If a modern threshing floor located in Bethlehem in the modern world can be used effectively in the 21st century, there's no reason why the threshing floor belonging to Araunah could not have been located within the City of David" (2017: 221-222).

On the previous page, there is a picture of a threshing floor near Bethlehem. This author/reviewer did a little experiment by Googling "Bethlehem" and "threshing floor" and then clicked on Google Image and *voila*, the very picture that Dr. Welty had in his article appeared. One can be certain that is how Dr. Welty found that picture as well.

That picture brought back pleasant memories. This reviewer knows exactly where that threshing floor is because while a student at the Institute for Holy Land Studies in Jerusalem, we visited it on the way to the Herodian. As a field-trip instructor at the Jerusalem Center for Biblical Studies, the Institute for Holy Land Studies (now Jerusalem University College), and the IBEX program for the Master's College, this reviewer would always stop at that threshing floor and discuss the story of Ruth and Boaz and the shepherds in the birth narratives of the Lord Jesus on the way to the Herodian.

The concluding section of Dr. Welty's article is entitled, "My Background and Standing to Comment on this Subject." In it he gives his academic pedigree and emphasizes his language skills of the Bible. He says: "I possess the academic qualifications to speak on the subject matter of the Hebrew and Greek grammar, syntax, and historical context of the biblical text" (2017: 236). In the final footnote, he addresses, without mentioning our names, Dr. Price and my lack of language skills. "At any rate, the *content* of their polemics against Dr. Cornuke display absolutely *no acquaintance* with biblical languages (at least I've never come across a single biblical quotation made by them from the original Hebrew, Greek, or Aramaic!)" (2017: 236, footnote 22).

Dr. Welty should be reminded that biblical languages are not the issue for the discussion of the location of the temples. The important disciplines for this study are the history, archaeology, and geography of Jerusalem, the Temple Mount, and the City of David which, by the way, are this author/reviewer's areas of expertise.

Let us return to the picture Dr. Welty has in his article. This threshing floor is situated just below the Arab village of Za'tarah. The village is located on the top of a hill and situated two kilometers to the northeast of the Herodian. Off in the upper left hand side of the picture, one can just barely see the three towers on the Mount of Olives about 11-12 kilometers away. Dr. Welty states of the picture: "It depicts a threshing floor in the foreground, the agricultural fields leading off into the background. Both the fields and the threshing floor are distinctively *not* on the apex of a hill." What is not noticed is between the threshing floor and the fields, off in the distance, is the Nahal Darga (or Wadi Darga). The bottom of the wadi (a dry river bed) is about 80 meters below the threshing floor. While the threshing floor is not at the "apex" of the hill, it is in an elevated position to get the gentle evening breeze needed to thresh the wheat from the chaff, unlike an alleged threshing floor in the Jerusalem City of David near the Gihon Spring which does not get a gentle westerly breeze in the evening.

Dr. Welty also asserts: "The threshing floor depicted is located near Bethlehem, Israel, not more than a kilometer or two from the old City of David!" One can assume that when he says "old City of David," he is referring to Bethlehem, the original City of David. This threshing floor is actually six kilometers, as the dove flies, from the Church of the Nativity in Bethlehem which is built over the ancient mound of Bethlehem.

While ancient languages are important for Biblical studies; a working knowledge of the history, archaeology, geography, and agriculture of the Bible is also important. Firsthand knowledge of the Land of the Bible is also crucial. If Dr. Welty had known the Land, he would not have made his concluding paragraph where he said: "If a modern threshing floor located in Bethlehem in the modern world can be used effectively in the 21st century, there's no reason why the threshing floor belonging to Araunah could not have been located within the City of David." This reviewer can speak from first-hand knowledge that this threshing floor is not "in Bethlehem" as Dr. Welty claimed, but six kilometers outside of town. It can also be said that the threshing floor went out of use in the 1990s with the introduction of mechanical threshers. A threshing floor near the Gihon Spring would not have gotten the gentle westerly breeze in the evening. If it did (but it doesn't) the chaff from the threshing would be blown into the only water source for the City of David, the Gihon Spring. That is not good for the drinking water.

## Was the Tabernacle at the Gihon Spring When Solomon Was Anointed King (1 Kings 1: 39)?

Cornuke believes, based on 1 Kings 1: 39, that the Ark of the Covenant was in the Tabernacle at the Gihon Spring in the City of David (2014: 75-76, 107; 2017: 75-76, 111). "So Zadok the priest, Nathan the prophet, Benaiah the son of Jehoiada, the Cherethites, and the Pelethites went down and had Solomon ride on David's mule, and took him to Gihon. Then Zadok the priest took a horn from the tabernacle and anointed Solomon. And they blew the horn, and all the people said, 'Long live King Solomon!'" (1 Kings 1: 38-39).

**Reviewer's Recollection:** I was explaining Cornuke's position to Dr. Gabriel Barkay, a strong advocate of the Temples of Solomon and Herod being on the historical Temple Mount and the co-director of the Temple Mount Sifting Project. We read the passage in the New King James Version of the Bible where the word "tabernacle" is used in verse 39. Goby looked puzzled by the word "tabernacle" until he said, "Let's look at this word in the Hebrew text." I had the passage in Hebrew so he read it. When he got to verse 39 he excitedly exclaimed, "That's it! The text does not say 'Tabernacle,' nor refer to the Tabernacle, but only to a tent!" Now I looked puzzled. Goby went on to explain, "When the Hebrew Bible speaks of the Tabernacle it uses the words '*Oh-hel mo-ed*' (Wigram 1978: 27-29), usually translated "Tent of Meetings," where God met with His people. In this passage, only the word '*oh-hel*', tent, is used. The words "Tents of Meeting" are not used in this passage." So an ordinary tent covered the place where Solomon was anointed. Another word that is used for the Tabernacle is *Mish-kahn* (Wigram 1978: 770-771).

That made sense now. During the summer of 1979 I worked for a few weeks in Area G of the City of David excavation, just above the Gihon Spring. By mid-morning the glaring sun was brutally hot and the temperature was excruciating. The text in 1 Kings 1 does not say what time of day or what time of year Solomon was anointed. But the tent at the Gihon Spring was a reception tent to shade the participants from the sun or to protect them from the rain during the anointing ceremony. The Tabernacle was not located at or next to the Gihon Spring when Solomon was crowned king. It was situated above the spring on the summit of the ridge of the City of David.

**"Not One Stone Left upon Another"**

Cornuke's book quoted Matthew 24: 1-2 and comments: "Christ's words clearly state that the entire temple, each and every stone, will be dug up, dislodged, and tossed away. It is interesting to note that there are massive stone blocks by the thousands in the wall supporting the Temple Mount platform. Was Jesus wrong in His prophesying that not one stone would remain standing?" (2014: 44; 2017: 41).

The Lord Jesus was not wrong in His prophecy. What did Jesus actually say? "Then Jesus went out and departed from the Temple [*ierou*], and His disciples came to Him to show Him the buildings of the Temple [*ierou*]. And Jesus said to them, 'Do you not see all these things? Assuredly, I say to you, not one stone shall be left here upon another, that shall not be thrown down'" (Matthew 24: 1-2). "Then as He went out of the Temple [*ierou*], one of His disciples said to Him, 'Teacher, see what manner of stones and what buildings are here!' And Jesus answered and said to him, 'Do you see these great buildings? Not one stone shall be left upon another, that shall not be thrown down'" (Mark 13: 1-2). "Then, as some spoke of the Temple [*ierou*], how it was adorned with beautiful stones and donations, He said, 'As for these things which you see, the days will come in which not one stone shall be left upon another that shall not be thrown down'" (Luke 21: 5-6). When each of the accounts are read in the three Synoptic gospels, it is observed that only the Temple and the buildings on the Temple Mount will be destroyed. The Lord Jesus said nothing about the Temple platform enlarged and constructed by Herod the Great because it is not a building.

What buildings were the disciples pointing to when Jesus said they would be destroyed? On the north side of the Temple, going west to east, there is the Chamber of the Hearth, the Gate of Jeconiah, a rinsing chamber, the Gate of the Offering for Women, a salt chamber, the Gate of the Flame, the Chamber of the Lepers, the Northern Gate, and the Chamber of the Woodshed. On the south side of the Temple, going west to east, there is the Kindling Gate, a wood chamber, the Gate of the Firstling, the Golah chamber, the Water Gate, the Chamber of Hewn Stone, the Chamber of the House of Oil, the Southern Gate, and the Chamber of the Nazarites. For a map, the reader can see Ritmeyer 2006: 345; for pictures of models, see 2006: 141, 218, 349, 372, 373; see also Netzer 2008: 141. There was also the Royal Stoa at the southern end of the Temple Mount (Josephus, *Antiquities* 15. 411-415; LCL 8: 199-201; Ritmeyer 2006: 90-94; Netzer 2008: 164-171).

In 70 C.E., the Temple and the surrounding buildings were destroyed, but the retaining walls were not the subject of the disciples' observations, thus the prophecy of the Lord Jesus did not include the platform on which the Temple was built. The Lord Jesus said nothing about the enclosure wall of the Temple Mount, although a significant portion of its perimeter structures were included in the Roman destruction. His prediction of the Temple and the surrounding buildings being destroyed was fulfilled – 100 percent to the letter, yet Jesus predicted nothing about the retaining wall built by Herod the Great.

## A Perfect Fit?

Cornuke tried to argue that the Temple of Herod was a "perfect fit," situated on a large square platform, 500 cubits by 500 cubits, over the Gihon Spring and part of the City of David. The book stated: "Josephus also confirms (in *Wars* V.5.2) that the temple was square-shaped. The historical Temple Mount/Dome of the Rock platform, however, is not square at all, but a trapezium that measures 1,041 feet on its north wall, 1,596 feet on its west wall, 929 feet on its south wall, and 1,556 feet on its east wall" (2014: 109; 2017: 113).

There are several factual errors in this quote. First of all, the citation from *Wars* 5 says nothing about the Temple being square; the correct quote is actually found in *Antiquities* 15. Second, the square mentioned by Josephus was actually the measurement of the platform that Solomon's Temple was originally built upon and not Herod's Temple (Ritmeyer 1992: 27; 2006: 140). Josephus is quite clear on this point. He wrote: "The hill [where Herod's Temple was built] was a rocky ascent that sloped gently up toward the eastern part of the city to the topmost peak" (*Antiquities* 15.397; LCL 8: 193). Two geographical points are to be noticed. First, Herod's Temple was on the topmost peak, a reference to the top of the Temple Mount, not down the slopes over or near the Gihon Spring. Second, Jerusalem of the Second Temple Period included the area of the Western Hill and today's Christian Quarter. From these areas, the Temple Mount is the eastern part of the city.

Josephus then described the hill on which Solomon's Temple was built in these terms: "This hill our first king, Solomon, with God-given wisdom surrounded with great works above at the top. And below, beginning at the foot, where a deep ravine runs around it, he surrounded it with enormous stones bound together with lead. He cut off more and more of the area within as (the wall) became greater in depth, so that the size and height of the structure, *which was a square*, were immense, and the great size of the stones was seen along the front surface, while iron clamps on the inside assured that the joints would remain permanently united. When this work reached the top of the hill, he leveled off the summit, and filled in the hollow spaces near the walls, and made the upper surface smooth and even throughout. **Such was the whole enclosure, having a circumference of four stades, each side taking up the length of a stade**" (Antiquities 15. 398-400; LCL 8:193; Ritmeyer 2006: 138-145, 165-205; emphasis added). It is important to note again the geographical terms "at the top" and "the top of the hill," not down the slopes in the City of David as Cornuke's book contends. The square platform was built by Solomon or one of the later Judean kings, but not by Herod the Great as the book stated (Ritmeyer 2006: 141).

The book cited "Shanks, p. 69" as the source for the 500 by 500 cubits square platform information (Cornuke 2014: 203, footnote 6; 2017: 113). It was actually found in another Shanks' book (2007: 69, 192, footnote 15) where Shanks footnoted Dr. Leen Ritmeyer's excellent article on the location of the original Solomonic Temple (1992: 24-45, 65-66), but apparently not consulted or at least not interacted with by Mr. Cornuke for his book. The measurement of 500 cubits also comes from tractate *Middoth* ("measurements") of the *Mishnah*. "The Temple Mount measured five hundred cubits by five hundred cubits. Its largest [open] space was to the south, the next largest to the east, the third largest to the north, and its smallest [open space] was to the west" (2.1; Danby 1985: 591; brackets in original). Cornuke is correct to state that Tractate Middot is the oldest portions of the Mishnah (2014: 109; 2017: 113; contra Welty's statements 2017:216-217). What he does not mention is that parts of the tractate contain statements by rabbis and sages living in the first century C.E. and were eye-witnesses to the Temple of Herod. In all probability, the 500 cubit is a reliable statement based on firsthand knowledge of the Temple.

The cubit used by Solomon was the long (royal) Egyptian cubit that measured 52.5 centimeters or 20.67 inches long (Barkay 1986: 37; Ritmeyer 1992: 33). Thus, the First Temple square platform was 262.5 meters (861 feet, almost three football fields in length) on each side. (In the Second Temple Period, ca. 400 B.C.E. to 70 C.E., the cubit was about 50 cm.)

**Personal Recollection:** I did a very revealing exercise by taking the "Ordnance Survey of Jerusalem" topographical map (1864-65) by Captain Charles Wilson of the British army and cut a square out of a piece of paper that was 861 feet on the English foot scale. I placed the square 600 feet south of the Temple Mount, according to the scale, and had the square parallel to the Temple Mount. Cornuke's alleged twin-bridge that was 600 feet between the Antonia's Fortress and the Temple Mount was connected from the southwest corner of the present-day Temple Mount to the northwest corner of the Temple complex as shown in the drawing in the book (2014: 142; cf. 2014: 62; 2017: 145; cf. 2017: 61; blue line on diagram of Figure 1). What the imagined square in the book (red square on diagram) covered was very revealing. Besides part of the City of David, it also covered the entire Kidron Valley and part of the Silwan Village on the western slopes of the Mount of Olives. As will be shown below, the illustrations in the book did not even follow its own written calculations!

Geographically, this square platform over the Gihon Spring (red square on diagram of Figure 1) makes no sense for the location of Solomon's or Herod's Temple and it is impossible for the location of the Temple platform for three reasons. First, the First Temple platform would have covered the Iron Age houses in the residential area on the eastern slopes of the City of David, also known as Shiloh's Areas G and E, and Kenyon's Area A, that were built after the time of Solomon (Shiloh 1984: 17-20). Were these houses dug into the basement of the platform after the construction of the First Temple by Solomon? Second, part of the Silwan Village, which was an Iron Age necropolis for Jerusalemite administrators, would have also been covered (Ussishkin 1993). It would be impossible to hew Iron Age burial caves in the Silwan escarpment after the Solomonic platform was built. Third, it would dam up the Kidron Valley and create a lake to the north of the Temple complex. Unless of course, Solomon or Herod the Great engaged in a monumental construction project by putting huge sewer pipes under the Temple platform to allow the water from the Kidron Valley to flow through or underneath the Temple complex and down the Kidron Valley to the Dead Sea. But there are no records in the Bible, in Josephus' works, the rabbinic sources, or archaeological evidence of any such sewer system or man-made lake.

In reality, Herod expanded the Temple platform so it was considerably larger than the 500-cubit First Temple platform and this is consistent with the literary sources. During the Seleucid, Hasmonean, and Herodian periods the Temple Mount platform was enlarged, thus making the Temple Mount in the days of Herod the Great much larger than the square platform of King Solomon (Ritmeyer 1992: 30-31; Patrich and Edelcopp 2011: 17-37). This is the trapezoid-shaped Temple Mount platform, cited in the first paragraph of this section, which is seen today.

The "perfect fit" of a square of 500 cubits on each side does, however, fit very well on the historical Temple Mount, called by scholars the "Ritmeyer Square" (see green square on diagram; for an excellent summary of this square on the Temple Mount, see Ritmeyer 1992: 27; 2006: 139-145, 238-239). Mr. Cornuke's (as well as Ernest Martin's) idea that the temples were over the Gihon Spring collapses on this one point alone and it was not the Romans who dismantled this imagined square platform – it was the facts on the ground and on the maps that dismantled this theory!

### Ancient Garbology and the Location of the Temple

Ancient garbology is the study of ancient trash. Israeli archaeologists have spent much time, energy, and resources, excavating the ancient garbage dump of Jerusalem on the eastern slope of the City of David. Much can be learned about what the people ate, how they viewed ritual purity, sacrifices on the Temple, and the waste management operation of the Romans.

The book's imagined 500 by 500-cubit Herodian square (red on diagram) would have covered the eastern slope of the City of David that was an active city garbage dump during the Second Temple Period. In an important and fascinating article by Professor Ronny Reich and Dr. Eli Shukron, the recent excavators of the City of David, they have described the city-dump on this slope in these terms: "In almost every excavated area, an extremely thick layer of loose debris just under surface [was encountered]. This layer is made of earth, loose rubble, small stones and a large amount of broken artifacts (mainly pottery shards with fragments of stone and glass vessels, coins, etc.), as well as broken animal bones. It seems to be ordinary household garbage, which was dumped down the slope, as is characterized by the slanting bedding lines of the debris. These bedding lines have a constant gradient of approximately 32 degrees, and they show occasional sorting of the components according to mass and size" (2003: 12).

Reich and Shukron summarized the size and date of this dump by saying: "The mantle of debris covers the entire eastern slope of the southwestern hill (the City of David). This area of debris is at least 400 meters long on the North-South axis (i.e., the length of the hill), and 50-70 meters wide on the West-East axis (i.e., the length of the slope). A modest estimate will show that we deal here with a huge deposit which measures, at least, 400 x 50 x 10 m = 200,000 cubic meters. According to a preliminary reading of the artifacts retrieved from the debris, the greater part of this amount was accumulated during a period of time that extends approximately from the middle of the $1^{st}$ century B.C.E. to the year 70 C.E., i.e., over approximately 100-120 years" (2003:14; see also Bouchnik, Bar-Oz, and Reich 2004: 71-80, 50*; Reich and Bar-Oz 2006: 83-98, 14*-15*; Bar-Oz 2007: 1-12; Reich 2011: 219-221; Spiciarich, Gadot, and Sipir-Hen 2017: 98-117; Gadot 2018: 36-45, 70).

In reality, an active city garbage dump that was in continuous use during at least the last 100 years of the Second Temple Period covered the area where the book claimed the 500 x 500 cubit Temple platform was standing. Herod the Great would not have built a temple over an active garbage dump that continued to be in use the whole time his temple existed. The Temple must have been located elsewhere.

## A "Superiority" Complex?

In this section of the book, several factual errors were made, and one mistake was copied and repeated from a secondary source (2014: 37-39; 2017: 33-36). The section began by calling the Dome of the Rock "the Mosque of Omar" (see also 2014: 8, 19; 2017: 2, 15). The Dome of the Rock is not a mosque and Omar did not build it. This shrine was built by the Umayyad Caliph 'Abd al-Malik (685-705 C.E.). Its octagonal shape, patterned after two known Christian churches in the area, indicated that it was a commemorative building, and not a mosque (Grabar 1959: 37).

Professor Moshe Sharon of the Hebrew University in Jerusalem and an expert on Arabic and Islamic history observed that: "The Dome of the Rock was not a mosque, it was a shrine, and it no doubt was built to honor and commemorate the rock over which the dome itself was raised." He goes on to suggest that: "The most important memory involved the Jewish Temple built by Solomon; the Muslims believed the rock of the Dome of the Rock was a vestige of Solomon's Temple" (2006: 42).

Sharon documented the fact that the earliest Muslims in Jerusalem believed the Dome of the Rock was the location of Solomon's Temple, and they learned of the location of this Temple from the local Jewish population. Sharon stated: "[The] Dome of the Rock was built by the early Muslims to symbolize the renewal of the Temple. The new holy structure thus served as a physical refutation of the Christian belief that the site should remain in desolation. Similarly, early Jewish midrash, though composed some 60 years after the building of the Dome of the Rock, hails the Muslims as the initiators of Israel's redemption and praises one Muslim ruler as the builder of the 'House of the Lord'" (2006: 44; also see his earlier article,1992: 56-67).

This goes contrary to the statement in the book that the Muslims did not build the Dome of the Rock because of any former Jewish Temple (Cornuke 2014: 39). In actual fact, that's **exactly** why the Muslims built the Dome of the Rock, because it was the place of the former Temple of Solomon.

Mr. Cornuke's book goes on to quote Dr. Myriam Rosen-Ayalon as saying: "the buildings [plural] on the Temple Mount were, 'Conceived in a manner and setting meant entirely to overwhelm and overshadow the Christian shrine, (which is the Church of the Holy Sepulcher).'" (2014: 39; 2017: 35). The book then cited the footnote on page 7 of her *Qedem* 28 volume describing the early Islamic monuments on the Haram al-Sharif ("Noble Sanctuary"), the Arabic name for the Temple Mount. The quote in the book actually came from page 11 of Hershel Shanks' book, *Jerusalem's Temple Mount*. Cornuke's book even copied the mistake that Shanks made citing Rosen-Ayalon's book. Shanks said that the buildings (plural), referred to the buildings on the Temple Mount, when in fact, Rosen-Ayalon wrote an "Islamic monument" (singular) and was referring specifically to the al-Aqsa Mosque, not the Dome of the Rock or any other buildings on the Temple Mount (1989: 4-7). Did the author of the book, *Temple*, actually consult Dr. Rosen-Ayalon's important work on the architecture of the Haram?

Cornuke's book also claimed that the Mosque of Omar [sic] "is thought by Muslims to be the third most holy place in Islam" (2014: 19; 2017: 15). This is also factually incorrect. The Al-Aqsa Mosque is the third holiest shrine in Islam, not the Dome of the Rock. The reader will remember that when Anwar Sadat, the president of Egypt, went to Jerusalem to make peace with Menachem Begin, the prime minister of Israel, he went to Al-Aqsa Mosque to pray and not the Dome of the Rock.

The tenth century C.E. Muslim historian, Muqaddasi, was also quoted, but a footnote for this source is not given in the book for this quote (2014: 38; 2017: 34-35). This reviewer observed that the quote also came from page 11 of Shanks' book, but Cornuke's book only quoted Shanks book, a secondary source, and not the original sources footnoted by Shanks (Grabar 1976: 55; Goitein 1982: 177). These two articles should have been consulted as well.

The author of the book did not verify what Shanks wrote in his book, but just copied his inaccurate statement. He should have looked up Rosen-Ayalon's book and caught Shanks' mistake himself, rather than repeat the inaccurate statement.

### The Nuba Inscription

In the fall of 2016 a new discovery was announced that added another nail to the coffin of the historical Temple Mount deniers. It was a 1,000+ year old Arabic inscription that was discovered by Assaf Avraham and Peretz Reuven on a wall of the Mosque of Nuba, a village near Hebron.

The translation of the text is as follows:

> In the name of Allah, the merciful god. This territory, Nuba, and all its boundaries and its entire area, is an endowment to the Rock of 'Bayt al-Maqdis' and the al-Aqsa Mosque as it was dedicated by the commander of the faithful, Umar iben al-Khattab, for the sake of Allah the almighty.

There are at least three things to notice about this inscription. First, the Arabic words *Bayt al-Maqdis* is equivalent to the Hebrew words *Beit Ha-Mikdash* and is translated "Holy Temple" or "House of the Sanctuary." The Muslims equated the Dome of the Rock with the locations of the temples on the historical Temple Mount. Second, there is a reference to the two buildings, the Dome of the Rock and the Al-Aqsa Mosque, found on the Haram al-Sharief of the historical Temple Mount. Finally, the inscription was dedicated by the commander, Umar iben al-Khattab, the Islamic leader who conquered Jerusalem from the Byzantine Christians in 638 C.E.

There are contemporary Islamic references to the Bayt al-Maqdis. Several of them are as follows:

> "I would regularly pray with Ibn-Dahar in Bayt- al Maqdis, when he entered, he used to remove his shoes."
> "Anyone who comes to Bayt al-Maqdis only for the sake of praying inside it – is cleansed of all his sins."
> "I entered Bayt- al Maqdis and saw a man taking longer than usual for his bows."
> "The rock that is in Bayt al-Maqdis is the center of the entire universe." This reference is based on a Jewish understanding that the Stone in the Dome of the Rock was the center of the universe.

Even as recent as 1925 the guide book for the Haram esh-Sharif acknowledged the Dome of the Rock was built over the location of Solomon's Temple. It says, "Its identity with the site of Solomon's Temple is beyond dispute. This, too, is the spot, according to universal belief, on which 'David built there an altar unto the Lord, and offered burnt offerings and peace offerings' (2 Samuel 24:25)" (Anonymous 1925: 4).

## What Was the Origin of the Octagonal Shape of the Dome of the Rock?

In the appendix of the book, Welty challenges this reviewer's assertion that the Dome of the Rock was a commemorative building. He contends that:

> Its octagonal shape indicates that it is modeled after the Temple of Baal-bek in Lebanon. It was definitely not a commemorative building. Instead, it was a part of larger worship center dedicated to pagan deities. That's why the Umayyad Caliph built the structure as a mosque. An astute reader will note the parallels between the site layout at Baal-bek and the Temple Mount ruins. The Muslim Dome of the Rock occupies the same relative position as did the octagonal structure at Baal-bek. The modern Al-Aqsa Mosque occupies the same relative position on the Temple Mount as did the Temple to Bacchus at Baal-bek. The Caliph's building program was intentional in this regard (Cornuke 2017: 227).

Whether there are parallels between the site layout of the Dome of the Rock and the octagonal structure at Baal-bek can be debated. The question is, "Why do you have to go 200 plus miles to the north of Jerusalem to find a parallel when you can go three and six miles to the south of the Dome of the Rock and find two octagonal structures, which in all probability the Dome of the Rock was patterned after?

Two Islamic scholars, writing in the *Palestine Exploration Quarterly*, correctly dismiss two octagonal churches as possible parallels in Jerusalem, i.e. the Church of the Holy Sepulchre and the Church of the

Ascension on the Mount of Olives. They concluded their article by saying:

> Yet, there is no record of any other important building built
> with an octagonal shape anywhere in the Islamic world
> during this period of a thousand years. This confirms the
> view presented in this paper that the Dome of the Rock
> needed to be octagonal to reflect the unique religious
> scenario that was believed to be happening only in the
> location where it was being built and will not be repeated
> anywhere else (Islam and al-Hamad 2007: 126; cf. Rosen-
> Ayalon 1989: 12).

In 1992 the Jerusalem municipality was widening the Jerusalem-
Hebron Road when ancient remains were discovered north of the Mar
Elias Monastery. It was excavated by the Israel Antiquities Authority
under the directorship of Rina Avner (Avner, Lavas, and Rosidis 2001:89*-
92*, 133-137; 2003: 173-186; see also Avner 2010 and 2011). The site was
identified as the Kathisma Church and Monastery dedicated to the place
that Mary, the Theotokos, rested on her way to Bethlehem to give birth
to the Lord Jesus. This event is recorded in the apocryphal *Protoevengelion
of James* 17: 2-3.

The octagonal Kathisma Church was built in 456 C.E. and
patterned after the octagonal Constantine the Great Church of the
Nativity in Bethlehem that was built in 333 C.E. The octagonal church
was replaced during the reign of Emperor Justinian (525-565 C.E.).
When the Dome of the Rock was built in 691-692 C.E., only the
Kathisma Church was standing (Avner 2010: 37). Avner, the excavator
of the Kathisma Church, observed that: "The architectural similarities
between the Church of the Kathisma and the Dome of the Rock appear
in the following features: both are octagonal in their exteriors, their plans
each consist of a central space with a hallowed rock, and both have two
octagonal concentric belts around that central space" (2010: 38). It is not
surprising to see the parallel between these two buildings because the
supervisors of the building of the Dome of the Rock resided in Jeru-

salem and would have been familiar with the Kathisma Church (Avner 2010: 43). There is also an octagonal church built on the top of Mount Gerizim in 484 C.E. and is also dedicated to Mary "the Mother of God" (Theotokos) (Magen 1990: 333-342).

The excavator, Avner, suggested that the Umayyad caliph, abd al-Malik, wanted to "construct a monument [the Dome of the Rock] that transmitted an anti-Christian statement. For the Dome of the Rock was designed to surpass in beauty the shrines from which both its plan and architecture derives. Furthermore, it was meant to express the emergence of a new faith that rejects a basic tenet of Christian belief – the divinity of Christ – as well as the veneration of his mother, Mary, as 'God Bearer'" (2010: 44).

## Throughout History the Jewish People Knew Where the Temple Was Located

Cornuke's assertion that in the fourth century C.E. people did not know where the temples had been located (Cornuke 2014: 9, 35; 2017: 3, 31). The Jewish people **knew** exactly where the temples were because they had unbroken knowledge from 70 C.E. as to where the temples had stood on the historical Temple Mount.

Professor F. M. Loewenberg, professor emeritus of Bar Ilan University, in an important article entitled, "Did Jews Abandon the Temple Mount?", documents the history of the Jewish people and their attachment to the historical Temple Mount. He points out that: "The destruction of the Second Temple in the year 70 C.E. did not spell the end of Jewish activities on the Temple Mount. For many centuries, Jews continued their attachment to the site by maintaining a physical presence on the mountain. And when they were prevented from doing so, they prayed three times a day for the speedy renewal of the sacrificial services in a restored temple." He goes on to say: Despite the conventional wisdom that the Jewish people were banished from this holy site, the evidence suggests that Jews continued to maintain a strong connection to and frequently even a presence on the Temple Mount for the next two thousand years. Even when they were physically prevented from ascending the site, their attachment to Har Habayit remained strong and vibrant." He then proceeded to document the Jewish presence on the historical Temple Mount throughout the Roman rule (70-300); the Byzantine period (300-618); the Early Muslim rule (638-1099); the Crusader Kingdom of Jerusalem (1099-1187); the Ottoman empire (1516-1856); and up until modern times. He concluded: "Even after the Roman armies destroyed the temple in 70 C.E., the Jews never abandoned the site. No matter what obstacles or decrees others placed in their way, Jews continued to ascend and pray at or near the area where the temple once stood." (Loewenberg 2013).

### *Miqwaʾot* **Around the Historic Temple Mount**

Cornuke described the discovery of the alleged coin from 20 C.E., but he does not indicate it was discovered in a *mikvah* (ritual bath) and the implications of the location of this and other ritual baths around and possibly on the historic Temple Mount (Reich 1989; 1990; 1999; Regev 2005: 194-204; Adler 2006: 209-215; Mazar 2002: 46-49, 61). Part of the Jewish ritual before one entered the Temple was to immerse oneself in a ritual bath. "None may enter the Temple Court for [an act of the Temple] Service, even though he is clean, until he has immersed himself" (Mishnah *Yoma* 3:3; Danby 1985: 164; Aviam 2014: 124-126).

Why are there so many *mikvaot* [Hebrew plural] or Jewish ritual baths on or in close proximity to the Temple Mount (Zweig 2008: 295-296, 49*, Plate 1A-1B) if the site was only the Antonia Fortress controlled by the Gentile Romans? Most Jewish people would not be visiting the Fortress so there would be no need to immerse themselves in these *mikvaot*. These *mikvaot*, however, would make perfect sense where they are if Jewish people wanted to immerse themselves in the ritual baths just before entering Herod's Temple on the historical Temple Mount.

## CONCLUSIONS

It was not this author/reviewer's intention to write a book-length review. There are numerous other topics that were misunderstood in Cornuke's books that have not been discussed. For example, the meaning of the Greek word *tagma* (2014: 48; 2017: 45); the "Flawed Theory" (2014: 49-51; 2017: 46-48); the "Mount is the Fort" (2014: 51-52; 2017: 48-50); Benjamin of Tudela, Eusebius, and Hecateus of Abdera (2014: 71-72; 2017: 69-71); Aristeas (2014: 83-84; 2017: 85-86); Tacitus (2014: 84-85; 2017: 86-87); the Temple Scroll (2014: 85-86; 2017: 87-88); the cleansing stream for the high priest's ritual cleansing (2014: 87-88; 2017: 89-91); the number of soldiers taking the Apostle Paul to Caesarea (2014: 90-95; 2017: 93-98), the simple answer to this problem is, however, that the 470 Roman soldiers were part of a reinforcement unit that came up to Jerusalem for the Feast of *Shavuot* (Pentecost) and were returning to Caesarea after the feast was over; King Herod Agrippa II's view into the Temple area (2014: 108; 2017: 112-113); and Nehemiah's Walls (2014: 121-123; 2017: 125-127; but see Ritmeyer and Ritmeyer 2005 for an excellent scholarly discussion of these walls).

The subtitle of the books say: "*Amazing New Discoveries that Change Everything About the Location of Solomon's Temple.*" As was shown in this chapter, the so-called "amazing new discoveries" do not change anything about the location of Solomon's Temple. It was still originally located up on the Temple Mount. Because of his lack of archaeological training and his lack of understanding of the archaeological, geographical, historical, and biblical information of Jerusalem and the historical Temple Mount, Cornuke's books do not change anything about the location of Solomon's or Herod's temples. They were still originally located on the historical Temple Mount.

These are not "highly-researched" books as the back covers of the books claim, nor are they carefully researched and written. As was shown above, there was a serious lack of any scholarship and the author did not grasp the archaeology, topography, geography, and literary sources of the ancient city of Jerusalem. Only a handful of secondary sources were used, but they were not critically read or followed-up on to check to see if those authors had gotten their facts correct.

The book cover also asks the provocative question: "Could history be so stunningly wrong?" The simple answer is "No." History is correct on the original location of the temples on the historical Temple Mount in Jerusalem. The facts are: Solomon's and Herod's temples were on the historical Temple Mount in Jerusalem. It is those individuals who try to move the temples to the City of David above the Gihon Spring who are so stunningly wrong. The facts are: The probability of the temples being above the Gihon Spring in the City of David is ZERO. Mr. Cornuke has produced no credible historical, archaeological, geographical, geological, or biblical evidence for his claims. This is the greatest archaeological blunder of all time. Case closed!

## REFERENCES

### Ancient Sources
Danby, Herbert. 1985. *The Mishnah*. Oxford: Oxford University.
Josephus. 1980. *Jewish Antiquities*. Books 15-17. Vol. 8. Trans. by R. Marcus. Cambridge, MA: Harvard University. Loeb Classical Library 418.

### Modern Works
Adler, Yonatan. 2006. "The Ritual Baths Near the Temple Mount and Extra-Purification Before Entering the Temple Courts: A Reply to Eyal Regev." *Israel Exploration Journal*, 56/2: 209-215.
Anonymous. 1925. *A Brief Guide to the Al-Haram al-Sharif*. Jerusalem: Supreme Moslem Council.
Aviam, Mordechi. 2014. "Reverence for Jerusalem and the Temple in Galilean Society." *Jesus and Temple*, pp. 123-144.
Avigad, Nahman. 1980. *Discovering Jerusalem*. Nashville, TN: Thomas Nelson.
Avner, Rina. 2003. "The Recovery of the Kathisma Church and Its

Influence on Octagonal Buildings." *One Land – Many Cultures*, pp. 173-188.

Avner, Rina. 2010. "The Dome of the Rock in Light of the Development on Concentric Martyria in Jerusalem: Architecture and Architectural Iconography." *Muqarnas*, 27: 31-49.

Avner, Rina. 2011. "The Initial Tradition of the Theotokos at the Kathisma: Earliest Celebrations and the Calendar. *The Cult of the Mother of God in Byzantium*, pp. 9-29.

Avner, Rina, George Lavas, and Irini Rosidis. 2001. "Jerusalem, Mar Elias – the Kathisma Church. *Excavations and Surveys in Israel*, 113: 133-137, 89*-92*.

Barkay, Gabriel. 1985. "Northern and Western Jerusalem in the End of the Iron Age." Unpublished PhD thesis. Tel Aviv University (Hebrew with English abstract).

Barkay, Gabriel. 1986. "Measurements in the Bible-Evidence at St. Etienne for the Length of the Cubit and the Reed." *Biblical Archaeology Review*, 12/2: 37.

Barkay, Gabriel and Zachi Zweig. 2007. "New Data in the Sifting Project of Soil from the Temple Mount: Second Preliminary Report." *City of David. Studies of Ancient Jerusalem*, pp, 27-67 (Hebrew).

Barkay, Gabriel and Zachi Dvira. 2015. *Temple Mount Sifting Project*. Jerusalem: Temple Mount Sifting Project.

Barkay, Gabriel and Zachi Dvira. 2016. "Relics in Rubble. The Temple Mount Sifting Project." *Biblical Archaeology Review*, 42/6: 44-55, 64.

Bar-Oz, Guy. 2007. "Holy Garbage: A Quantitative Study of the City-Dump of Early Roman Jerusalem." *Levant*, 39: 1-12.

Borowski, Oded. 1987. *Agriculture in Iron Age Israel*. Winona Lake, IN: Eisenbrauns.

Bouchnik, Ram, Guy Bar-Oz, and Ronny Reich. 2004. "Animal Bone Remains from the City Dump of Jerusalem from the Late Second Temple Period." *New Studies on Jerusalem*, Vol. 10, pp. 71-80, 50* (Hebrew).

Bullock, C. Hassell. 2001. *Encountering the Book of Psalms. A Literary and Theological Introduction*. Grand Rapids, MI: Baker Academics.

Cornuke, Robert. 2014. *Temple: Amazing New Discoveries that Change Everything About the Location of Solomon's Temple*. Charlotte, NC: Lifebridge Books.

Cornuke, Robert. 2017. *Temple: Amazing New Discoveries that Changed Everything about the Location of Solomon's Temple*. Coeur d'Alene, ID: Koinonia House.

Feinberg, Paul M. 2016. "The Hidden Secret of Some Christians." *Prophecy in the News,* (April) 14.

Gadot, Yuval. 2018. "Holy Land(fill)." *Biblical Archaeology Review,* 44/1: 36-45, 70.

Garfinkel, Yosef and Madeleine Mumcuoglu. 2016. *Solomon's Temple and Palace: New Archaeological Discoveries*. Jerusalem: Bible Lands Museum.

Grabar, Oleg. 1959. "The Umayyad Dome of the Rock in Jerusalem." *Ars Orientalis,* 3: 33-62.

Hutzli, Jurg. 2011. "The Meaning of the Term *'ir dawid* in Samuel and Kings." *Tel Aviv,* 38/2: 167-178.

Islam, M. Anwarul and Zaid F. Al-Hamad. 2007. "The Dome of the Rock: Origin of Its Octagonal Plan." *Palestine Exploration Quarterly,* 139/2: 109-128.

Loewenberg, F. M. 2013. "Did Jews Abandon the Temple Mount?" *Middle East Quarterly,* 20/3: 37-48.

Magen, Yitzah. 1990. "The Church of Mary Theotokos on Mount Gerizim." *Christian Archaeology in the Holy Land. New Discoveries*, pp. 333-342.

Martin, Ernest. 2000. *The Temples that Jerusalem Forgot*. Portland, OR: ASK Publications.

Mazar, Eilat. 2002. *The Complete Guide to the Temple Mount Excavations*. Jerusalem: Shoham Academic Research.

Mazar, Eilat. 2009. *The Palace of King David. Excavations at the Summit of the City of David. Preliminary Report of Seasons 2005-2007*. Jerusalem and New York: Shoham Academic Research.

Na'aman, Nadav. 2012b. "Five Notes on Jerusalem in the First and Second Temple Periods." *Tel Aviv,* 39/1: 93-103.

Netzer, Ehud. 2008. *The Architecture of Herod, the Great Builder*. Grand

Rapids, MI: Baker.

Patrich, Joseph and Marcus Edelcopp. 2011. "Four Stages of Development of the Temple Mount." *New Studies in the Archaeology of Jerusalem and Its Region*. Collected Papers, Vol. 5, pp. 17-37 (Hebrew).

Regev, Eyal. 2005. "The Ritual Baths Near the Temple Mount and Extra-Purification Before Entering the Temple Courts." *Israel Exploration Journal*, 55/2: 194-204.

Reich, Ronny. 1989. "Two Possible *Miqwa'ot* on the Temple Mount." *Israel Exploration Journal*, 39/1-2: 63-65.

Reich, Ronny. 1990. "Miqwa'ot (Jewish Ritual Immersion Baths) in Eretz-Israel in the Second Temple and Mishna and Talmud Periods." Unpublished Ph.D. dissertation. Jerusalem: The Hebrew University (Hebrew).

Reich, Ronny. 1999. "Design and Maintenance of First-Century Ritual Immersion Baths." *Jerusalem Perspective*, 56: 14-19.

Reich, Ronny. 2011. *Excavating the City of David. Where Jerusalem's History Began*. Jerusalem: Israel Exploration Society.

Reich, Ronny and Guy Bar-Oz. 2006. "The Jerusalem City Dump in the Late Second Temple Period: A Quantitative Study." *New Studies on Jerusalem*, Vol. 12, pp. 83-98, 14*-15* (Hebrew).

Reich, Ronny and Eli Shukron. 2003. "The Jerusalem City-Dump in the Late Second Temple Period." *Zeitschrift des Deutschen Palastina-Vereins*, 119/1: 12-18.

Ritmeyer, Leen. 1992. "Locating the Original Temple Mount." *Biblical Archaeology Review*, 18/2: 24-45, 64-65.

Ritmeyer, Leen. 1996. "Where the Ark of the Covenant Stood in Solomon's Temple." *Biblical Archaeology Review*, 22/1: 46-55, 70-72.

Ritmeyer, Leen. 2006. *The Quest. Revealing the Temple Mount in Jerusalem*. Jerusalem: Carta.

Ritmeyer, Leen and Kathleen Ritmeyer. 1989. "Reconstructing Herod's Temple in Jerusalem." *Biblical Archaeology Review*, 15/6: 23-42.

Ritmeyer, Leen and Kathleen Ritmeyer. 2005. *Jerusalem in the Time of Nehemiah*. Jerusalem: Carta.

Rosen-Ayalon, Myriam. 1989. *The Early Islamic Monuments of Al-Haram al-Sharif. An Iconographic Study.* Qedem 28. Jerusalem: Institute of Archaeology, Hebrew University.

Shanks, Hershel. 1986. "Excavating in the Shadow of the Temple Mount." *Biblical Archaeology Review*, 12/6: 20-38.

Shanks, Hershel. 2007. *Jerusalem's Temple Mount from Solomon to the Golden Dome.* New York: Continuum.

Sharon, Moshe. 1992. "The 'Praises of Jerusalem' as a Source for the Early History of Islam." *Bibliotheca Orientalis*, 49/1-2: 56-67.

Sharon, Moshe. 2006. "Islam on the Temple Mount." *Biblical Archaeology Review,* 32/4: 36-47, 68.

Spiciarich, Abra, Yuval Gadot, and Lidar Sapir-Hen. 2017. "The Faunal Evidence from Early Roman Jerusalem: The People behind the Garbage." *Tel Aviv,* 44/1: 98-117.

Ussishkin, David. 1993. *The Village of Silwan. The Necropolis from the Period of the Judean Kingdom.* Jerusalem: Israel Exploration Society and Ben-Zvi Institute.

Wigram, George. 1970. *Englishman's Hebrew and Chaldee Concordance of the Old Testament.* Grand Rapids, MI: Zondervan. Reprint of 1843 edition.

Zweig, Zachi. 2008. "New Information from Various Temple Mount Excavations from the Last Hundred Years." *New Studies on Jerusalem,* Vol. 14, pp. 293-355, 49*-50* (Hebrew).

# Jesus and the Decapolis: A New Understanding of the Role of Hippos/Susita

Dorothy Drummond

## INTRODUCTION

*Decapolis* was a regional name that everyone in the time of Christ would have understood, much as the similarly imprecisely defined term *Midwest* is understood. The term "Decapolis" referred to the territory associated with and loosely connecting ten ancient Greek trading cities in Palestine (Figure 1). It also referred to a culture, Greek and free-wheeling, with Jews, Nabateans, and other minorities in the blend. The New Testament mentions the Decapolis by name three times, but never with locational precision. An event that occurred within the Decapolis (without mentioning the name "Decapolis") appears one additional time.

With the exception of the much-older Scythopolis (Beit Shaan), Damascus, and Philadelphia (Amman), the cities of the Decapolis were all founded in the third century B.C.E. when Greek Ptolomies and Seleucids were vying for control of Palestine. Most of the original settlers were pensioned soldiers. All of the cities prospered as trade centers, linked by road with one another. Under Roman jurisdiction beginning in 63 B.C.E., the Decapolis cities were allowed semi-autonomy. Two of these cities, Hippos, utterly destroyed by an earthquake in 749 C.E. and now under excavation as an archaeologic site, and Scythopolis, now a thriving Israeli city again named Beit Shaan, were located within the area now occupied by the country of Israel. The remainder were scattered east, northeast, and southeast of the Jordan River, for the most part within modern Jordan: Pella, Dion, Gerasa, Gadara, Philadelphia (modern Amman), Raphana, Canatha, and Damascus.

When Scripture refers to the Decapolis in relation to Jesus' ministry, it can be assumed that the reference is to the territory surrounding those Decapolis cities closest to Galilee. Most particularly this could have included not only Hippos and Scythopolis but also Gadara or even but improbably Gerasa. This chapter will examine the site and circumstances of each account to determine where in the Decapolis events narrated in Scripture most probably might have occurred and where they probably did not occur.

## DECAPOLIS SITES RELEVANT TO THE GOSPEL

### Hippos

Hippos, known also by its Aramaic name of *Susita* (both translate to "horse"), was the Decapolis city nearest to the places in Galilee where Jesus preached (Figure 2.). At the time of Jesus, Hippos was a city occupying a plateau rising a thousand feet above the eastern shore of the Sea of Galilee. That plateau is on the western edge of Israel's Golan Heights. Directly across the Sea of Galilee to the west, was Tiberius. In the third century B.C.E., during the wars between the Seleucids and the Ptolemies, Hippos was a defensive site as well as a trading center. The Romans occupied it in 63 B.C.E., and it was an active trading city through Roman and Byzantine times. The site of Hippos fell into total neglect following the eighth century earthquake. Israel fortified it in the latter half of the twentieth century during the wars with the Arabs. Since 2000, it has been an active archaeologic site, revealing a main road (the Decumanus) running east-west the length of the site, Roman markets and shrines dating from the first to the fourth centuries, and Byzantine churches. Gradually, after seventeen seasons, the considerable extent of the city is being revealed (Figure 3).

During the time of Jesus, Hippos had its own small port on the Sea of Galilee, a switchback road winding up to the plateau, and on the east a road that connected it with other Decapolis cities. The Romans did little to lessen the autonomy within the Decapolis that Hippos had enjoyed under Greek rule. Hippos had its own coinage. However, Hippos is never mentioned by name in Scripture.

## Scythopolis

Scythopolis is south of the Sea of Galilee, near the Jordan River. Like Hippos, it is not mentioned in the Gospels. But this is understandable, in that most of Jesus' ministry takes place within the perimeter of the Sea of Galilee. Jesus could well have stopped at Scythopolis on his way to Jerusalem, but we have no evidence that he did.

## Gerasa, Gadara, and Gergesa

The Decapolis cities and/or regions that are named in the Gospels are Gerasa, Gadara, and Gergesa. Gerasa was an administrative city approximately 30 miles south of the Sea of Galilee. The people associated with Gerasa were called Gerasenes. Gadara, smaller but of regional importance, lay six miles south of the Sea of Galilee and separated from it by the deep gorge of the Yarmouk River. In some accounts, areas near Gadara are referred to as the Land of the Gadarenes. Gergesa was a small town on the eastern shore of the Sea of Galilee. It was not a Decapolis city. Its inhabitants were called Gergesenes. The similarity of the three names has led to confusion, as attested by differences that appear in various translations. In some versions, it is not the city but "the region of" the city that is cited.

## THE GOSPELS ACCOUNTS: A PLACE NAME CONFUSION

The Decapolis is mentioned by name in three instances in the Gospels, and by implication in a fourth. Confusion arises not only from differences as narrated by the Gospel writers but also from differences in various translations. Accounts in Matthew, Mark, and Luke tend to substantiate each other in reference to the Decapolis but differ in detail.

## "Large Crowds from . . . the Decapolis. . . ."

The earliest reference to the Decapolis in Scripture is in Matthew, Chapter 4, at the beginning of Jesus' ministry, as news of the Galilean prophet was spreading:

Matthew 4: 24      "News about him spread all over Syria. . . ."

Matthew 4: 25      "Large crowds from Galilee, the Decapolis, Jerusalem, Judea, and the region across the Jordan followed him."

At this stage in his ministry, Jesus was preaching in the towns on the northern shore of the Sea of Galilee. All were within the Roman province of Syria. If hearers came from Judea and Jerusalem, several day's hard walk away, they could have come as well from both near and distant parts of the Decapolis. Word spreads along roads, and the road from the Sea of Galilee to Hippos led directly to the other Decapolis cities. For the most part, inhabitants of the Decapolis were Greeks, but some Jews had settled there as well. Not only Jews, but curious Greeks also could have been drawn by the stories circulating about the Jewish prophet in Galilee. From where in the Decapolis did the "large crowds" come? Matthew does not say.

## Where Were the Pigs Sent Down-Slope?

Jesus and his disciples frequently went by boat from the northern shore of the Sea of Galilee to the eastern shore. On one occasion, they encountered a very troubled man, or in Matthew's version, two men. In the NIV translations given below, this event occurred in different places: in Mark's Gospel, in the region of the Gerasenes; in Matthew's Gospel, in the region of the Gadarenes; and in Luke's, in the region of

Figure 1. Decapolis Cities

the "Gerasenes across the lake from Galilee." Some ancient translations of Matthew name another site (v. 28), the region of the Gergesenes.

Mark 5: 1-20:

They went across the lake to the region of the Gerasenes. When Jesus got out of the boat, a man with an impure spirit came from the tombs to meet him. This man lived in the tombs, and no one could bind him anymore, not even with a chain. For he had been chained hand and foot, but he tore the chain apart and broke the irons on his feet. No one was strong enough to subdue him. Night and day among the tombs and the hills he would cry out and cut himself with stones.

When he saw Jesus from a distance he ran and fell on his knees in front of him. He shouted at the top of his voice, 'What do you want with me, Jesus, Son of the Most High God. In God's name don't torture me.' For Jesus had said to him 'Come out of this man, you impure spirits.' Then Jesus asked him, 'What is your name?' 'My name is Legion,' he replied, 'for we are many'. And he begged Jesus again and again not to send them out of the area.

A large herd of pigs was feeding on the nearby hillside. The demons begged Jesus, 'Send us among the pigs. Allow us to go onto them.' He gave the permission, and the impure spirits came out and went into the pigs. The herd, about two thousand in number, rushed down the steep bank into the lake and were drowned. Those tending the pigs ran off and reported this in the towns and countryside, and the people went out to see what had happened.

When they came to Jesus they saw the man who had been possessed by the legion of demons, sitting there, dressed,

Figure 2. Looking East from the Sea of Galilee about 1970, toward Susita Mountain, a Fortified Site. Kibbutz Ein Gev: Susita is Aramaic for "Horse.

Figure 3. Aerial View of Hippos Archaeological Site, Looking North

and in this right mind, and they were afraid. Those who had seen it told the people what had happened to the demon-possessed man, and told about the pigs as well. Then the people began to plead with Jesus to leave the region. As Jesus was getting into the boat the man who had been demon-possessed begged to go with him. Jesus did not let him but said 'Go home to your own people and tell them how much the Lord has done for you, and how he has had mercy on you.' So the man went away and began to tell in the Decapolis how much Jesus had done for him. And all the people were amazed.

Matthew 8: 28-34:

When he arrived at the other side in the region of the Gadarenes, two demon-possessed men coming from the tombs met him. They were so violent that no one could pass that way. 'What do you want with us, Son of God?' they shouted. 'Have you come here to torture us before the appointed time?' Some distance from them a large herd of pigs was feeding. The demons begged Jesus, 'If you drive us out, send us into the herd of pigs.' He said to them, 'Go!' So they came out and went into the pigs, and the whole herd rushed down the steep bank into the lake and died in the water. Those tending the pigs ran off, went into the town and reported all this, including what had happened to the demon-possessed men. Then the whole town went out to meet Jesus and when they saw him, they pleaded with him to leave their region.

Luke 8: 26-40:

They sailed to the region of the Gerasenes, which is across the lake from Galilee. When Jesus stepped ashore, he was met by a demon-possessed man from the town. For a long time this man had not worn clothes or lived in a house, but had lived in the tombs. When he saw Jesus, he cried out and fell at his feet, shouting at the top of his voice, 'What do you want with me, Jesus, Son of the Most High God? I beg you, don't torture me!' For Jesus had commanded the impure spirit to come out of the man. Many times it had seized him, and though he was chained hand and foot and kept under guard, he had broken his chains and had been driven by the demon into solitary places. Jesus asked him, 'What is your name?' 'Legion,' he replied, because many demons had gone into him. And they begged Jesus repeatedly not to order them to go into the Abyss.

A large herd of pigs was feeding there on the hillside. The demons begged Jesus to let them go into the pigs, and he gave them permission. When the demons came out of the man, they went into the pigs, and the herd rushed down the steep bank into the lake and was drowned.

When those tending the pigs saw what had happened, they ran off and reported this in the town and countryside, and the people went out to see what had happened. When they came to Jesus, they found the man from whom the demons had gone out, sitting at Jesus' feet, dressed and in his right mind, and they were afraid. Those who had seen it told the people how the demon-possessed man had been cured. Then all the people of the region of the Gerasenes asked Jesus to leave them, because they were overcome with fear. So he got into the boat and left. The man from whom the demons had gone out begged to go with him, but Jesus sent him away, saying 'Return home and tell how much God has done for you.' So the man went away and told all over town how much Jesus had done for him.

Of the three (possibly four) named sites where this story took place

(Figure 4), which one is the most likely?

1. The region of the Gerasenes, in Mark's account, is possible if the east shore of the Sea of Galilee fell under the administrative district of which Gerasa was the chief city. But the actual administrative boundaries are not known. Many translations say the event happened in Gerasa, and this is blatantly wrong. Gerasa, now the important archaeological site of Jerash, is located about 30 miles south of the Sea of Galilee, east of the Jordan River, on a gentle riverine terrace. There are no steep cliffs in or around Gerasa, and one could not sail from Galilee to Gerasa.

2. Matthew speaks of the region of the Gadarenes, referring to the Decapolis city of Gadara, about six miles to the south of the Sea of Galilee. In a sense, because Gadara was a minor administrative center, "the region of the Gadarenes" might be acceptable, but the account implies a specific place. Some versions of the text say that the event occurred in the city of Gadara, but this is quite impossible. Jesus came by boat from Galilee to the place where he met the demon-possessed man, and he could not have reached Gadara by boat. Gadara, now an archaeological site near the town of Umm Qeis, was six miles south of the Sea of Galilee, separated from it by the deep gash of the Yarmouk River, which feeds into the Jordan. Sited spectacularly at the top of a cliff that defines the south bank of the Yarmouk Gorge, it was a sophisticated city, drawing artists and poets from all over the Roman Empire. But it was no place for a herd of pigs.

3. Luke describes the region of the Gerasenes (from Gerasa) as being "across the lake from Galilee," and this description does not fit. There has never been a Gerasa on the Sea of Galilee.

4. By contrast, on the east side of the Sea of Galilee, four miles north of Hippos, there is a town called Kersa, probably a variation of the ancient name of Gergesa. Origin, writing in the third century, speaks of Gergesa as the place where the pigs ran down the slope. On one side of Kersa is a steep cliff, plunging directly into the sea. Ruins of a monastery in Kersa indicate that the church once revered this site. An alternative to Gergesa

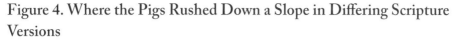

Figure 4. Where the Pigs Rushed Down a Slope in Differing Scripture Versions

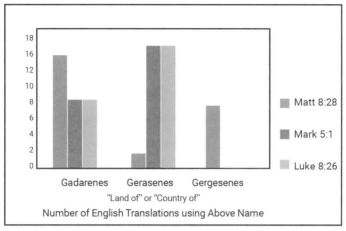

might possibly be the vicinity of Hippos, but there, the slope is not sufficiently steep, and it does not plunge directly into the sea. Any future translation should probably situate this story in Gergesa, and it would be proper to speak of the Gergesenes or the country of the Gergesenes. But, unfortunately, translations tend to perpetuate long-held errors.

## RE-ENTERING GALILEE BY WAY OF THE DECAPOLIS

Shortly after his return by boat to Capernaum, Jesus and his disciples visited Tyre and Sidon, two Phoenician cities on the Mediterranean coast. Tyre is approximately one long day's westward walk from Capernaum, while Sidon is some 22 miles north of Tyre. It is not certain that Jesus actually visited these two cities, for both Matthew and Mark say that he went into the "borderlands" of Tyre and Sidon. He could possibly have merely entered the eastern portion of the territory under jurisdiction of the two cities, that is, the part bordering on Galilee, or he could have reached the outskirts of the settled urban areas. It is reported in Scripture that in Tyre he had an encounter with a Syro-Phoenician (Canaanite) woman, but nothing is known of his visit to Sidon.

From Sidon, Jesus and his disciples returned to Galilee by way of the Decapolis. This would by no means have been the most expeditious way home, requiring a journey through the north of Galilee and into the Golan Heights. Roads existed for the journey, and once he reached the main Decapolis route heading southward from Damascus, he would have been able to stop in Decapolis villages on the return trip. Considering that those who had gathered to hear him had come also from the Decapolis, he could well have wanted to journey there, even if it meant taking the long way home. But then, at some point he would have had to turn west, to reach the Sea of Galilee. Here, the most probable route would have been to leave the Damascus-to-Philadelphia main road at the Hippos juncture, and then head towards and through Hippos and down the winding road to the Sea of Galilee. There at the small port of Hippos, Jesus and his disciples could have found a boat that would take them north to Capernaum.

The passage in Mark 7: 31 which attempts to say how Jesus got from Sidon to Galilee by way of the Decapolis, is variously translated:

> **New International Version:** *Then Jesus left the vicinity of Tyre and went through Sidon, down to the Sea of Galilee and into the region of the Decapolis.*
>
> **New Living Translation:** *Jesus left Tyre and went up to Sidon before going back to the Sea of Galilee and the region of the Ten Towns.*
>
> **English Standard Version:** *Then he returned from the region of Tyre and went through Sidon to the Sea of Galilee, in the region of the Decapolis.*
>
> **Berean Study Bible:** *Then Jesus left the region of Tyre and went through Sidon to the Sea of Galilee and into the region of the Decapolis.*
>
> **Berean Literal Bible:** *. . . he came through Sidon, to the Sea of Galilee, through the midst of the region of the Decapolis.*
>
> **New American Standard Bible:** *. . . and came through Sidon to the Sea of Galilee, within the region of Decapolis.*
>
> **King James Bible:** *. . . he came unto the sea of Galilee, through the midst of the coasts of Decapolis.*

**Christian Standard Bible:** . . . *he went by way of Sidon to the Sea of Galilee, through the region of the Decapolis.*

**Contemporary English Version:** . . . *and went by way of Sidon toward Lake Galilee. He went through the land near the ten cities known as the Decapolis.*

**Good News Translation:** . . . *and went on through Sidon to Lake Galilee, going by way of the territory of the Ten Towns.*

**Hoilman Christian Standard Bible:** *He went by way of Sidon to the Sea of Galilee, through the region of the Decapolis.*

**International Standard Version:** . . . *and passed through Sidon towards the Sea of Galilee, to the territory of the Decapolis.*

**NET Bible:** . . . *and came through Sidon to the Sea of Galilee in the region of the Decapolis.*

**New Heart English Bible:** . . . *and came through Sidon to the sea of Galilee, through the midst of the region of Decapolis.*

**Aramaic Bible in Plain English:** He went through Sidon and the territory of the Ten Cities to the Sea of Galilee.

**God's Word Translation:** . . . *and came through Sidon to the Sea of Galilee, within the region of Decapolis.*

**Jubilee Bible 2000:** . . . *he came by Sidon unto the sea of Galilee through the midst of the borders of Decapolis.*

**American KJV:** . . . *departing from the borders of Tyre and Sidon, he came unto the sea of Galilee, through the midst of the region of Decapolis.*

**American Standard Version:** . . . *and came through Sidon unto the sea of Galilee, through the midst of the borders of Decapolis.*

**Douay-Rheims Bible:** . . . *he came by Sidon to the sea of Galilee, through the midst of the coasts of Decapolis.*

**Darby Bible Translation:** . . . *he came to the Sea of Galilee, through the midst of the coasts of Decapolis.*

**English Revised Version:** . . . *and came through Sidon unto the sea of Galilee, through the midst of the borders of Decapolis.*

**Webster's Bible Translation:** *He came by way of Sidon to the*

*Lake of Galilee, passing through the district of the Ten Towns.*

**Weymouth New Testament:** . . . *he came to the sea of Galilee, through the midst of the region of Decapolis.*

**World English Bible:** . . . *and came to the sea of Galilee, through the midst of the region of Decapolis.*

**Young's Literal Translation:** . . . *he came unto the sea of Galilee, through the midst of the coasts of Decapolis.*

Although the route (# 3 in Figure 5) is unspecified, in the past, most commentators have assumed that Jesus returned to Galilee by way of Gadara. But as mentioned previously, a return by way of Gadara would have placed him on the south bank of the steep Yarmouk River gap and far from a boat-journey to Capernaum. No version mentions Hippos, the one site where the re-entry most probably could have occurred.

## FEEDING THE 4,000 IN THE DECAPOLIS

At this juncture, Mark states that Jesus was with a large crowd "in a remote place." With seven loaves of bread and a few small fish, Jesus fed 4,000 people there, then boarded a boat for Dalmanutha on the western side of the Sea, near Magadan. Could the crowd have gathered on the slope below Hippos, leading toward the sea? The city of Hippos could have accounted for the source of the crowd. A similar account in Matthew gives a slightly different version, omitting the trip from Sidon through the Decapolis, and placing Jesus on a mountainside along the Sea of Galilee. On the eastern side of the Sea of Galilee, in the region of the Decapolis near Hippos, the topography is steep enough to be described as mountainous, and the road leading from the Sea to the city on the crest of the plateau could have enabled a crowd to gather (Figure 6). Matthew and Mark both have Jesus leave by boat for the western shore of the Sea.

In Mark 8: 1-8, the passage reads:

During those days another large crowd gathered. Since they had nothing to eat, Jesus called his disciples to him and said, [2]'I have compassion for these people; they have already been with me three days and have nothing to eat. ³ If I send them home hungry, they will collapse on the way, because some of them have come a long distance.' ⁴ His disciples answered, 'But where in this remote place can anyone get enough bread to feed them?' ⁵ 'How many loaves do you have?' Jesus asked. 'Seven,' they replied.

⁶ He told the crowd to sit down on the ground. When he had taken the seven loaves and given thanks, he broke them and gave them to his disciples to distribute to the people, and they did so. ⁷ They had a few small fish as well; he gave thanks for them also and told the disciples to distribute them. ⁸ The people ate and were satisfied. Afterward the disciples picked up seven basketfuls of broken pieces that were left over. ⁹ About four thousand were present. After he had sent them away, ¹⁰ he got into the boat with his disciples and went to the region of Dalmanutha.

The account in Matthew 15: 29-39 reads:

²⁹ Jesus left there and went along the Sea of Galilee. Then he went up on a mountainside and sat down. ³⁰ Great crowds came to him, bringing the lame, the blind, the crippled, the mute and many others, and laid them at his feet; and he healed them. ³¹ The people were amazed when they saw the mute speaking, the crippled made well, the lame walking and the blind seeing. And they praised the God of Israel.

³² Jesus called his disciples to him and said, 'I have compassion for these people; they have already been with me three days and have nothing to eat. I do not want to send them away hungry, or they may collapse on the way.' ³³ His disciples answered, 'Where could we get enough bread in this remote place to feed such a crowd?' ³⁴ 'How many

## Figure 5. What Route Did Jesus Take to Get Back to Galilee?

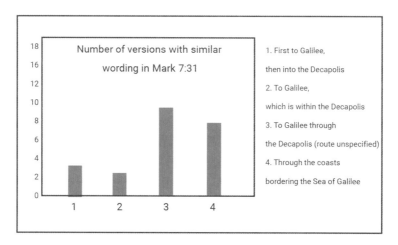

Number of versions with similar wording in Mark 7:31

1. First to Galilee, then into the Decapolis

2. To Galilee, which is within the Decapolis

3. To Galilee through the Decapolis (route unspecified)

4. Through the coasts bordering the Sea of Galilee

## Figure 6. Approaching Hippos from the East

Source: https://www.archaeological.org/

loaves do you have?' Jesus asked. 'Seven,' they replied, 'and a few small fish.'

[35] He told the crowd to sit down on the ground. [36] Then he took the seven loaves and the fish, and when he had given thanks, he broke them and gave them to the disciples, and they in turn to the people. [37] They all ate and were satisfied. Afterward the disciples picked up seven basketfuls of broken pieces that were left over. [38] The number of those who ate was four thousand men, besides women and children. [39] After Jesus had sent the crowd away, he got into the boat and went to the vicinity of Magadan.

Both Gospel writers distinguish between the feeding of 5,000 on a grassy slope near the north shore of the Sea and the feeding of 4,000 on a remote and probably rugged slope near the eastern slope of the Sea. Many scholars now think that the 4,000-episode was in the Decapolis and that the people in the crowd included many who were not Jews. A crowd from Hippos would have answered this description. The reference to the "God of Israel" in Matthew is suggestive of curious non-Jewish listeners.

## CONCLUSION

Although not mentioned in the Gospels, Hippos/Susita is the most likely Decapolis city associated with Jesus' ministry. The Decapolis played a small but essential role in the geography of places where Jesus walked. Most especially, it brought into contact with Jesus people who probably were not Jews. In this sense, along with the Syro-Phoenician woman in Tyre, the listeners from the Decapolis were the first non-Jewish people to encounter the teachings of Jesus.

## REFERENCES

Andrews, Samuel J. 1923. "The Demoniacs at Gergesa." *The Life of Our*

*Lord Upon the Earth Part III.* New York, NY:   Reproduced by and available through Amazon, 2017.

Editor. "Gadarenes, Girgesenes, Gerasenes," *Bible Gateway Dictionary.* www. Bible Gateway.com/resources/dictionaries.

Eisenberg, Michael. 2017. *Hippos of the Decapolis and Its Region: 18 Years of Research.* Haifa: Michmanim. December 27.

Hitchcock, Roswell D. 1869. "Gergesenes." *An Interpreting Dictionary of Scripture.* New York, NY: Prager.

Jol, Harry M., Gloria I. Lopez, Haim Cohen, and Michael Artzy. 2014. "Initial GPR Exploration Near the Anchorage of Kursi, Sea of Galilee, Israel." GSA Annual Meeting in Vancouver, British Colombia. October, Paper No. 95-8.

Meyers, Eric M. and S. Thomas Parker, Eds. 2016. "Decapolis." *The Oxford Encyclopedia of Archeological Excavations in the Near East.* Oxford Biblical Studies Online. Nov. 14.

*New International Version of the Bible.* 1983. Grand Rapids, MI: Zondervan/ Harper-Collins.

Segal, A., J. Mlynarczyk, M. Burdojewicz, M. Schuler, and M. Eisenberg. 2009. *Hippos-Susita: Tenth Season of Excavations.* Haifa: Zimmer Institute of Archaeology, University of Haifa.

Segal, Arthur and Michael Eisenberg. 2006. "The Spade Hits Susita" *Biblical Archaeology Review.* 32 (3): 41-51, 78. May-June.

# Israel and Phoenicia: Wary Neighbors Over Three Millennia

Dorothy Drummond

## INTRODUCTION

When Jesus visited Tyre and Sidon nearly two thousand years ago, the two Phoenician coastal cities already had been in existence for more than two millennia. Although the region now known regionally as the northern Levant and politically as Lebanon was called Phoenicia in Jesus' time, that term was then only about five hundred years old. It had been given to the region by the Greeks at the time when they were rivaling the Phoenicians for Mediterranean trade. *Phoenicia* means "Purple Land," a reference to the purple dye derived from the murex snail, for which the region was famous throughout the ancient world. Before that there was no regional name. There were only the names of its chief city-states: Byblos, Sidon, Tyre, and others. For most of the 3,000 years that Israel and Phoenicia have been neighbors, their relationship has been wary; yet during the time of David and Solomon, the two entities were in productive symbiosis.

### Kana'an/Canaan, From Expansive Occupance to Thriving Maritime Settlement

During the second millennium B.C.E., Phoenicia had been the prospering maritime edge of a large area occupied by the Kana'an, a Semitic people genetically cousins to the Hebrews. Linguists trace the origin of both people to Mesopotamia. In the second millennium, while the Hebrew tribes by tradition were toiling in Egypt, the Kana'an occupied land from the Mediterranean Sea eastward beyond the Jordan and from the Negeb north to Syria. The Kana'an are known in the Old Testament accounts as the Canaanites.

As the second millennium was drawing to a close, the Israelites were two hundred years into their tribal struggle to occupy the land that tradition told them was theirs from the time of Abraham. The Tribe of Zebulon had bordered on Sidon, and the tribe of Asher had claimed, but did not subdue, land that was within the territory of Tyre. Most of the Canaanites who once occupied the plateau, defeated in battles by the hardened nomadic Israelites, had retreated to the coastal littoral, and there they prospered.

Bordered on the east by the nearby Lebanese ranges, the coastlands offered only a narrow coastal plain suited to farming or grazing. Instead of farming, the Kana'an migrants turned to the sea, settling in and around Tyre, Sidon, and other coastal cities, and following their kinsmen in seafaring and craft traditions already a thousand years old (Figure 1). The Mediterranean was their lake. Kana'an mariners were accomplished traders, and Kana'an craftsmen spun fiber, dyed thread and wove cloth, hammered copper, combined tin and copper into bronze, and created objects of beauty from ivory and gold. In exchange for their wares, the Kana'an merchants purchased grain and olives, wine and dried fruit, and Kana'an mariners and traders carried raw materials and value-added products throughout the ancient world. Among their trading partners were the Israelites.

At the beginning of the first millennium B.C.E., Tyre and Sidon were the leading city-states in Canaan, and as such they were rivals. Sidon was older by far, and Tyre had been its daughter. Separated by only 26 miles, they were independent entities, in competition with one another for trade. Both faced the sea, and both maintained harbors. Both became the target of conquerors. From about 1000 to about 500, Tyre was in its

Figure 1. The Commercial Network of the Phoenicians

ascendancy, chiefly because of its geographical situation. Whereas Sidon faced the sea from an unprotected shoreline, Tyre used its mainland position only as an adjunct to its island headquarters, 600 yards offshore. The island was small, fortified with a wall, and favored with two sheltered harbors. Here lived both the craftsmen and the mariners. The mainland was tributary. But what the Tyrians and Sidonians lacked was foodstuffs and raw material.

## Kana'an Connections with Israel in the Reigns of David and Solomon

On the plateau to the southeast, by 1000 B.C.E. the Hebrews had learned to farm their good lands and pasture their hillsides. A few villages were becoming towns, a hierarchy of wealth and power was evolving, and the demand was growing for luxury goods. Merchants from Tyre and Sidon were plying their wares to the Hebrews. To pay for these imports, landlords levied taxes-in-kind on their tenants, and a measure of Hebrew grain and olive oil, honey, wine and wool entered trade. Threaded through the Old Testament are accounts of the contacts between the Hebrews and the people of Kana'an on the coast, mostly with the Tyrians and to a lesser extent with the Sidonians. The accounts reveal much about both communities.

The first biblical mention of Sidon is found in the Book of Judges, as "oppressors of Israel" (probably offering guerrilla resistance as the Israelites came to dominate the land). The first biblical mention of Tyre is in the story of David, who had been successful in battle. David was carving out an empire, and on the coast, a young Tyrian king named Hiram was impressed. David had managed to wrest a part of Jerusalem from the Jebusites, a Canaanite people who were still holding on. He wanted to build a palace there. But David and his men, skilled in battle, lacked the sophistication, let alone the building materials, to build a palace worthy of an up-and-coming monarch.

Hiram offered to help David. He had cedar from the mountains backing his territory, men to fell the trees and convert them to planks, teamsters and mariners to transport the planks by land and water, and craftsmen to build the palace. All these he offered David. David accepted, and in return he offered foodstuffs. The Tyrians built David's palace. David told Hiram that what he really wanted to do is build a sanctuary for the Ark of the Covenant, presently housed in a tent, and he had an idea for how the sanctuary should look. It should look like the temple that Hiram had built for Melqart, the god of Tyre. Hiram took an interest in David's God. David bought from the Jebusites a building site for the temple he wanted to build. But David had blood on his hands, the blood of battle, and his God did not allow him to build the sanctuary. When David died and his rule passed to Solomon, Hiram continued the relationship.

With Hiram's help, Solomon carried out David's plan and built the Temple in Jerusalem, but not before the materials to do so could be assembled. Bronze was essential. Tyrian fleets passed through the Pillars of Hercules into the Atlantic to reach the tin deposits of southern Britain, to be combined with copper from Cyprus and the mines of the Sinai to make bronze. Silver they could get from Tartessos (Tarshish) in Spain. Specially-built ships, called Ships of Tarshish, were designed to carry this heavy cargo. But Hiram, with a large sea-going fleet, also craved an outlet to the Red Sea and the Indian Ocean.

Figure 2. Solomon's Temple Built with Help from Tyre

## Tyre's Help in Building the Temple

Solomon had a southern port at Ezion-Geber (now Eilat), giving access to the Red Sea, but he lacked knowledge of the sea. At Ezion-Geber, Hiram helped Solomon to build a sea-going fleet, helped train his men, and also built his own fleet there. The combined sea-going fleets set out on a three-year voyage to eastern Africa and "Ophir." Most probably Ophir was in India or Sri Lanka. When they returned, the fleet was laden with gold, precious stones, ivory, and especially tropical hardwood. These materials, together with bronze and cedar wood, went into the building of the Temple. To manage the construction and its exquisite embellishments and to cast the bronze, Hiram sent Solomon skilled workers, led by his top craftsman, also known as Hiram, the son of a Hebrew woman and a Tyrian man.

The Temple was rectangular, 27 meters long by 9 meters wide, built of tropical hardwood (Figure 2). Most probably it was constructed as the Tyrians knew how to do it, for they had built a temple to Melqart. Solomon's Temple had an outer hallway, a central open courtyard, and a Holy of Holies. The walls of the inner sanctuary were covered with gold leaf. At the entrance to the Temple were two bronze pillars, 15 meters tall, probably similar to those of Melqart's temple chronicled by the third century Hellenistic observed Menander, who used papyrus records then still available in the archives of Tyre. Menander's writings are now lost to us, but Josephus was able to draw on them in the first century C.E.

Hiram's craftsmen working on the Temple constructed the following, as recorded in 1 Kings 7: 13-50:

> Two winged creatures, wings outspread, in the Holy of Holies, of olive wood
> An altar of bronze
> Two bronze entrance columns, 15.5 meters tall
> A bowl-shaped capital on top of each column
> A design of interwoven chains on each capital
> 400 bronze pomegranates in two rows of a hundred each around each capital
> Ten bronze carts
> Thirty gold basins
> A thousand silver basins
> A large bronze tank to hold water
> Twelve bronze bulls to support the tank
> Pots, shovels, and bowls of bronze

To build the Temple Solomon needed hordes of unskilled workmen as well as the craftsman that Hiram supplied. For this purpose, Solomon pressed into service Canaanites still living in the land.

What did Hiram get in exchange for all his help? In addition to foodstuffs, wool, and hides, and continued access to the Red Sea, Solomon gave him title to 20 villages in Galilee, adjacent to the northern part of Hiram's territory. But after he saw the villages, Hiram was disappointed.

With sarcasm, he asked, "So these, my brother, are the towns you have given me." For this reason the area came to be called "worthless."

To strengthen the bond between Sidon and Israel, Solomon entered into a matrimonial alliance with Sidon. In this way Ashteroth (Asherah/Astarte), goddess of the Phoenicians, entered Israel along with gods of the other "foreign" wives who lived in Solomon's palace.

### Israel and Kana'an During the Divided Kingdom

Tyre is next mentioned in Scripture about a half-century after Solomon's domain had split into the Northern Kingdom of Israel and the Southern Kingdom of Judah which occurred in 933 (Figure 3). At this point the Kingdom of Tyre, now Tyre-Sidon, was prospering under the rule of a king named Ethbaal. His agrarian neighbor, the kingdom of Israel, was ruled by King Omri. The two kings had complementary interests. The newly affluent urban class in Israel's growing cities and towns were markets for the wares of Tyre, while Tyre could benefit not only from the output of Israel's fields and pastures but also from access to the ancient Kings Highway trade route to the east of Israel. Relations between Ethbaal and Omri were so good that they agreed that their children should marry.

After Omri died, his son Ahab succeeded him, and as promised he took the Tyrian princess Jezebel as his wife. For Israel, the marriage was a disaster. Jezebel brought with her into Israel the priests of the goddess Asherah, and she had the prophets of Ahab's God murdered. In allowing Jezebel to have her way, it may well have been that Ahab was trying to cement an alliance with her father at a time when the Assyrians were threatening. For Israel, this alliance would have helped. But Ethbaal, secure in his island fortress and unafraid of the Assyrians, saw no benefit in a military alliance. Jezebel's fortunes declined after the God of the prophet Elijah defeated the prophets of Baal-Asherah. Jezebel survived her husband's reign but was eventually herself murdered.

Figure 3. Israel and Phoenicia after the Death of Solomon

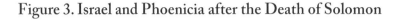

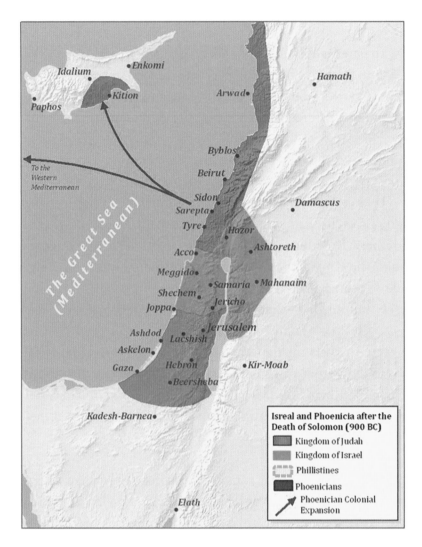

Figure 3. Israel and Phoenicia after the Death of Solomon

Meanwhile, in the Southern Kingdom of Judah, Tyrian influence spread when Ahab's daughter by Jezebel, Athalia, was married to King Jehoram in a treaty arrangement to heal the breach between the Northern and Southern kingdoms. Athalia (who may have been Ahab's sister instead of his daughter) proved to be as much of a tyrant as Jezebel. She looted Solomon's Temple to build a monument to the Tyrian god Melqart. After seizing the throne of Judah briefly, she met the same fate as Jezebel.

## The End of Cordial Ties with Tyre

With the death of Athalia, the political connections between Tyre and Israel/Judah ceased. Tyre used its special island fortress position and its trade ties to make peace with the Assyrians, offering tribute in goods in exchange for freedom from direct rule. The Northern Kingdom, by contrast, was totally eliminated before the beginning of the seventh century, and the Assyrians carried off their people into permanent exile. The Assyrians also ravished the Southern Kingdom, but at the last minute, miraculously, they retreated. Jerusalem was saved and the Southern Kingdom lived on for another century. Contacts with Tyre continued, for the name Tyre appears often, and always in inimical terms.

From this time on, nothing that is said of Tyre in the Old Testament is positive. The power and wealth and widespread trade of Tyre are acknowledged, but the wickedness of the city merits God's wrath. Isaiah, writing probably while the Assyrians were threatening, prophesied (wrongly at the time) that "Tyre is destroyed and left without house or harbor." Joel, writing a hundred years later and just before the Exile, excoriated Tyre for selling the people of Judah as slaves to the Greeks. By this time Tyre was marketing slaves taken by the Assyrians and others. Presumably, some were from the vanquished Northern Kingdom as well as ravished areas of the Southern Kingdom. Ezekiel, exiled to Babylon at the beginning of the sixth century, railed against Tyre: "By the abundance of your trading you became filled with violence within, and you sinned…. You corrupted your wisdom for the sake of splendor…. You defiled your sanctuaries by the multitude of your iniquities." Ezekiel was certain the Babylonians would annihilate Tyre.

But the dire prophesies of Tyre's destruction by Isaiah in the eighth century and Ezekiel in the sixth century were premature. Although the land portion of Tyre fell victim, neither the Assyrians nor the Babylonians were able to destroy the Tyrian island fortress through seige. When the Judeans returned from 80 years of exile in Babylon, they found Tyrians in the land they must reoccupy. The Tyrians brought dried fish to sell, but probably not luxuries. The returned Judeans were an impoverished lot. And it may well be that after years of siege, Tyre was no longer able to produce finely crafted goods. Scripture does not indicate. But it does mention that Tyrians and Sidonians were among those who rebuilt the Temple. They lived among the Judeans under Persian rule.

## Phoenicia under Persian and Greek Rule

Tyre and Sidon in this period (530-330) were under first Persian rule, then Greek rule. The small Canaanite city-states and their territory came to be known in Greek writings as *Phoenicia*, and this name eventually prevailed (Figure 4). Under the Persians the Phoenician cities continued to trade, and the Persians used Tyrian nautical skills to build and help man their fleet in wars with the Greeks. But the starch had gone out of Phoenician polity. The Assyrians had badly damaged Sidon, and the Babylonians had laid a prolonged siege to Tyre, weakening the fortified island to such an extent that it never again dominated the Mediterranean. Its colony of Carthage thrived in the western Mediterranean for another three centuries, but largely out-of-touch with Tyre, the motherland.

In 333 Alexander appeared on the scene to contest Persian rule, and he knew he first had to subdue the Phoenician cities on his way to Egypt. He had no difficulty with Sidon, which surrendered without a fight. But Tyre resisted. Alexander was obsessed with Tyre. When its offshore fortress could not be reached by Greek arrows, and its walls and its navy withstood the challenge of siege, Alexander gave orders to his engineers: Build a causeway, 600 meters long, to connect the mainland with the island. It took seven months, for the channel was deep. At last Greek soldiers rushed across the completed causeway and in 332, massacred the Tyrians and razed the city. Ancient Tyre was no more.

From Tyre, Alexander proceeded to Jerusalem, still on his way to Egypt. He was welcomed by the Jewish citizens, and his soldiers did no damage. He allowed Persian law to continue, and in the realm of religion he had nothing to say. From then on, Greeks began to set up communi-

Figure 4. Phoenicia

Source: *National Geographic.*

ties in Palestine. Whether under the Egyptian Ptolemies or the Syrian Seleucids – the Greek kingdoms that followed Alexander – Greek ideas clashed with Judean ways, and the two peoples kept to themselves. The ties with Phoenicia were broken. However, wandering Tyrian merchants continued to offer dried fish, but the elegant commerce of the ancient past was over.

### Tyre and Sidon, the Cities That Jesus Visited, under Roman Rule

But Tyre did not disappear. Currents broadened the causeway, and people of Canaanite blood once again occupied the city. The city's maritime fortunes receded under the jurisdiction of the heirs to Alexander, first the Egyptian Ptolemys and then the Syrian Seleucids. The Romans took over Phoenicia in 63 B.C.E., and their engineers were impressed with the harbor at Tyre that in earlier times had served the city so well. They deepened the harbor and made Tyre the leading port in the eastern Mediterranean. Tyrian boatbuilders built the Roman fleet, as they had once built the Persian fleet. Once again Tyre became known for Tyrian Purple and for craftsmanship. Sidon, too, began to flourish, and the Romans built an artificial harbor there.

Secure under Roman rule, Tyre and Sidon were cosmopolitan entrepots, and the people who lived there were open to new ideas. These were the cities that Jesus and his disciples probably visited. Both Matthew and Luke say that Jesus went into the "borderlands" of Tyre and Sidon. In the first century, there was no travel barrier between Syro-Phoenicia of which Tyre and Sidon were a part and the Galilee ruled by Herod Antipas, where Jesus spent most of his ministry. In fact, the western part of Galilee was part of Syro-Phoenicia. Some Syro-Phoenicians had heard of Jesus. When Jesus preached to crowds in Galilee, among them were listeners from Tyre and Sidon. At one point Jesus had compared the faith of Tyrians and Sidonians favorably with that of the people of Bethsaida. In the borderland of Tyre he encountered a Greek-speaking Syro-Phoenician woman, a Canaanite (in other words, a Gentile), and healed her daughter. His disciples wanted him to push her away, but

Figure 5. Satellite Image of Tyre

Source: 2009 ORION-ME.

Jesus let the woman make her point: His ministry was to those who have faith, and not only to the Jews. From Tyre he traveled on to Sidon before returning to Galilee. Obviously, Jesus considered Phoenicia within the realm of his concern. Its inhabitants included the first of Gentile believers to be mentioned in Scripture. Thirty years later, the Apostle Paul put in at Sidon on his way from Caesarea to Rome.

## Two Thousand Years to the Present: Phoenicia and Israel

Today, two thousand years later, Phoenicia is now the country of Lebanon. The Lebanese people--descendants of the Phoenicians--retain the genes of the Canaanites who thrived as craftsmen and traders in the time of Hiram and Solomon. The ports of Tyre and Sidon are fairly silted and now handle only small fishing boats (Figure 5). Sidon has swelled to a population of 164,000 while Tyre's population is 135,000. They are Lebanon's third and fourth cities in size. Beirut, the capital, with a metropolitan population of 3.2 million, is much larger. Tourism in Tyre and Sidon is of some importance, but the only evidence of antiquity is Roman, and it is considerable. The largest hippodrome in Roman Asia was in Tyre. Nothing, however, remains of the Phoenicians. In recent centuries, the Lebanese have emigrated to distant lands as small tradesmen, a legacy of their ancestral past.

A small part of the population of Tyre and Sidon is Maronite (Catholic) Christian, a legacy of the earliest first-century converts and of the dominance of Christianity during the three centuries of Byzantine rule. However, most of the population is Shi'a Muslim and has been since the seventh century C.E. During the Crusader period in the twelfth century, the port of Tyre traded with Venice and Genoa and was one of the main Crusader entry points to the Holy Land. In the following centuries, Phoenicia became something of an Ottoman backwater.

French rule followed World War I, and for a few decades Beirut thrived as the cosmopolitan banking and tourist center of the Middle East. Palestinian refugees fled into southern Lebanon in 1948, and many of them are still housed in crowded UNRWA refugee settlements in and around Tyre and Sidon. For a while in the 1970s and 1980s, Lebanon was the headquarters of Palestinian resistance.

In 1982, with help from Lebanese Christian parties, Israel forced the Palestinian troops to leave Lebanon. For security, however, Israel occupied the southern part of the country, including Tyre and Sidon. Israeli troops pulled out in 2000, but the northern border of Israel is only 20 miles from Tyre. Israeli settlements near the border in Galilee are on guard against incursions from the north. Hezbullah, the Shi'a army that got its start in the southern region of Tyre and Sidon but now literally controls all of Lebanon, is heavily supported by Iran. Today, Israel considers Hezbullah one of its greatest threats.

For more than three thousand years, the peoples of Phoenicia and Israel have been wary of one another. They still are.

## REFERENCES

Drummond, Dorothy. 2013. "Ezekiel's Tyre" and "The Oracles Against Tyre." In William A. Dando, Caroline Z Dando and Jonathan J. Lu, Eds. *Geography of the Holy Land: New Perspectives.* Kaohsiung, Taiwan: Holy Light Theological Seminary Press, pp 174-200.

Finkelstein, Israel and N. Na'aam. 1994. *From Nomadism to Monarchy: Archaelogical and Historial Aspects of Early Israel.* New York, NY: Biblical Archaeological Society.

Golden, Jonathan M. 2009. *Ancient Canaan and Israel: An Introduction.* New York, NY: Oxford University Press.

Halpern, B. 1983. *The Emergence of Israel in Canaan.* Riga, Latvia: Scholars Press.

Mascati, Sabastian. 1999. *The World of the Phoenicians.* London: Phoenix Giant.

Noll, K. L. 1992. *Canaan and Israel in Antiquity.* Princeton, NJ: Princeton University Press.

Stern, Ephraim. 2017. "Phoenicia and Its Special Relationship with Israel." *Biblical Archaeology Review,* 43:6 November/December.

_____. 2000. *The English Standard Version Bible.* New York, NY: Oxford University Press.

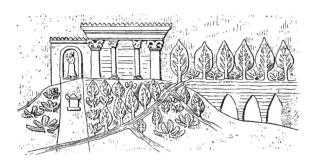

# PART THREE

## Urban Food Security, Urban Warfare, and

## Famine

*. . . sit under one's own vine and one's own fig tree' was a proverbial expression among the Israelites to denote peace and prosperity*

1 Kings 4: 25; Micah 4: 4; Zechariah 3: 10

Food requirements of the Roman Empire, agricultural specialization, improvements in the road network, and advancements in food processing led to a rural-to-urban migration which shifted many Israeli farmers from food-producing subsistent barter or local market economies to limited food-consuming monetized Empire-wide economies. In a land of "milk and honey," within one of the most supportive climatic-types for growth of life-supportive nutritious foods, Palestine was converted to a land of people surviving on vitamin and mineral-deficient diets and experiencing debilitating health problems under Roman and Herod the Great's rule. A small reduction in the availability of low cost basic foods increased diet-based health problems and led to deaths by starvation and disease. This resulted in great political discontent, assassinations, riots, revolution, and war. Millions died in the process. Food and food deprivation issues were so important to the residents of the Promised Land that more than 500 Scripture passages in the Bible are devoted to food.

Warfare in the Bible almost always had a religious or ideological basis. The term "war" is mentioned more than 140 times and "peace" 260 times in the Bible. Siege warfare brought out the most brutish and bestial nature of human beings. William A. Dando and Lara M. Dando introduce Part Three with a chapter on urban food security, siege warfare, and famine in the Holy Land. Jonathan J. Lu then provides insights into the conquest of Canaan and Israelite urban warfare practices. In his chapter, Perry G. Phillips uses maps to describe the urban-based defense strategies of Judean kings. This chapter is followed by William A. Dando and Caroline Z. Dando's chapter in which they define the term "parable" and demonstrate how Jesus utilized the parable to mold his message through events in an agricultural year and in difficult rural food times. Shifting emphasis, William A. Dando and Bharath Ganesh Babu review food security in the Roman Empire, faith-based response to urban famine needs, and the 46 C.E. famine in Jerusalem. Finally, William A. Dando and Lara M. Dando describe urban warfare in Samaria and Jerusalem during periods of civil unrest and siege warfare.

# Religion and Siege Warfare in the Holy Land

William A. Dando and Lara M. Dando

## INTRODUCTION

All societies depend on a common ideology for their unification and existence. Societies are bonded by a set of beliefs, sentiments, and values that set them apart from other societies. In some societies, religion, humans' belief in a supreme being that arouses their feelings of awe, security, piety, and dependence, is an all-pervading force. A religion produces a distinct attitude towards life. International political differences often have a religious or belief undertone. Those leading nation states believe that their way of life or religion is a source of power that guides them or aids them in warfare. Warfare, as described in the Bible, almost always had a religious or ideological basis. The earliest known account of a military campaign was that of an Egyptian invasion of Canaan in the twenty-fourth century B.C.E. The Holy Land was not a rich or populous area of the world. However, its location became a prize for a wide array of conquerors.

### Judaism

There have been countless periods of intense discrimination and wars between countries because of religious or belief differences and antagonisms. In recent years, discord between Semitic groups in the Middle East has led to great loss of life and even possible threat of a World War. Among the Semitic tribes that wandered through steppes and desert margins of the Middle East 3,900 years ago were the ancestors of the Jews and Moslems of today. Abraham and his people set out from Ur in southern Mesopotamia, settled briefly in Palestine, went to Egypt, and returned to Palestine and Arabia. What distinguished the Hebrews from other groups in the Middle East at that time was their commitment to one god. This exclusive monotheism, together with strict ethical and civil laws, welded the Jews and later the Moslems into distinct and closely knit religious communities (Figure 1).

The end of the ancient Jewish state came in 586 B.C.E. when "many gods-believing" (polytheistic) Babylonian conquerors invaded Judea, destroyed Jerusalem, and sent the Jews into exile. They did return later, but the Jewish revolt against the Romans in 70 C.E. led to their complete dispersal from the land promised by their God to Abraham. From 70 C.E. until the end of the eighteenth century, Jews in Europe suffered personal humiliation, discrimination, expulsion, or massacres (Broek and Webb 1968).

## Christianity

Under intense oppression, most Jews believed that nothing could save them but the Messiah. They differed, however, on how this "kingdom on earth" might come about. Some believed by force of arms and others by spiritual regeneration. In approximately 4 B.C.E., a child (Jesus) was born in Bethlehem, Judea, who was eventually called the Messiah (Figure 2). According to Scripture, Jesus' teaching contained many elements of Judaic thought, but it was based on love of God, ethical thought, and a message of hope for all people on earth. A convert of Jesus, Paul gave Jesus' gospel to the downtrodden of the Greco-Roman civilization and

provided an organization that welcomed all. Actively persecuted until the early 300s C.E., Christianity became the state religion of the Roman Empire. The spread of Islam greatly affected Christianity in North Africa, the Middle East, and parts of Asia.

Christianity became the prominent religion in Western and

Eastern Europe in 1300. However, it lost most of the Iberian Peninsula to Islam in 712. Moslem rule lasted there from 700 to almost 1500. In 1600, religious strife in Europe centered on issues of religious authority, Roman Catholic Church dogma, and interpretation of the Scriptures. Demands and movements for church reform were common in all countries of Roman Catholic Europe. The break from Rome led to the establishment of national Protestant churches. It has been suggested that the rise of the middle class in northwestern Europe, associated with capitalism and free enterprise, led to Protestantism. Protestantism has been defined as a set of religious values including compliance of the teachings of Jesus Christ, hard work and thrift, individual freedom and fair competition, the profit motive based on strict moral ethics, and denial of the non-Bible-based commandments and dogma of the Roman Catholic Church.

## Islam

*Islam*, meaning "submission to God," had its origin in Mecca, the main transfer point on ancient caravan routes from southern Arabia to Syria. Mohammed, the founder, combined elements of Judaic and Christian dogmas and ethics into a new religion. The keystone of this religion was "there is no god but Allah." Mohammed taught that Allah had revealed Himself to previous prophets but insisted that he had received the definitive truth. His revelations were written down and gathered in the Koran. At the time of Mohammed's death (632 C.E.), all of Arabia was under his rule. In less than 100 years, Arab Moslem expansion conquered lands from the Atlantic Ocean to the borders of India. They conquered thriving Christian nations and vibrant Jewish communities. In the following centuries, Islam spread to India, Central Asia, Southeast Asia, and parts of Africa.

Islam was born in the desert. The Koran and Islam reflect this environment and harshness of survival in a severe water-scarce land. The victorious Arab armies brought Islam and Arab culture to the new physical environments and cultural areas which they controlled. If Christians and Jews of these conquered areas surrendered peacefully but resisted conversion to Islam, they were given protection as non-citizens upon payment of a tax. Those who resisted Islamic rule were converted to Islam at "sword's point" (Makhlouf 1988).

## INITIAL ANTAGONISMS

These three major religions, Judaism, Christianity, and Islam, had their origins in the Holy Land. Judaism and Jewish religious practices, including circumcision, temple worship, dietary laws, commandments, and 613 *mitzvots* (or commands) that all faithful Jews were required to follow, limited widespread international acceptance. Christianity brought freedom from these laws to those who believed in one God, freedom from human traditions and human restrictions not given by God. Islam, revealed to Mohammed through revelations, was gathered into a holy book, the *Koran*. It contained not only religious doctrines and rules of worship but pronouncements on worldly matters. The Koran is the fountainhead of Moslem law. All who observe the defined "Five Pillars of Faith" were considered brothers in the Moslem community – a community without restrictions of color or caste.

## HISTORIC CAUSES OF WAR IN THE HOLY LAND

Located on the main land bridge between Eurasia and Africa and controlling access to the Mediterranean Sea from Mesopotamia, the Holy Land was the site of constant wars by rival empires and religious zealots with dreams of earthly kingdoms (Figure 3). The term "war" is mentioned 140 times in the Bible and the term "peace," 257 times. The books of Joshua and Judges describe early Israelite warfare against the Canaanites and Philistines as simple events (Dando and Babu 2013). David and Solomon's military ventures were larger in scope and resulted in the formation of a large and powerful "Kingdom of Israel." The division of Solomon's kingdom into Israel in the north and Judah in the south weakened both, as did continuous warfare between the two kingdoms. Assyria, a nation devoted to an ideology of war, captured Israel and deported thousands of Israelites in 721 B.C.E., and in 586 B.C.E., the

Babylonians captured Judah and did the same.

The invasion into the region by Alexander the Great in the fourth century and the capture of the Persian Empire brought some relief for the Jews. However, when Alexander died, his empire was divided and two of his successors fought six "Syrian wars" over the Holy Land. A Jewish revolt against their Greek ruler, Antiochus IV, over religious issues and persecution in 167 B.C.E. resulted in an independent Jewish state which survived until 37 B.C.E. Internal divisions in Judea in 37 B.C.E. led the Romans to depose the last Hasmonean ruler in favor of Herod the Great. The Jews did not like Roman rule or Herod and they rebelled. In every instance, Roman military forces triumphed despite remarkable defenses at places such as Jerusalem and Masada. Eventually the Jewish remnants were dispersed throughout the Mediterranean world and the Middle East. At the time of the collapse of the Roman Empire, less than 5 percent of the world's Jews lived in Palestine (Goodrick and Kolenberger 1981).

## SIEGE WARFARE: A BASIC DEFENSE TACTIC

Historically, a facet of urban warfare was creating a protracted total shortage of food in an urban center that would cause widespread diseases and food-deficit deaths from starvation for a large segment of those who sought safety behind urban defense fortifications/walls. Siege warfare brought out the most bestial and brutish nature of human beings. If the city defenses failed, the enemy looted, raped, and killed or took as slaves the members of the garrison and civilians (Kerrigan 2015).

Only eleven famines took place in ancient Israel between c. 1850 B.C.E. and 70 C.E. The first five famines were essentially rural and related primarily to shortages in pasturage. The last six famines claimed many, many lives and occurred in urban centers – all were created by invading armies and siege warfare. The most terrifying incidents of human suffering and depravity were recorded in Samaria, the capital of Israel, and in Jerusalem, the capital of Judea. In the Holy Land, with its

Figure 1. The Battle Between the Israelites and Amalekites

Source: Illustrators of the 1728 Figures de la Bible, Gerard Hoet (1648 – 1733) and others, published by P. de Hondt in The Hague in 1728, Wikimedia Commons

arid and semi-arid climates, where water was scarce and people clustered around water sources, warfare was and will be primarily focused on urban centers and rural settlements (Windrow 2009).

Military geographers believe that the greatest disadvantage the ancient Hebrews had in their efforts to conquer the land promised to them was their lack of understanding about siege warfare (David 1998). Canaan was a land of walled cities controlling water sources and trade routes. Fortified Canaanite cities were not totally captured until 300 years later, and the Hebrews initially were forced to settle in the sparsely populated central mountain core. Once Joshua's army and Moses' followers were dispersed in the highlands, the Philistine city-states along the Mediterranean coastal plain became a constant military threat. Philistine military technology was also advanced, and they had weapons made of iron. Hebrew hill-men's military equipment was made primarily of bronze, consisting of simple daggers and swords. It was not until approximately 1020 B.C.E., under Saul, a nation-protecting leader and king, were the Hebrew soldiers organized and modernized into a small professional army. Saul's successor, King David, expanded Saul's army into a regionally powerful army competitive in the Near East. Although King David was a very successful military commander, one of his major successes was the conquest of the strongly fortified and inaccessible city of the Jebusites, Jerusalem. In a study of siege warfare in ancient Israel, three military sieges seemingly stand out as the best examples of successful sieges and how non-combatants in captured cities were treated or fared, including Jerusalem in 1,000 B.C.E.; Lachish in 701 B.C.E.; and Masada in 73-74 C.E.

### Jerusalem, 1,000 B.C.E.

Jerusalem had existed as a city and fortress from the fourth millennium (Figure 4). At the time of David, it was the home of the Jebusites, a Canaanite tribe related to the Hittites and Amorites. Although David's army was small and ill-equipped, it was loyal, battle-tested, and experienced. However, Jerusalem was a natural fortress. Located on the crest of a mountain, at a height of about 2,500 feet on a natural rock escarpment, it was well defended and had solid walls, stout gates, and strong towers. David did not have military equipment to breach the walls, and his troops were vulnerable to arrows and missiles launched by the defenders. He did have archers and rock slingers. After hearing the taunts and derisive jeers from the defenders, David launched a diversionary assault on the walls. Then he commanded his main force, under the cover of archers and rock-slingers, to make a sudden mass rush at what he perceived to be the weakest section of the city wall. His troops managed to secure this segment of the city wall and were able to withstand a fierce counterattack.

After desperate close-quarter fighting, the defenders retreated, David's men entered the city, and the inhabitants surrendered. David did not kill the defeated city dwellers or the Jebusite king. Instead he treated the defeated defending garrison leniently and paid landowners for private land seized in the capture of the city. David made Jerusalem the capital of a united Israel. The city's location, between the northern tribe and the southern tribe of his kingdom and commanding the main trade routes between them, was of great benefit to subsequent kings of Israel (Dougherty *et al.* 2008).

## Lachish, 701 B.C.E.

Judah became subordinate to the Assyrians after they destroyed the northern state of Israel in 724 B.C.E. Hezekiah, the farsighted king of Judah, quickly began to defend his country by refortifying Jerusalem, guaranteeing its water supply in case of a siege and improving the defenses of cities and towns throughout Judah. He also requested support from Egypt if Judah was invaded. When King Sennacherib of Assyria did invade Judah in 701 B.C.E., King Hezekiah did not attempt to attack the Assyrian army. He hoped that Judah's many strong fortresses would wear down the Assyrians until they gave up and retreated from Judah. Initially it seemed that Judah might be spared. An Egyptian relief force arrived, ambushed Sennacherib's army, and for a short period of time, halted the Assyrian invasion. Unfortunately, the Assyrians were able to regroup and renewed their invasion into Judah.

The first major obstacle Sennacherib faced was Lachish which blocked a major western approach to Jerusalem (Smith 1884). Lachish was a formidable fortress built on a high steeply sloped mound. Surrounding the city was a double line of walls with square towers at regular intervals. The walls were constructed of solid stone, and wooden barriers were built on top of them to protect defending archers. All the surrounding slopes leading to the walls were paved with smooth slabs of rock making the slopes very difficult to climb. Only one narrow road led to the city making a massive assault impossible, and the gate to the

Figure 2. Jesus Entering Jerusalem

Source: The story of the Bible from Genesis to Revelaton, Wikimedia Commons

city was defended by two strong towers. Sennacherib's engineers began the siege by constructing a ramp near Lachish's main wall and close to the main gate. The defenders attempted to stop construction of the ramp utilizing arrows, spears, and rocks tossed down on the construction crew. The attackers' archers attempted to reduce the loss of workers by sniping at the defenders' archers. After the ramp had been completed, the attackers pushed a huge siege tower up the ramp and broke down a section of the wall. At the same time, Assyrian soldiers assaulted the city walls at other sites with siege rams and scaling ladders. Following several days of bloody hand-to-hand combat, the attackers entered the city and began the slaughter of the city defenders and male inhabitants. The victors looted the city. The captured leaders of the city were impaled, and artisans, women, and children were sent into Assyrian exile as slaves. Sennacherib then led his army to Jerusalem and began another siege. However, the defenses of Jerusalem were not tested because, according to the passage in 2 Kings 19: 35, "... that night the angel of the Lord went forth and slew a hundred and eighty-five thousand in the camp of the Assyrians, behold these were all dead bodies." Sennacherib fled Judah and returned home. He had captured 46 forts in Judah and deported 200,150 enslaved Judeans to Assyria (Herzog and Gichon 1997).

## Masada

The Jewish revolt against the Romans, begun in 66 C.E., ended in 70 C.E. with the storming of Jerusalem and the destruction of the Temple. However, small pockets of Jewish rebels remained and were captured, one by one. One Jewish fortress did hold out against the Romans. In this fortress, approximately 1,000 Jews, led by Eleazar ben Yair, were surrounded by over 7,000 Roman troops from the Tenth Legion. Masada, a last-resort refuge for King Herod in case he was deposed by Jewish revolutionaries, was built on a high mesa in the southern desert of Judah near the Dead Sea (Mould 1936). It had been captured by zealot rebels early in the rebellion and was now their final refuge. The last Roman campaign of the rebellion was to capture Masada and destroy it as a sanctuary for harassing raids in the surrounding area. The task fell to Lucius

Figure 3. Palestine in the Time of Christ

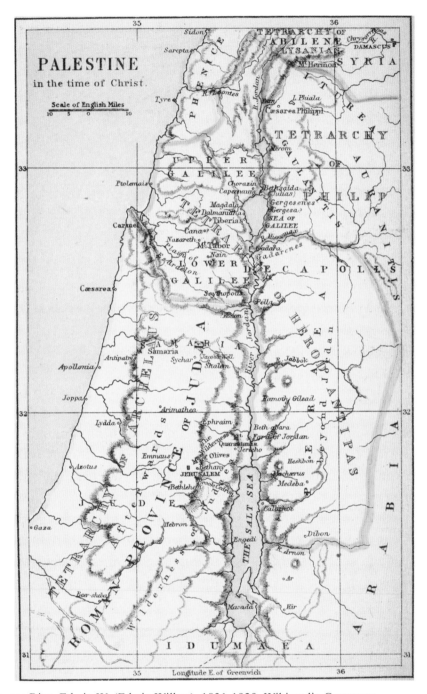

Source:Rice, Edwin W. (Edwin Wilbur), 1831-1929, Wikimedia Commons

## Figure 4. Jerusalem in the Time of Solomon

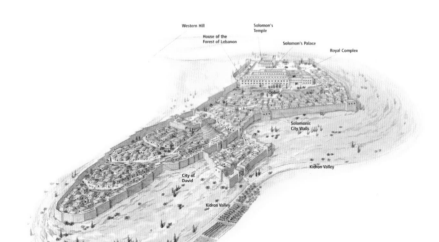

Flavius Silva, newly appointed Procurator of Judea.

The term *Masada* means "fortress" in Hebrew. It was formidable and well stocked with water, food, and weapons. There was no easy approach to this fortress from any direction, and there were only three narrow and difficult to climb paths to the top of the mesa. A wall had been constructed around the complete edge of the mesa, and heavily fortified gates guarded the top of each path (Tzu 2009).

In 72 C.E., the Romans surrounded the mesa, built eight camps and a wall connecting them, and attempted to starve the defenders to surrender. This tactic failed, and the Romans began a methodical, well-planned siege operation. The Romans were in no hurry, because Judah had been pacified. There were no threats to the Roman supply lines and no chance of relief for the defenders. Those defending Masada knew that if they surrendered, they would be crucified as a warning to others who might consider rebelling against Roman rule. They also knew that there was no escape for them (Hart 1967).

Silva made the decision to construct a gigantic ramp, employing Jewish slave labor and Roman soldiers. Construction began in the autumn of 73 C.E., and the ramp was completed in the spring of 74 C.E. The ramp enabled the Romans to push a siege tower up to the walls of the fortress. Once the battering ram reached the wall and created a breach, Roman soldiers entered Masada. The defenders did their best to prevent the Romans from entering the inner defenses of the fortress including constructing a second wall inside the fortress. However, the wall could not hold back the attackers. Soon it became obvious to all within Masada that the fortress would fall to the Romans, and all alive would be executed or crucified in a gruesome manner to demonstrate the futility of challenging Rome. Suicide was determined to be the only alternative. However, Judaism frowned upon suicide. The rebels conceived a way of killing each other until at the end, only one zealot had to kill himself. Apart from two women and five children who had hidden, there were no survivors left in Masada. The capture of Masada was the end of the Jewish Revolt of 66-74 C.E.

## WARFARE IN THE HOLY LAND FROM 74 C.E. – 1918

Almost all of the Jewish population of the Promised Land that were not massacred in the bloody Jewish Wars of 66-74 C.E. and in the Bar Kokhba rebellion of 132-135 C.E. were sold into slavery and deported to where slave labor was needed in the Roman Empire (Figure 5). The slow but complete economic, social, and political break-up of the Roman imperial system in 476 C.E. and the confusion and the bitter hostility between European cultural groups created a political vacuum that enabled the Moslem armies to conquer all of the Middle East, North Africa, and Spain by 720 C.E. Political and religious confusion in Western Europe led to the development of the "feudal system" and religious wars. Religious strife in the Moslem-controlled lands of the Middle East and North Africa produced countless local wars and revolutions. The Roman Church became a political body and political entity using the traditions of the Roman Empire as the basis for unity in Europe.

Figure 5. Titus and Plundering of the Temple

Source: https://en.wikipedia.org/wiki.

Meanwhile the Moslem Empire, from the Atlantic Ocean to South Asia, began to disintegrate. Fanatic "Green Flag" Moslems from Egypt captured Jerusalem from the moderate Moslems and interfered with Christian access to the Holy Sepulcher. The orthodox Seljuk Turks invaded the Middle East, destroyed the Byzantine army, and captured most of the lands controlled from Constantinople. Pope Urban II called for a "holy war," a crusade to rid the Promised Land and particularly Jerusalem, of the Moslems. On July 15, 1079, Jerusalem was captured. The slaughter of Moslem inhabitants was terrible – the blood of the conquered ran down the streets of the city. In 1147, the second crusade expanded Christian control of more land that became part of the Kingdom of Jerusalem. Saladin, a Kurdish Moslem and ruler of Egypt, preached a *jihad* or holy war of united Moslems against the Christians controlling Jerusalem and in 1189, Jerusalem was retaken. That same year, a third crusade failed to retake Jerusalem from Moslem control. Many crusades followed including a sixth crusade in 1228 when King Frederick II negotiated the surrender of part of the Kingdom of Jerusalem to him.

The Christians lost Jerusalem again in 1244 to the Sultan of Egypt. It was not until 1918, when the city was captured by a mixed force of French, British, and Indian troops, did Jerusalem become free of Moslem control (Wells 1956).

## MODERN CAUSES OF WAR IN THE HOLY LAND: 1918 TO THE PRESENT

The British, believing that they would govern post-World War I Palestine, issued a declaration advocating Palestine be the homeland for the Jews. The Balfour Doctrine of 1917 stated that the Jews would have a homeland and Arab rights were not to be lessened. Arabs in the Middle East began to fear the increase of Jews in their land during the interwar period. Soon the Arab Palestinians considered the British as anti-Arab and resented that other Arab mandates were given independence. When World War II ended, Jews in large numbers left Western Europe and settled in Palestine. The newly created Jewish Army, formed in part from Britain's Jewish Brigade, assisted new settlers relocate. The Palestinians received no payment for their land or homes. In response, they fled to other Arab countries, and the Arabs prepared for war against the new Jewish nation.

On May 14, 1948, Israel declared its independence. One day later, Arab nations surrounding Israel declared war. A hastily mobilized Israelite army responded with vigor. The Arab forces' invasion plan was to push the Jews into the Mediterranean Sea. The well-trained and British-equipped Jordanian Arab Legion advanced across the Jordan River and occupied the West Bank; Egyptian forces occupied the Gaza Strip; and Syria occupied the Golan Heights. Israeli forces made Jerusalem the focal point of their defense plan, and the Jordanians were only able to capture the eastern half of the city including the Temple Mount. The United Nations negotiated a peace settlement in 1949 in which Israel gained control of 50 percent more territory than they would have received under the old plan. However, the Old City of Jerusalem remained in Arab control. Israel survived the first attempt to eradicate them from their new homeland.

Nevertheless, the Arabs were determined to destroy this new nation. In 1956, Egypt blockaded the Straits of Tiran, Israel's outlet to the Red Sea, and its primary access to petroleum. Israel responded by invading Egypt and seizing the Sinai Peninsula and the Gaza Strip. The Egyptians were defeated. The Syrians, amazed and angry, continued to harass Israel and began to shell Israelite settlements from the Golan Heights. In response to numerous provocations, on June 5, 1967, Israel launched a surprise air attack on targets in Egypt, Jordon, and Syria. The war lasted only six days, and the Arabs accepted a U.N. Security Council ceasefire. From this defeat of Arab military forces, Israel gained the Sinai Peninsula, the Gaza Strip, the Golan Heights, and all lands west of the Jordan River – including all of Jerusalem (Figure 6).

The Jews were the winners of the initial Israeli-Palestinian wars, but the issue of a Jewish nation, surrounded by Arab nations, led to a much larger conflict. Leaders of Arab nations called on Moslems to fight a *jihad* or holy war against Israel. Al-Qaeda, an international move-ment founded by Osama bin Laden, promoted terrorism against Israel and against West European nations that supported Israel – especially the United States. Many oil-rich Arab rulers supported the actions of Al-Qaeda and terrorism as a means to destroy Israel. Moderate Moslems do not believe that jihad means war against Jews, Christians, or unbe-lievers (Drummond 2002). Many believe that it means a struggle or crusade against misrepresentation of God's word and radical Zionism.

## FUTURE WARFARE IN THE HOLY LAND

In an analysis of military actions in the Holy Land over the past 3,000 years, researchers have found that wars were multifactored in origin and can be grouped into three broad categories, i.e., (1) conflicts over control of the land bottleneck between ancient and modern empires and territories; (2) conflicts over control of the main land transportation and trade routes between Africa and Eurasia; and (3) conflicts over the control

Figure 6. Jerusalem Under Siege – 1967

Source: https://www.thenation.com/article/historians-war-six-day-war/.

of the minds and souls of believers (religions and ideologies). Wars of the future in the Holy Land will be continuous, cruel, and devastating to combatants and non-combatants, and engendering wars and acts of terrorism outside the Holy Land. Preventive wars will be necessary as instruments of "balance of power" politics. The problem of deterring war in the Holy Land, terrorism throughout the world, and eventually World War III, is as multifactored as the origins of war. It will require continuous international cooperation in commerce and trade, education, political activity and aspirations and military actions, legal practices to maintain tranquility between local and universal goals, cultural respect, and human good will.

Wars now fought in the Middle East and the Holy Land are insurrections against the world community and could lead to a nuclear war and the extinction of humankind on Earth. Present day misguided jihads are an endless and vicious form of modern indiscriminate urban warfare. They include unspeakable terrorism, suffering, and death to countless non-combatants, indiscriminate suicide bombings, absolute social disruption, use of worldwide social media, disregard for common decency, and internationally accepted codes of warfare, and a commitment to the extermination of cultures and non-believers. To eliminate this scourge, new military approaches and confidence-destroying tactics must be devised, new military training programs created, and new military hardware invented and utilized. The world needs endless peace and not endless war.

## REFERENCES

Broek, Jan O. M. and John W. Webb. 1968. *A Geography of Mankind.* New York: McGraw-Hill Book Company, pp. 128-132.

Dando, William A. and B. G. Babu. 2013. "Weather, Climate, and Warfare in Ancient Israel: 1900 B.C. to A.D. 70." In Dando, William A., Caroline Z. Dando, and Jonathan J. Lu, Eds. *Geography of the Holy Land: New Insights.* Kaohsiung, Taiwan: Holy Light Theological Seminary Press, pp. 259-289.

David, Saul. 1998. *Military Blunders: The How and Why of Military Failure.* New York: Carroll and Graf Publishers, pp. 62-71.

Dougherty, M. J., M. E. Haskew, P. G. Jestice, and R. S. Rice. 2008. *Battles of the Bible: 1400 B.C.--A.D. 73.* London: Amber Books Ltd, pp. 6-10, 122-131, and 206-215.

Drummond, Dorothy. 2002. *Holy Land Whose Land?* Seattle: Educare Press, pp. 195-197.

Goodrick, Edward W. and John R. Kolenberger III. 1981. *The NVI Complete Concordance.* Grand Rapids: Zondervan Publishing House, pp. 193-194 and 986-987.

Hart, B. H. Liddell. 1967. *Strategy.* London: Faber and Faber (A Signet Book), pp. 240-246, and 285.

Herzog, C. and M. Gichon. 1997. *Battles of the Bible.* London: Greenhill Books, pp. 19, 199-215.

Kerrigan, M. 2015. *Dark History of the Bible.* London: Amber Books, Ltd, pp. 111-132.

Makhlouf, G. 1988. *The Rise of Major Religions: The Human Story.* Englewood Cliffs, NJ: Silver Burdett Press, pp. 8, 24-35, and

36-47.

Mould, Elmer W. K. 1936. *Essentials of Bible History*. New York: The Ronald Press Company.

Smith, William. 1884. *A Dictionary of the Bible*. Chicago: The John C. Winston Company, p. 340.

Sun Tzu. 2009. *The Art of War*. London: Arcturus Publishing Limited, pp. 100-111.

Wells, H. G. 1956. *The Outline of History*. Volume II. New York: Garden City Books, pp. 533-554.

Windrow, M. 2009. *The Great Sieges*. London: Quercus Publishing Plc., pp. 9-20.

# The Conquest of Canaan and the Ai Campaign[1]

Jonathan J. Lu

## INTRODUCTION

Once the children of Israel entered into the "Promised Land" by crossing the Jordan River (Joshua 3-4), they gathered together at Gilgal. It was here that they celebrated the second Passover after they left Egypt; the first Passover had been observed in the Wilderness of Sinai (Deuteronomy 9: 1-5). They also renewed the covenant with Jehovah by performing the rite of circumcision (Joshua 5: 2-9). They took a few days, after all the excitement, to sort out important matters. For instance, the land into which they entered was neither empty nor devoid of people; the Canaanites were already there. Clashes and wars were likely to happen. With their full intention to occupy the land, the Israelites had to think wisely in charting their future course of action.

The Canaanites were higher in cultural achievements. They had already built cities with fortifications. The Israelites had to decide whether it would be wise for them to try to attack the Canaanite cities or simply to settle down quietly in the countryside. If taking the cities was considered to be the first order of priority, then which cities should be taken first? In the process of conquering the land, what would be their best strategy? In the individual encounters, what would be their best tactics? For these and other important matters, they had to consult with each other. Indeed, their commander, Joshua, met "the Commander of the Lord's army," and presumably, consulted also with him (Joshua 5: 14).

As a result of these consultations, the Israelites decided to take Jericho first and then to penetrate onward by way of Ai and Bethel, directly up to the hill country of the Central Highland to reach the region around Shechem, especially Mt. Ebal and Mt. Gerizim (Deuteronomy 27: 11-26; Joshua 8: 30-35; see Figure 1). There were, however, other routes by which one could reach the Shechem area. After the capture of Jericho, for example, they could have moved northward along the Jordan valley, and then followed Wadi Tirza (modern name) northwestward to the old "Patriarchs' Way" to reach Shechem (Har-El 1982, 87-101). Instead, they first made a humiliating attempt of attackng Ai. The attempt was to go from Jericho by way of Ai to the Central Highland.

Why by this way? Were there some strategic reasons which made them go up directly to the Central Highland from Jericho? Why was Ai so important that it warranted their first attack after Jericho? How was Ai taken? Or what tactics did the Israelites use to capture Ai? These then are some of the questions this chapter endeavors to answer. However, before looking into these questions, it is necessary to discuss a few theories concerning the conquest of Canaan and the settlement thereof by the Israelites.

## THREE THEORIES

With respect to the occupation or settlement of Canaan by the Israelites, scholars have advanced two interesting models in addition to what was recorded in the Bible. The Bible portrays the invasion of Canaan by the Israelites in a series of lightning military campaigns. It was en masse, systematic, and progressive: beginning with the defeat of the Amorite kings, Sihon and Og of Bashan, in Transjordan and ending with the destruction of the "allied" of Jabin in Upper Galilee. As a matter of practice, the Israelites, after conquering and destroying a Canaanite city, would build anew another city on top of the ruins. They also captured the environs of these cities and settled upon them. For this reason, this traditional, biblical approach is called by scholars, "the Conquest Model" (Malamat 1982: 25; Gottwald 1979: 192-203).

# Figure 1. Ai, the Gateway to the Central Highlands and Shechem

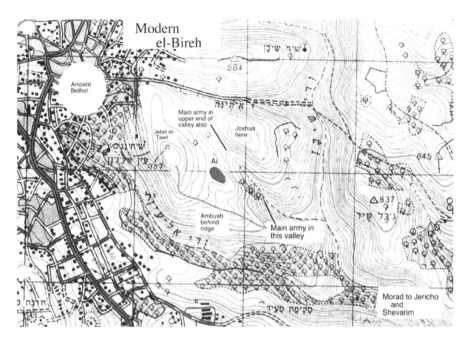

Source: Livingston, David. http://davelivingston.com/battleai.htm

In 1925, a German scholar, Albrecht Alt, initiated an idea that the settlement of the Israelites in Canaan was accomplished through a more subtle process of peaceful immigration that led to the settlement of the land (Alt 1967: 175-221; Noth 1960: 68-84; Weippert 1971: 128-29). According to Alt and as quoted in Weippert, individual clans of Israelites, as nomads (as some have alluded them to be), lived with their herds in the fringe area between the desert and the sown land. They were forced to penetrate into the cultivated land in summer when natural vegetations ceased to grow. They came with the understanding and permission of the owner of the cultivated land to graze their flocks in the harvested fields and in the woods. Only gradually and slowly did the Israelites expand into other parts of the land. It was by this process of immigration or infiltration that the Israelites achieved their "territorial expansion" (Weippert 1971: 6). For this reason, this approach is known as the "Immigration or Infiltration Model" (Gottwald 1979: 204-209).

This school of thought has gained quite a wide acceptance by scholars, among whom are several contemporary Israelis. Specific mention should be made of the late Professor Yohanan Aharoni who cited the peaceful relations between the Patriarchs and various cities as examples and who spoke convincingly of the transformation of the Israelites over several generations and through different stages, from semi-nomadic life into that of the sedentary farmers (Aharoni 1979: 191-275).

Another theory was advanced to interpret the occupation of Canaan by Israelites. This theory was initiated by George E. Mendenhall (1962: 66-87) who was of the opinion that:

> the Hebrew conquest of Palestine took place because a religious movement and motivation created a solidarity among a large group of preexistent social units, which was able to challenge and defeat the dysfunctional complex of cities which dominated the whole of Palestine and Syria at the end of the Bronze Age.

This idea was further developed by Norman K. Gottwald (1979: 210) who suggested that the Israelites who entered Canaan were:

> in fact composed in considerable part of native Canaanites who revolted against their overlords and joined forces with a nuclear group of invaders and/or infiltrators from the desert.

For this reason this theoretical model is known as "the Revolt Model" (Gottwald 1979: 210-219).

The approach by this writer, however, is based on the Conquest Model because of the following reasons. First, the field of geography of the Bible is unique in that it is based entirely on one book, the Bible (Lu 1979 & 1990). An approach as such, developed specifically for this field, should logically have its primary focus on the Bible. Second, the Bible tells that during a certain specified time, the Israelites entered into the land of Canaan, destroyed many of its cities, rebuilt and settled on them, and lived sometimes side by side with the Canaanites. Excavations today prove that archaeological evidences, by and large, do support the records found in the books of Joshua and Judges (Yadin 1982: 17-23). Furthermore, the *leitmotif* that runs throughout the Bible is one that holds that the land must be taken by military efforts. To this, the conquest model offers the closest parallel. Moreover, the model is found to be consistent with critical examinations of the biblical text.

## THE STRATEGY

The Israelites crossed the Jordan River from the east on the tenth day of the first month (Joshua 4: 19). It was in the spring, and "the spring was the season when wars usually began" (I Chronicles 20: 1, LB). Having observed the Passover and recovered from the wounds of circumcision at Gilgal, it was time for them to go forth to conquer and to possess the land as the Lord had directed.

Not far to the west of Gilgal, stood the city of Jericho, a formidable and heavily fortified Canaanite city. It was situated at the hub of the plains of Jericho as the most important regional center. Jericho posed a challenge to the Israelites. To test their military skills and to assure their corporate morale, they had to try to take Jericho as their first military objective in Canaan.

The instruction given to Joshua by the Lord, (Joshua 6: 2-5), was for all the men of war, as well as the priests, to march around the walled city of Jericho once a day for six days, and then seven times on the seventh day before they shouted for attack in battle. In the processional march, the armsbearing soldiers were to march in silence before the seven priests who were to blow their seven trumpets of rams' horns continually while marching. They were followed, in turn, by other priests carrying the Ark of the Covenant. Then after the Ark, came the rear guard.

Such an operation is highly psychological. In military terminology, it is called "conditioning" – conditioning the enemy by attracting their attention to the same repeated "field exercises" until the enemy's vigilance has relaxed and then strike them with a sudden and decisive blow. Furthermore, like modern Israeli military operations, the ancient Israelites knew also the importance of and how to employ the techniques of intelligence gathering and reconnaissance to avoid peril and to assure victory. In fact, while the Israelites were yet at Shittim, two spies had already been sent out by Joshua to "scout the land, especially Jericho" (Joshua 2: 1), to find out particularly the morale of the enemy. On this very matter, the great Chinese military strategist, Sun Tzu, wrote in his chapter on "Attack by Stratagem," that the purpose was to "know the enemy and know yourself, and you can fight a hundred battles with no danger of defeat [sic]" (Hart 1967: 28; Wu 1992: 55 and 209).

Careful reconnaissance, psychological warfare, and Divine help, coupled with an *esprit de corps* and a deep sense of purpose, were the decisive factors in the Israelites' victory. And the city of Jericho fell literally before them (Joshua 6:15-21). This first military action was a great success and their morale was elevated. A wise general would naturally take advantage of the momentum thus created, and Joshua again sent out agents to spy around Ai and its vicinity.

## Invading the Central Highland

Joshua's intention was to go directly up to the hill country of the Central Highland. There were several strategic reasons that the Israelites would want to get up to the highland as soon as possible. From a geographic point of view, namely terrain, the Central Highland offered the following advantages. First, the Israelites were militarily inferior to the Canaanites who, at that time, were already using chariots in their armed forces. The chariots found their operation optimum in the plains, but were rather restricted in the hilly country. By taking the mountains first, the Israelites would avoid exposing themselves unnecessarily and defenselessly to the Canaanite chariotry on the plains. Second, the

Israelites were lightly armed; the Central Mountain Massif would be a natural fortress on which they could depend to withstand the onslaught of the heavily armed Canaanites. Third, the mountainous terrain would preclude the deployment of heavily-armed Canaanites on the one hand, and give the lightly-armed Israelites, on the other hand, an opportunity to make up their deficiencies by a combination of stealth, cunning, daring, and mobility. Fourth, by keeping themselves to the mountains and away from the plains and the sites of the *Via Maris*, the Israelites would invite little danger of Egyptian interference (Herzog and Gichon 1978: 29-30; Malamat 1979: 25-52).

There were geopolitical considerations. First, while many fortified Canaanite city-states were located on the coastal plains and in the Jezreel and Jordan valleys, only a few were found in the highland (Cohn 1981: 27). The highland region would thus seem to offer the least resistance once the Israelites got to it. Second, the Canaanite city-states in the Central Highland had suffered a prolonged period of Egyptian military attack and colonial subjugation by thirteenth century B.C.E. Therefore, they were vulnerable to attack by the Israelites (Malamat 1979: 31; Malamat 1982: 29). Third, there were also ethnic disunities, animosities, as well as political and social differences among the Canaanite citys-tates. This was another situation which the Israelites did exploit (Malamat: 1982: 29).

"International" geopolitics of the time might also help them make the decision to hasten to the highland. First, the king of Shechem, it was reported, was working in league with the Israelites (the 'Apiru). He even admitted that one of his sons had actually joined the 'Apiru (Aharoni 1979). This alliance may help to explain two things: (1) Why there seems to be no conquest of the Shechem region in the biblical accounts. (2) The fact that soon after the destruction of Ai, Joshua was able to immediately build an altar to the Lord on Mt. Ebal (Joshua 8: 30) to fulfill what Moses had instructed him to do (Deuteronomy 11: 26-29; 27: 413). Second, the city-states in the Central Highland were not well organized "internationally." This explains the fact that Gibeon, Chephirah, Beeroth, and Kiriah-jearim were able to make treaties independently with the Israelites, while all the kings beyond the Jordan in the hill country and in the lowland conspired and gathered together to fight Joshua and Israel (Joshua 9: 1, 2; Malamat 1979: 29). Furthermore, the forested hill country of the Central Highland at that time probably was still sparsely populated. It not only offered less capability to curb the advancement of the Israelites but also, in fact, offered the best possibility for the Israelites to find room to settle (Alt 1967: 219-220).

## By Way of Ai

The aforementioned seemed to be the strategic reasons that the Israelites chose to first invade the Central Highland. Now there are several routes by which one could reach various parts of the Central Highland. The decision, however, was to reach this part of the Central Highland by way of Ai and Bethel. But why, among other possible alternatives, was Ai chosen to be approached first?

From a physiographic point of view, the Central Highland includes both the Judean Hills and the Samaria Hills. While the Samaria Hills centered around Shechem, the Judean Hills could be subdivided further into three subregions. These are, in order from the south, the Hebron Hills, the Jerusalem Hills, and the Bethel Hills, with the southern portion being the highest, and the Bethel Hills, in which Ai and Bethel are located, being the lowest. Farther north, the highland rises again into the Samaria Hills (Orni and Efrat 1973: 58-62).

The Bethel Hills region, which was allotted to the tribe of Benjamin because of its being the lowest portion on the Central Highland, is also known as the "Saddle of Benjamin." It is situated directly west of Jericho on the Central Highland. There are two major wadis, W. Makkuk and W. Qilt, leading down from the Bethel Hills to join the Jordan River, passing north and south of Jericho respectively. Perhaps, it was because of this "saddle" situation, together with relatively easy accessibility, that the Israelites chose to approach this part of the highland first.

Furthermore, Bethel was one of the three places on the Central Highland where the Patriarchs had actually lived. These places were, from north to south:

Shechem (Genesis 12: 5, 6; 33: 18-20; 35: 4),
Bethel (Genesis 12: 8; 13: 2-4; 28: 18, 19), and
Hebron (Genesis 13: 18; 23: 2, 15-17; 35: 27; 49: 29-32).

These "home-towns" naturally were the places the "returning" children were anxious to visit first. But both Hebron and Shechem were quite a distance farther to the south and north; only Bethel was situated to the west of Jericho.

Moreover, Bethel was located at the crossroads where the valley paths, leading up from Jericho, met the "Patriarchs' Way." Since Ai was located on the eastern edge of the Bethel Hills and occupied a look-out position, it naturally was the first target of attack by the Israelites. The Bible does not say which valley (wadi) or mountain slope the Israelites took to approach Ai. Of the two wadis near Jericho that reach the eastern slopes of the Bethel Hills, Wadi Qilt swings farther south to join its upper course, Wadi Suweinit, to reach the vicinity of modern Ramallah. Whereas Wadi Makkuk leads directly west to the hills and its upper course (or branch), Wadi el-Jaya, passes the north side of et-Tell to reach Bethel (modern Beitin). Therefore, it is possible that the Israelites might have followed Wadi Makkuk or along its slopes to reach Ai by Wadi el-Jaya (Kraeling 1956: 135).

## THE CONQUEST OF AI

The intelligence report about Ai was optimistic. There even was an air of over-confidence. "It was a small city," reported the spies, "and it won't take more than two or three thousand of us to destroy it; there is no point in all of us going up there" (Joshua 7: 3 LB). But something terribly wrong had happened. The Israelites were defeated by men of Ai at their first attempt although the casualties were relatively light – only thirty-six men died in battle. What went wrong?

## Problem in Communication and Breakdown in Discipline

Their defeat in the first attempt to capture Ai was shocking to the Israelites. There was a tremendous psychological setback. On the one hand, "the hearts of the whole congregation melted, and became as water" (Joshua 7: 5, RSV). On the other hand, the heart of the Commander trembled at thinking of the possible outcome of being surrounded by the Canaanites when they heard about this defeat (Joshua 7: 9). So Joshua cried out to the Lord for a possible answer.

The Lord's verdict was very concise: Israel has sinned (Joshua 7: 10-26). Sin leads to defeat. If victory was to be won, the sin must be dealt with. And so, Achan and all of his household – everything – were brought to the Valley of Achor (i.e., the valley of trouble or calamity). They were stoned to death and burned. Then the Lord ceased from his anger.

The Bible, with its emphasis on the moral issue and spiritual value, is very succinct about this matter. Malamat, however, based on a military point of view, attributed this defeat to "a major intelligence blunder" and "a breakdown in discipline" (1982: 30-31). According to him, the spies had erred on two counts. First, they underestimated the enemy's strength by saying "It was a small city" (i.e., there are not too many people in that city). In reality, Ai had 12,000 inhabitants (Joshua 8: 25). But size alone does not determine the strength of a military force. Second, they couched their report with military counsel by suggesting that "it won't take more than two or three thousand of us to destroy it." In military games, field agents give only reports, not counsel. Decisions on military operations belong not to field agents but exclusively to those in command.

From a historical perspective, military victory was often followed by looting, burning, and perhaps also with raping, unless the soldiers were rigid in discipline. The "sin of Achan" in the case of Jericho, according to Malamat, was due to "a breakdown in discipline at the time of the conquest of Jericho – specifically, to Achan's taking of loot which was under divine ban." This author, however, has the opinion that Achan did not pre-meditate to loot before the conquest of Jericho.

Furthermore, the miraculous defeat of Jericho and this glorious victory might have had its psychological effect on the command – perhaps no less than on the ranks. Elevated confidence tends to encourage over-looking the minute details which produce ignorance. There are three ways in which a ruler can bring misfortune upon his army, so writes Sun Tzu , in his chapter on "Attack by Stratagem": "when ignorant that the army should not advance; when ignorant of military affairs; [and] when ignorant of command problems" (Hart 1967: 28; Wu 1992: 51-53). In this case, Joshua was ignorant on two out of these three counts. He was ignorant of the fact that there was a breakdown in discipline, a command problem, and he was ignorant enough to order an advance of his troops when there was an inaccurate intelligence report. The result, as it may be expected, was defeat.

The setback at this first attempt on Ai, nevertheless, had its sobering effect. More important than intelligence gathering were discipline and morale. On the front line in the battlefield, the problem of disobeying an order often resulted in capital punishment for the offenders. And so, not only Achan, but also his entire household, were stoned to death. But how would Joshua restore the morale of his army?

The Israelites' past success had won for themselves a special place in the eyes of the Canaanites – "fear fell upon the Canaanites and all the inhabitants of the land melt away" before the Israelites (Joshua 2: 9). If these Canaanites heard about the defeat of the Israelites by the men of Ai, they might think of the invading Israelites as a bunch of "paper tigers"(a term used often in Chinese culture). Not only the image of the Israelites and the reputation of their commander-in-chief were at stake, but the Canaanites might also come, as in Joshua's own words, "and surround us, and cut off our name from the earth" (Joshua 7: 9). Under such circumstances, what should Joshua do? He must act and act quickly with confidence for a total victory in order to restore the morale of his army and to maintain his image among the Canaanites. The ancient Chinese strategist, Sun Tzu, writes in his chapter on "Use of Energy" that, "order or disorder depends on organization and direction; courage or cowardice on postures (circumstance); strength or weakness on dispositions"(Hart 1967: 30; Wu 1992: 87). Joshua realized that he must pick up his courage, reorganize his situation, and recondition his dispositions. This was exactly what he did, and he was once again ready to launch another attack (before the news of his defeat spread) – only this time, he used a new tactic.

## The New Stratagem

Quoting from Sun Tzu again:

Those skilled at making the enemy move, do so by creating a situation to which he must conform; they entice him with something he is certain to take, and with lures of ostensible profit they wait him in strength (Hart 1967: 30; Wu 1992: 86-88).

This statement by Sun Tzu summarizes well the stratagem of Joshua's second attempt on Ai. This time, as the Lord had instructed (Joshua 8: 1), Joshua took "all the fighting men" with him and went up to Ai. He then chose thirty thousand mighty men of valor and sent them forth by night. And he commanded them, saying:

Behold, you shall lie in ambush against the city, behind it; do not go very far from the city, but hold yourselves all in readiness; and I, and all the people who are with me, will approach the city. And when they come out against us, as before, we shall flee before them; and they will come out after us, till we have drawn them away from the city,... then you shall rise up from ambush, and seize the city... and when you have taken the city, you shall set the city on fire, doing as the Lord has bidden (Joshua 8: 48 RSV).

Quoting from Liddell Hart, Malamat (1982: 31) called this tactic an "indirect approach." When the plan mentioned above was executed, even Joshua himself was perhaps surprised, for as we read, "*there was not a man left* in Ai or Bethel, who did not go out after Israel: *they left the city open*, and pursued Israel" (Joshua 8: 17 italics added by the author for emphasis).

Then the Lord told Joshua to stretch out his spear. This he did as a signal. And the men waiting in ambush got out from their hiding place,. They ran and took the city and set it on fire. When the men of Ai looked back and saw the smoke of their city go up to the sky, they immediately lost their strength to pursue. Then Joshua and his men turned back on the pursuers and smote them. Having set the city of Ai on fire, the ambushers also came forth to attack the men of Ai, who were by then caught between the two forces. At the end, no one survived or escaped (Joshua 8: 18-22). It was by this stratagem that Ai was taken.

Several things should be noted from the process of this operation. First, there were considerable calculated risks involved. The whole army was split into two: one for ambush, the other for decoy. Second, there was a feigned retreat or controlled flight. Third, there was precise timing and coordination. As Tzu has written:

> When the strike of a hawk breaks the body of its prey, it
> is because of timing. Thus the momentum of <u>one</u> skilled
> in war is overwhelming and his attack precisely regulated
> (Hart 1967: 30; Wu 1992: 84-85).

The decoy force must regulate its pace of fleeing: to keep a safe distance from the pursuers and yet to retain an optimum distance away from the city. Then there was a prearranged signal which coordinated the precise timing of capturing and burning the city, as well as the counter attack by the fleeing force. Fourth, in all of these doings, secrecy and alertness were superbly executed. The ambush position was set up by night: they were to take cover "behind the city and were to "hold themselves in readiness."

Finally, as Sun Tzu writes in his chapter on "Disposition of Military Strength," "the experts in defense conceal themselves as under the ninefold earth; those skilled in attack flash forth as from above the ninefold heavens" (Hart 1967: 29; Wu 1992: 63). The Israelites did take good advantage of the "ninefold earth." First, the ambush force was to take cover "behind" the city [from the perspective of Jericho at which the instruction was given]. This is to say that they were to hide in the ravine on the west side of the city of Ai. If et-Tell which Marquet-Krause (1933-35) and the Joint Expedition (1964-70) excavated, indeed was Ai, then the ambush force really did conceal themselves well. For Wadi el-Jaya, which led from et-Tell (Ai) to Bethel, passed on the north side of et-Tell and was open to view when one looked down from Bethel toward Ai. It was, therefore, not very good for the purpose of taking cover. But on the west (behind), it concealed well (Callaway 1975: 36-52; 1976: 18-30).

Likewise, the main force which Joshua led also must have taken good advantage of the terrain. First, when they approached the city of Ai, they must have approached it from a slope that was conspicuous from Ai. This would have the effect of holding the attention of the men of Ai who guarded the city and of distracting them from any suspicion that there might be an ambush. Then, when they fled, they must have fled in a terrain that was not too steep in slopes with its orientation toward the south. There were two possible advantages of doing this: (1) By fleeing on a south-sloping terrain, it would enable the scout of the ambush force, hiding in the ravine on the west side of the city, to easily see Joshua when he stretched out his spear as the signal of attack. (2) When the time had come for the fleeing force to turn back and attack the pursuers, they would not have to fight the enemy from the deep slopes below a rather difficult and disadvantageous position.

## SUMMARY

In this chapter, the author has briefly summarized three models with respect to the conquest of Canaan by the Israelites toward the end of the thirteenth century B.C.E. Of the three models presented, this author prefers the traditional biblical model which portrays the conquest through a series of military campaigns in a decisive and lightning-like manner.

The author then explores several reasons that may account for the strategic move of the Israelites who went directly to the hill country of the Central Highland shortly after they had crossed the Jordan River and immediately after the fall of Jericho. These include the advantages of the mountainous terrain in the Central Highland; the geopolitical and international situations of the time; the sociogeographic conditions in the highland such as ethnic disunities, animosities along socio-ethnic lines; as well as the region's relatively sparse population at that time. With respect to the Ai campaign, the author suggests several reasons why the Israelites chose to take the Jericho-Ai-Bethel route to get to the Central Highland while other possible routes were available.. As to the capture of Ai, there were two attempts. The first attempt failed miserably, due probably to the problem of communication and, more importantly, the problem of discipline. The second attempt was a great success because, first, the problem of disobedience and sin had been dealt with severely and, second, the employment of a new stratagem. The stratagem of "indirect engagement" involved some calculated risks, precise timing, good coordination, secrecy, and high spirit. But the Israelites also exercised their skill in taking good advantage of the terrain.

The Ai stratagem was so successful that the ruse became a model for the case of Gibeah several years later (Judges 20: 29-35). However, there are some scholars who prefer to believe that it was the experience at Gibeah that actually served as a model for the Ai campaign because of the silence of the archaeological evidence at et-Tell (Ai) (Weippert 1971: 128-129; Aharoni 1979: 210). Unfortunately, this suggestion would complicate the chronology of these and other biblical events. For those who are not willing to accept, for example, Aharoni's notion that the conquest of Ai was a purely aetiological story lacking historical tradition, this author would like to offer two questions for further consideration:

(1) Is it possible that there might be errors in dating the excavated materials? (2) Is it possible that there might be other nearby sites which could possibly be identified as Ai but are still awaiting excavation or discovery? In order to be able to answer the second question positively, more field work of a geographic nature must be conducted at the Bethel-Ai region. Nevertheless, it is interesting to note that some of the ancient arts of warfare discussed in this chapter and elsewhere (Yardin 1967: 396-414), have been repeated or adopted by the contemporary Israeli military strategists.

## ENDNOTES

[1] This chapter, now revised, first appeared in *Geography of the Holy Land: Perspectives*, Volume I.

## REFERENCES

Aharoni, Yohanan. 1979. *The Land of the Bible: A Historical Geography*. Translated from Hebrew by A. F. Rainey, 2nd ed. Philadelphia: The Westminster Press.

Alt, Albrecht. 1967. *Essays in Old Testament History and Religion*. Translated by R. A. Wilson. Garden City, New York: Doubleday & Co., Inc.

Callaway, Joseph A. 1975. "Ai." In Michael AviYonah, Editor, *Encyclopedia of Archaeological Excavations in the Holy Land, Vol. 1*. Englewood Cliffs, New Jersey: Prentice Hall, Inc.

_____1976. "Excavating Ai (et-Tell): 1964-1972." *Biblical Archaeologist*. March 1976: 18-30.

Cohn, Robert L. 1981. *The Shape of Sacred Space: Four Biblical Studies*. American Academy of Religion, Studies in Religion No. 23. Chico, California: Scholar Press.

Gottwald, Norman K. 1979. *The Tribes of Yahweh: A Sociology of Religion of Liberated Israel 1250-1050 B.C.E.* Maryknoll, New York: Orbis Books, 1979.

_____1982. "Were the Early Israelite Pastoral Nomads?" *Biblical*

*Archaeology Review,* 12: 27.

Har-El, M. 1982. "The Routes of the Patriarchs." In Ariel, ed., *A Review of Arts and Letters in Israel. Jerusalem.*

Herzog, Chaim and Mordechai Gichon. 1978. *Battles of the Bible: A Modern Military Evaluation of the Old Testament.* New York: Random House.

Kraeling, Emil G. 1956. *Rand McNally Bible Atlas.* Chicago: Rand McNally & Company.

Lu, Jonathan J. 1990. "The Role of Geography in the Settlement of Israelites in the Central Highland and in the Capture of Ai Under the Leadership of Joshua." Paper presented at the conference on the Role of Geography in Jewish Civilization: Perceptions of Space, Place, Time, and Location in Jewish Life and Thought.

Lu, Jonathan J. 1979. "Geography of the Bible as An Academic Subject in Geography." *ERIC Reports.* Microfiche. March 10, 1979, ED 161 811: 5.

Malamat, Abraham. 1979. "Conquest of Canaan: Israelite Conduct of War According to Biblical Tradition." *Revue Internationale d'Histoire Militaire.* 42: 255-2

_____1982. "How Inferior Israelite Forces Conquered Fortified Canaanite Cities." *Biblical Archaeology Review,* 12: 24-35.

Mendenhall, George E. 1962. "The Hebrew Conquest of Palestine." *The Biblical Archaeologist,* 25: 66-87.

Noth, Martin. 1960. *The History of Israel.* Revised translation by P. R. Ackroyd of the Second edition of *Geschichte Israels'.* New York: Harper and Row, Publishers.

Orni, Efraim. and Elisha Efrat. 1973. *Geography of Israel.* 3rd ed. Philadelphia: The Jewish Publication Society of America.

Ryrie, Charles C. 1978. *The Ryrie Study Bible.* New American Standard Translation. Chicago: Moody Press.

Sun Tzu. *The Art of War.* Translated from Chinese by General S.Griffiths in Adrian Liddell Hart (as prepared by Sir Basil Liddell Hart), editor, 1976. *The Sword and the Pen: Selections from the World's Greatest Military Writings.* New York: Thomas Y. Crowell Company.

Weippert, Manfred. 1971. *The Settlement of the Israelite Tribes in Palestine:*

*A Critical Survey of the Recent Scholar Debate.* Translated from German by James D. Martin. London.

Wu, Jeou-Lung, *et al.*, eds. 1992. *Sun Zi: The Art of War: An Interpretive Review.* Taipei, Taiwan: The Li-Ching Cultural and Educational Foundation. (In Chinese, with English inserts).

Yadin, General Yigael. 1967. "For by Wise Counsel Thou Shalt Make Thy War." In G. H. Liddell Hart, 2nd Rev. Ed., *Strategy.* New York: Frederick A. Praeger, Publishers.

_____ 1982. "Is the Biblical Account of the Israelite Conquest of Canaan Historically Reliable?" *Biblical Archaeology Review,* 12: 17-23.

# Defenses and Wars of the Judean Kings

## Perry G. Phillips

## INTRODUCTION

King David fought many wars to unite the nation of Israel and to protect it from its enemies.[1] After David's death – and with direct intervention by David himself[2] – the united kingdom transitioned to his son, Solomon. Unfortunately, in spite of David's admonition to Solomon to obey the Lord with all his heart, mind, and soul,[3] Solomon eventually fell into idolatry as a result of his marriage to many "foreign women."[4] As such, the Lord brought about a division in Solomon's united kingdom, but only after Solomon's death in the time of his son Rehoboam.

Because of bad decisions by the young Rehoboam (2 Chronicles 13: 6, 7), the ten northern tribes split away from his kingdom. Concurrently, surrounding enemies took advantage of Israel's breakup and rebelled against Rehoboam. What was Rehoboam to do?

Rehoboam's efforts to fortify his southern kingdom of Judah will be summarized in this chapter.[5] A brief description will show how his actions reflect the geography of Judah in terms of major approaches in and out of his kingdom. These approaches remained constant throughout the reign of subsequent kings, which means that Rehoboam's initial fortifications remained relevant throughout Judah's history. That is, as a result of their strategic importance, Judah's kings continued to use the same fortresses right up to the exile of Judah to Babylon.

In this chapter the importance of these fortresses will be indicated by means of the history of the battles surrounding them. The emphasis will be on the strategic region to the west of Jerusalem (the lowlands or the Shephelah), for this was always the major incursion route into Judah and most in need of defense. Finally, in this author's mind, there is no better way to visualize these wars than in maps, so what follows is, in effect, a short atlas of the wars of the Judean kings with emphasis on the battles in this significant region.

### Rehoboam's Fortification of Judah

In 2 Chronicles 11: 5-12, Rehoboam's establishment of the fortified cities is narrated:[6]

> Rehoboam lived in Jerusalem and built cities for defense in Judah. Thus, he built Bethlehem, Etam, Tekoa, Bethzur, Socoh, Adullam, Gath,[7] Mareshah, Ziph, Adoraim, Lachish, Azekah, Zorah, Aijalon and Hebron, which are fortified cities in Judah and in Benjamin. He also strengthened the fortresses and put officers in them and stores of food, oil and wine. He put shields and spears in every city and strengthened them greatly. So he held Judah and Benjamin.[8]

King Rehoboam's fortifications are shown on Map 1, and this map will serve as the base map for what follows. The fortified cities, in effect, are "signposts" on the military health of Judah. Activity outside of the area of the fortresses signifies Judah's ascendency. Conversely, battles at the fortresses or inside the line of fortresses signify losses to Judah. One immediately notices that most of the fortresses are west and south of Jerusalem. The wilderness and the Rift Valley served as natural defenses on the east (see Figure 2).

Although Trans-Jordanian entities occasionally attacked Judah (e.g., Moab, Edom; Map 5 below), major conquering armies avoided

**Figure 1. [Map 1] Rehoboam's Fortifications (in blue with orange dot).**
This map serves as the base map for what follows. Base map was formed using Bible Mapper 5.0 (http://biblemapper.com)

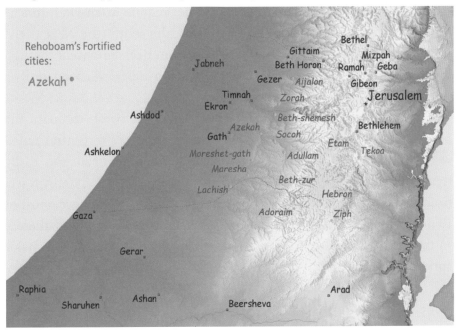

**Figure 2. View Looking East Across the Wilderness of Nebi Musa.**
Note the ruggedness of the wilderness – a good defense for Judah's eastern border. (Photo by Perry Phillips).

attacks from the east across the Rift Valley.[9]  To be sure, Judah faced antagonism from the Northern Kingdom of Israel, and they fought several wars amongst themselves. Generally, however, the border between Israel and Judah was stable, so Judah did not require extensive fortifications along its northern border.[10]  As for Judah's south (the Negev), the main approach to Jerusalem from Arad and from Beersheva went through Hebron, and fortifying Hebron along with Ziph appeared adequate.

Rehoboam's main concern was from the west through the Shephelah (lowlands), for in this direction approaches to central Judah were, from a geographical/topographical standpoint, open and easily traversed by foreign armies. Wide valleys (Figure 3) made for easy travel from the Mediterranean coast to the Judean countryside; hence, most of Rehoboam's fortresses protecting these approaches were found there.[11] In this chapter, the focus will be on the Shephelah since it was the major approach into Judah.

## Rehoboam and Shishak

To begin with, Rehoboam's defenses protected Judah from local incursions. They did not, however, protect him from Shishak's invasion from Egypt. As mentioned by Phillips (2013: 299), Shishak made an "end-run" around the fortresses.[12] Map 2 shows Shishak's attack. Rehoboam learned his lesson – despite outstanding fortresses, true defense of Judah depended upon obedience to the Lord (2 Chronicles 12: 5, 8).

## King Asa Expands to the West

After Asa's religious reform[13] (2 Chronicles 14: 2-5), he turned his attention to expanding his kingdom to the west. "He built up the fortified cities of Judah, since the land was at peace" (2 Chronicles 14: 6). Although not mentioned explicitly, these cities may have suffered earlier damage from Shishak, but whatever the case for their dilapidation, Asa realized their importance and strengthened them.

**Figure 3. A Typical Valley in the Shephelah. Looking east from Lachish.** Note the broad valley bordered by rounded hills leading to the hill country of Judah on the horizon (Photo by Perry Phillips).

**Figure 4. [Map 2] Shishak's Invasion Routes into Judah (blue arrows).** He avoided Rehoboam's fortress cities with an "end-run" around them.

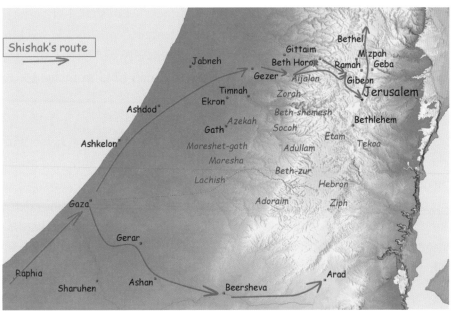

Figure 5. [Map 3] Asa's Battles with Zerah the Cushite

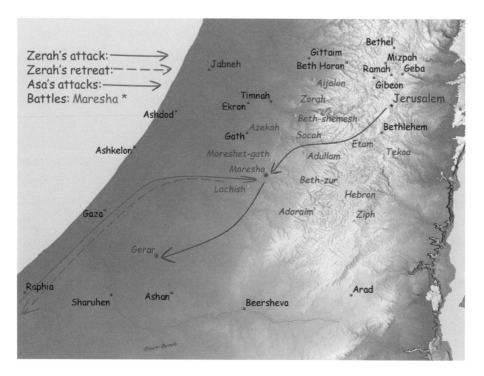

Soon after the buildup of "these towns" with "walls around them, with towers, gates and bars" (2 Chronicles 14: 7), Zerah the Cushite attacked Judah at the "Valley of Zephathah near Mareshah [Maresha]." Despite Zerah's numerical superiority, Asa defeated Zerah and chased him and his forces all the way to Gerar, destroying this city and its surrounding towns and hauling off loads of spoils back to Judah (2 Chronicles 14: 12 –15). Map 3 depicts the battles.

Despite Asa's defeat of the Cushites, he fell out of favor with the Lord by not depending upon God to help him overcome the attack against him by Baasha, king of Israel (1 Kings 15: 18-22). Instead of absorbing the lesson of trust that saved him at Maresha, he hired the king of Syria to attack Baasha from the north, thereby relieving Baasha's siege against Judah. Asa then fortified his northern flank by building up Mizpah and Geba (1 Kings 15: 22; 2 Chronicles 16: 1, 6, see Map 4).

**Figure 6. [Map 4] Baasha's Attack on Ramah and Asa's Rebuilding of Mizpah and Geba Using Material from Ramah.** Note how these cities control the major crossroads north of Jerusalem, which, of course, Asa as king of Judah needed to control at any cost. One often refers to this region as *the Central Benjamin Plateau.*

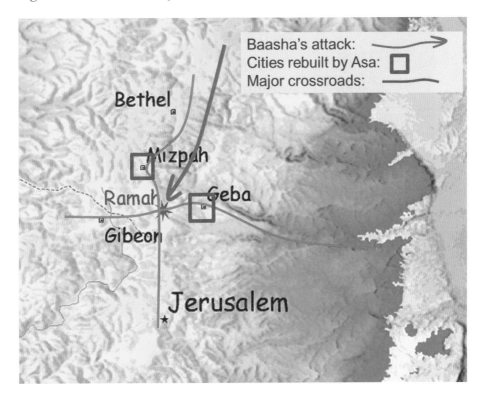

### Jehoshaphat Strengthens Judah

From Asa's son, Jehoshaphat, one learns that faithfulness to the Lord is the *sine qua non* of a healthy Judah. Jehoshaphat greatly improved the moral/ethical/spiritual health of his kingdom, but he realized that a strong military works in conjunction with godly obedience, so "he built forts and store cities in Judah and had large supplies in the towns of Judah. He also kept experienced fighting men in Jerusalem" (2 Chronicles 17: 12, 13). As a result, "the fear of the Lord fell on all the kingdoms of the lands surrounding Judah, so that they did not go to war against Jehoshaphat" (v. 10).

**Figure 7. [Map 5] A Coalition of Inhabitants from the East Attack Judah Across the Lisan.** Jehoshaphat meets them near Tekoa south of Bethlehem.

Figure 8. [Map 6] Philistines and Arabs (from Ethiopia) Invade Judah and Take away Spoil during Jehoram's Reign

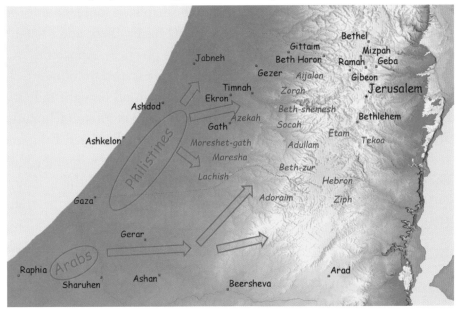

Scripture does not list Jehoshaphat's fortresses, but geography dictates that they would have been the same fortresses constructed initially by Rehoboam, especially the ones to the west against the Philistines who, instead of fighting with the king, brought him gifts instead (v. 11). Jehoshaphat's obedience and his western fortifications did not, however, deter an invasion from the east. A combined force of Moabites and Ammonites, with some of the Meunites,[14] invaded Judah from the east across the Rift Valley coming from the direction of Edom (See Map 5).[15] Jehoshaphat and the people prayed to the Lord for deliverance, and the enemies of Judah destroyed themselves, leaving plenty of booty for the inhabitants of Judah to take back to their homes in Jerusalem (vv. 20-30).

Jehoshaphat later entered into a disastrous alliance with Israel's king Ahaziah and was rebuked for involving himself with the north's wicked king (vv. 35-37), but overall, Jehoshaphat provided prosperity and safety to Judah.

## Jehoram's Evil Degrades Judah

From the heights to the depths! Jehoshaphat's son, Jehoram (or Joram), turned away from the Lord, murdered his brothers, and brought condemnation upon Judah with his idolatrous practices. Apparently, he was a brave and competent warrior in the way he escaped from his attack upon Edom (2 Chronicles 21: 9), but his spiritual fall brought military disasters upon his nation. The Philistines, who brought gifts to Jehoram's father Jehoshaphat, invaded Judah, as did Arabs who bordered Ethiopia (see Map 6). The invaders carried away much spoil – even members of Jehoram's own household in Jerusalem. Fortresses are nothing if not accompanied by strong faithfulness on the part of the king. Jehoram reigned eight years and died a horrible death (abdominal cancer?) "to no one's regret" (2 Chronicles 21: 18-20).

## Ahaziah: He Should Have Stayed Home

Jehoram's son, Ahaziah, took over Judah after the death of his father, but his spiritual character was no better than his predecessor. "He did evil in the sight of the Lord like the house of Ahab, for they were his counselors after the death of his father, to his destruction" (2 Chronicles 22: 4). Ahaziah took part in a war against Aram (Syria) with King Joram of Israel, but he was killed by Jehu when the latter rebelled against Joram and killed him and Ahaziah upon assuming kingship of Israel (2 Kings 9: 27-30). As for Judah during the time of Ahaziah, nothing is mentioned concerning battles. Ahaziah ruled for one year, and apparently Judah was stable during this time.

## Joash: Escapes as an Infant, Murdered Later in Life

Following the murder of Ahaziah by Jehu, Ahaziah's mother Athaliah attempted to rid Judah of all of her son's descendants and rule the kingdom alone. Thankfully, however, Jehosheba, Ahaziah's sister, rescued Joash, Ahaziah's youngest son. Eventually, with the help of the high priest Jehoiada, Joash became king.

Figure 9. [Map 7] Hazael, King of Aram, Conquers Gath, and That Opens the Way to Jerusalem

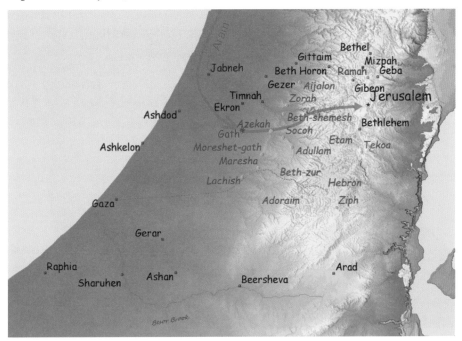

Joash started well: He repaired the Temple (2 Chronicles 24: 8-14; 2 Kings 12: 1-13) and remained faithful to the Lord as long as Jehoiada guided him. Upon the latter's death, however, Joash turned away from the Lord. As a result, Hazael, king of Aram (Syria), came all the way south and attacked Gath before turning towards Jerusalem (2 Kings 12: 17; see Map 7).

With this breach in Judah's defenses, Hazael subsequently went to Jerusalem and departed only after Joash paid much ransom. So odious was Joash's response and his faithlessness to the Lord (he even murdered Jehoiada's son [2 Chronicles 24: 20-22]) that his own officials assassinated him (2 Kings 12: 20, 21).

## Amaziah – Like Father, Like Son

Amaziah started well following the good aspects of his father Joash. In his strength he invaded Edom and captured the stronghold of

## Figure 10. [Map 8] The Activities of King Amaziah

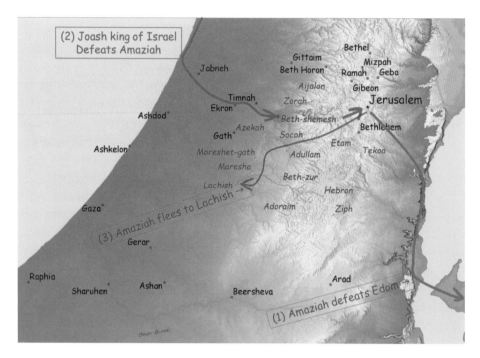

Sela (2 Kings 14: 7; 2 Chronicles 25: 11, 12).[16] In his pride, however, he challenged Israel's king Jehoash (or Joash) to a contest. Jehoash encouraged Amaziah to stay home and enjoy his victory against Edom, but Amaziah refused and met Jehoash in battle at Beth-shemesh. The result proved disastrous for Amaziah and for Judah.

Joash followed his victory at Beth-shemesh with an assault on Jerusalem that resulted in the destruction of a portion of Jerusalem's wall and the giving over of much booty to Jehoash. Repeating the history of Amaziah's father, "they" (officials again?) conspired against Amaziah. He fled to Lachish, but was caught and murdered there (see Map 8).

### Uzziah (Azariah): Judah Back on Top

The book of Kings says little about Amaziah's son Uzziah[17] (2 Kings 15: 1-7), but 2 Chronicles fills in the details. Uzziah did "right in the sight of the Lord" (2 Chronicles 26: 4) most of his life. Uzziah

Figure 11. [Map 9] Uzziah Expands Judah's Rule Deep into Philistine Territory

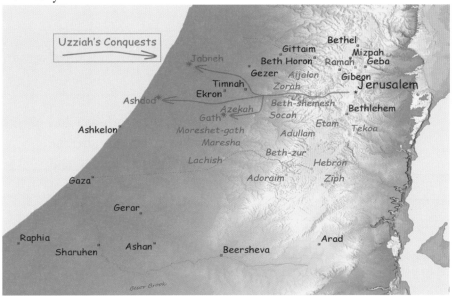

reigned 52 years and he expanded Judah's territory deep into Philistine territory – conquering Gath, Jabneh, and Ashdod (see Map 9). He also built up the port of Ezion-geber on the north end of the Red Sea.[18] Unfortunately, like so many kings before and after him, he fell into pride. He attempted to offer incense in the Temple – an offering relegated only to priests – and was stricken with leprosy as judgment. Consequently, he lived out his remaining days in a separate house, cut off from others and from the Temple (2 Chronicles 26: 16-21).[19]

## Ahaz: Big Reversal in Judah's Fortunes – for the Worse

What one generation will do! Ahaz, Jotham's son, was as evil as it gets in Judah. To wit:

> But he walked in the ways of the kings of Israel; he also made molten images for the Baals. Moreover, he burned incense in the valley of Ben-hinnom and burned his sons in fire, according to the abominations of the nations whom the Lord had driven out before the sons

of Israel. He sacrificed and burned incense on the high places, on the hills and under every green tree (2 Chronicles 28: 2-4).

Needless to say, the Lord brought calamity upon Judah by way of surrounding enemies:

> [A]gain the Edomites had come and attacked Judah and carried away captives. The Philistines also had invaded the cities of the [e]lowland and of the Negev of Judah, and had taken Beth-shemesh, Aijalon, Gederoth, and Soco with its villages, Timnah with its villages, and Gimzo with its villages, and they settled there (28: 17, 18).

Map 10 shows Ahaz's dire straits.

To protect himself from his enemies, Ahaz sought help from Assyria, but Assyria afflicted him rather than help him (v. 20). In spite of this, Ahaz became even more unfaithful. He closed the Temple of the Lord, built innumerous altars around Judah, and sacrificed to other gods. Both the political and the spiritual conditions in Judah sank to the depths of despair.

## Good King Hezekiah

The situation in Judah did not improve until Ahaz's son Hezekiah inherited the kingdom. Hezekiah immediately instituted religious reform in Jerusalem and in Judah (2 Chronicles 29; 31). He also invited the remnants of the northern tribes to join him in Jerusalem to celebrate the Passover (30: 1-12, 18):

> Thus Hezekiah did throughout all Judah; and he did what was good, right and true before the Lord his God. Every work which he began in the service of the house of God in law and in commandment, seeking his God, he did with

Figure 12. [Map 10] Ahaz's Unfaithfulness Brings Disaster upon Judah as Local Enemies Invade and Settle

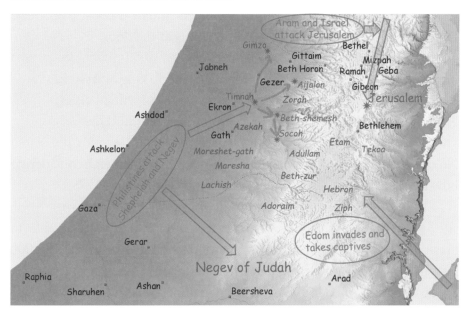

Figure 13. [Map 11] Sennacherib Attacks Hezekiah's Fortresses in the Shephelah, Especially Lachish. The Assyrian attack on Jerusalem failed, and Sennacherib beat a hasty retreat to Nineveh.

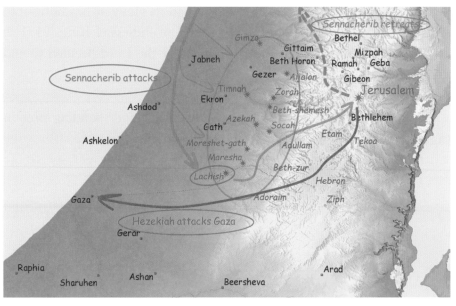

all his heart and prospered (31: 20, 21).

One would think at this point life in Judah was back on track. However, in spite of the reforms, the wolf was at the door:

> After these acts of faithfulness Sennacherib king of Assyria came and invaded Judah and besieged the fortified cities, and thought to break into them for himself (32: 1).

No doubt Sennacherib invaded Judah through the Shephelah considering how much he gloated over the fall of Lachish (See Map 11).[20]

Lachish became Sennacherib's prize since he was not able to break into Jerusalem. According to Scripture, the Lord destroyed 185,000 Assyrians,[21] which forced Sennacherib to return to Nineveh (2 Kings 19: 35, 36). There he died at the hands of two of his sons (v. 37; cf. Isaiah 37: 36-38).

## From Hezekiah to the Exile

The reforms of Hezekiah did not last long. No sooner did Hezekiah's son, Manasseh, take over that the nation plunged headlong into idolatry led by Manasseh himself. His sins were endless (1 Kings 21: 1-9; 16-18; 2 Chronicles 33: 1-9) to the point that the Lord decided to end the Judean kingdom forever.

Eventually, after his exile by the Assyrians and spending time in captivity in Babylon, Manasseh came to his senses:

> When he was in distress, he entreated the Lord his God and humbled himself greatly before the God of his fathers. When he prayed to him, he was moved by his entreaty and heard his supplication, and brought him again to Jerusalem to his kingdom. Then Manasseh knew that the Lord was God (2 Chronicles 33: 12, 13).

Manasseh spent the rest of his life rebuilding Jerusalem and the Temple. He was not able to undo all the evil that befell Judah because of his earlier idolatry, but at least Jerusalem was safe. It is not known, however, how the rest of his kingdom fared, for Scripture remains silent on activities outside of Jerusalem. As such, one can only assume that Judah was relatively quiet during the latter part of Manasseh's reign.

Manasseh's son, Amon, succeeded him as king. Amon, unfortunately, brought back the idolatry of his father's earlier reign, but he lasted only two years before his servants conspired against him and he was eliminated.

## Josiah – The Last Good King

Josiah was the last king of Judah during somewhat stable times. Scripture mentions no wars during the reign of Josiah against surrounding nations. Rather, Josiah's main interest was spiritual renewal in Judah and in the Northern Kingdom.

Josiah began his reform while still a youth (2 Chronicles 34: 3-7). He broke down the altars of Baal, destroyed the Asherim poles,[22] and broke the cast images of the pagan gods. He not only cleansed Judah, he also cleansed the tribes of Ephraim, Manasseh, and Naphtali in the north, and the tribe of Simeon to the south. One of his major accomplishments was to destroy the altar at Bethel that Jeroboam I built after the monarchy split and he became king of the Northern Kingdom. This was the altar whose destruction the unnamed prophet from Judah foretold (1 Kings 13).

Scripture describes Josiah's rehabilitation of the Temple in great detail (2 Kings 22: 3-7; 2 Chronicles 34: 8-13). During this time the workers found the "book of the law of Moses" (2 Kings 22: 8-22; 2 Chronicles 34: 14-28),[23] and after reading this book, King Josiah and his court deeply humbled themselves, carried out a "covenant renewal" along with other reforms (2 Kings 23: 1-3; 2 Chronicles 34: 29-32; 2 Kings

23: 4-20; 2 Chronicles 34: 33), all ending with a monumental Passover celebration (2 Kings 23: 21-27; 2 Chronicles 35: 1-19).

Unfortunately, external affairs brought about Josiah's death. In his haste to impede Neco (Necho), king of Egypt, on his way to Mesopotamia, Josiah met his death at Megiddo. The death spiral of Judah followed.

### Last Days of Judah

From the death of Josiah (609 B.C.E.) until the exile of Judah (586 B.C.E.), Judah suffered spiritual, economic, and political ruin. Some of Josiah's sons became puppet kings, first under the rule of Egypt and then under Babylon. Surrounding nations began to encroach upon Judah, thus weakening the nation until King Nebuchadnezzar of Babylon conquered Judah and exiled its people to Babylon. During the conquest by the Babylonians, the last reference to the fortresses of Judah – namely Azekah and Lachish, can be found. To wit:

> [T]he army of the king of Babylon was fighting against Jerusalem and against all the remaining cities of Judah, that is, Lachish and Azekah, for they alone remained as fortified cities among the cities of Judah (Jeremiah 34: 6, 7).

Interestingly, the Lachish Ostraca mention the same event:

> May Yahweh cause my lord to hear reports of good news this very day. And now, according to all that my lord sent thus your servant has done. I have written upon the tablet according to all that [you] have sent to me. And with respect to what my lord sent concerning the matter of Beth-Harapid, there is no man there. As for Semakyahu, Shemayahu has seized him and taken him up to the city. Your servant cannot send the witness there today; rather, it is during the morning tour that [he will come (to you)].

Figure 14. [Map 12] Nebuchadnezzar Eliminates the Fortresses of Azekah and Lachish Before Attacking and Destroying Jerusalem

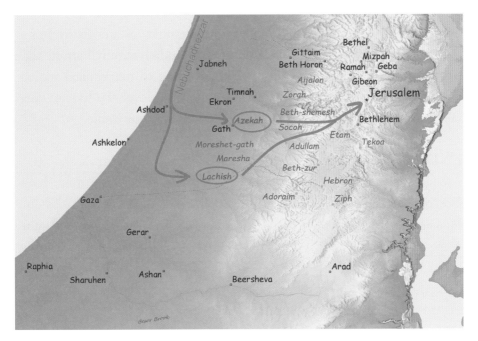

> Then it will be known that we are watching the (fire)-signals of Lachish according to the code which my lord gave us, for we cannot see Azekah.[24]

Apparently, someone between Jerusalem and the Shephelah was able to observe the signal fires of Azekah and of Lachish and was able to report that Azekah had fallen before the fall of Lachish, a great confirmation of Jeremiah's history. Map 12 shows the military situation.

## CONCLUSION

The history of the fortifications of Rehoboam and of subsequent Judean kings provides geographical lessons on the defense of Judah. Geographically, every Judean king knew his territory well and made plans for its defense that one cannot gainsay. The kings' fortresses straddled major inroads into Judah from the Shephelah to the west, from the biblical Negev to the south, and from the Aravah/Dead Sea region to the east. Each king not only constructed lines of defense, he also provided food, implements, and leadership for their effectiveness in time of war. That is the geographical/political aspect to the fortifications.

Unfortunately, successful defense of Judah required more than strong fortifications. Trust in Yahweh, according to the biblical writers, had to be the foundation of all defense, and at this level, the Judean kings failed. Consequently, the fall of their kingdom was inevitable.

## ENDNOTES

[1] See "Narrative" under "David" in *https://en.wikipedia.org/wiki/David.*

[2] Adonijah, David's fourth son, attempted to take over the kingdom, but he was thwarted when Bathsheba – Solomon's mother – and the prophet Nathan interceded with King David who decreed that Solomon would succeed him as king (1Kings 1).

[3] 1 Kings2: 1-9. Subsequent history of Judah is, in effect, a history of the practical outcomes of following or of rejecting David's advice.

[4] 1 Kings 11: 4.

[5] For details, see Phillips (2013: 290-292).

[6] For a discussion of the historicity of the text, see Phillips (2013: 299).

[7] Probably Moresheth-Gath since Gath itself is a major Philistine city (Cf. Rainey 2006: 170.

[8] Scripture quotations taken from the *New American Standard Bible* ® (NASB). Copyright © 1960, 1962, 1963, 1968, 1971, 1972, 1973, 1975, 1977, 1995 by The Lockman Foundation. Used by permission www.lockman.org.

[9] In the Second Temple Period, Vespasian drove south along the Rift Valley with one branch of his army, the other branch traversing the coastal highway.

[10] Albeit a few battles of note took place (1 Kings 14: 30; 1 Kings 15: 22; 2 Chronicles 16: 1, 6 [Map 4]). In this chapter the concentration will be on battles centered about Judah's fortifications established by Rehoboam and maintained by subsequent Judean kings. The battles between the kings of Israel and Judah make for a separate study.

[11] For more detailed descriptions of the geographical terrain of these fortresses, see Phillips (2013: 293-299.

[12] One thinks of Germany's end-run around the Maginot Line in World War II by going through Holland and Belgium instead of a direct attack on France.

[13]Asa was Rehoboam's grandson.

[14]According to the Septuagint, some Hebrew manuscripts have "Ammonites." Edomites also appear to have been part of the group (Cf. v. 10).

[15]Some manuscripts have "Aram," but "Edom" makes more sense since the place names of En Gedi and Tekoa appear in the narrative. Most likely, the invasion force crossed the narrows at the "tongue" (Lisan) of the Dead Sea.

[16]Amazingly, Amaziah captured the "gods" of Edom and brought them back to Jerusalem and worshipped them. As the prophet told him, if these gods were not able to protect Edom, what made Amaziah think that they would protect him? Amaziah discounted the prophet's advice, and his idolatry led to his undoing (2 Chronicles 25: 14-16).

[17]Also called Azariah.

[18]Near present-day Elath.

[19]During this time, "Jotham his son was over the king's house judging the people of the land" (v. 21). 2 Chronicles 27 relates Jotham's exploits – conquering the Ammonites and "he built cities in the hill country of Judah, and he built fortresses and towers on the wooded hills" (v. 4). No doubt he kept up the prevailing fortresses of Judah to the west.

[20]2 Kings 18: 7-8 states that "the Lord was with [Hezekiah]; wherever he went he prospered. And he rebelled against the king of Assyria and did not serve him. He defeated the Philistines as far as Gaza and its territory, from watchtower to fortified city." A question of chronology arises: What is the relationship between the time of Hezekiah's defeat of the Philistines and the attack upon Judah by Sennacherib? It appears that there were two phases of Sennacherib's attack. First, Hezekiah rebels against Sennacherib and pays him to leave ("I have done wrong"; 2 Kings 18: 14). At this time Hezekiah defeats the Philistines. But later, when Sennacherib returns, Hezekiah prepares for battle (2 Chronicles 32: 1-9), especially for the defense of Jerusalem after Sennacherib destroys the fortified cities of the Shephelah.

As for the question of whether Sennacherib attacked Jerusalem once or twice, see Cogan (2001).

[21]Herodotus places the story in Egypt, but most scholars believe he is relating the attack of Sennacherib upon Jerusalem. For the quote from Herodotus, see http://www.perseus. tufts.edu/hopper/text?doc=Perseus:text:1999.0126:book=2:chapter=141.

[22]Female goddess consort of Baal.

[23]Some believe this to be Deuteronomy; others believe that the priests in Josiah's time generated the "book of the law" to enhance their position at the Temple in Jerusalem. This has been called "D" in the so-called "JEDP" theory. Analyzing the origin of the book takes us too far afield for this chapter, but the interested reader can refer to Arnold (2003). For the record, this author does not buy into a late origin for Deuteronomy.

[24]Lachish Ostracon #4 (http://www.bible.ca/ostraca/Ostrace-Lachish-Letters-
Jeremiah-YHWH-Egypt-Fire-Signals:Azekah-weakening-hands-nebuchadnezzar-
587BC.htm.)


## REFERENCES

Arnold, B. T. 2003. "Pentateuchal Criticism, History of" in *Dictionary
of the Old Testament Pentateuch*, eds. T. D. Alexander and D. W.
Baker. Downers Grove: InterVarsity Press, pp. 622 – 31.

Bible Mapper 5.0 *(*http://biblemapper.com*)*

Cogan, M. 2001. "Sennacherib's Siege of Jerusalem: Once or Twice?" in
*Biblical Archaeology* Review, 27:1 ( January/February). Available
online at: http://cojs.org/sennacherib-s_siege_of_jerusalem-_
once_or_twice-_mordechai_cogan-_bar_27-01-_jan-feb_2001.

David. 2018. Wikipedia: *The Free Encyclopedia*. Retrieved 24 February
from https://en.wikipedia.org/wiki/David.

Herodotus. 1991. *The Histories*. http://www.perseus.tufts.edu/hopper/text
?doc=Perseus:text:1999.01.0126:book=2:chapter=141.

Lachish Ostracon #4 (http://www.bible.ca/ostraca/Ostraca-Lachish-
Letters-Jeremiah-YHWH-Egypt-Fire-Signals-Azekah-
weakening-hands-nebuchadnezzar-587BC.htm.)

*New American Standard Bible*® (NASB). Copyright © 1960, 1962, 1963,
1968, 1971, 1972, 1973, 1975, 1977, 1995 by The Lockman
Foundation. Used by permission. www.Lockman.org.

Phillips, P. 2013. "Rehoboam's Defenses for Judah in the Tenth-Ninth
Centuries B.C." *Geography of the Holy Land: New Insights*, eds. W.
A. Dando, C Z. Dando, J. J. Lu. Kaohsiung, Taiwan: Holy Light
Theological Seminary Press, pp. 290 – 315.

Rainey, A. and R. S. Notley. 2006. *The Sacred Bridge*. Jerusalem: Carta.

# Parables: Food, Agriculture, and Feeding the Cities

William A. Dando and Caroline Z. Dando

## INTRODUCTION

The Bible begins with the creation of the world and the molding of man in God's own image. He gave man a companion and the two, dominion over everything that moved over the earth. He also gave them herb-bearing seeds, trees that yielded fruit that could be consumed, and animals and birds for meat. Adam and Eve were placed in the Garden of Eden. They did not need to labor because God had provided sustenance that only needed gathering. Unfortunately, they sinned and were driven from the Garden of Eden. To sustain their bodies, they were required to work by the "sweat of their brow" to produce wheat for their bread, tend animals for their meat, and nurture grapes for their wine (Genesis 1: 1-36; Figure 1). Humans multiplied but with adequate food to sustain life (Daniel-Rops 1962). At times, food was scarce due to war, weather perturbations, soil fertility depletion, and failures in food preservation techniques (1 Kings 8: 37-40; Figure 2). Initially, plants made up 70 to 80 percent of their diet. What they ate to sustain their bodies reflected their way of life, lack of permanent homes (they were nomads), and interaction with indigenous farmers (Genesis 27: 4-33).

## SURVIVING BY THE SWEAT OF THEIR BROW

In the time of the post-exile period, 1150 B.C.E. – 63 C.E., which included Jesus' lifetime on earth, those living in Roman Palestine were primarily subsistence farmers, animal herders, shopkeepers, craftsmen,

Figure 1. Subsistence Agriculture in Ancient Israel

and fishermen. Their diet evolved to include foods that were eaten in Egypt, selected Canaanite foods, traditional Hebrew foods, and new foods brought into the Promised Land by traders, military ventures and occupations, and government actions (Numbers 11: 32; 1 Samuel 26: 20). Large villages and towns became centers of agricultural-based industries or places that grew specialty commercial crops. The three principal products of the Jewish farmer were "wine to gladden the heart of man, oil to make his face shine, and bread to strengthen man's heart" (Psalms 104: 15). The life of a farmer was difficult, required continuous daily effort and hard labor with no long periods of rest and relaxation. The Gezer Calendar in approximately 925 B.C.E. describes a mixed farming system and an agricultural year divided into monthly activities (Baly 1957):

His two months are [olive] harvest;
His two months are grain planting;
His two months are late planting;
His month is hoeing up of flax;
His month is barley harvest;
His month is harvest and festivity;
His two months are vine tending;
His month is summer fruit.

Those who lived in Roman Palestine produced a great variety of plants, animals, and fish. Plants made up 70 to 85 percent of most people's diets. Quality of an average person's diet depended on their ability to purchase or barter food, the season of the year, profits from the food sold or requisitioned, and where they lived. Food served in a Jewish house could include items from the following list and found in Figure 3 (Dando *et al.* 2005).

1. Bread, Rice, and Parched Grain – wheat, barley, rye, millet, and chickpeas
2. Beverages – wine, vinegar, beer, milk, juices
3. Fruit – olives, grapes, raisins, dates, figs, carob, lemons, apricots, oranges, apples, pomegranates, melons, mulberries
4. Animal Products – milk, cheese, yogurt, butter, sweet fat
5. Meat – sheep, goats, cattle, oxen, chickens, geese, doves
6. Wild Game – partridge, quail, geese, pigeons, hart, gazelle
7. Fish – more than fifty varieties
8. Vegetables – beans, lentils, cucumbers, squash, onions, garlic, leeks, lettuce, peas
9. Nuts – almonds, pistachios, walnuts
10. Condiments – mint, carob, dill, rue, cumin, olive oil, mustard, coriander, saffron, cinnamon, salt, anise
11. Other – locusts, honey, eggs

## Jesus' Ministries

Jesus taught and ministered to those with the greatest needs primarily in rural places, villages, towns, and selected cities. Those who initially expressed the greatest interest in his message were followers of John the Baptist, the poor, the outcasts, widows and widowers, the ill and handicapped, and the elderly. Few could read and Jesus had nothing for them to read. Many were blind and most had been taught by repetition of stories, myths, legends, and fables. Jesus said "The reason I speak in parables is that 'seeing they do not perceive, hearing they do not listen, nor do they understand'" (Matthew 13: 13-14). He was a masterful story-teller and parable composer. Many contend that he developed teaching by parables to its highest form. After testing various methods to deliver his message, such as a fable, a short story not based on fact with a moral message; allegory, a symbolic narrative where every sentence had a meaning in itself; simile, a vivid metaphor drawn from life and designed to refocus the mind of a hearer to a productive thought; and myth or invented story concerning imaginary beings and things, Jesus determined that parables were an effective means of presenting the "word" to a story-loving people in a way that they could understand. Also, the parables he presented were focused on the socioeconomic activities of the surrounding "preacher points" and "miracle sites" and the perceived needs of those who came to him.

Hunger years and famines were unexpected and irregular cultural hazards that claimed the lives of many who dwelled in Roman Palestine. Most famines were associated with military actions and sieges of large cities and towns. Hunger, dietary deficiency diseases, and despondency were pervasive as the Romans requisitioned or purchased the highest quality foods for shipment to Rome for their legions and retired military personnel settlements. Jewish noblemen and religious leaders as well demanded the finest foods. The urban rich Jews and the Romans dined well while the poor in small towns, villages, and cities suffered from undernutrition and malnutrition. Nathan's parable of the rich man's greed and the poor man's lamb (2 Samuel 12: 1-7), Naboth's vineyard, Ahab's

# Figure 2. Climates of Ancient Israel

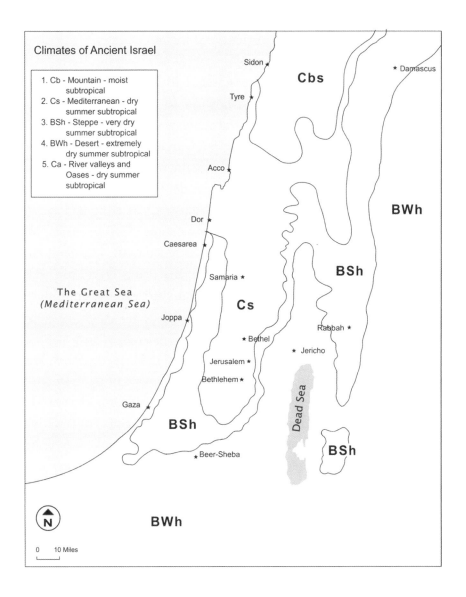

Climates of Ancient Israel

1. Cb - Mountain - moist subtropical
2. Cs - Mediterranean - dry summer subtropical
3. BSh - Steppe - very dry summer subtropical
4. BWh - Desert - extremely dry summer subtropical
5. Ca - River valleys and Oases - dry summer subtropical

Sidon

Damascus

Cbs

Tyre

Acco

BWh

Dor

Caesarea

Samaria

BSh

The Great Sea
(Mediterranean Sea)

Cs

Joppa

Rabbah

Bethel

Jericho

Jerusalem

Bethlehem

Dead Sea

Gaza

BSh

BSh

Beer-Sheba

N

BWh

0    10 Miles

greed, and Jezebel's murder of Naboth  (1 Kings 21: 1-17) are examples of the cruelty and injustices in Jewish society that were compounded by Roman prejudice and arrogance in Jesus' time.

### Parables: A Treasure Store of Agricultural Insights

Twenty-two parables were selected to be included in Table 1, and the majority were taken from Matthew. In most Bibles, only 39 are accepted as parables, but a few biblical scholars claim that there are only 27 while some believe that there are 59. Variations in the numbers of parables included in the Old and New Testaments vary for many reasons, including the year the translation was made, the translation used, the language in which the original Bible was written, changing and evolving meanings of words, and discoveries of new manuscripts or scrolls. Most scholars claim that only two parables were recorded in the Old Testament: Nathan's story of the poor man's one lamb, chastising David for his lust for Bathsheba (2 Samuel 12: 1-14), and Isaiah's story of the unproductive vineyard, bad grapes, and unfaithful Jews (Isaiah 5: 1-7).

To complicate matters more, not every book in the New Testament includes the same parables or the same number of parables. In the *New Revised Standard Version of the Bible*, Matthew records eleven; Mark, two; Luke, seventeen; and John, none. Matthew was a tax collector while Mark was a self-made scholar and companion of Peter. Luke was a physician and John was a fisherman. Variations in parables included in the books written may reflect each author's background and the audience to whom each author wrote. It appears that the Gospel of Matthew was written for non-Christian Jews and from a Jewish viewpoint; the Gospel of Mark for Greek Christians; the Gospel of Luke for Gentiles and new followers of Jesus including Romans; and the Gospel of John for world Gentiles. Parables found in the Gospels of Matthew, Mark, and Luke focus, in most part, on issues and problems common to the Roman province of Galilee. However, no true parables are found in the Gospel of John; his thrust was more for the urbane and for those who lived in Judea.

# Figure 3. Agricultural Regions of Ancient Israel

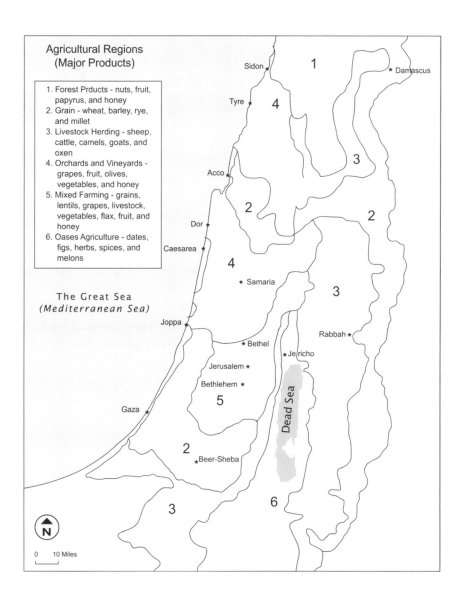

Agricultural Regions
(Major Products)

1. Forest Prducts - nuts, fruit,
   papyrus, and honey
2. Grain - wheat, barley, rye,
   and millet
3. Livestock Herding - sheep,
   cattle, camels, goats, and
   oxen
4. Orchards and Vineyards -
   grapes, fruit, olives,
   vegetables, and honey
5. Mixed Farming - grains,
   lentils, grapes, livestock,
   vegetables, flax, fruit, and
   honey
6. Oases Agriculture - dates,
   figs, herbs, spices, and
   melons

The Great Sea
(Mediterranean Sea)

**Table 1. Parables of Familiar Concerns and Happenings of Rural Dwellers Provide Understanding into Jewish Agricultural Year** (Base is the Gezer Calendar)

| |
|---|
| **Two Summer Months of Fruit Harvest (olives, figs, pomegranates, pistachios, nuts)**<br>— A Tree and Its Fruit (no good tree bears bad fruit) (Matt. 7: 15-20)<br>— A Fig Tree, Young Leaves, Agricultural Seasons, Signs (Matt. 24: 32)<br>— A Farmer and His Sons (vine care needs and reluctant sons) (Matt. 28: 32)<br>— Vineyard Work and Unhappy Laborers (workers' pay by owners) (Matt. 20: 1-17) |
| **Two Fall Months of Early Grain Planting and Two Winter Months of Late Grain Planting**<br>— Mistreatment of Farm Workers (servant plowing fields plus. . .) (Luke 16: 19-31)<br>— Sowing Seeds on Good and Bad Ground (seed survival) (Luke 8: 4-8)<br>— Sowing Only the Best Seeds (good seed, good soils, good harvest) (Matt. 18: 3-9)<br>— Salt of the Earth and Its Taste (lost taste and lost value) (Matt. 5: 13)<br>— Mixed Agriculture and Dietary Diversity (Matt. 13: 34-36)<br>— Food Needs, Famine, and Pigs (bean pods to the fatted calf) (Luke 15: 11-32)<br>— Weeds (Tares) Among the Growing Wheat (wise judgement/good yields) (Matt.: 13: 13-24)<br>— From Small Seeds, Great Plants Grow (the mustard seed, etc.) (Matt. 13: 31-32) |
| **One Late Winter Month of Cultivating and Nurturing Plants (including flax)**<br>— Completing the Life Cycle of a Plant (seed, plant, yield) (Mark 4: 26-29) |
| **One Late Spring Month of Barley Harvest**<br>— A Great Agricultural Year, Good Yields, New Barns (a rich and insensitive fool) (Luke 12: 11-21) |
| **One Month of Early Summer Wheat Harvest and Festivity**<br>— Sheep and Goats (good and evil, failure to feed the hungry) (Luke 12: 16-21)<br>— New Wine and Old Bottles (new wine properly stored) (Matt. 9: 17)<br>— Leaven Bread (small acts can result in amazing results) (Matt. 13: 33) |
| **Two Summer Months of Vine Tending, Tree Care, and Neglected Tasks**<br>— A Misplaced Fig Tree in a Vineyard (did not produce figs for 3 years) (Luke 13: 6-9)<br>— A Fig Tree with No Figs (Jesus claimed it had no value) (Matt. 21: 17-19)<br>— A Lost Sheep (the joy of finding something of value lost) (Matt. 18: 12)<br>— Wicked Tenants (tenants refused to share crops with the land owner) (Luke 20: 9-15)<br>— The Rich Man and the Beggar (results of not sharing one's good fortune (Luke 16: 19-31) |
| **One Month of Summer Fruits and Vegetables** |

Figure 4. Jesus and the Syrophonecian Woman

## LOCATING, IDENTIFYING, SORTING, AND CLASSIFYING PARABLES

Finding and conducting a content analysis of parables is a difficult and time-consuming task. However, it is possible to group the parables of Jesus into three broad categories: (1) Promise of a divine kingdom to come. (2) Roman Palestine's Jewish agriculture, the most disturbing preacher point or miracle site socioeconomic and environmental issue; daily or reoccurring problems in the lives of the disheartened and destitute men and women (Figure 4). (3) Religious and governmental corruption; surviving under the yoke of a harsh Roman occupation and Herod's cruel rule; hunger and disease.

In the time of Jesus, Roman Palestine was divided into four official political divisions. Galilee and Judea were basically Jewish, the Decapolis was basically Greek, and Samaria was basically Samaritan (Table 2). There was great historic animosity between the Jews and the Samaritans. Jesus avoided Samaria because of its Hellenistic culture, citizens' worldly materialism, and racial/religious conflicts. Yet at least two visits are recorded in Luke and once he was rejected as he was passing through on his way from Galilee to Jerusalem (Luke 9: 52-56).

## DIVINE INSTITUTION OF LABOR

Idleness was despised and condemned in the Scriptures. An idle man was condemned as a useless public danger. The farmer and farming were considered divine appointments. The rabbis stressed that Yahweh ordained that His people were to be tillers of the soil and caregivers to animals. Palestine, at the time of Jesus, was essentially an agricultural and pastoral nation whose economy and life were based on the land. Rural matters take up a large portion of the Scriptures, and the parables of Jesus reflect this. Jesus was a countryman's son. Most of his parables and sayings are related directly to those who lived on the land. His parables are a treasure chest and a source of agricultural knowledge. If read carefully, life in rural Palestine in the time of Jesus appears before one's eyes.

## Table 2. A Brief Geography of Parables*

| Galilean Ministry | Judean Ministry | Decapolis Ministry | Samaritan Ministry |
|---|---|---|---|
| Tares (weeds) | Rich Fool | Prodigal Son | Children and Dogs |
| Sower/Plant Growth | Barren Fig Tree | | |
| Mustard Seed | Lost Sheep | | |
| Salt and Earth | Prodigal Son(?) | | |
| Leaven Bread | Rich Man/Poor Man | | |
| Fig Tree | Wicked Tenant | | |
| Farm Laborer | Fig Tree/ Climate | | |

*The general locations in Roman Palestine where Jesus taught with parables are primarily in two of the four political divisions (Halley 1965; Hammond 1990; Lockyer 1991).

The parables that Christ used of dry land farming and pastoral life were evocative to his listeners, because they were intimately well acquainted with that life. However, there was a vast difference between the standard of living of a great landed proprietor and a small-town merchant or rural farmer who worked his own piece of land. Overall, the Holy Land which God had given to His chosen people kept them adequately fed and healthy – until the coming of exploitive conquerors like the Romans and evil dictators like Herod.

## REFERENCES

_____. 1990. *The Holy Bible. New Revised Standard Version.* Ezekiel 4: 16-17.

Baly, D. 1957. *The Geography of the Bible: A Study in Historical Geography.* London: Lutterworth Press, p. 301.

Dando, William A., Caroline Z. Dando, and Jonathan J. Lu, eds. *Geography of the Holy Land: Perspectives.* Kaohsiung, Taiwan: Holy Light Theological Seminary Press, p. 463.

Daniel-Rops, Henri. 1962. *Daily Life in the Time of Christ.* New York, NY: Hawthorne Books, Inc., pp. 262-282.

Halley, Henry H. 1965. *Halley's Bible Handbook.* Grand Rapids, MI: Zondervan Pulishing House, pp. 428-475.

Hammond. 1990. *Atlas of the Bible Land.* Canada: Hammond World Atlas Corporation, pp, 36-37.

Jeremias, J. 1966. *Rediscovering the Parables.* New York, NY: Charles Scribner's Sons, pp. 71-87.

Lockyer, Herbert. 1991. *All the Teachings of Jesus.* New York, NY: Harper and Row, p. 305.

Lockyer, Herbert. 1963. *All the Parables of the Bible.* Grand Rapids, MI: Zondervan Publishing House, pp. 9-23.

# Food Security in the Roman Empire and Faith-Based Response to Human Needs: The 46 C.E. Famine in Jerusalem

William A. Dando and Bharath Ganesh Babu

## INTRODUCTION

Faith, i.e., belief and trust, is based on evidence of things not seen, along with confidence, conviction, and substance of things hoped for. It is a mind-set that certain statements and events are true, and it serves as motivation for action and believing in things when common sense tells a person that he or she should not. Faith without seeking knowledge, having trust, and implementing action is meaningless. The new Christian Church's first faith-based response to human needs on a vast scale was manifested in the Jerusalem famine of 46 C.E. Hunger and famine were unexpected, irregular, cultural hazards that claimed the lives of many who dwelled in the Holy Land between 1850 B.C.E. and 70 C.E. Cultural decisions, religious antagonisms, civil strife, and war were the major factors in life-taking famine formation. The classic means of famine survival was to walk away from the place or region of absolute food scarcity to an area where food was available. In almost all cases of famine in ancient Israel, food was available within a few days walk from the famine center or region. Of the eleven major famines that occurred in 1850 B.C.E. to 70 C.E., the first five were rural famines, primarily characterized by lack of pasture grass, and these famines impacted animals most severely. The last six famines took place in urban areas and affected humans specifically.

Thus, the most appalling and shocking catastrophic famines occurred in major urban centers. The tenth biblical famine was a life-taking event that took place in Jerusalem when Rome controlled all of the lands along the shores of the Mediterranean Sea – including the Holy Land (Dando 1983: 231-249).

## THE ROMAN EMPIRE AND THE JEWISH DIASPORA

With the formation of the Roman Empire and *Pax Romana*, the movement of peoples throughout the Mediterranean world was made easier. Jews spread to the west, beyond Italy (Figure 1). They also were able to spread eastward through the Parthian Empire to India, and a sizeable community had established itself in Babylonia. The main areas of concentration, however, remained in Judea, Syria, western Asia Minor, and Egypt where Alexandria had become a major center of Greco-Jewish culture (Dowley *et al* 1997: 67-70).

Emperor Augustus brought peace, prosperity, and stability to the Roman Empire. By the time of his death in 14 C.E., the frontiers of the Empire had been made secure: the Danube River became the northern frontier and a series of buffer states protected Asia Minor and the eastern Mediterranean from the Parthians in the east. Some of these states were "client" kingdoms which acknowledged Roman dominance in return for Roman protection. Further conquests by Emperor Trajan (Dacia, Arabia, Armenia, and Mesopotamia) expanded the imperial boundary to its maximum extent in 116 C.E.

An extensive program of road building enabled a Roman citizen to travel safely and quickly from Britain to Mesopotamia (Figure 2). A citizen needed no languages other than Latin and Greek, no passport, and only the Roman *denarius* for currency.

Jews in the Inter-Testament period came to be far more numerous outside Palestine than those in Palestine. Colonies of Jews grew strong in every land and in all the major cities in the Roman world. In the time of

Figure 1. The Jews in the Roman Empire in the First Few Decades of the New Millennium

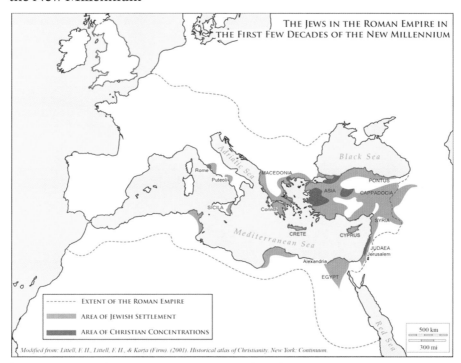

Source: Modified from F. H. Littell and Karta (Firm). 2001. *Historical Atlas of Christianity.* New York, NY: Continuum.

Christ, the number of Jews in Egypt was estimated at one million.

Also, very large numbers of Jews could be found in Damascus and Antioch. They influenced the socioeconomic growth and development of wherever they lived, and their religion, Judaism, was influenced by the religious thought of these nations (Cohn-Sherbok 1994: 49; Ward 1952: 66).

## THE RAPID SPREAD OF CHRISTIANITY AND THE RELIGION'S IMPACT ON FAMINE RELIEF

An understanding of the diffusion of Christianity is very essential to the comprehension of famine relief in the world since 46 C.E. Rather quickly this humble religion developed in an obscure segment of

Figure 2. The Roman Transportation System at the Time of Claudius

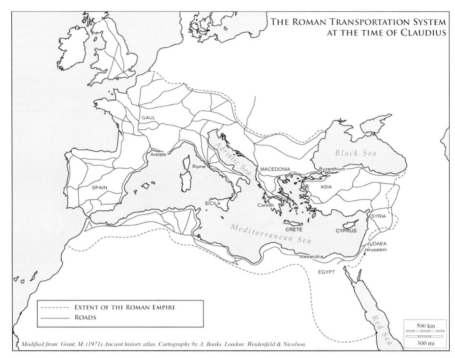

Source: Modified from M. Grant. 1971. *Ancient History Atlas*. Cartography by A. Banks. London: Weidenfeld & Nicolson.

the Roman Empire, derived vigor from opposition, and eventually spread to all corners of the world. It is amazing that the Christian faith achieved a remarkable victory over the established religions of the earth owing to the convincing evidence of the doctrine itself. The message was embodied in the story of the life, teaching, deeds, death, and resurrection of Jesus Christ. The growth of the Christian Church was a factor of its message, the zeal of its believers, the doctrine of a future life, the power of faith, the pure and austere morals of believers, and the discipline of the members of the Church that bonded them into a unified religious body, the Christian Church, initially in the heart of the Roman Empire (Gibbon 1994: 446-511).

The Jews languished under the Assyrian and Persian monarchies, emerged from obscurity under the successors of Alexander the Great, multiplied to become an influenced segment in the eastern Mediterranean lands, and then spread to the lands surrounding the coast of the Mediterranean Sea and into Africa and Asia. The Jews refused to merge or be assimilated into the many cultures and religions of the ancient world. Their sullen obstinacy with which they maintained their beliefs and customs marked them as a distinct religious group. Neither the violence of Antiochus, the conniving of Herod, the politeness of Augustus, nor the madness of Caligula could deter their zeal and devotion to the God of Abraham, Isaac, and Jacob. Judaism, as a formal religion, was admirably fitted for defense; it was never designed to attract masses of proselytes. It was basically a single family whose laws and traditions separated a chosen people from the rest of humankind. The obligation of preaching to the Gentiles the tenets of the faith of Moses was not included in the Law. Descendants of Abraham alone were the heirs to the Covenant (Table 1).

While the Jews shunned the society of strangers, the more liberal zeal of a religious denomination with its foundation in Judaism, i.e., Christianity, embraced Gentiles and began to spread to the known world (Table 2). Christianity, based on the unifying strength of the Mosaic law, presented to the Gentiles without the fetters and stressing the unity in God for all humankind, was embraced by the poor and the rich alike. The divine authority of Moses and the prophets was stressed, as were predictions of the coming of the Messiah. Judaism's ceremonial law was succeeded by spiritual worship that blended well into all cultures and was attractive to freeman and slave, to the Greek and to the barbarian, and to the Jew and the Gentile. It became a sacred duty of a Christian to spread the good news of Jesus Christ among friends, relatives, and strangers (Little 2005: 142).

It was natural that the rites and rituals of Judaism be observed in an off-shoot church that was founded shortly after the death of Christ. Christ's followers were first called Christians in Antioch. The bonds of the Temple and the most difficult aspects of Jewish religious culture for Gentiles to accept took time to be modified and embraced. However, when numerous and wealthy churches were established in the great cities of the Empire, in Antioch, Alexandria, Ephesus, Corinth, and Rome, the

## Table 1. Spreading the Gospel by a Chosen Few

The transition to the Christian mission was not the result of conscious deliberations and solemn discussions among the early Church leaders in Jerusalem. It was more an obvious extension of the work being done with non-Christian Jews. The momentous step of preaching to the Gentiles was taken independently by Paul. Those involved in spreading the Gospel to non-Jews included:

1. **Peter** – preached in Jerusalem, throughout Palestine, Babylon, and Rome. He was martyred by Nero in Rome.

2. **John** – preached in Asia Minor, Macedonia, Corinth, Ephesus, seven churches in Asia, Samaria, and Patmos Island. He died in Ephesus.

3. **Matthew** – preached in Palestine and taught in neighboring foreign countries including Greece. He was beheaded – the first disciple martyred.

4. **James** – preached in Palestine. He was beheaded by Herod Agrippa in 44 C.E.

5. **Andrew** – preached in Asia Minor, Greece, and Scythia. He was martyred in Patrae, Archia by crucifixion.

6. **Phillip** – preached in Phrygia, Caesarea, and Samaria. He was martyred in Hieropolis, Phrygia.

7. **Bartholomew** (Nathaniel) – preached in Parthia, Armenia, and India. He was martyred in Armenia; flayed alive and crucified head-downward.

8. **Thomas** – preached in Syria, Parthia, and India. He was martyred by a lance.

9. **James** (brother of Jesus) – preached in Palestine and was a church administrator in Jerusalem. He taught in Egypt and was martyred by stoning in 62 C.E.

10. **Thaddeus** – preached in Edessa, Syria, Arabia, Mesopotamia, Armenia, and Iran. He was martyred by being speared repeatedly and then stoned.

11. **Simon** – a zealot and member of the Kaneweak sect, preached in Armenia and Iran. He was stoned to death and then sawn into pieces.

12. **Paul** – preached in Cyprus, Rhodes, Asia Minor, Asia, Bithynia, Macedonia, Greece, Italy, Rome, Eastern Europe, and Spain. He was martyred by beheading in 66 C.E. in Rome on orders from Nero.

new covenant and the new interpretation of the Law as presented by Christ in his sermon on the Mount eased cultural obstruction to Gentiles joining the family of God. Of specific concern of religiously-minded seekers of a way was the uncertainty of the immortality of the soul and life after death. While the Jewish Sadducees piously rejected immortality of the soul, the Jewish Pharisees did believe in the immortality of the soul. Pharisees believed in fate, predestination, angels, spirits, and an after-death state of rewards and punishments. The doctrine of future life and immortality obtained sanction of divine truth from the authority and example of Jesus Christ. The promise of eternal happiness on condition of adopting Christianity resulted in converts to Christianity from all walks of life.

The message of hope and belonging, the zeal of the believers, the doctrine of a future life, and the miraculous powers of the primitive Christian Church attracted converts from the established religions of the age. Supernatural gifts, such as speaking in tongues, visions and prophecy, expelling demons, healing the sick, raising the dead, and miraculous cures ascribed to Christians who had faith were desired by segments of society who lacked hope and lived a life of want. The most curious and most credulous of pagans were often persuaded to become a member of this new church which asserted the possession of attributes not held by other religions. Absolute faith in the miracles ascribed to Jesus Christ and his disciples, plus faith in those who had received the Holy Spirit, impressed non-believers to join the new church.

Early Christians demonstrated their faith by living virtuous lives, doing good works, and serving as examples to be emulated. Following the examples of Jesus Christ, early Christian missionaries lived and worked alongside those who were converted and understood the temptations and the struggles to survive in a cruel society. Through faith those who were imperfect and had not lived blameless lives emerged from sin and despair to the hope of immortality and a special place of rest and solace. New converts, when admitted to the sacraments of the church, were bound by solemn obligation to abstain from theft, robbery, adultery, perjury, and fraud. Their serious devotion to the teachings of Jesus Christ inured them with chastity, temperance, respect for others, concern for the less advantaged, and strictest integrity. Their mutual charity, unbreakable confidence, and high morals, combined with humility and patience, set them apart from most people at that time.

The new religion which threatened the established religions of

## Table 2. A Postulated Chronology in Acts of the Apostles

| | |
|---|---|
| c. 29/30 C.E. | Death of Jesus (rose from the dead and made 10 or 11 recorded appearances to his disciples) |
| 30/31 C.E. | Formation of the Church in Jerusalem (50 days after Jesus' resurrection and 10 days after his ascension in Heaven) |
| 31 C.E. | Stoning of Stephen and Dispersion of the Church |
| 32 C.E. | Conversion of Saul (Paul) |
| 34 C.E. | Paul's First Visit to Jerusalem after His Conversion |
| 35 C.E. | Peter's Conversion of Cornelius, the Roman Gentile |
| 42 C.E. | Reception of Gentiles into the New Church in Antioch |
| 46-48 C.E. | Paul's First Missionary Journey (Galatia) |
| 46 C.E. | The Jerusalem Famine |
| 46 C.E. | Paul's Second Visit to Jerusalem |
| 50 C.E. | Council of Jerusalem |
| 51-53 C.E. | Paul's Second Missionary Journey (Greece) |
| 54-57 C.E. | Paul's Third Missionary Journey (Ephesus) |
| 57-58 C.E. | Paul in Macedonia, Corinth, and Philippi |
| 58 C.E. | Paul in Jerusalem |
| 58-60 C.E. | Paul in Caesarea |
| 61 C.E. | Paul's Voyage to Rome |
| 61-63 C.E. | Paul in Rome |

Sources: Henry H. Halley. 1959. *Halley's Bible Handbook*. Grand Rapids, MI: Zondervan Publishing House, pp. 559-560; D. I Lanslots. 1980. *The Primitive Church (the Church in the Days of the Apostles)*. Rockford, IL: Tan Books and Publishers, Inc., p. 91; Halford E. Luccock. 1942. *The Acts of the Apostles*. Chicago and New York: Willet, Clark and Co., pp. 1-164.

the Empire, was obliged to adopt internal governing policies, appoint administrators and ministers, select individuals to set and maintain philosophical standards and church rituals, and set the goals and objectives of the new Christian commonwealth. It was necessary to bring together all the various approaches in the interpretation of Jesus Christ's message into one sound and accurate book of discipline – to create a dynamic, all inclusive, unified religious body based on the teachings of Jesus Christ.

Churches that were founded in the cities of the Roman Empire were initially united only by ties of faith and belief in one God and his son, Jesus Christ. The need for discipline, direction, or clarification of doctrine was supplied by missionaries or prophets. Soon it became apparent that a more formal approach to church governance and direction were needed and the public functions of the new church were solely entrusted to established and approved ministers and bishops. These early bishops were considered men of high repute and the honorable servants of a free people believing in one God. Bishops, the wise men of the new church, resolved controversies of faith and discipline with the assistance of debate, prayer, and the presence of the Holy Spirit. From a loose alliance of dispersed churches evolved a unified religion, administrated by insightful individuals, selected in an informal election process. Unity in tenets and ritual from diversity of interpretations, derived from cultural differences, evolved into an international religious entity based on their agreement in the message and teachings of Jesus Christ.

The Christian Church grew out of the character of its members. They possessed a burning zeal, death-defying faith, untiring industry, singleness of purpose, patient suffering, sublime courage, and profession of a message of love and hope through the church as one body – a church founded on the union of believers bonded by faith.

## FOOD SECURITY IN THE ROMAN EMPIRE DURING THE RULE OF EMPEROR CLAUDIUS I, 41-54 C.E.

The Roman Empire was a political structure differing from any of the empires that preceded it. Great changes in the texture of human society and in the conditions of social interrelationships had been going on for centuries. The flexibility and the transferability of money were becoming powers for political and cultural control and socioeconomic advancement. Transferability altered the relations of rich men to the state and their poorer fellow citizens. This new empire, the Roman Empire, was not the creation of a mighty conqueror. It grew out of a foundation laid by a republic. The introduction of money increased the power of the usurer and the difficulties of the borrowing debtor. It eventually led to a division of the people into the aristocratic (wealthy) and the common citizens (poor) who were called, in Rome, patricians and plebeians. These two groups made up the Roman state and were its citizens; the slaves and outlanders were not considered part of the state. Free peasants or plebeians dispersed over the countryside were not only excluded from public office but from inter-marriage with the patrician class who lived primarily in fortified towns. The patricians made use of their political advantages to grow rich through war and conquests at the expense of not only the defeated enemy but also the poorer plebeian whose farm was neglected and who fell into debt serving in the Roman army (Garnsey 1988: 271).

Life in the Roman Empire became a struggle between those who had – the patricians – and those who had very little – the plebeians. The plebeians won a greater share in the government and the wealth coming to Rome as the Empire grew in military power and political stature. The plebeians' use of "general strikes" and threats of mass violence won them privileges and rights. The strikes of the plebeians and the "aristocratic" or patricians often led to famines such as the one in 440 B.C.E. After the sack of Rome by the Gauls in 390 B.C.E. and the recovery by the plebeians who suffered severely from the after-war usury and profiteering by the patricians from whom they were forced to borrow funds to rebuild their houses and outbuildings and restock their farms, the struggle between classes abated. Trade and taxes from territories controlled by Rome led many plebeians to become wealthy. Laws were changed to permit inter-marriage and social mixture became common. New social classes were emerging with fresh approaches to old problems. These classes included freedmen, freed slaves, artisans, traders, and merchants. Roman citizenship, a coveted award, was extended and grew cautiously but steadily. Garrisons of full citizens were established at strategic sites, and many new towns and cities were established. As the Roman Empire expanded and prospered, the need to keep communications open was realized and a system of roads, sea lanes and ports, and the spread of Latin bonded the Empire together. The first of high roads (highways), the Appian Way, linked the city of Rome to the heel of Italy in 312 B.C.E. According to the census of 265 B.C.E., the population of the Empire exceeded 300,000 citizens. In 89 B.C.E., all free inhabitants in Italy became Roman citizens (Niebuhr 1844: 3, 123, 269).

The taste of plunder and the jealousy of Carthage's sea power led the wealthy decision makers of the Empire in Rome to instigate an "offensive defensive" war with Carthage that began in 264 B.C.E. and ended in 202 B.C.E. Victorious in battle, the rich decision makers in Rome destroyed the city of Carthage, demanded that the Carthaginians all be removed ten miles from the sea and surrender all territory they controlled, and salted their land, making it impossible to grow crops. The Romans, in essence, murdered the city of Carthage and then did the same to Corinth when it tried to limit Roman trade monopolies. Many subsequent wars were fought and won. Ordinary Roman citizens lost their sons, became impoverished, and slowly drifted to cities for employment, food, and shelter. From the end of the wars with Carthage to the Christian era (specifically the great political genius, Emperor Constantine the Great, centuries later), the ignorance of the common people led to the dissolution of a Roman-style republic to control by emperors or caesars (Evans 1981: 428-442).

There emerged in Rome and throughout the Empire a "cash-and-credit-using" system. Money had been utilized in various places and nations in the world for centuries. However, its use and means of transferring money was recognized by the leaders of Rome as providing a liquid medium for trade and enterprise. Its use changed trade and commerce profoundly. The effect of money was to give people freedom of choice, movement, and leisure, and it expanded commercial opportunities. With the use of money, those who had wealth ceased to be tied to land, house, stores, flocks, and herds. The release of this untethered wealth stimulated commerce, trade, and the general economic health of the Roman world. No longer were debts paid exclusively by bars of precious metals, stocks of goods, or heads of cattle. The big cities before Rome were trading and manufacturing cities, specifically Corinth, Carthage, Syracuse, and Alexandria. Rome was not a trading or manufacturing center; it was a political and financial center. It imported profits and tributes, and very little went out from Rome in return. New freedoms, expanded opportunities, and enhanced power in Rome were based on their "cash-and-credit" monetary system. The eastward expansion of the Roman Empire was largely a hunt for treasures in strong-rooms or temples to keep pace with the need for money. There was a Roman proverb, "*Pecunia non olet*"(money does not stink).

The Roman "cash and credit" monetary system was augmented by a method of moving money by a bill of exchange drawn upon an individual, a family, a financial group, a close-knit international monetary exchange, or rudimental bank; it was payable on demand. This simple but effective method of transferring funds had evolved slowly in the Middle East and eastern Mediterranean, was refined somewhat by Jewish traders, and proved very useful in international, national, and regional commerce and in transferring money to the Temple. Basically a practical method of circulating credit evolved. A "check" became, among the Jews particularly, a negotiable instrument and a written order to reimburse a seller for a product or service. It could be transferred to another person or entity by endorsement.

Most checks were "order" checks, reading "pay to the order of . . ." requiring the person whose name was on the check, known as the "payee," to endorse the check before it was paid. Most checks were not paid in currency but by debiting or crediting deposits. When a check was presented for payment, it was carefully examined, and then the date, signature, and endorsement were noted to determine that the writer of the check had sufficient funds to "cover" the check or to extend credit based on rudimental credit reports. Forms of a "cashier's check" and a "certified check" were used frequently by financial institutions or "banks" against itself and were signed by the cashier or some other bank officer. It was equivalent to cash and unquestioned as money exchange. Checks had a lower risk of loss by theft; they eliminated the need to transport heavy gold or silver great distances; and they provided a receipt. The early development of banking practices, checks, and letters of exchange made credit an important monetary medium in commerce and trade. The Jews in 46 C.E. had in place a means of transferring funds and paying debts by use of "letters of credit" or checks. Also the Jews' linguistic and financial skills won them responsible positions in local administrative and in local or regional business and commercial activities.

Claudius, seeking funds to finance the Roman government, army, and grain purchases to feed Rome's large urban population, was a conscious expansionist of the Empire. He annexed Thrace, Lycia, Judea, and Maurentania. Claudius invaded Britain, put much of the island under his control, and added the Orkneys to the Empire. Also he built a harbor and granaries at Ostia near Rome to ensure the support of the citizens of Rome, for their allegiance was only gained and kept by a substantial retainer of grain. Once when they thought that he had failed them, they made their position clear to Claudius by pelting him with a shower of stale bread crusts (Levick 1990: 878). The city of Rome had grown in population far beyond that which could be sustained from the farms, orchards, and vineyards of Italy. Rome had to be supplied grain, oil, and wine from Sicily, Egypt, Africa, Spain, and to some extent, Judea (Hammond 1946). Egypt alone, when it fell under Roman political control in 30 B.C.E., provided one-third of Rome's annual grain supply – approximately 135,000 tons of grain (Mayerson 1997). In years of high yields, wheat was stored in public and private granaries to cover shortages in the event of a low-Nile area flood. Stored surpluses of grain from Egypt and North Africa made it possible for the Roman government to meet food crises in Italy and other provinces of the Empire. Two-thirds of the land cultivated in Egypt was solely dependent on Nile water and planted only to grain crops (Kessler and Temin 2007: 308-332 and Levick 1978: 79-105).

## FAMINES IN THE ROMAN EMPIRE DURING THE RULE OF CLAUDIUS I, 41-54 C.E.

In the days of Claudius Caesar, no less than four different famines were mentioned by ancient historians. He began his reign in 41 C.E. and ruled for 13 years. He was poisoned by one of his wives, Agrippina, who wanted to place her son Nero on the throne. During Claudius' reign, at least four famines occurred, one of which was particularly severe in Judea. The **first famine** took place in Rome in the first and second years of his reign, 41-42 C.E. It was triggered by difficulties in importing grain from Egypt. To prevent this from happening again, Claudius constructed a state-of-the-art port at the mouth of the Tiber River at Ostia, a convenient and dependable passage from the new port to the city of Rome. The **second famine** took place in the years 45, 46, and 47 C.E., and it was very severe in the fifth and early sixth year of his reign. It was one of the most devastating famines in Judean scholars' recollections. Jerusalem languished, but help did not come from Rome to any degree nor was there any remedy proposed to ease the famine. This famine claimed the most lives in 46 C.E. The coastal cities of Judea endured the food shortages relatively well. They sold what food surpluses they had stored and secured what they needed to diversify their diets from sea-going commercial vessels. Those who lived far inland from the Mediterranean Sea, given the prohibitive cost of land transportation, survived on what they produced, on what they could buy to augment their diet, and on famine foods. The greatest loss of life occurred in inland cities such as Jerusalem. Some food was available in Jerusalem, but the food was so expensive, the poor could not afford to buy the food that they needed to sustain life. The **third famine** occurred in Greece in the eighth and ninth years of Claudius' reign, 48 and 49 C.E. Wheat prices increased six times that of normal years. Food was available to those who could afford to buy it. The poor suffered horribly and many died. The **fourth famine** took place in the latter years of Claudius' reign, 51-52 C.E. This famine created havoc, and large numbers of those who lived in Rome starved to death. Priests in the city's temples deemed this famine a "divine judgment" (Vincent 1905: 222-223; Levick 1990: 109-111, 179-184; Wells 1984: 3, 123, 269).

The causes of the famine in Jerusalem, particularly in 46 C.E., were complex, yet the procedures to remedy the disaster were simple. The death of Herod Agrippa in 44 C.E. ended a period of relative tranquility in Judea. Judea reverted to the status of a Roman province, and the administrators were not knowledgeable of Jewish culture at that time. They fostered tensions between the rich and the poor in Jerusalem and Judea; civil disobedience was ubiquitous, social cohesiveness was weakened, and these combined to precipitate the rise of political rebels, religious prophets, and holy men who roamed the country. Civil strife and anti-Roman insurrections took place in most cities of Judea. Those Christians, who could, fled Jerusalem and Judea for other Jewish colonies of a sort, in cities within the Roman Empire and Asia. One destination was Antioch (Argubright 2003: 41-44; Grant 1985: 29-34).

Claudius I initially had made Herod Agrippa king over all the districts that his grandfather had ruled. Once more the Jews had their own king, a popular monarch, a Pharisee, and a strict Jew. He died in 44 C.E. and the rule of the procurators was restored. Under the rule of Cuspius Fadus, many patriot bandits were captured and killed. Theudas, who claimed to be a prophet and led a minor revolt against Roman authority, was captured and beheaded. After Fadus came Tiberius Alexander, an apostate Jew from Egypt. The next procurator, Ventitius Cumanus (48-52 C.E.) provoked the Jews to riot. A massacre took place in the Temple and there was a clash between Samaritans and Galileans. Cumanus ultimately was banished by the Emperor and replaced by Felix (52-60 C.E.) under whom the revolutionary movement grew in intensity. Claudius' selection of procurators accelerated the movement of Jewish Christians from Jerusalem and Judea.

Antioch, on the Orontes River, ranked as the capital of the East, and was the seat of the imperial legate of the Roman provinces of Syria and Cilicia. According to Josephus, it was the third largest city of the Roman Empire, second only to Rome and Alexandria. Its culture was chiefly Greek. Antioch was a very important city of commerce; its port on the Mediterranean Sea was Seleucia. The center of gravity of Christianity rapidly passed from Jerusalem to Antioch. Tradition closely associates Peter with the city, naming him as its first bishop. Christianity in Jerusalem was not destroyed after the death of Stephen – it was dispersed. Barnabas was a very important figure in the early church; he was the leader in the movement which resulted in the transference of the Church's headquarters from Jerusalem to Antioch. Paul's work in the Church and in Antioch was primarily because of the support and encouragement of Barnabas. Other Christians left Jerusalem and joined those in Antioch, including a prophet named Agabus. He reported that the Holy Spirit had empowered him to predict that a great famine was about to take place throughout the world in the days of Claudius Caesar. Both Tacitus in his *Annals XII*, 43 and Suetonius in *Claudius* 18, confirmed that there were several famines in Claudius' reign, 41-54 C.E. Josephus in *Antiquities XX*.5 mentions one in Judea which was at its worst, circa 46 C.E. Crops had failed in many Roman Empire food-producing regions due to excessive rainfall, flooding, and disease, along with problems in Roman agricultural organization and the urban food supply system. A breakdown of the Roman Empire's transportation network enhanced urban food shortages. There were great losses of human life. The members of the Antioch church, every man according to his ability, decided to contribute to the first Christian Church Famine Relief Fund and sent the cash to help their fellow Christians and others who lived in Judaea. They did not want to send cash by post, but chose Barnabas and Paul to be bearers of the aid (Swete 1905: 202-214; Yamauchi 1980: 193-202).

Other faith-based famine relief came from those who ascribed to Judaism. Josephus reported that:

> About this time it was Helena, queen of Adiabene, and her son Izates changed their course of life, and embraced the Jewish customs. Monobazazus, the king of Adiabene, fell in love with his sister Helena, and took her to be his wife, and begat her with child. . . when his son was born he called him Izates. . . . he openly placed his affections on . . . Izates.

The brothers of Izates were envious and hated him for his father's open preference for him. His brothers' hatred forced Monobazazus to send his beloved first son to Abennerig, king of Charax-Spasini, to protect him. Izates married Samacha, Abennerig's daughter, and eventually became king of Charax-Spasini.

The story continues that:

> . . . the king's mother, when she saw that the affairs of Izates' kingdom were in peace, and that her son was a happy man, and admired among all men, . . . had a mind to go to the city of Jerusalem, in order to worship at the temple of God which was very famous among all men, and to offer her thank-offerings there. So she desired her son to give her leave to go thither. . . gave her a great deal of money, and she went down to the city of Jerusalem. Now her coming was of great advantage to the people of Jerusalem; for whereas a famine did oppress them at that time. . . . many people died of want of what was necessary to procure food. . . . queen Helena sent some of her servants to Alexandria with money to buy a great quantity of corn [wheat], and others of them to Cyprus to bring a cargo of dried figs. . . . and as soon as they were come back . . . she distributed the food to those who were in want of it. . . . When her son Izates was informed of the famine, he sent a great sum of money to the principal men in Jerusalem (Josephus 1960: 84, 415-416).

## FACTORS THAT CONTRIBUTED TO THE JERUSALEM FAMINE OF 46 C.E.

Eleven famine periods in almost 2,000 years are not excessive. They do reflect a physical environment and a socioeconomic system conducive to support human food needs. Food consumed in the nomad tents and houses of those who lived in ancient Israel was varied, nutritious, and more than adequate in times of peace, in reasonable weather or a normal agroclimatic year, and in times of uninterrupted inter-regional and international trade. However, food was scarce in portions of ancient Israel at times, due to droughts, frosts, hail, soil loss or soil depletion, insect infestations, plant diseases, questionable food preservation techniques, greed, food hording, and war. Hebrews, Israelites, and Jews prized their food, gave food as gifts, and dreaded food scarcity and famine. Providing food to someone who hurt you or who was an enemy was considered a superlative good deed. There was never a nationwide food shortage in ancient Israel, and there was no reason for a crop failure to trigger a famine (Dando 2012: 6-8).

C. R. Little, in a 2005 study of Paul and biblical missions for a church in the twenty-first century, reported:

> We have clear evidence that there was an unusually high Nile during the reign of Claudius, indeed a one-hundred-year flood (eighteen cubits high) in A.D. 45, which in turn flooded the fields where the grain grew in Egypt, thus causing a severely late grain harvest but also one below normal size. By August-November of 45, the price of grain had jumped to more than twice that of any other recorded price in the Roman period before the reign of Vespasian because it was known what sort of bad crop was in store by the end of the year. A.D. 46 was going to be a very bad year for those depending on buying grain to make bread. Indeed, the effects of the famine were likely to stretch into 47 because of grain hording once the severe grain shortage in Egypt became widely known (142).

Furthermore, the Jewish sabbatical year in which the land lay fallow may have fallen in the period of excessive rainfall and flooding in Roman Empire food-producing regions. Also, there was a double increase in Roman taxes and a political priority of feeding the citizens of Rome at the human cost of famine deaths in other segments of the Empire.

# AGABUS AND GUIDELINES FOR CHRISTIAN FAMINE RELIEF

There was an interval in Jewish history, according to Professor H. B. Swete writing in 1905, when it was commonly believed that prophecy was dead. Yet the Christian era opens with a revival of formal prophecy in Jerusalem. Among many recognized early prophets were Zacharias, Simeon, Hannah, John the Baptist, and Jesus. As the early Christian Church began to form, it incorporated scribes, teachers, and prophets through whom the voice of God could make himself heard again. The early Christian prophets were men capable, through the Spirit, of guiding believers to new fields of life and thought. But in the Christian Church as well as in the Jewish synagogue, the prophetic spirit found expression chiefly in the words of individuals charged with special gifts. The first definite reference to Christian prophets occurred in Acts 11: 27. Shortly before a famine in the time of Claudius, about 44 or 45 C.E., a band of prophets went down from Jerusalem to Antioch. One of the prophets from Jerusalem, named Agabus, foretold the coming of a horrible life-taking famine in Jerusalem in the near future; the famine took place the next year (Swete 1905). Believing and trusting and based on evidence not seen, the Christians in Antioch immediately responded. Members of the new Christian Church in Antioch determined that, according to their ability, each would contribute to a Jerusalem relief fund. After all donations were received, they were carried to the Church elders in Jerusalem by Barnabas and Paul (*Holy Bible* 1989: 136). For many years afterwards, "prophets and teachers" ministered in the church at Antioch.

Famine relief funds from Antioch to the elders of Jerusalem to purchase food for those who were starving from the famine were not used to covert people to Christianity; famine relief was "missionary-activity" motivated. Money carried to Jerusalem by Barnabas and Paul was a faith-based compassionate response to a humanitarian need. The famine relief act was also an offer for closer ties with the Church in Jerusalem, a gesture for the missionaries and teachers which the Church in Jerusalem had sent to Antioch and a demonstration of the bond of common faith that linked all Christian churches together. To some extent, the relief funds reflected the respect and veneration of the Jerusalem Church, and they did serve as a model and provided guidelines for future Christian famine relief. Apparently there was no famine or food shortages in Antioch because if there had been, the members of the Antioch Church would not have been able to send famine relief to Jerusalem. Also since they did not send food but cash to Jerusalem, food must have been available to purchase in Jerusalem.

The famine in Jerusalem and Judea extended for years and terrible economic problems plagued those who lived there. The Jerusalem Church survived the horrors of the 46 C.E. famine year, but the food problems that followed took their tolls (Hammond 1946). Christian churches that had been established in other cities of the Roman Empire also took up collections to meet the needs of the Judean churches. Paul, teaching in Corinth, guided the Corinthian Church's famine relief mobilization. He believed that relief of the poor was a critical aspect of Christian life. In 1 Corinthians 16: 1-4, Paul wrote:

> Now the matter about the money to be raised to help God's people in Judea; you must do what I told the churches in Galatia to do. Every Sunday each of you must put aside some money, in proportion to what he has earned, and save it up, so there will be no need to collect money when I come. After I come I shall send the men you have approved, with letters of introduction, to take your gift to Jerusalem. If it seems worthwhile for me to go, then they will go along with me.

Corinth was a bustling political and commercial center in the main transportation routes from Rome to the eastern Roman provinces. Pagan religious and worldly ethics flourished among its polyglot population of mixed nationalities and races. In his second missionary journey Paul spent almost 18 months in Corinth. While in Ephesus, after leaving Corinth, he wrote a letter to the Corinthians offering guidance on how

Christians should act and solve problems – including aid to other Christian congregations and to the poor in other provinces of the Roman Empire. He stressed the motivations for sharing liberally with those in need. He wrote in 2 Corinthians 8: 1-5 and 13-14:

> We want you to know, brothers, what God's grace has done in the churches of Macedonia. They have been severely tested by the troubles they went through; but their joy was so great that they were extremely generous in their giving, even though they were very poor. I assure you, they gave as much as they could, and even more than they could. Of their own free will they begged us and insisted on the privilege of having part in helping God's people in Judea. . . . it is only fair that you should help those who are in need. Then, when you are in need and they have plenty, they will help you. In this way both are treated equally.

Paul stressed proportional giving, did not require any particular amount or percentage of income, asked members to give according to their means, and insisted that a heart of cheer and gladness accompany Christian giving (2 Corinthians 9: 7). There was hunger in Corinth at that time, but the Corinthians had enough food, relatively inexpensive food, to survive. He did not expect the Corinthians to give beyond their means, but to just live the faith.

## IMPACT OF THE NEW CHRISTIAN CHURCH'S HUNGER AND FAMINE RELIEF POLICIES

The new Christian Church's first international hunger and famine relief program was an outgrowth of a prophecy by a member of the Jerusalem Church to members of the Christian Church in Antioch. Agabus predicted a famine would claim the lives of many who lived in Jerusalem and Judea. The famine did occur, it was a three-year famine, and it was most devastating in Jerusalem in 46 C.E. Based on their faith in Agabus's prediction, funds were raised from members of the church. The first Christian Famine Relief Fund was based on church members giving according to their ability to those according to their need. Barnabas and Paul made the initial famine-relief visit to Jerusalem in 46 C.E. and delivered a monetary gift from the church at Antioch. At that time, the Jerusalem Church members expressed the hope that the believers in the new Christian churches outside of Judea would continue to remember those in Judea.

Paul was deeply committed and eager to raise funds for the relief effort (Galatians 2: 10). The collection effort was successfully completed in 57 C.E. The churches in Macedonia and Achaia were pleased to make contributions for the poor in Jerusalem as were those churches in Berea, Thessalonica, Derbe, Asia, Philippi, Lystra, and Corinth. A more than ten year hunger-famine relief campaign to aid the poor in Jerusalem and Judea was in response to persistent food shortages, double taxation by the Romans, over-population aggravated by diaspora Jews returning to Jerusalem to die and be buried there, a steady increase in widows and elderly in need of assistance, and a precarious Palestinian economy administered by inept Roman officials. The Jerusalem Church Relief Fund served as a visible expression of the interdependence of Christian believers worldwide and a tangible representation of the heart of the Christian message, i.e., in Jesus Christ is neither Jew nor Greek, neither slave nor free, neither male nor female (Galatians 3: 28; Beitzel 1985: 179).

Since the beginning of the Christian Church, shortly after the death of Jesus Christ, the Church has been deeply involved globally in human health and welfare through many programs of relief, rehabilitation, and service – including issues of hunger and famine. Most Christian churches follow the model and guidelines set by the Antioch Church in about 43 and 44 C.E. They try to:

1. Seek and address human needs in the spirit of Jesus Christ;
2. Provide immediate relief of acute human need and respond to the suffering of persons in the world caused

by natural, ecological, cultural, and political turmoil;

3.  Work cooperatively with appropriate giving units, inter-denominational agencies, and philanthropic groups;

4.  Administer aid while preserving the dignity of persons without regard of religion, race, nationality, or gender; and

5.  Assist and train relief fund coordinators/administrators to means of addressing emerging and ongoing issues related to the root causes of hunger and famine.

From its inception, the Christian Church strongly has affirmed the right of everyone on earth to have access to safe and nutritious food and the fundamental right of everyone to be free of hunger and secure from death by famine.

## REFERENCES

Argubright, John. 2003. "The Famine of Acts Chapter 11." *Bible Believer's Archaeology. The Search for Truth.* Volume 2.  Kearney, NE: Morris Publications.

Beitzel, Barry. 1985. *The Moody Atlas of Bible Lands.* Chicago: Moody Press.

Biblos. "Acts 11: 28-30" <http: //bible.cc/acts/11-28.htm>.

Cohn-Sherbok, Dan. 1994. *Atlas of Jewish History.* New York: Routledge.

Dando, William A. 2012. *Food and Famine in the 21ˢᵗ Century.* Volume 2. Santa Barbara: CA: ABC-CLIO.

Dando, William A. 1983. "Biblical Famines, 1850 B.C.-A.D. 46: Insights for Modern Mankind." *Ecology of Food and Nutrition.* Vol. 13, No. 4.

de Ste Croix. 1981. *The Class Struggle in the Ancient Greek World from the Archaic Age to the Arab Conquests.* London: Duckworth Press.

Dowley, Tim, Alan Millard, David Wright, and Brian Stanley. 1997. *The Baker Atlas of Christian History.* Grand Rapids, MI: Baker Books.

Evans, J. K. 1981. "Wheat Production and Its Social Consequences in the Roman World." *The Classical Quarterly, New Series.* Vol. 31, No. 2.

Garnsey, P. 1988. *Famine and Food Supply in the Graeco-Roman World.*

Cambridge, England: Cambridge University Press.

Gibbon, Edward. 1994. *The History of the Decline and Fall of the Roman Empire.* Volume 1. London: The Penguin Press (Allen Lane).

Grant, Michael. 1985. *The Roman Emperors: A Biographical Guide to the Rulers of Imperial Rome 31 B.C.-A.D. 476.* New York: Charles Scribner's Sons.

Hammond, Mason. 1946. "Economic Stagnation in the Early Roman Empire." *The Journal of Economic History, Vol. 6 Supplement: The Tasks of Economic History,* May.

*Holy Bible: New Revised Standard Version.* 1989. Oxford, England: Oxford University Press.

Isbouts, Jean Pierre. 2007. *The Bible World: An Illustrated Atlas.* Washington, D.C.: National Geographic.

Josephus, Flavius. 1960. *Josephus: Complete Works.* (translated by William Weston). Grand Rapids: MI: Kregel Publications.

Kessler, David and Peter Temin. 2007. "The Organization of the Grain Trade in the Early Roman Empire." *Economic History Review.* Vol. 60, No. 2.

Levick, Barbara M. 1990. *Claudius.* New Haven and London: Yale University Press.

Levick, Barbara M. 1978. "Antiquarian or Revolutionary? Claudius Caesar's Conception of His Principate." *The American Journal of Philology.* Vol. 99, No. 1, Spring.

Little, C. R. 2005. *Mission in the Way of Paul: Biblical Mission for the Church in the Twenty-First Century.* New York: P. Lang Publishing.

Mayerson, Philip. 1997. "The Role of Flax in Roman and Fatimid Egypt." *Journal of Near Eastern Studies.* Vol. 56, No. 3, July.

Niebuhr, Barthold G. 1844. *The History of Rome.* Volume 3 (translated by William Smith and Leonhard Schmitz). Philadelphia: Lea & Blanchard.

Rostovtzeff, M. 1926. *The Social and Economic History of the Roman Empire.* Oxford, England: The Clarendon Press.

Scrimshaw, Nevin S. 1987. "The Phenomenon of Famine." *Ann. Rev. Nutr.* Vol. 7, pp. 1-22.

Swete, H. B. 1905. "The Prophets in the Christian Church." *The Biblical*

*World.* Vol. 26,   No. 3, Sept.

Vincent, Marvin Richardson. 1905. *Word Studies in the New Testament.* Volume 1. New York: Charles Scribner's Sons.

Ward, Baldwin H. 1952. *Pictorial History of the Bible and Christianity.* Wilton, CN: Year.

Wells, Colin. 1984. *The Roman Empire.* Stanford, CA: Stanford University Press.

Yamauchi, Erwin M. 1980. "Ancient Ecologies and the Biblical Perspective." *Journal of American Scientific Affiliation.* Vol. 32, No. 4, Dec.

## ACKNOWLEDGEMENTS

The authors wish to thank the following people for their assistance and suggestions in improving this chapter and for their kind words of support: The Rev. Tom True, Terre Haute District Superintendent of the United Methodist Church; Col. Gene Palka, Chairperson, Dept. of Geography and Engineering at the U. S. Military Academy at West Point; Mrs. Marion Dusenberry, Biblical Scholar and Adult Bible Class Teacher, Newell, PA; Prof. Ken Dawes, University of North Dakota and Adult Sunday School Teacher at University Lutheran Church, Grand Forks, ND; the Rev. Dana Newhouse, Trinity Lutheran Church, Terre Haute, IN; Mr. Steve Hardin, Reference/Instruction Librarian, Cunningham Library, Indiana State University, Terre Haute, IN; and Professor Jonathan Lu, Holy Light Theological Seminary, Kaohsiung, Taiwan.

# Urban Famines in Samaria and Jerusalem During Periods of Civil Unrest, Food Plundering, and Siege Warfare

William A. Dando and Lara M. Dando

## INTRODUCTION

The term "war" may be defined in many ways, and accepted definitions of this term reflect the times in which it is occurring, the area or site of the conflict, and its duration and magnitude. Armed conflicts of dominant nations with primitive people are called "pacifications," "military expeditions," or "exploitations." Armed conflicts with weak or militarily unprepared states are called "interventions" or "reprisals." An armed conflict within a nation is called a "rebellion" or "insurrection." In any case, if the resistance to the invaders or the insurgents achieves a magnitude of scope and life-taking, the event is called a "defensive response" or a "defensive war." War is primarily an extra-legal activity in which a nation, group, sect, or tyrant attempts to subjugate and rule others for the benefits of the winner of the hostilities or to defend themselves from aggression or change. A war may be a "cold war" without hostilities or a "hot war" that is costly, claims many lives, and at times, destroys objects of cultural achievement or exterminates a cultural group (Table 1). Military battles and events can cost the lives of millions of military personnel and millions of unarmed non-combatants. War is not a new concept. In ancient Israel, military conflicts were frequent, claimed many lives, eradicated cultural groups, and destroyed countless villages, towns, and cities. War is mentioned 140 times in the Bible. Ancient Israel's problem was its location across international trade routes and age-old war paths between

Egypt and Assyria/Babylon. Its attraction was its agricultural products. War in ancient Israel resulted in debilitating hunger, starvation, pestilence, rural or urban famine, and death. It also caused great national economic and refugee problems for surrounding non-warring states (David 1998).

War-induced rural food shortages and famines rarely capture the attention of those who record history. Albeit, war-induced sieges, involving the defense of a city or fortress ramparts, cleverly designed walls and towers, moats and pits, withstanding repeated assaults, while the defenders and entrapped citizens slowly dwindle stores of food, water, and defense hardware, do attract those who read history. Urban warfare's significance is a matter of impact, magnitude, and duration. The term "siege" is mentioned 48 times in the Bible. Long sieges, in most cases, created urban famines. An urban famine is a protracted total shortage of food in an urban center causing widespread diseases and food-deficit deaths from starvation for a large segment of the urban population. It brings out the most bestial and brutish nature of human beings. As the siege wears on, the defenders' hope for a relief force slowly diminishes, along with daily increasing anxiety, fear, and desperation. The defenders slowly absorb the realization that if the city defenses fail, the enemy takes all – including the lives of the garrison and the civilians whom the garrison is protecting. The reasons for invading forces to attack and lay siege to a city are many, including that the city or fortress usually provides a haven for military personnel and a base for military operations. In addition, if the city is well provisioned and withstands the siege, failure to capture it may decide the outcome of the whole campaign (Windrow 2009).

In times of war, when invading enemies ravaged the country-side, cities offered refuge to farmers and rural villagers who would flee their devastated and looted homes, bringing their families and possessions, including animals, inside the perceived protection of the walls. This exacerbated the balance between active defenders and the number of non-combatants who had to be fed. In biblical times, invaders often annihilated, expelled, or enslaved whole populations. They subjected cities to wholesale massacre, rape, looting, and arson.

## Table 1. Introduction and Definitions

| | |
|---|---|
| **The Problem** | — Location<br>— Agricultural Surpluses |
| **Urban Famine** | A protracted total shortage of food in an urban center causing widespread disease and food-deficit death from starvation for a large segment of the urban population. |
| **Food Plundering** | Requisitioning or taking basic foods from a rural food-producing population and the poor to feed the elite and urban food consumer. |
| **War** | — Fighting, destruction, and killing carried on by armed forces between nations or within nations.<br>— Types of war included:<br>  – Pacifications or expeditions<br>  – Interventions<br>  – Reprisals<br>  – Rebellions or insurrections<br>  – Defensive response<br>  – Cold wars |

## URBAN FAMINE IN A PROMISED LAND

There were only eleven famines in ancient Israel between c. 1850 B.C.E. and 70 C.E. recorded in the Bible and in the works of Roman and Greek historians. Dating of famines is approximate and determined with prudent reserve. The first three biblical famines associated with the Patriarchs, Abraham, Isaac, and Jacob, are simply stated historic facts. It may be assumed that they were only partial in extent and time. The fourth famine took place during the life of Ruth and in the area centered on Bethlehem. The fifth famine occurred in the days of King David. It lasted three years and the number of deaths was unreported. The sixth famine took place in Israel and was particularly severe in Samaria during the time of Elijah and King Ahab. It was induced by drought and made worse by the actions of King Ahab and Queen Jezebel. The seventh famine, a seven-year famine, occurred in Israel during the reign of King Jehoram in the time of Elisha. The eighth famine was recorded in Israel during the siege of Samaria, during the rule of King Jehoahaz. This famine was made more horrible by rampant cannibalism. The ninth famine reached its horrible apex in June and July, 587 B.C.E., while under a 30-month siege by King Nebuchadnezzar of Babylon. Jerusalem was sacked, men of distinction put to death, and those who survived were deported to Babylon. The tenth famine in 46 C.E. initiated the beginning of the end as the home of a self-governing people ruled by the descendants of Abraham. This famine occurred primarily in Judea and was focused on Jerusalem during the reign of Emperor Claudius (Figure 1). Famine relief by overseas Jews and Christians reduced the number of lives lost. The last major famine recorded in ancient Israel took place in Jerusalem in the reigns of emperors Nero and Vespasian. General Titus laid siege to Jerusalem, created a horrendous urban famine, captured the city, killed hundreds of thousands in Jerusalem, and destroyed the city in 70 C.E. The first five famines recorded in the Bible were essentially rural and related primarily to shortages in pasturage. The last six famines claimed many, many lives and occurred in cities (urban centers). The most terrifying incidents of human suffering and depravity were recorded in Samaria, the capital of Israel and in Jerusalem, the capital of Judea.

**Example 1. Samaria: Capital of Israel – the Famine of 853 B.C.E.**

*Introduction*

Samaria (meaning watch mountain) was an ancient city, situated 36 miles north of Jerusalem in a beautiful and fertile, wide basin-shaped valley, six miles in diameter. It was encircled by high hills, near the eastern edge of the great coastal plain bordering the Mediterranean Sea. In the center of the basin was an oblong hill with steep yet accessible sides and a flat top. This hill was chosen by King Omri as the site of the Kingdom of Israel's capital in 925 B.C.E. (1 Kings 16: 23, 24). Samaria, located on the chief north-south route through the "hill country," did become the beautiful capital of the ten tribes. The city was surrounded by a land of rich soils that produced wheat and barley, vines and fig trees, pomegranates and olive trees, and honey – a land of prosperous farmers. King Ahab built a temple to Baal as well as an ivory palace there (1 Kings

Figure 1. Central Judea and Southern Samaria

Source: http://www.bible-history.com/maps/palestine_nt_times.html

16: 32-33). Isaiah, who lived in Jerusalem and prophesized in Judah, immortalized Samaria's glorious beauty. He called Samaria "the head of Ephraim," located in a lush "fat" valley (Isaiah 28: 1-4). The city was besieged by Syrians in 901 B.C.E. (1 Kings 20: 1), in 853 B.C.E. (2 Kings 6: 24-27), and in 722 B.C.E. (2 Kings 17: 5-6). King Sargon of Syria did capture Samaria in 723, but he did not destroy the city. The possessor of Samaria was considered king of Israel (Isbouts 2008). Samaria achieved its greatest splendor during Roman times. Herod the Great renamed the city Sebaste.

## Benhadad's Siege

In 853 B.C.E., Benhadad, King of Damascus, led a large Aramaean (Syrian) army against King Jehoram (Joram). Jehoram, after being informed of the size of the invading army, concluded that his smaller army could not defeat Benhadad. He retreated to Samaria, closed all the gates, and relied on the strength of the city walls for his safety and for the safety of the city's population, the refugees who fled there, and his remaining army. Benhadad decided, after seeing the site of the city and the imposing walls surrounding Samaria, that he would modify his attack plan and save the lives of thousands of his soldiers. He would capture the city and its inhabitants not by a frontal attack or use of engines of war, but by creating an urban famine. Thus, he surrounded Samaria, cut off access to food and water supplies, and severed communications with any hoped-for relief forces (Mould 1939).

## Famine

Soon all the basic foods in the city were consumed, and what remained was sold at a very high price. People without money for food began to starve. Famine foods were consumed and an ass' head was sold at an extremely high price of eighty shekels of silver and a sextary (kor) of dove's dung (a substitute for salt) for five shekels of silver. The famine became so severe and so many people starved to death that King Jehoram feared that a starving person in the city might betray the city to the enemy.

Figure 2. Jerusalem in Its Glory: 46 C.E.

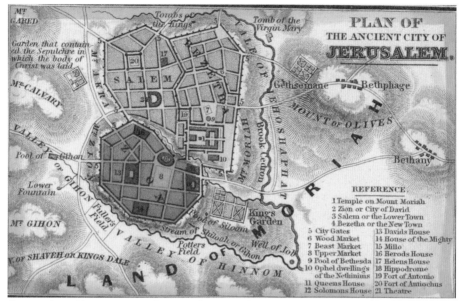

Source: http://captainjamesdavis.net/2014/03/12/history-of-jerusalem-from-142-bc-to-70-ad-with-the-closing-scene-of-the-fall-of-jerusalem/

Figure 3. Urban Famine in Jerusalem, Capital of Roman Judea, 46 C.E.
A few dined well; most suffered from Roman food plundering.

Source: https://kidskonnect.com/history/roman-food/

Each day, he walked around the city walls to determine if the walls were stable and not weakened from within. One day, while making his rounds, he was met by a woman crying out, "Have pity on me, my lord." Thinking that she was about to ask for something to eat, he told her that he had no food to give her. She replied that she did not want food, only justice. She explained that she had made an agreement with a neighbor friend that they should kill their children and eat them. She agreed, killed her son, and they ate his flesh. However, when it was her friend's turn to kill her son so that they could eat his flesh, the neighbor refused and hid her son. The story of the woman who had killed and ate her son greatly upset and grieved King Jehoram. He tore his garment and cried out with a loud voice (2 Kings 6: 24-31).

*Famine Broken*

Deeply disturbed by the number of Samarians who had died from hunger and from fighting amongst themselves for food, King Jehoram planned to surrender the city to King Benhadad. Surprisingly Benhadad's army fled in great panic from their positions and their camp in the middle of the night. They believed that they heard the sounds of a great relief army of Hittites and Egyptians, hired by King Jehoram. The Aramaeans deserted their weapons and war animals, their cattle, tons of wheat and barley, and much gold and silver. Jehoram learned of the attacking army's flight from four lepers who had been denied safety behind Samaria's walls and were living outside the walls. With great caution, Jehoram sent out scouts, who found that the enemy's siege positions and camp were deserted and vast quantities of war material, food, and wealth had been left behind (2 Kings 7: 3-20). The siege of Samaria by King Benhadad was broken when he and his army fled the country. The next day, in the market place, a measure of wheat sold for one shekel and two measures of barley for one shekel (Keller 1956).

## Example 2. Jerusalem: Capital of Roman Judea – Famine of 46 C.E.

*Introduction*

A holy city for 35 to 40 centuries, Jerusalem (meaning *city of peace*) was the nation's capital and the chief city of Palestine in 46 C.E. As a primate city in the Middle East, it was different from most capitals because it was not located on a river, it had no sea harbor, and it had no control over caravan routes or networks. In contrast to Samaria, Jerusalem was situated in a rocky, barren, rugged, stony region of scrub and thin pastures – a land of shepherds rather than farmers (Figure 2). Jerusalem was not on the main road between Babylon and Egypt, nor the main roads from the Mediterranean Sea to the Dead Sea and the Arabian deserts. It was located on a mountain top and possessed a reliable water supply from two ancient springs, one termed Gihon and the other, En-rogel (Jacob's well). Its Temple area was the principal place of Hebrew worship from the days of David and Solomon to the destruction of the city by Titus in 70 C.E. Centrally located, 32 miles from the Mediterranean Sea, 18 miles from the Jordan River, 20 miles from Hebron, and 36 miles from Samaria, on the edge of one of the highest tablelands of the country at an elevation of 2,550 feet, Jerusalem was higher and more remote than any other great Middle Eastern capital in history (Brodsky 2005).

As a mountaintop city, Jerusalem had only two main roads leading to it. One road led from the Jordan Valley via Jericho and the Mount of Olives, a north and east route, and the other, from the Mediterranean Sea and the coastal plain, up to the high ground of Gibeon, then turning south to Jerusalem via Ramah and Gibeah, a west to south route. The city of Jerusalem was located on Mount Zion, a western hill, and Mount Moriah, an eastern hill (2 Chronicles 3: 1). Mount Moriah was the site of the Temple. The tower-fortress Antonia was attached to the northwest angle of the Temple. The city was besieged no fewer than 17 times, twice it was razed to the ground, and the walls were leveled four times.

Unified ancient Israel was a "land of milk and honey." The foods available and consumed in the tents and homes of Abraham and his descendants were varied and nutritious and more than adequate in times of peace, domestic tranquility, and reasonable agroclimatic years (Genesis 27: 4-13). Israelites in the pre- and post-exile periods (1150 B.C.E. – 63 C.E.), primarily subsistence farmers and animal herders, large noble estate owners, prosperous commercial farmers and pastoralists, consumed foods similar to that which were eaten in Egypt, Babylon, and Canaan (Numbers 11:32; 2 Samuel 26: 20). Those who lived in the Promised Land during the reigns of Herod and his sons and Roman occupation (63 B.C.E. until the destruction of Jerusalem in 70 C.E.) produced a great variety of agricultural products. Albeit, the highest quality foods were consumed by Herod and his family, nobles, military personnel, wealthy merchants, and religious leaders or they were exported to Rome. Food plundering, i.e., requisitioning or taking by political/economic means needed basic foods from a rural food-producing population and the poor to feed elite and urban food consumers, was the *modus operandi* of Roman occupation. In a land producing and exporting great quantities of superior quality food products, the amount and composition of the common peoples' diet deteriorated. Scarce food years, hunger, and regional famines were frequent – especially in areas of Judea.

The quality of life and the deprivation of the peoples of Roman Israel reached its nadir or lowest point after the death of Jesus and during the reign of Claudius, between 41 and 54 C.E. Famines not only occurred within Roman-occupied Israel but also within numerous areas in the Roman Empire. Food plundering in Roman Israel during the reigns of the Herods converted the "land of milk and honey" to a land of poverty, discontent, disease, hunger, and famine. Those who lived in Galilee, Samaria, and Judea were undernourished and malnourished, suffering from vitamin and mineral deficiency diseases on an epidemic scale. Hatred of Herod and his family was only exceeded by the Jews' loathing of the Romans. Civil disturbances and Roman vicious responses created an air of menace, despondency, and gloom in Roman Palestine.

*Famine of 46 C.E.*

A major famine during Claudius' reign took place in the years of 45, 46, and 47 C.E. The 46 C.E. famine in Palestine was one of the most devastating famines in Judean scholars' recollections. Tens of thousands of Jerusalem's residents starved to death. Jerusalem languished, but no food relief came from the Romans and no remedy was proposed to ease the famine. The coastal cities in Palestine endured the food shortages relatively well, and the dwellers of the coastal plains and small hill country survived with minimal loss of life. The greatest loss of Jewish life occurred within the inland mountain cities such as Jerusalem. Some food was available in Jerusalem, but the food was of low quality and very expensive. The rich and well-placed people survived – the poor who had no money to buy food died (Figure 3).

*Ending the Famine*

The causes of the famine in Jerusalem in approximately 46 C.E. were complex, socioeconomic, and political. The Roman administrators and Herodian nobility had fostered tensions in Jerusalem and Judea. Civil disobedience was widespread, social cohesiveness was broken, armed revolutionaries roamed the countryside, political assassinations abounded, and anti-Roman insurrections took place in most cities. The solution to ending the famine in Jerusalem was simple: provide food or means to secure food for the poor. Members of the Antioch Church of Christ, every man according to his ability, contributed to the first Christian Church Relief Fund. They sent letters to Christian churches or cells throughout the Roman Empire and asked for "cash" donations to buy famine relief food. Contributions to the fund were made in gold, silver, or checks. Barnabus and Paul were chosen to be the bearers (from Antioch to Jerusalem) of the aid (Swete 1905: 202-214; Yamaguchi 1980: 193-202). Other faith-based famine relief came from synagogues or from those who embraced Jewish customs. Queen Helena of Adiabene went to Jerusalem, saw the need, and sent some servants to Egypt to buy great quantities of wheat and other servants to Cyprus to buy dried figs. When the wheat and figs arrived, she distributed the food free to those who were in need. Many others who learned of the famine did the same (Josephus 1981, Book II: 415-416). Except for human prejudice and greed, there was no reason for the 46 C.E. famine in Jerusalem (Dando 2013).

**Example 3. Jerusalem: Capital of Palestine – Famine of 70 C.E.**

*Introduction*

In the period between 40 and 70 C.E., Roman administrators of Palestine generated great antagonisms that provoked widespread Jewish unrest. Roman reprisals to civil disturbances and open revolt increased the followings of the Zealots and deepened the hatred of Roman occupation. Inter-ethnic violence and rebellion spread throughout Palestine. In 67 C.E., hard-line Governor Gessius Florus provoked life-taking riots in Jerusalem. He could not put an end to the violence and had to withdraw from the city. Zealots, in blood-seeking rage, took control of Jerusalem, massacred pro-Roman citizens, and killed every Roman soldier of the garrison that occupied the Antonia Fortress. In response, the governor of Syria, Cestius Gallus, marched on Jerusalem, occupied the northern suburbs, failed to capture the Temple complex, and was forced to withdraw. During the retreat to Syria, the legion of Cestius Gallus was defeated by the Zealots and Jewish guerrillas. In 67 C.E., Emperor Nero gave command of Roman military forces to General Flavius Vespasian. Vespasian sent his son and aide, Titus, south to Alexandria to mobilize Legion XXII. Then Vespasian went west to Macedonia where he assembled Legion V and east to Syria where he prepared Legion X for military action. All three legions marched to Acre (Ptolemais, a seaport city 13 miles north of Mount Carmel) where they united into one large combined motivated military force of approximately 50,000 men. He invaded Galilee and Samaria, killing all who resisted and burning any village, town, or city that would not surrender without a siege.

Figure 4. The Siege of Jerusalem

Source: https://en.wikipedia.org/wiki/Titus

Figure 5. Soldiers Parading in Rome Celebrating Their Victory over the Jews

Source: Sodabottle (Own work)
https://commons.wikimedia.org/wiki/File%2C_Diaspora_museum_2.jpg

About this time, Emperor Nero died in Rome. He died without a successor, so army generals vied for Nero's throne throughout 69 C.E. While Nero's successors were fighting each other for the throne, Vespasian's troops in the east proclaimed him as emperor in 69. His allies from the Danube legions defeated the last general (Vitellians) fighting for the throne, and Vespasian then sailed for Rome to take the throne. He entrusted his son Titus to crush the Jewish Revolt with seven legions – four that Titus commanded and three that Vespasian had commanded. Titus marched on Jerusalem from the north in April, 70. He positioned two legions to the north of the city, a legion to the east on the Mount of Olives, and a legion west, facing the citadel of Herod's palace. These legions were positioned facing critical military objectives. The Roman siege army with their auxiliaries and allies was expanded to about 70,000 men while the defenders had perhaps 23,000 men.

The Jewish defenders initiated the battle for Jerusalem by an early sortie towards the Roman camps, inflicting significant casualties and rejecting Titus' terms for peace. In May, Titus launched his first attack on the newly built third wall, just north of Herod's citadel. On the fifteenth day of the siege, the western wall was breeched and quickly, the second wall was breeched. The entire second wall was captured and demolished. After the capture of the third and second walls, the Temple Mount and the Antonia Fortress were exposed to attack. Titus had built four new siege towers near the Antonia Fortress and one against Herod's citadel. They failed. Titus then ordered construction of a continuous palisade all around the east, south, and west remaining walls. The newly constructed walls cut off outside sources of food for the city. Food shortages in Jerusalem soon caused hunger, starvation, and then a horrible famine in the city. Defending soldiers began to loot and brutalize non-combatant city dwellers. Cannibalism became rampant. Famine pain drove deserters out of the city to surrender. Those who managed to escape from the city were captured and crucified by the Romans.

The second phase of Titus' plan to capture Jerusalem was the demolition of the Antonia Fortress and to use its rubble to extend their ramp into the northwest corner of the Temple Court. After a brief battle, the Antonia Fortress was captured. Six days later, the ramp was completed, and Roman troops and cavalry were brought into the Outer Court. Gates of the Inner Court were then burned down. Starving defenders made a desperate sortie or surprise attack from the surrounded Temple Mount, but they were unsuccessful. The survivors of the sortie withdrew inside the Temple. Overwhelmed, the valiant defenders of the Temple could not stop the Roman soldiers from entering the Temple Court. By accident, the sanctuary was set afire, and the last defenders died in the fire that consumed the Temple (Figure 4).

Although the Temple was destroyed and the sanctuary fell in mid-August, fighting continued for three more weeks. The city of Jerusalem was completely sacked and partially razed on September 7. It only took Titus approximately five months to destroy the "city of peace" (Figure 5). Possibly 500,000 died in the siege from famine, 500,000 died from inter-city strife and military action, and 97,000 captured defenders were sent to the amphitheaters of Roman cities or to Rome for display (Josephus 1981, Book VI: 589).

The siege and destruction of Jerusalem and the Jewish Temple led to the complete eradication of the Jewish state. The revolt against Rome was an impossible geopolitical task, and defense of Jerusalem was a fatal flaw. The defenders had no hope for relief from an outside force, and they did not have the food, military hardware, or military skills necessary to succeed. Even more so, the defenders fought against each other, and they brutalized civilian non-combatants.

## CONCLUSION

The tale of two cities, Samaria and Jerusalem, is one of initial joy, peace, and prosperity, then war, siege, and famine. Samaria, with unified defenders and able leaders, was able to withstand destruction; conversely, Jerusalem was completely destroyed and leveled a number of times. Both cities served the needs of their people both spiritually and politically, were well located, and were the repositories of cultural artifacts most revered by the people whom they served. As remarkable episodes of heroism and defiance, each of the three siege famine examples selected above were turning points in history. Also, all are examples of how men and women have stood firm hoping to claim victory against overwhelming odds and evil oppressors (Klawans 2015).

The questions any decent and concerned citizen of the world asks in the twenty-first century are why must we employ war in our arsenal of geopolitics and why is famine an accepted military tool to subjugate a people or place? Famines rarely claim the lives of national leaders, generals, or military personnel. Famines, and particularly urban famines where siege is the military weapon employed, kill the innocent, the poor, and those with health problems. In the first decades of the twenty-first century, we have great hunger and unrecognized starvation in the part of the world that was the birth place of three major religions: Judaism, Christianity, and Mohammedanism. It is also the region of modern urban famines in 2019.

## REFERENCES

Brodsky, Harold. 2005. "The Site of the Jerusalem Temple." In Dando, William A., Caroline Z. Dando, and Jonathan J. Lu, Eds. *Geography of the Holy Land: Perspectives.* Kaohsiung, Taiwan: Holy Light Theological Seminary Press, pp. 201-220.

Dando, William A. 2013. "Faith-Based Response to Human Needs: The A.D. 46 Famine in Jerusalem." In Dando, William A., Caroline Z. Dando, and Jonathan J. Lu, Eds. *Geography of the Holy Land: New Insights.* Kaohsiung, Taiwan: Holy Light Theological Seminary Press, pp. 357-378.

Dando, William A. 2005. "Food and Famine in Ancient Israel." In Dando, William A., Caroline Z. Dando, and Jonathan J. Lu, Eds. *Geography of the Holy Land: Perspectives.* Kaohsiung, Taiwan: Holy Light Theological Seminary Press, pp. 300-322.

Dando, William A. 2013. "The Jerusalem Famine of A.D. 70: A Horrible

Tribute to Human

Failings." In Dando, William A., Caroline Z. Dando, and Jonathan J. Lu, Eds. *Geography of the Holy Land: New Insights.* Kaohsiung, Taiwan: Holy Light Theological Seminary Press, pp. 143-158.

David, Saul. 1998. *Military Blunders.* New York: Carrol & Graf Publishers, pp. ix-x, 1.

_____. 1989. *Holy Bible: New Revised Standard Origin.* Nashville: Thomas Nelson Publishers.

Isbouts, Jean-Pierre. 2008. *Young Jesus.* London: Sterling Publishing Company, Inc., pp. 20, 102, 108, 120.

Josephus, Flavius. 1981. *Complete Works.* Translated by W. Neil. New York: The Ronald Press Company, specifically Book II, pp. 415-416, and Book VI, "The War of the Jews," p. 589.

Keller, Werner. 1956. *The Bible as History.* New York: William Morrow and Company, pp. 231-235, 249-250.

Klawans, Jonathan. 2015. "A Crisis of Faith in the Wake of the Temple Destruction." *Biblical Archaeology Review.* Vol. 41, No. 6, November/December, pp. 26, 78.

Mould, Elmer. 1939. *The Essentials of Bible History.* New York: The Ronald Press Company, pp. 27-28, 249, 288, 322, 328, 431.

Swete, H. B. 1905. "The Prophets in the Christian Church." *The Bible World.* Vol. 26, No. 3, September, pp. 202-214.

Windrow, Martin. 2009. *The Great Sieges.* London: Quercus History, pp. 7-11.

Yamaguchi, Erwin M. 1980. "Ancient Ecologies and the Bible Perspective." *Journal of American Scientific Affiliation.* Vol. 32, No. 4, December, pp. 193-202.

# PART FOUR

## Epilogue

At one time in the history of Geography, an old discipline that describes the earth and the activities of its inhabitants, many geographers ascribed to Determinism. This approach to research and writing stressed that the physical environment directed and controlled human decision-making and molded the actions of all who lived there. Some wrote that the physical geography and specifically weather and climate determined the distribution of population, the historical development of a people, socioeconomic progress, national characteristics, and religious thought. The concept of physical determinism was soon modified, and an anthropogeographic line of thought, a method of thinking and seeking human consequences from the environment of a place, emerged – in essence, geographic cause and effect. The international spread of geography as an academic discipline in colleges and universities and international research and intense field work eliminated deterministic thought and led to a viewpoint that humans innately had the abilities to make wise decisions and the collectively unrestrained ingenuity to resolve issues so that they, to a certain extent, would have dominion over all the world.

The Bible records that humankind was created and initially dwelled at a place in an earthly rural paradise called Eden. It also recorded the history of a chosen people as they progressed from hunters-gatherers, homeless nomads, rural clusters of people, to village, town, and city dwellers. The Bible concludes with humankind living in a stupendous magnificent place – a holy city – a new Jerusalem. Human "Alpha to Omega" is traced from rural dwellers to city dwellers, the beginning and the ending of a human settlement continuum. This book modestly describes an evolution in progress and concludes with the contention by Jonathan J. Lu that few of the disputes, conflicts, and human-made problems are unsolvable – including the solution to the unending Arab/Israeli conflict. This chapter is followed by a note of the significance of place by Ronald R. Boyce.

# Looking Back to 2002: Katsav, Arafat, and a Biblical Solution to the Arab/Israeli Conflict

Jonathan J. Lu

## Introduction

There's been enough suffering on both the Palestinian and Israeli sides. We have to put an end to it.

Moshe Katsav, President of the State of Israel, *Jerusalem Post*, August 7, 2001

Few of the disputes/conflicts in the contemporary world proved to be as intractable as that of the Arab-Israeli conflict in the Middle East (Drysdale and Blake 1985: 263). According to Held, the conflict has many facets, dimensions, and perspectives. It involves territorial disputes, conflicting historical claims, ethnic confrontations, ethical dilemmas, religious implications, ideological differences, political hostilities, economic competitions, geographical ramifications, emotional contentions, and military skirmishes (Held 1989: 169-72).

Battah and Lukacs (1988: 1-3) discussed a two-dimensional conflict: the inter-communal conflict and the interstate conflict. The former involves two ethnic communities (Israelis and the Palestinians); the latter involves two political states (Israel and Arab). The inter-communal conflict has two sub-dimensions which this author would call the intra-territorial conflict between the Jews and the Palestinians inside

Israel-Palestine, and the extra-territorial conflict between the Israelis and the forces that help support the Palestinian National Authority (NPA) outside Israel-Palestine.

The Arab-Israeli conflict also has many perspectives with many sub-perspectives. "From any perspective," says Held (1989: 172), "the problem and its ramifications have caused a tragic number of casualties, prolonged human suffering, extensive physical destruction, and explosive divisiveness as well as retardation of development and a waste of human and other resources." What is this Arab-Israeli conflict, really? What was the cause? What has been done to resolve or alleviate the conflict? What have been the obstacles? After briefly discussing each of these questions, this chapter will propose a solution from a biblical perspective, called "A Biblical Solution." Based on biblical teachings and principles, this chapter will discuss: (1) a historical account of the Jews and the Canaanites/ Philistines living together; (2) God's command of allotting land to resident aliens as an inheritance; and (3) the Jewish, Muslim, and Christian concepts of "love your neighbor."

## ARAB-ISRAELI CONFLICT: WHAT IS IT?

Simply put, the Arab-Israeli conflict merged as one of competing nationalism (Schulze 1999: 92), laying claim by the two peoples, Israeli Jews and Palestinian Arabs, both of who insist on the rights to the same piece of land. This land was known as the Land of Canaan (Gen. 11: 31), the Land of Israel (e.g., 1 Samuel 13: 19), the Land of the Philisia (Zephaniah 2: 5) or the Filastin Land, *al-Ard al-Muqadassa* (the "Holy Land" in Arabic), and the Promised Land. Today, this land is called by those who live here as Palestine, Eretz Israel (or simply *Ha'Aretz*, "the Land"), Palestine-Israel, or Israel-Palestine. Christian scholars outside this region have called it "the Holy Land" (e.g., Smith 1894; Ogden and Chadwick 1990), or "the Land of the Bible" (Aharoni 1967 & 1979; Figure 1).

The conflict is far from being simple. The whole issue and the nature of this conflict are rather complex and the solution to this conflict involves complicated situations. Garfinkle (1991: 1-4) discusses the nature of this complex conflict from four different perspectives as follows:

First, there are the involvements of various factors. To be sure, there is the Jewish state of Israel whose existence is at the very center of the entire affair. But there are also Jewish communities throughout the world to whom the survival of the state of Israel is extremely important. Then, there are the Palestinian Arabs who, though not having a state of their own at the present, believe, nevertheless, that the existence of their own state is victimized by the existence of Israel, by the intervention of the past imperial and the present super-powers, by the inter-discord of their Arab brothers, and even by the betrayal of their own self-proclaimed leaders. In addition, there is also the involvement of other Arab states, adjoining or disjoining Israel, who oppose the existence of Israel because of religious affinity with Arab Muslims.

Second, there is a complicated "all-or-nothing" nature in this conflict. Until very recently, almost all of Israel's Arab neighbors did not feel that Israel had the right to exist in Palestine, thus, their "dedication" to push Israel into the "Great Sea." On the other hand, there were hard-core Zionists and Israeli supporters who vehemently denied the political aspiration of the Palestinian Arabs.

Third, there is a complex cause-and-effect resulting from the legacy and modern foreign influences. On the one hand, the idea of Zionist movement was impregnated on foreign soil, born in the European ghetto, and nurtured by European foreign policies. On the other hand, the rise of Arab nationalism was inspired by European ideologies, supported by European encouragement of Arab opposition to Turkish overlords, and shaped by European intrusive hegemony of the region's affairs. It is interesting to observe that Arabs who lived on this land for thousands of years identified their loyalties with family, clan, tribe, and religion rather than with a nation. The Jews who lived in Diaspora for an even longer length of time, identified their nationhood with religious conviction. To them, national consciousness is more dependent on the strength of religious

Figure 1. Canaan's Second Millennium B.C.E.

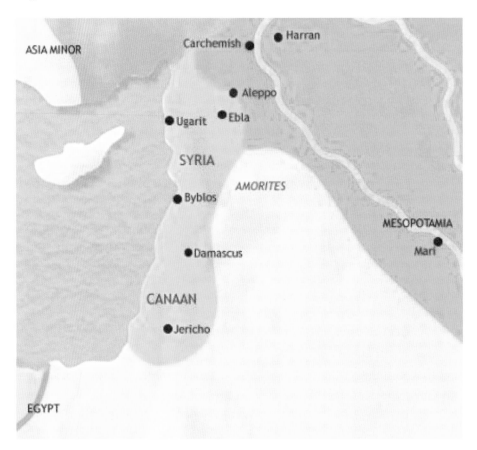

belief than on "physical presence" (Garfinkle 1991: 3).

Finally, there are theological and historical prejudices. The State of Israel is overwhelmingly Jewish; and the aspired Palestinian state is overwhelmingly Muslim. But this Jewish-Israeli and Muslim-Palestinian-Arab relationship has a common yet complex historical and theological root that could be traced back to the time of Abraham and to the origin of Islam in the seventh century. Thus, it has been observed that down through the historical lane, despite the recent conflict, the Israeli Jews have less rancor with Palestinian Arab Muslims than with European Christians.

The situations described by Garfinkle have improved since the

Camp David Accord in September 1978 and the Israeli-Egyptian Peace Treaty in 1979. These were followed by the Reagan Fresh Start Initiative of 1982, the Madrid Conference of October 1991, and, on September 13, 1993, the first Israeli-Palestinian Agreement, known as the "Declaration of Principles" or "Oslo (I) Accord" signed in Washington, D.C. In this document, the "legitimate and political rights" were mutually recognized. It was further agreed by both to "strive to live in peaceful coexistence and mutual dignity and security and achieve a just, lasting and comprehensive peace settlement and historic reconciliation through the agreed political process" (as quoted in Schulze 1999: 119 and <www.israel.org/mfa/go.asp>). On March 5, 1997, Mr. Yasser Arafat told the Jewish leaders in New York City that the Palestinian Covenant was changed, and it no longer called for the destruction of Israel in Palestine.

### The Arabs and the Jews

Ethnically, the popular notion is that Arabs and Jews both belong to the same Semitic race. Therefore, the term "anti-Semitism" is a misnomer because this term was coined by Wilhelm Marr, a German, in 1879 to denote anti-Jews in Central Europe at that time. However, Goitein was of the opinion that the term denoted a closely related language group that includes Hebrew and Arabic (Goitein 1955: 19). Another popular belief holds that Jews and Arabs are cousins having been descended through Isaac and Ishmael (*Ismā'īl* in Arabic). The Bible does support the notion that Abraham (*Ibrāhīm* in Arabic) was the father of both Ishmael and Isaac (Genesis 16: 1-3, 15-16; 17: 1-27; 18: 9-14; 21: 1-21). However, whereas the Bible recognizes that the Jews are the descendants of Isaac; it does not explicitly indicate that Arabs are the descendants of Ishmael. The current notion is that the term "Arab" is not ethnic nor racial. It denotes that anyone who speaks Arabic is an Arab. Furthermore, while the descendants of Ishmael may be of Arabic origin, not all Arabs are the descendants of Ishmael.

Nevertheless, there is also an idea that Arabs are "cousins" of Israelites. The idea is of a Jewish origin, based on Isaiah 21: 13 where it mentions an Arab tribe, Dedanim. *Dedanim* comes from the same root word as *dodanim*, meaning "cousins." The Arabs themselves have accepted this cousin-relation with the Jews. The acceptance, perhaps, is due to the teaching of Muhammad as recorded in the Koran (2: 125 and 2: 127) where it mentions that Ibrahim enjoined his son Ismail to purify the Ka'ba of Mecca and, together, they raised its foundation (Khatib 1986: 24-25; Zhou 1958: 29). From this, it was interpreted that Ibrahim was not only the physical ancestor of the Arabs, but also the co-founder of Islam (Goitein 1955: 22-23). However, there is little real hard evidence that all Arabs are the descendants of Ismail.

It is also believed that there are cultural affinities between the Jews and the Arabs as manifested in similarities in social patterns and outlooks, in the common motif in the history of the two peoples during the classic periods, and even in their common heritage of suffering. Jewish thought and philosophy were systematized under the Arab-Muslim influence, and even Jewish law and religious practice were formulated under the same (Goitein 1955).

Some scholars seem to have found evidence that the Hebrew language developed its grammar and vocabulary on the Arabic model. Without the parallelism of the Arabic language that is preserved in various ways down through the ages, the revival of ancient Hebrew into a modern language "would be entirely unthinkable" (Goitein 1955: 8). With such a close relation and affinity between the Jews and the Arabs, the question may be raised here as to why there are so many animosities and so much antagonism?

## ARAB-ISRAELI CONFLICT: WHAT CAUSED IT?

To answer the question of what caused the Arab-Israeli conflict, one must go back in history and define it from a time reference. Scholars generally mark World War I as the starting point (e.g., Cohen 1987; United Nations 1990). Others would trace its origin back to "the closing years of the 19th century" (e.g., Arafat 1974: 7), when the first "Zionist

Congress" convened in Basel, Switzerland in 1897 (Moore 1974).

According to Professor Abboushi, there was no such political entity as a Palestine before World War I. It was the McMahon-Hussein Correspondences of 1915, the Sykes-Picot Agreement of 1916, and the Balfour Declaration of 1917 that set the stage for the continuing rise of Arab Nationalism and the Zionist activities that led to the initial Palestinians-Zionists conflict. These and subsequent events, such as the San Remo Conference of 1920 that gave Britain the Mandatory authority over Palestine, the approval of the Mandate Agreement for Palestine by the League of Nations in 1922, and the Operationalization of the Agreement in 1923 were the primary forces for the gradual realization of a "Jewish National Home in Palestine" (Abboushi1990: 1-10).

Abboushi was of the opinion that "Israel was a military fact before it became a political reality, and it was primarily the military fact that gained political recognition for the Jewish state." According to him, the creation of the Jewish state of Israel ended the Palestinian-Zionist conflict and began the Arab-Israeli conflict. In other words, the inter-communal conflict was transformed into the inter-state conflict.

At first, the Arabs used military force in an attempt to prevent the political reality of Israel in the 1948-49 war. This military option continued in the ensuing years, and reached its failure climax in the 1967 war. As a result, the inter-state nature of the conflict was once more transformed into inter-communal (Battah and Lukacs 1988: 1-3). Having failed in military attempts, the Arabs were now inclined to use politics. If politics failed, warned Abboushi, the Arabs would have to again resort to military activities to challenge Israel in the battlefields (1990: 197).

Many of the pre-1948 incidents seem to have been caused by emotional upheaval and lack of communication as exemplified by the 1929 disturbances (*ibid.* 37-39). For the deep-rooted causes, one may list clash of nationalism, territorial disputes, ethnic or religious strife, aspiring ideologies, coupled with religious self-righteousness and sanctification

(Alexander 1973: vi), sociological differences in attitude toward land and labor (Shafir 1989; Abboushi 1990: 46), imperialist intrusion, and extension of the East-West conflict, and even American foreign policy (Smith 1992).

If the Arabs, indeed, are the descendants of Ishmael, according to popular belief, then this author would venture to say that the seed of the Arab-Israeli conflict was planted a long time ago. At the age of 85, Abraham, whose name was Abram, was promised to have an offspring as numerous as stars in the heavens (Gen. 15: 5) when he was still childless without an heir. Abraham's wife, Sarai, who "had borne him no children," begged Abraham to sleep with her maidservant, Hagar, so that she might "build a family through her" (Genesis 16: 2, NIV). Hagar bore Abraham a son when he was 86 years old and Abraham named him Ishmael. This son, however, was born not through promise but according to the flesh (Galatians 4: 23, RSV).

When Abraham was 99 years old, God told him to change the name of his 89 years old wife to Sarah and promised him to have a son by her (Genesis 17: 15-16). Indeed, Sarah "bore Abraham a son in his old age" of one hundred years, and he named him Isaac (Genesis 21: 2-5). It was at the weaning feast of Isaac when Sarah saw Ishmael "mocking" that she told Abraham "to get rid of that slave woman and her son;" for she said, "that slave's son will never share in the inheritance with my son Isaac" (Genesis 21: 9-10, NIV). By this, Ishmael was expelled from Abraham's household and was severed from the inheritance promised to Abraham.

Thus, the seed of the conflict between the "heirs" of these two half-brothers was sown. From the biblical account, we do not see any more contacts between Isaac and Ishmael, from the latter's expulsion until more than 70 years later when "Abraham breathed his last and died." Then "Isaac and Ishmael, Abraham's two sons, buried him in the cave of Machpelah" (Genesis 25: 8-9). Jack Cohen found these "the most startling, soul-stirring verses in the Bible" (J. Cohen 1987: 167). Cohen also raised a very interesting question on what might have been the result if Abraham, instead of expelling Ishmael and his mother, insisted on holding the family together (*ibid.*. 169).

The direct cause of the contemporary Arab-Israeli conflict, however, is the establishment of a "Jewish national home in Palestine." Wars broke out immediately after the declaration of the establishment of the State of Israel on May 14, 1948. The war was between the Israeli soldiers and the Arab volunteers first and thereafter with the regular armies from the Arab countries. The conflict intensified in the ensuing years. Major wars broke out in 1957, 1967, 1973, and 1982 between the State of Israel and the Arab states, including Lebanon.

It was the belief of Ben Gurion in the 1950s that peace with the Arab world would come only after Israel hit it over the head until it was persuaded that Israel was too resolute and too strong to beat (quoted in Morris 1999: 666). Based on what was happening in the 1990s, Morris saw some truth in Ben Gurion's prognosis (*ibid.* 666-669). Perhaps, this was also the perception of then Israeli Prime Minister, Ariel Sharon, when he expressed his opinion that "it wouldn't be possible to reach an agreement with them before the Palestinians are hit hard . . .If they aren't badly beaten there won't be any negotiation" (<www.pna.gov.ps2001>).

Benjamin Natanyahu, in his book *A Durable Peace,* concluded, that "if the central aim of the Jewish people during its exile was to retrieve what had been lost, then the purpose now is to secure what has been retrieved" (Natanyahu, 1993: 398). The question is "what's the extent of what has been retrieved" and would Israel be satisfied with this?

## SUGGESTIONS FOR AND EFFORTS TOWARD PEACE IN THE MIDDLE EAST

The outcome of military actions since 1948-49 reveals only one thing: the solution to the Arab-Israel conflict cannot be resolved through the showing of forces in the battlefield. They can only result in loss of more lives, in increasing sufferings, and in more refugees. The conflict, it is obvious, has to be settled through diplomatic negotiations.

## Negotiations

It is to be expected that in the process of negotiation there would be obstacles. Schulze mentions that "asymmetry of power and legitimacy between negotiating parties is particularly obvious." Schulze, however, recognizes that "symmetry alone does not guarantee successful negotiations." Other obstacles to negotiations include: the fate of Jewish settlers in the West Bank and Gaza Strip, the status of Jerusalem, the release of Palestinian prisoners, violence by extremists, different perceptions of the time frame, and scale of concession. Conditions required for negotiation and compromise, according to Schulze, include: (1) a firm conviction that conflicts cannot be resolved by means of military actions, (2) a third-party mediation, and (3) a window of opportunity (Schulze, 1999: 92-96). To these, this writer would add a fourth, a genuine desire by both parties, for settling a just, honorable, and permanent peace based on equity.

These conditions, except for the last one, had not been lacking in the process. When the violence erupted despite mediations, it was still far from reaching an abatement. One could not help but wonder about the sincerity or genuine desire for peace by both parties. The deadlock seemed to focus on insisting by Mr. Sharon, a complete stopping of Arab suicide bombings, and on the insistence by Mr. Arafat, of complete stopping of violence by Jewish settlers within the West Bank and Gaza Strip. It may have been a bit unrealistic to expect the complete stopping of suicide bombings as these activities were beyond the control of President Arafat. Concomitantly, the Office of the Prime Minister in Israel could not exercise full authority over the settlers' violence. It added a new demand of the complete withdrawal of the IDF before negotiations could begin.

The negotiation experiences so far, observed Schulze (*ibid.* 96), have been characterized by a refusal to scale back maximum demands, to prioritize objectives, and by a lack of willingness to compromise. If violence was still perceived to be the only leverage, violence would continue. Degeneration of human mind, heart, and desire was the culprit. Negotiations, based on genuine desires, require a good faith, and it is risky. The question was if it was worthwhile to try?

## Mediations

Mediations by third-party countries and resolutions by the United Nations Security Council (Resolutions 242 and 338) did not produce any meaningful results in a peace settlement in the Middle East. In recent years, scholars have made several suggestions toward solving the Arab-Israeli conflict. It was deemed that superpowers' involvement in the Arab-Israeli conflict was motivated by their "sphere of interest," and they could result in further complications. Galtung, therefore, proposed a "conflict management" system to involve not only the United States and the United Nations, but also the Soviet Union (1988: 323). However, with dissolution of the Soviet Union, this suggestion obviously needed to be reconsidered.

Alexander, on the other hand, criticized oversimplification of the causes and the un-objectiveness of scholars whose opinions often led to confusion and to hindrances to peace. He then suggested, as a solution, to look at the simultaneous interplay between the actors and the factors. The former included: individual, state, non-state, regional, and international; the latter included: economic, political, social, cultural, and religious factors (Alexander 1973: 4).

Since Israel may be considered as the oldest and the youngest brother in the family of people in the Middle East, Goitein felt that Israel should take the lead in settling the conflict. As the oldest brother, Israel was obligated to be indulgent with the younger members of the family. He should have "a sober, objective, and even sympathetic attitude toward the Arabs." As the youngest member of the family, Israel must learn from his senior the social habits of traditional Arabs. However, Goitein further suggested that Israel deserved, as the oldest, a little consideration and even reverence; and, as the youngest, encouragement and even help from the Arabs (Goitein 1955: 233-234).

Bailey suggested an impartial mediation through "face-to-face" encounters (Bailey 1990). Earlier, Reisman proposed to set up "Power Diplomacy." By this, he meant, the interference of external superpowers. The purpose was to help create conditions for "minimum order" in the region, to lower the level of overt violence, to neutralize the initiators of unrest, and to resolve the major moral and human problems in the most possible equitable manner (Reisman 1970: 78).

Saul Cohen anticipated the Middle East to become a geographically unified unit. To him, Israel's present and future was inextricably entwined with not only the Palestine Arabs, but also with the war and peace strategies of Egypt, Jordan, Lebanon, Syria, Iran, and Iraq. Therefore, he suggested that there could only be a "Middle Eastern strategy" for the United States and the United Nations, for Iraq and Egypt, for Turkey and Iran, and for Jordan and Israel (1992: 5).

Galtung felt that toward the settlement of the Arab-Israeli conflict there had been "no peace process nor the intention of having one." He pointed out that the "imposed" agreement such as Camp David Accord, and the "peace by piece" practice were not a real peace process. To him, there remained only three rival images: (1) a one-state solution which involved the absorption of the Palestinians as first class citizens within Israel; (2) a two-state solution with the creation of an independent Palestinian state anchored in the West Bank and Gaza; and (3) a confederate solution based on some kind of Israeli/Palestinian partnership, perhaps with Jordan becoming a "Benelex" of the Middle East (1988: 321-324). Galtung had some faith in the "confederate solution" which he believed to be a better idea.

Beilin analyzed "the Arabs of Israel" and seemed to feel the impracticality of the one-state solution. He then laid down some principles for consideration in future negotiations. These included: social justice, equal value of all human beings, reduction of social differentials, and an obligation to give every individual the opportunity for self-discovery and self-fulfillment. What he proposed here was "an extension of freedom of choice in all areas--economic, religious, educational – and a concerted effort to remove deprivation" (Beilin 1999: 256-260).

In an article written for *The Washingtonians* and later condensed in the *Reader's Digest*, author Lydia Strohl raised the question: "If medicine can use religion and faith, why can't politics?" (Strohl 2001: 108). Perhaps, it is time to look into religion for a possible solution.

Having analyzed distinctive handicaps and definite assets of the role that Christians could play in the current Arab-Israeli conflict, Epp felt that Christians should be involved in what he called "prophesying ministry" toward the peace effort in the Middle East. By prophesying, it was meant "the bold proclamation of the will of God in every practical and relevant term." This included proclaiming justice for the Palestinian Arabs, advocating security for the Jews, restraining the superpowers, and boosting the role of the United Nations. As peacemakers, Epp challenged Christians to render their sacrificial deed by laying down their lives for their friends and enemies. They should be willing to stand by and help the Palestinian farmers as they braved the Israeli jets and to stand with the Israeli Kibbutzim and other settlements being shelled by the Arabs (Epp 1970: 231-265). However, what Epp advocated was humanitarian concerns for a suffering people, he did not say much about settling the conflict.

Moshe Katsav, former President of the State of Israel once said, "There's been enough suffering on both the Palestinian and Israeli sides. We have to put an end to it." (*Jerusalem Post*, August 7, 2001). To put an end to the conflict was the desire of many for sure. The question was "how."

# THE NEED FOR A BIBLICAL SOLUTION

To find a solution to the conflict, one must have a real under-standing of the problem. At the core of the conflict, there lies a contest for control of the same piece of land by the Israeli Jews and the Palestinian Arabs (Supra). For the Palestinian Arabs, their claim to the land is based on their continuing presence, at least since the seventh century C.E. For the Jews, their claim to the land is based on the history of the Hebrew tribes who have intermittently lived in the land. They occasionally ruled the land from the second millennium B.C.E. until their expulsion from Jerusalem in 135 C.E. Furthermore, as recorded in the Bible (e.g., Genesis 15: 18), their claim is also based on the promise made by their God, Yahweh, to their forefathers (Gerner 1991: 3).

As mentioned earlier, Jack Cohen, assuming that Arabs are descendants of Ishmael, raised an interesting question as to what might have happened if Abraham, instead of expelling Ishmael, decided to hold the family together (Supra). The question was very relevant because it has cropped up again in the current meetings of the descendants of the two long-separated half-brothers. The descendants of Isaac and Ishmael are once again together on the same common ancestral land. If the quarrel results from the incompatible claims of the two peoples for the same parcel of land that is promised in the Bible, we must look into the Bible for the possible solution. The author will identify three areas for consid-eration.

Before getting to that, one must ask first, what is meant by the "Biblical Solution?" Let it be understood, that the Bible referred to here is the Judeo-Christian Bible. It contains an Old as well as a New Testa-ment. The title of this chapter implies that solving this conflict lies in the principles and teachings found in the Judeo-Christian Bible. The process involves faith and trust, love and forgiveness, repentance and reconcilia-tion. It requires genuine sincerity and openness and a willingness to sacri-ficially take the first possible risky step. It is not "if you do that, we'll do this." The spirit is this: all being considered, we will do this for the benefits of all of us, even though you might not see the point at this moment, we are willing to take the risk with the hope that you will respond positively in time.

The three areas mentioned here are as follows: (1) The principle of living together in peace; (2) The principle of allotting the land for an inheritance; and (3) The principle of loving God and one's neighbor.

## The Principle of Living Together in Peace

Ethical questions aside, the Israelites and the Canaanites were once living together on the same piece of land during the major part of five centuries after the Israelites had crossed the River Jordan and entered into the "Promised Land." The situation was created by "balance of power." Since none of the tribes of Israel were able to expel the Canaanites out of the lands designated to them by Joshua, they had to live together with the Canaanites and for practical purposes, in peace. Thus, we read for example: "But the Jebusites, the inhabitants of Jerusalem, the people of Judah could not drive out; so the Jebusites dwell with the people of Judah in Jerusalem unto this day." (Joshua 15: 63). "Yet the sons of Manasseh could not take possession of those cities, and the Canaanites persisted in dwelling in that land" (Joshua 17: 12; see also Judges 1: 27-35). During the days of Judges, despite the presence of so much enmity, Samson was able to move freely through the land of the Philistines, even to the major city of Gaza (Judges 13: 24, 25; 16).

## The Principle of Allotting the Land for an Inheritance

This principle was given by the Sovereign Lord to prophet Ezekiel whose prophesies we read: Thus says the Lord God: "These are the boundaries by which you should divide the land for inheritance among the twelve tribes of Israel . . . You shall allot it as an inheritance for yourselves **and for the aliens who reside among you** and have begotten children among you. They shall be to you as native-born sons of Israel; with you they shall be allotted an inheritance among the tribes of Israel. In whatever tribe the alien resides, there you shall assign him his inheritance, says the Lord God." (Ezekiel 47: 13, 22-23, RSV; author's emphasis)

Let us ask first, "Who are these resident aliens?" Then let us note further that this is a command of the Sovereign Lord. The resident aliens, under the current context, are none other but the Palestinians. The instruction in the prophesy of Ezekiel is that these aliens should be treated as native-born sons of Israel; they should be allotted an inheritance among the tribes of Israel. In other words, these aliens may live in the same community as neighbors. This is a nice and ideal situation. However, in the case of today's Israel, it is almost impossible for the Jews and the Arabs to live next door to each other. For this reason, if these aliens were to receive land as an inheritance, according to the Lord's command, they probably would have to be in the West Bank or in the Gaza Strip. And this is what the Palestinians are aspiring for.

With a policy of "Land for Peace" already in place, this solution seems to be workable. One major obstacle might be the Israeli concern for security. This was a legitimate concern for the Israelis, which Mr. Arafat had not adequately addressed. In his address, "The Palestinian Vision of Peace," Mr. Arafat almost just mentioned the question of security in passing when he said, "The Palestinian vision of peace is an independent and viable Palestinian state on the territories occupied by Israel in 1967, living as an equal neighbor alongside Israel with peace and security for both . . ."(Arafat 2002). The biblical solution to this sort of thing is to not make a big case out of it, but to just ask for clarification and then go on to build a stronger relationship based on that "good faith."

**The Principle of Loving God and One's Neighbor**

Love is a splendid thing; it avails very much. The definition of love is clearly defined in the New Testament (especially in the First Epistle to the Church in Corinth, Chapter 13). To be sure, the Law of Moses spoke of "eye for eye and tooth for tooth" (Figure 2). The reason behind this approach was to take away the sin and evil from the Land. However,

Figure 2. Hezbollah Planning Imminent Invasion of Israel's Northern Galilee in 2015

the message on love abounded. In Deuteronomy, one reads: "You shall love the Lord your God with all your heart, and with all your soul, and with all you might" (6: 5). In Leviticus, one finds; "But you shall love your neighbor as yourself: I am the Lord" (19: 18).

To most people, loving God is not hard to understand. But many would probably have to ask: "Who is my neighbor?" (Luke 10: 29). Reading from Luke 10: 25-27, if not carefully, one probably would think that one should love those who are less fortunate like the one being beaten. On careful reading of the text, one realizes that the neighbor in this incident is the one who shows mercies. The truth is that if one has not experienced mercies extended to him, he is likely unable to show mercy to another. In our case of Arab-Israeli relations, may the descendants of Father Abraham who all received mercy, learn how to extend a merciful hand toward others. This writer longs to see that that day would come soon when all descendants of Abraham travel together in life's path with happiness and joy.

## CONCLUSION

To have peace in Israel-Palestine, it is imperative that the Jews in Israel follow the instruction of Yahweh to give the aliens, the Palestinians, the right to the land. Living side by side in peaceful coexistence was both an historical fact during the major part of Joshua's time, it is also the heart's desire of Yahweh as revealed through the words of his prophet, Ezekiel.

In an address, President Arafat expressly said: "Israel's peace partner is, and always has been the Palestinian people. Peace is not a signed agreement between individuals – it is **reconciliation** (author's emphasis) between people" (Arafat Feb 3, 2002). Mr. Arafat hit it right: RECONCILIATION!

In the Old Testament, reconciliation required the spilling of blood through sacrifice of animals. In New Testament time, Christ the Lamb of God was a sacrifice for all. "While we were enemies we were reconciled to God by the death of His Son" (Romans 5: 10). For this Arab-Israeli conflict, many lives have been sacrificed, and much blood has been spilled. One should only mention Anwar Saddat, Yizack Rabin, soldiers, civilians, innocent women, and children; and don't forget, suicide bombers. Hasn't enough blood been spilled? If negotiations then and now achieved nothing, blood would have been spilled in vain. May our hearts not be so callous that these lives were sacrificed for nothing!

As one meditates upon the occasion when Isaac and Ishmael trod together on the same ground to bury "their father Abraham in the Cave of Macphelah," one wonders if the destiny of these two peoples is to be together only in sadness? Or is their relationship to be found only in bitter memories of ancestral rivalry? Can the two peoples acknowledge and accept their common origin and build a new life together, founded on mutual respect of each other's differences that have accumulated over the years? The answer to this question is an unquestionable *Yes,* though with a condition--at the fulfillment of the prophesized promise spoken of by

Ezekiel: "A new heart will I give you, and a new spirit I will put within you; and I will take out of your flesh the heart of stone and give you a heart of flesh" (Ezekiel 36: 26). It is our hope that the day of fulfillment of this promise is now!

## REFERENCES

Abboushi, W. F. 1990. *The Unmaking of Palestine*. Brattleboro, Vermont: Amana Books.

Aharoni, Yohanan. 1967 and 1979. *The Land of the Bible: A Historical Geography*. Translated by A. F. Rainey. Philadelphia: The Westminster Press.

Alexander, Yonah. 1973. *The Role of Communications in the Middle East Conflict: Ideological and Religious Aspects*. New York: Praeger Publishers.

Arafat, Yasser. 1974. "Palestine Lives." Address given at the 29th Session of the United Nations General Assembly, November 13. San Francisco: Peoples Press.

Arafat, Yasser. 2002. "The Palestinian Vision of Peace." The Palestine Ministry of Information (February 3) <www.minfo.gov.ps/pal_news/english/1802-02.htm>

Bailey, Sydney D. 1990. *Four Arab-Israeli Wars and the Peace Process*. New York: St. Martin's Press.

Battah, Abdalla M. and Yehuda Lukacs. 1988. "Introduction," in Yehuda Lukacs and Abdalla M. Battah, Eds. *The Arab-Israeli Conflict: Two Decades of Change*. Boulder, CO: Westview Press.

Beilin, Yossi. 1999. *Touching Peace: From Oslo Accord to A Final Agreement*. London: Weidenfeld & Nicolson.

Cohen, Jack. 1987. *The Reunion of Isaac and Ishmael*. New York: The Reconstructionist Press.

Cohen, Michael J. 1987. *The Origins and Evolution of the Arab-Zionist Conflict*. Berkeley, CA: University of California Press.

Cohen, Saul B. 1992. "Middle East Geopolitical Transformation: The Disappearance of a Shatterbelt." *Journal of Geography*. 9: 1 (2-10).

Drysdale, Alasdair and Gerald H. Blake. 1985. *The Middle East and North*

*Africa: A Political Geography.* New York: Oxford University Press.

Epp, Frank H. 1970. *Whose Land Is Palestine?* Grand Rapids, MI: William B. Eerdmans Publishing Company.

Galtung, Johan. 1988. "The 'Peace Process' Twenty Years Later: Failure Without Alternative?" in Yehuda Lukacs and Abdalla M. Battah, Eds. *The Arab-Israeli Conflict: Two Decades of Change.* Boulder, CO: Westview Press.

Garfinkle, Adam M. 1991. "Genesis." Chapter 1, in Alvin Z. Rubinstein, ed. *The Arab-Israeli Conflict: Perspectives.* New York: Harper Collins Publishers Inc.

Gerner, Deborah J. 1991. *One Land, Two Peoples: The Conflict Over Palestine.* Boulder, CO: Westview Press.

Goitein, Solomon D. 1955. *Jews and Arabs: Their Contacts Through the Ages.* New York: Schocken Books Inc.

Held, Colbert C. 1989. *Middle East Patterns: Places, Peoples, and Politics.* Boulder, CO: Westview Press.

Hudson, Michael C. 1984. *Alternative Approaches to the Arab-Israeli Conflict: A Comparative Analysis of the Principal Actors.* Washington, D. C.: Center for Contemporary Arab Studies, Georgetown University.

Khatib, M. M. 1986. *The Bounteous Koran: A Translation of Meaning and Commentary*, Authorized by Al-Azhar (Religious Institution). London: Macmillian Press, Ltd.

Lukacs, Yehuda and Abdalla M. Battah. 1988. *The Arab-Israeli Conflict: Two Decades of Change.* Boulder, CO: Westview Press.

Moore, John Norton, Ed. 1974. *The Arab-Israeli Conflict*, Vol. III: Documents. Princeton, NJ: Princeton University Press.

Morris, Benny. 1999. *Righteous Victims: A History of Zionist-Arab Conflict, 1882-1999.* New York: Alfred A. Knoff.

Natanyahu, Benjamin. 2000. *A Durable Peace, Israel and Its Place Among the Nations.* New York: Warner Books.

Ogden, D. Kelley and Jeffrey R. Chadwick. 1990. *The Holy Land: A Geographical, Historical and Archaeological Guide to the Land of the Bible.* Jerusalem: Barry Segal International Ltd.

Reisman, Michael. 1970. *The Art of the Possible: Diplomatic Alternatives in the Middle East.* Princeton, NJ: Princeton University Press.

Rubinstein, Alvin Z. 1984. *The Arab-Israeli Conflict: Perspectives*. New York: Praeger Publishers.

Rubinstein, Alvin Z. 1991. *The Arab-Israeli Conflict: Perspectives*. New York: Harper Collins Publisher Inc.

Savir, Uri. 1998. *The Process: 1,100 Days That Changed the Middle East.* New York: Vintage Books, 1998.

Schulze, Kristen. 1999. *The Arab-Israeli Conflict*. London and New York: Addison Wesley Longman, Ltd.

Shafir, Gershon. 1989. *Land, Labor and the Origins of the Israeli-Palestinian Conflict: 1882-1914*. New York: Cambridge University Press.

Shi, Tze-Zhou, Translator and Commentator. 1958. *Guo-yu Gu-Lan-Jing (Mandarin Koran)*. Authorized by Taipei Mosque Committee. Zhong-Hua Con-Shu Wei Yuan Huei.

Smith, Charles D. 1992. *Palestine and the Arab-Israeli Conflict*. 2nd Ed. New York: St. Martin's Press.

Smith, George Adam. 1894. *The Historical Geography of the Holy Land*. London: Hodder & Stoughton Ltd.

Strohl, Lydia. 2001. "Why Doctors Now Believe in Faith Healing?" *Readers Digest.* (May), pp. 108-115

United Nations. 1990. *The Origins and Evolution of the Palestine Problem: 1917-1988*. New York: United Nations.

# The Significance of Place in the Bible

Ronald R. Boyce

Events in the Bible do not unfold on an empty canvas or a *tabula rasa*. The panorama of change is not painted on a sterile, flat, featureless plain. It ripples with rocks and rills, mountains, valleys, and hills; rivers and springs; forests, grasslands, and deserts; fish-filled lakes and stagnant seas. It is a physical landscape, on which many find solace, "tongues in trees, books in running brooks, sermons in stone. . . ," lines from Shakespeare's *As You Like It*, Act II, Scene 1. It is teaming with plants, animals, and people. Each happening is built upon the leavings of those preceding -- roads and bridges, farms and cities; some places seemingly sacrosanct, others condemned. Therefore, past happenings inscribe indelible, but obscure, imprints on the landscape, producing a palimpsest which then affects future events.

Hence, places are a critical part of full understanding. These places are clues that provide necessary information. In biblical hermeneutics, there are no *ceteris paribus* (other things being equal) assumptions. This contrived device may work well for understanding the axioms of plane geometry, and even for Central Place Theory, but it is hostile to biblical understanding. It results in a text without a context. Abraham, Isaac, and Jacob traversed a land, filled with cities, mountains, deserts, plains; their nomadic existence was dictated by the rains and the provisions of nature. The Hebrews entered the land of Canaan which was already fully occupied and rich with a cornucopia of crops.

Thus, the places themselves are an essential part of fully understanding of the text. The places chosen, the paths taken to them, and the time and distance travelled are all important clues. The places – the where – are deliberately, selectively, and symbolically suitable to illustrate particular information critical for comprehensive understanding. The position of a place relative to other places often provides meaning to the progressive parade of the human race on the road to Sychar and beyond. For example, Jesus must have passed Bethel and Shiloh – two sacred cities of great historical significance – on the path through the hill country from Jerusalem to Sychar. But neither are mentioned. Yet their omission is obvious and raises the question of why, but this important biblical silence is unnoticed by the spatially ignorant.

Geographers have long noted that, if one plots on a map places of interest, overlaying other assumed correlatives, associations become apparent. Of course, these similar patterns may not be causal, but coincidental, even peripheral. Nonetheless, they cause the observer to summon theses ripe for examination. For example, logic alone – following-up hunches – may suggest that there may be a causal connection between the positioning of passes, rivers, and routes and the placement of towns and cities situated along these routes. Productive agricultural areas might logically be associated with an abundance of towns and villages. Thereby, biblical study benefits from the same procedure as secular study. An understanding of place is not only greatly enriched by noting spatial similarities, but concepts and questions often are apparent, which were earlier concealed, as candidates for further study.

Even deceptively small geographical information in Scripture is usually important. Whenever such things as direction taken, days travelled, and even time of leaving and arriving are mentioned, usually only by a word or two, these are provided for a purpose. The Bible does not contain any insignificant information, spatial or otherwise, but is sometimes frustratingly parsimonious. To their peril, many simply skip over these tidbits of information without giving them a thought or like extensive genealogies and the plethora of places listed. However, to ignore or miss seemingly small things results in the missing of large things. If nothing else, it abridges the Scriptures and results in the gaining of only a skimpy understanding.

The importance of what is **not** stated in Scripture, revealed by geographical study, often raises questions and suggests answers. For example, Abram's trek from Haran to the Plain of Moreh, a distance of 500 miles, is covered in only three verses (Genesis 12: 4-6). His travel from the Plain of Moreh to Egypt, another 300 miles, also only receives three verses (Genesis 12: 8-10). Why? If one examines the physical geography – e.g. the climate, vegetation, and topography – enlightenment immediately occurs. The distance from Haran to Egypt is over 800 miles, a distance similar to that between Saint Louis and Denver. Such a trip, with a wandering, feed-encumbered herd of sheep and goats, must have taken many months. Yet, these are the only statements given. Even the route taken, except for the mention of Shechem and Bethel, is unspecified.

Thereby, geographical evidence provides convincing proof of the significance of Shechem, Bethel, and Ai, the only towns mentioned in the trek of Abram from Haran to Egypt. Technically, when Abram left Haran on the Belikh River, approximately fifty miles from the Euphrates, he took his first steps toward the land which God would show him. He left with his goods, servants, family, and animals. But when he crossed the Euphrates River about a week later, he entered the Promised Land (Genesis 15: 18). It might be expected that he would erect a memorial of the event, much as Joshua did when he crossed the Jordan River into Canaan (Joshua 4: 3), but the Scriptures say nothing. In fact, the 500-mile trip from Haran to Shechem must have taken months and surely passed near very important places such as Mount Herman (over 9,000 feet), Damascus, and the Jordan River (below sea level), before they reached the rising slopes leading to a flat valley near the twin peaks of Mount Ebal and Mount Gerizim (each about 3,000 feet high). The Plain of Moreh (Oaks) was adjacent to them and the city of Shechem, on its west. The Plain of Moreh was located in a strip of "dry forest," grassland sprinkled with oaks, about five miles wide, of a "dry forest" zone. The landscape was semi-arid, having about twenty inches of rainfall annually. It looked similar to the grassy, hilly, oak-laden landscape of countless early Western movies. This narrow strip of land runs along the leeward side of the hill countries of Ephraim and Judah from just north of Shechem, almost to Beersheba. Rains come from the west. Most of the precipitation to Canaan is orographic (mountain caused). As air is forced up and over the hill country (windward side), precipitation increases with elevation. However, as the air descends on the leeward side, rainfall decreases until desert occurs. Thereby, this "Goldilocks" zone for grazing was created by physical geography. Even so, surely this was not the first grassy place Abram had encountered on the route from Haran.

But even good valleys are soon exhausted with continuous grazing, and Abram moved south to an area in the "dry forest" valley between Bethel and Ai. The Scriptures report these stops in only three verses (Genesis 12: 8-10). At both places, Abram built an altar and again received a confirmation of the covenant. And upon Abram's return to Canaan, he camped at the Plain of Mamre, in this same special dry forest zone near Hebron. The omission of other places is astounding and instructive.

Obviously, the selection of all the places mentioned and not mentioned is deliberate and is meant to be studied. Therefore, the exhortation to "**study** to show yourself approved by God" (2 Timothy 2: 15; emphasis added by author) applies to a good geographical understanding of the Bible.

432

# Geography of the Holy Land: Jerusalem, Regional Cities, Small Towns, and Rural Places（瞭解聖城與聖地）

版權者：William A. Dando

發行人：Jonathan J. Lu（呂榮輝）

出版者：聖光神學院出版社（Holy Light Theological Seminary Press）

　　　　河南二路二號（No. 2, Henan 2nd Road）

　　　　臺灣高雄市新興區 80050（Kaohsiung 80050, Taiwan）

　　　　電話：886-7-9537333（TEL: 886-7-9537333）

　　　　傳真：886-7-9537090（FAX: 886-7-9537090）

　　　　網址：http://www.holylight.org.tw

　　　　郵政劃撥：42048138 號；戶名：聖光神學院出版社

登記證：行政院新聞局局版臺學字第 6211 號

承印者：前程出版社（電話：886-7-7268399）

封面設計：Bharath Ganesh Babu

出版日期：2019 年 9 月初版

定價：新台幣 750 元（美金 USD25.00）

國際標準書碼：ISBN 978-986-91747-8-7（精裝）

---

國家圖書館國際標準書號資料

---

Geography of the Holy Land: Jerusalem, Regional Cities, Small Towns, and Rural Places（瞭解聖城與聖地）

Copyright Holder: William A. Dando

Editors: William A. Dando

　　　　Caroline Z. Dando

　　　　Jonathan J. Lu

Publisher: Jonathan J. Lu

Published by : Holy Light Theological Seminary Press

　　　　2, Henan 2nd Road, Kaohsiung 80050 Taiwan

Published for: Bible Geography Specialty Group

　　　　The Association of American Geographers

　　　　Washington, D. C.,

　　　　U. S. A.

ISBN: ISBN 978-986-91747-8-7（精裝）